aph
Workout Book

The Complete Paragraph Workout Book

Carolyn H. Fitzpatrick
University of Maryland—Baltimore County

Marybeth B. Ruscica
St. Vincent's College of
St. John's University

D. C. HEATH AND COMPANY
Lexington, Massachusetts   Toronto

Cover Credit: Eldorado Canyon, Colorado, John P. Kelly/The Image Bank

Photo Credits: p. 1: William Meyer/Click/Chicago; p. 21: Christopher Brown/Stock, Boston; p. 23: Renee Lynn/Photo Researchers, Inc.; p. 41: Dean Abramson/Stock, Boston; p. 61: Chester Higgins, Jr./Rapho/Photo Researchers, Inc.; p. 85: Sam Pierson, Jr./ Photo Researchers, Inc.; p. 117: Rapho/Photo Researchers, Inc.; p. 137: John Blaustein/Woodfin Camp & Associates; p. 167: UPI/Bettmann Newsphotos; p. 189: William Meyer/Click/Chicago; p. 205: Kenneth Murray/Photo Researchers, Inc.; p. 231: Alan Dorow/Archive Pictures, Inc.; p. 233: Mark Antman/The Image Works; p. 241: Tim Davis/Photo Researchers, Inc.; p. 253: Charles Harbutt/Archive Pictures, Inc.; p. 267: Tim Davis/Photo Researchers, Inc.; p. 279: Lehtikuva/Pentti Kushkinen/Woodfin Camp & Associates; p. 303: Tim Davis/Photo Researchers, Inc.; p. 319: Tom Cheek/ Stock, Boston; p. 325: Tim Davis/Photo Researchers, Inc.; p. 331: Anestis Diakopoulos/ Stock, Boston; p. 337: Joe Epstein/Design Conceptions; p. 351: Joe Epstein/Design Conceptions; p. 361: John Griffin/The Image Works; p. 369: UPI/Bettmann News-photos; p. 379: Eli Reed/Magnum.

Published simultaneously in Canada.

Printed in the United States of America.

International Standard Book Number: 0-669-20039-5

10 9 8 7 6 5 4 3 2 1

Acknowledgments

Russell Baker, excerpts from *Growing Up* by Russell Baker. Copyright © 1984 by permission of Contemporary Books, Inc. "Little Red Riding Hood Revisited" by Russell Baker, 1/13/80. Copyright © 1980 by the New York Times Company. Reprinted by permission.

Claude Brown, excerpted from *The Children of Ham* by Claude Brown. Copyright © 1976 by Claude Brown. Reprinted with permission of Stein and Day Publishers.

Jacques Cousteau, excerpts from *The Shark* by Jacques Cousteau with Philippe Cousteau. Copyright © 1970 Jacques Yves Cousteau. Reprinted by permission of Doubleday & Company, Inc.

S. I. Hayakawa, "How Dictionaries Are Made" from *Language in Thought and Action,* fourth edition by S. I. Hayakawa. Copyright © 1978 by Harcourt Brace Jovanovitch, Inc. Reprinted by permission of the publisher.

Michael Kelly, "Teach Bike Riding in One Hour," originally published in *Parents* magazine. Copyright © 1987 by Michael H. Kelly. All rights reserved. Reprinted by permission of the author.

Walter Laqueur, "Reflections on Terrorism" by Walter Laqueur. Copyright Fall 1986 by the Council on Foreign Relations, Inc. Reprinted by permission of *Foreign Affairs,* Fall 1986.

Sara Levitan and Clifford M. Johnson, *Second Thoughts on Work.* Copyright © 1982, reprinted by permission of W. E. Upjohn Institute, Kalamazoo, MI.

Margaret Mead and Rhoda Metraux, "On Friendship" by Margaret Mead and Rhoda Metraux, *A Way of Seeing.* Copyright © 1966, 1970 by Margaret Mead and Rhoda Metraux. Reprinted by permission of William Morrow & Company.

John Steinbeck, excerpt from *The Grapes of Wrath* by John Steinbeck. Copyright 1939, renewed © 1967 by John Steinbeck. Reprinted by permission of Viking Penguin Inc.

Lytton Strachey, excerpt from *Queen Victoria* by Lytton Strachey. Copyright 1921 by Harcourt Brace Jovanovich, Inc.; renewed 1949 by James Strachey. Reprinted by permission of the publisher.

E. B. White, excerpt of approx. 550 words from pp. 121–122 of "Here Is New York," copyright © 1949 by E. B. White. Both reprinted by permission of Harper & Row Publishers, Inc.

Theodore H. White, excerpt of approx. 850 words from pp. 41–43 of *In Search of History* by Theodore H. White. Copyright © 1978 by Theodore H. White. Reprinted by permission of Harper & Row Publishers, Inc.

Preface

We have designed *The Complete Paragraph Workout Book: A Concise Guide to the Writing Process* to meet the diverse needs of student writers enrolled in college composition classes. Suitable for developmental students, this text examines the writing and reading processes for the paragraph and essay; moreover, the text provides a review of grammar and punctuation.

The Complete Paragraph Workout Book begins with the assumption that all writers must read their own prose and that of others. By incorporating certain reading skills as they write, students can become better writers and place writing in the shared social context in which it must exist. Composing employs two skills that, as Peter Elbow states, "are so different that they usually conflict with each other: creating and criticizing." As writers, students must be allowed the freedom to invent, explore, and discover ideas as they develop paragraphs or essays. As readers, students must be able to criticize their own prose in order to address an audience with a specific purpose, determine an effective rhetorical strategy, organize details, and create an appropriate tone. In addition, students must be able to criticize the prose of others to test the validity of information presented, to determine the effectiveness of rhetorical strategies, and to respond to another's message.

Too often, student writers view their prose as the end product of several hours' work. They fail to see that writing, if it is to be meaningful, must address an audience that will respond. Within this mutual social context of writer and audience, composing becomes communication, not the mere recording of words upon a piece of paper. By encouraging student writers to be aware of their own prose and that of others, we believe that these students will increase their desire and ability to communicate with others and will take necessary risks to share ideas.

To confront the two problems of creating and criticizing, *The Complete Paragraph Workout Book* integrates reading strategies and the writing process. These strategies will facilitate student writers' abilities to understand and analyze their own prose as they compose and to recognize how other writers communicate effectively, convincingly, and honestly. Examining the writing process, Part One is arranged in a developmental sequence from the introductions to the reading process ("To the Student") and the writing process (Chapter One) to a final discussion of the essay. Part One incorporates related reading strategies within each chapter on the writing process. In "Creating Topic Sentences," for example, students identify and generate topic sentences by recognizing the distinction between fact and opinion. Students also learn that the placement of a paragraph's topic sentence is determined by the writer's purpose. In addition, this text provides selected readings. Throughout the book, exercises present various types of writing, from academic textbooks to prose by professional writers as well as students, to indicate the social nature of writing. In Chapters Two through Seven, students can explore rhetorical strategies through model paragraphs and writing assignments. These assignments will motivate students to find their own solutions to writing situations and will allow students to use their own experience to respond to the writing of others. Chapter Nine ("The Essay") reinforces the writing process and identifies reading strategies for essays. For instance, students learn to summarize, critique, and evaluate essays; they then apply these strategies to revisions of their own work. Moreover, this chapter includes a wide variety of essay writing assignments that motivate students to apply their knowledge of composing strategies to rhetorical situations. The assignments at the end of the chapter also ask students to respond to the pictures provided in this text.

A review of traditional grammar, Part Two encourages students to edit their papers carefully after they have revised drafts. These grammar chapters are keyed to editing strategies introduced for the paragraph in Chapter Five ("Revising") and for the essay in Chapter Nine of Part One. Material within the chapters of Part Two is arranged sequentially. Each chapter contains clear learning objectives and a step-by-step explanation of a particular problem. Sentence exercises immediately follow each explanation, so that students can apply their newly acquired knowledge. In addition, we encourage students to construct their own rules and sentences. Such practice in identifying concepts and in developing sentences helps students apply principles they have learned. Practice sentences follow blocks of material and allow students to test accumulated knowledge on the sentence level before they edit paragraphs and essays.

The Complete Paragraph Workout Book offers instructors and student writers flexibility. Since students can vary greatly in their abilities to compose and criticize, an instructor can develop an individual approach for each class by selecting from the wide variety of exercises. As they deem appropriate, instructors can employ the writing strategies in Chapter Two through Seven either in the order presented or at the end of discussion of the paragraph. The *Instructor's Guide* provides additional teaching suggestions for reading strategies, checklists for rhetorical strategies, evaluation forms for peer groups, reading levels for model paragraphs and essays, and answers to objective exercises.

We wish to thank Paul A. Smith, our editor, as well as Laurie Johnson and Renée Mary, our production editors, at D. C. Heath for their guidance and support. We are also grateful for the valuable comments of the manuscript readers: Janet M. Carnesi, State University Agricultural and Technical College at Farmingdale, New York; Domenick Caruso, Kingsborough Community College; Irene Lurkis Clark, University of Southern California; Anthony DiMatteo, New York Institute of Technology; Phyllis T. Dircks, Long Island University—C. W. Post Campus; Donnasue Farrell, Manatee Community College; Christopher Cole O'Hearn, Los Angeles Harbor College; Charles Piltch, John Jay College of Criminal Justice; Irwin Weiser, Purdue University; and William F. Woods, Wichita State University. Moreover, the Learning Resources Center of the University of Maryland—Baltimore County kindly allowed us to test the book during a summer course. Finally, we wish to thank our students. We are especially indebted to those who have kindly allowed their essays to be reprinted here: Fernando Dela Cruz, Wayde Minami, Chris Broden, Bill Heschl, Larry Mathena, Dan Estrada, Shellie Smith, and Yvonne Schaberg of the University of Maryland—Baltimore County; and William McCann, Mansur Shomali, Reginald Meneses, Will Baird, Thomas Lee, Matt Wolf, and Joe Liberatore of Loyola High School, Towson, Maryland.

Carolyn H. Fitzpatrick
Marybeth B. Ruscica

Contents

4 *Organizing Details*   85

5 *Revising*   117

6 *Achieving Coherence*   137

7 *Diction*   167

8 *Style*   189

9 *The Whole Essay*   205

PART II   GRAMMAR REVIEW   231

1   *Verbs I: The Present, Past, and Future Tenses*   241

2   *Verbs II: The Perfect Tenses and the Progressive Forms*   253

3   *Verbs III: The Finer Points—Voice, Mood, Verbals, and Style*   267

4   *Subjects, Verbs, and Prepositional Phrases*   279

To the Student

Effective reading gives power. Active, reflective reading allows you to comprehend materials better, increase your knowledge, and save time and effort. You, as an active reader, will analyze both the items that comprise a textbook or essay and their functions within the text. You will, for example, analyze an author's intended audience and tone as well as the validity of his or her point of view and the accuracy of the supporting details. You will, as your analytical ability increases, read with greater comprehension and ease. Synthesis—that is, incorporating the material you have read into your own knowledge—increases your understanding of complex situations and ideas. Analytical reading also saves time, for you will not have to reread the passage to remember the material. Finally, as a bonus, analytical reading can help improve your writing. In the composing process, this analytical ability will enable you to evaluate and critique your own writing and that of others. Skillful reading, therefore, makes you an active reader, a thoughtful writer, and a powerful communicator.

The Communication Process

Communication, a social process, involves a sender and a receiver in an endless series of activities and roles. For communication to occur, the sender (a speaker or writer) transmits a message to the receiver (an audience or reader). Communication, however, does not end when the receiver reads the message. Through posing questions, the receiver can, frequently, become a sender either by asking the speaker to respond to these questions or by answering them. The chart shown on page 3 indicates the social, reciprocal nature of communication as each participant, in turn, assumes the roles of sender and receiver.

In effect, senders begin the communication process by constructing a message that they then transmit to an audience. Hence, communication becomes a social activity. This audience will analyze the sender's information and reconstruct the message in light of the audience's own background, education, and experience. At that point, receivers synthesize the new information, presented by the sender, with their own experience. If the receiver has

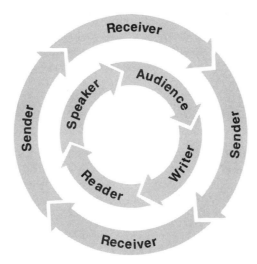

no immediate use for the newly acquired knowledge, the communication process temporarily comes to a halt; it begins again when the receiver utilizes that knowledge to construct a new meaning. The receiver can become a new sender by communicating this new message either to the original sender or to a new audience. This action reinforces the reciprocal nature of communication. The chart below depicts the complex web of elements that contribute to successful communication.

COMMUNICATION PROCESS ACTIVITIES

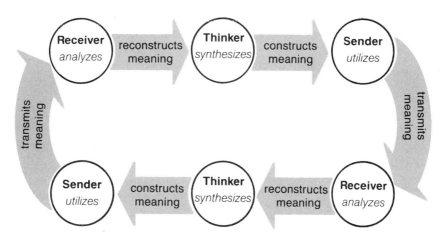

You assume many roles when you communicate: you think, read, and write. To communicate with power, you must actively assume these roles. In this chapter, you will begin to develop analytical reading skills; you will learn to think about what you read and to evaluate essays by previewing, skimming and, in the end, analyzing them.

READING AS THINKING

Analytical reading is not a passive activity. While you might believe that you read effectively when you watch television, listen to the radio, talk with friends, or perform other tasks, you do not. Certainly, some types of reading can be accomplished as you are performing other tasks; for example, you can read the directions for a recipe as you complete the instructions, and you can check the television guide as you watch a program. However, you will not retain this information. Analytical reading allows you to remember and use what you read. Because it does so, analytical reading requires your complete concentration. In this way, analytical reading differs from the type of reading you might do when you read a billboard, a sales display, the comics in the newspaper, or even the message on your cereal box in the morning. In reading tasks like these, you do not consciously analyze the message you are receiving; often, you are simply keeping your eyes busy as you take a long trip, hunt for bargains, look for amusement, or try to awaken.

Analytical reading requires that you carefully think about the material you are reading. In effect, this type of reading demands that you enter into a dialogue with the author of the passage. Why did the author make a particular statement? Why did the author insist that his or her point of view was the correct one? What details did the author use to support this opinion? Are these details accurate? By asking questions like these when you read, you become an active, effective reader.

Usually, efficient readers have a specific goal when they read. For example, they might read a chemistry text to understand a particular process or read a play to understand the plot and the characters' motives. Inefficient readers lack these goals. They believe, instead, that one reads only because the passage was assigned by the instructor. Hence, they do *not* consciously think about what they are reading and often must reread the same passage to understand its meaning. Active readers, however, know their reason for reading.

READING PURPOSE

Individuals read for three major reasons: entertainment, information, and rejection.

1. When you read for *entertainment*, you want a pleasurable pastime. Consider, for example, the types of materials you read when you are on vacation. You may choose a horror story, a romance novel, a detective or mystery novel, or science fiction. You want to be scared, excited, or surprised by your material. In general, however, you will not use the material you are reading for any purpose other than daydreaming. As a matter of fact, the material will probably be stored in your short-term memory, where it will be available for you to recall its details for a short period of time; later, you will forget most of the specific details and remember only that you read the piece. Often, short stories, novels, and magazine articles provide your entertainment.

2. When you read for *information*, you want to learn; you are interested in using the material either to acquire specific information (the current unemployment figures, for instance) or to increase your general knowledge (the operating procedures for your computer, for example). Depending on your intended use of the information, you will store the details either in your long-term memory, where it will always be retained, or in your short-term memory, where it will be retained for a limited time and then forgotten. Most of your academic reading falls into this category; you read newspapers, textbooks, nonfiction books, and articles for information.

3. When you read for *rejection*, you judge the usefulness of the material to you. For example, if you were researching information for a term paper, you would probably scan a number of books for information. Based upon your cursory reading of a piece, you would decide whether the material would be useful to your research. In this case, you would reread the piece to gain information. If the piece presents material that you already know, then you would not read the piece carefully. If the piece proves useless, then you would reject a second reading of it. When you glance through professional journals, newsletters, newspapers, and magazine articles in search of new information, you read for rejection. You will later reread those pieces that offer information, but you will skip those pieces that do not appear informative or interesting.

Your purpose in reading influences the way you read and your reading rate; therefore, you should understand your goals in reading a particular piece before you actually read it. Answers to the following questions will help you determine the types of reading you currently do and the effectiveness of your reading.

1. Why do I read? _____

_____

2. When I read, what am I trying to achieve? _____

_____

3. What is my goal when reading? _____

_____

4. Under what conditions, in what environment, do I read? _____

_____

5. How much do I remember after I have read? _____

_____

6. How long does it take me to read? _____

_____

7. How do I actually read? What is my method? _____

_____

Now, think about your answers. What do they indicate about your reading habits?

1. When I read, my purpose(s) is (are) _____

2. When I read, my goal(s) is (are) _____

3. When I read, my retention is _____

4. When I read, my rate is _____

As you have probably recognized by now, reading purpose, rate and type are intertwined; your purpose and goal influence the type of reading you will do and the rate at which you will read.

READING GOALS AND RATES

To be an active reader, you must think about the information being presented to you and why this information is important to you. Therefore, you must state goals about your reading. Once you have pinpointed your reason for reading, you can determine the appropriate type of reading to achieve your goal, and you can read at the appropriate rate. The chart on page 6 depicts the relationships among reading purpose, goal, type, and rate.

Purpose for Reading	Goal	Type of Reading	Reading Rate
Entertainment	Store in short-term memory	General	Average
Information	Store in short-term memory	Previewing	Fast
	Store in long-term memory	Skimming	Fast
		Scanning	Fast
		Studying	Slow
Rejection	Store in short-term memory	Skimming	Fast

When you read for entertainment (general reading), you read at your normal rate (about 300–400 words a minute), and you store the information in your short-term memory. When you read for information, your reading rate will be slow (if you need to study the material) or fast (if you are reading for background information or to locate a specific detail). When you read for rejection, you skim; this reading type requires a fast rate and short-term memory. Consequently, before you read, first decide *why* you are reading. Since your coursework demands that you remember material for use in class, on tests, and later in a career, this chapter will focus on reading for information and the analytical ability necessary for this process.

PURPOSE AND AUDIENCE

In addition to identifying your goals, you must consider the characteristics of the audience for whom the material is written. Does the writer address the message to professionals in the field or to someone who wants a general overview of a situation? Is the audience unfamiliar with the material, or is it someone who requires a thorough examination of the topic? Obviously, the author's view of his or her intended audience influences style, organization, information, tone and vocabulary, and message.

A number of familiar situations confirm that an author addresses a particular audience. If you have ever received a letter from a political candidate, then you probably recognized that the message was designed to convince you of the candidate's merit. The author of the letter might have addressed you in a friendly manner and attempted to enlist your support of his or her candidacy. Obviously, the author will present only the positive aspects of his or her career and will not include information on his or her more controversial political opinions. A letter from the candidate's opponent, however, will contain different facts and argue for a different conclusion. Consider, too, the different audiences for whom advertisements in magazines and on television are designed. Advertisers know that their products will appeal to a section of the population if the advertisements emphasize the feature most likely to attract that group. Look, for example, at various magazines, each designed to reach a different audience; the advertisements will address the magazine's audience and its needs. The same product may, however, be advertised in a number of ways to appeal to different groups. In academic textbooks, the audience's familiarity with the material obviously dictates the author's details and purpose. Consider an advanced mathematics text; it is designed solely for a reader who has some experience in basic and intermediate math. The text, however, would be useless for someone who has just learned how to divide whole numbers. In the same manner, some academic journals are written for professionals in particular disciplines; hence, their writers employ the language used within the field when they prepare manuscripts for publication. These examples verify that an author constructs a message for a specific audience with a specific purpose in mind.

Once you have identified the author's purpose and audience, re-examine your own reading purpose to see how your goal and reading type and rate are affected. If the material addresses novices and you are an expert in the field, then you will probably read for rejection. However, if the material addresses a general audience, then you might just scan the piece for a specific detail. In other words, the author's purpose and audience influenced his or her communication and will affect your analysis of the material. Thus, identifying the author's purpose and intended audience can help you decide what *your* goal and reading type and rate will be.

EXERCISE 1   Consider your most probable reason for reading each of the following materials. Then determine the audience for which the material was written and the most appropriate type of reading you should do.

	Reason	Audience	Type
1. A page in the phone book			
2. Chapter 4 in *Economics: Public and Private Choices*			
3. Business section of Sunday's newspaper			
4. "The Lottery" by Shirley Jackson			
5. Today's television schedule			

The Reading Process

To evaluate a textbook's or an essay's usefulness to you, you should employ the stages in the reading process: previewing, skimming, and analyzing.

PREVIEWING

When you begin the reading process, you preview a textbook or an essay. Previewing helps you decide whether or not a specific article, book, or chapter will provide useful information.

A **preview** is an introduction, an overview. Think of a movie preview; it provides an overview of the movie's plot, characters, and action. However, it does not tell the entire story. The preview may last for five minutes, while the movie lasts for ninety. Similarly, a reading preview provides an introduction to the material's contents, structure, and purpose; however, the preview does not condense the entire book, chapter, or essay. Although reading the material may take an hour or more, previewing it may take only five minutes.

You preview to develop a general understanding of the material and its organization. You can then decide to reject the material if the information is not relevant or is already familiar to you, or you can decide to read the material more thoroughly. In the latter case, previewing will make your actual reading more efficient because you will already know the major topics, their relationships, and the ultimate emphasis of the piece. Although it initially requires a few extra minutes, previewing can ultimately save you time.

Since you preview to identify ideas and to begin thinking about the topic, you do not need to read the entire piece. To preview, look only at the major parts of the piece.

- First, look at the piece's source and the date. You need to recognize any possible biases and inaccuracies. Consider, for example, two possible articles on nuclear disarmament, one published in *The Nation* and the other in *National Review*. Although the articles address the same topic, they will be written from different perspectives and directed towards different audiences. The article in *The Nation* will represent a liberal political stance and be addressed to liberal readers; however, the article in *National Review* will represent a conservative political stance and be addressed to conservative readers.

  To test your ability to identify biases, consider the topic *health care costs*. How would the topic be treated by the *Washington Post*? To what audience would an article on this topic be directed? Consider the same topic discussed in *USA Today*. From what perspective would the article be written? What is the author's intended audience? (If you are unfamiliar with these newspapers, then locate them in the library, and read several articles in each one.)

  In addition, you should note the publication date to determine how current the information is. While some fields offer sound information from over several centuries of research, other fields rely upon information gathered within the past decade. Consider, for example, the field of computer science. Although articles from the 1940s would be correct and valuable, they do not reflect the advances in computer technology made within the past decade. On the other hand, philosophers often return to the ancient Greeks for information about the nature of matter and of humankind. Read the following titles and copyrights of books published on the care of premature infants, a field that has been transformed by improvements in technology. Which book should be used as a resource for a seminar paper to be presented as part of a continuing-education course for nurses?

  > *Born Premature*, copyright 1962
  >
  > *Too Small, Too Soon,* coypright 1985

  Obviously, the book published in 1962—which has not been updated—no longer provides current information on premature infants. Doctors have learned a great deal about how to treat premature infants within the past twenty years. Therefore, researchers would gain more current information if they studied the more contemporary book.

- Second, read the full title and subtitle of the book; the titles will identify the subject matter and indicate how the subject will be analyzed. Also, note the author's name and any additional information, such as academic degrees or experience, about him or her. You may be able to discern whether the author is a recognized expert in the field and whether this analysis follows a specific ideological viewpoint. Consider these examples of titles and authors.

  > *The Fall of the Bastille: An Insider's Account* by Jean-Jacques L'Enfantant
  >
  > *Highlights of the French Revolution* by Donald J. Pasomtory, B.A., Lecturer, Alcatraz College

  Since the subtitle of L'Enfantant's book indicates that he was present during the revolution, his book would probably be more useful in discussing observers' reactions to the event. Pasomtory, however, has had the advantage of almost two hundred years of scholarship concerning the specific causes of the French Revolution. His degree (B.A.) indicates that he has completed his college education. More than likely, though, he is not a recognized expert in the field because he has not completed a graduate degree in history.

- Third, read all of the subheadings, and turn them into questions. This method provides a purpose for subsequent reading, and it will help you determine what information you, as a writer, should provide for your audience. In addition, the subheadings will allow you to determine a structure for the article and enable you to organize your facts. The following chart indicates the types of questions you could ask after you have read the subtitles in a chapter in an economics textbook.

Subheadings	Questions	Information
Real property tax	What is the real property tax? How is it calculated? What are its advantages and disadvantages?	Definition of Term
Value-added tax	What is it? How can it be implemented? How successfully does it enhance revenue?	Advantages and Disadvantages
Sales tax	How does it affect consumption? Does it alter buying habits of consumers?	Popular Image

- Fourth, look at any charts, graphs, pictures, and visual aids. These visual representations clarify difficult material and condense information. In addition, they will alert you to the level of difficulty of the material. Consider the following chart depicting the changes in consumer borrowing over nineteen months.

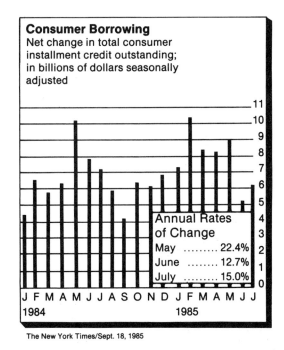

The New York Times/Sept. 18, 1985

The New York Times/Sept. 18, 1985. Copyright © 1985 by The New York Times Company. Reprinted by permission.

Can you imagine trying to write a description of all the numbers and ratios? Your description would require much more space than three inches of a newspaper column and would be far more complex for the reader.

EXERCISE 2 To practice your skill, preview the article, "The Meaning of Work," on page 13. Consider the article's usefulness if you were to write an essay on the same topic addressed to an audience with little background information in that field. Finally, answer the questions below.

1. Does the source have any obvious biases that might influence the presentation of the material? _____

2. Is the information current? _____

3. Are the authors experts in the field? Do they represent a specific philosophical interest? _____

4. Does the article include more subtopics than you are prepared to discuss? Is the organization helpful to you, or does it hinder your reading? _____

_____

5. Are there any visual aids? If so, are they useful? If not, would graphs or charts be appropriate in this article? _____

_____

6. Finally, does the article warrant further reading? Can it help you expand your knowledge? Will it be useful to you as a writer? _____

_____

If you answer *yes* to the last set of questions, then you should proceed to the next step in the reading process: skimming. However, if you reject the article because you believe it is not useful, then you have finished processing the article. Although your involvement with that article has ended, the communication process has not. You can now either find another article to preview for its usefulness or rethink your approach to the entire topic.

COMMUNICATING

SKIMMING

Skimming allows you to grasp the essential elements of a reading selection quickly. While requiring only five to ten minutes, skimming provides you with the fundamentals of the topic. When you skim, you glance quickly at an article. Therefore, skimming requires speed and does not allow a detailed reading. Skimming will, however, give you an overview of an article's main idea, support, organization, and conclusions.

Readers skim for two purposes: information and rejection. You skim for information when your preview has convinced you of the material's usefulness but you lack a sufficient amount of time to read the material thoroughly. By skimming the article, you can identify the main ideas and understand the author's line of reasoning. Skimming is valuable when you are reviewing a chapter before a class or test, doing research for a term paper, or exploring a new subject.

On the other hand, if your previewing has left you uncertain about an article's value, then skimming can help you decide whether the article warrants a thorough reading. When researching a topic, you do not read every article available on the topic; some will not be applicable to your interests. You can, however, determine a potential source's usefulness by skimming it. Then you can reject any source that does not suit your purpose, and you can carefully read those that do. Similarly, as a professional, you must be aware of current trends and discoveries in your field, but you usually will not have the time to read everything. Skimming will help you decide when to expend your time and effort more effectively.

To skim, you must read less. Instead of reading every word in an article, you can skim for the main idea; consequently, you "finish" the article more quickly than if you had read it thoroughly. Ideally, your skimming rate should be twice your average reading speed. However, skimming has one disadvantage: decreased comprehension. You cannot possibly answer questions on the details of the article since skimming demands that you omit reading the entire piece. Therefore, you comprehend only 50% of a piece you have skimmed, compared to 70% to 80% of a piece you have read completely.

Skimming demands actual reading—as quickly as possible—of the following parts of the material:

1. the introductory paragraphs (usually the first and second in a piece),
2. the first sentence in each following paragraph (usually the paragraph's topic sentence, identifying the paragraph's main idea), and
3. the concluding paragraphs (usually the last two in a piece).

Since you skim to determine the general lines of the author's argument, you want to recognize the main and supporting ideas in the piece. In the introduction, the author usually states a thesis, which identifies the passage's main idea. In a similar manner, the author will frequently reiterate this message in the conclusion; skimming those final two or three paragraphs reinforces your understanding of the thesis. Often, the body of the essay provides support for the author's main idea; consequently, by reading the first sentence in each body paragraph, you understand the essay's organization and supporting elements.

When you finish skimming a selection, you should know its contents. You should be able to discuss the author's message, even if you cannot delineate the fine points of the argument. With this knowledge, you can decide whether the author's information can be used as a basis for your own writing. If so, then you should analyze the article further. However, if you have gleaned all the relevant material from the piece during your skimming, then there is no need to spend more time on it. You can continue your research by skimming another promising article.

EXERCISE 3 To practice this skill, skim "The Meaning of Work" on page 13. Then answer the following questions.

1. What is the authors' main idea? _____

2. What arguments do they use to support the main idea? _____

_____

3. What conclusion, if any, do the authors draw? _____

_____

4. Do the authors offer any solution to a stated problem? _____

_____

5. Based on your skimming, write a short, preliminary summary of the authors' main

   idea and supporting arguments. _____

_____

_____

_____

_____

6. If you were to respond to this piece, would your intended audience know this

   information already? Specify an audience for your response. _____

_____

_____

7. Would your audience need to know this information? What, specifically, would the

   audience need to know? _____

_____

_____

8. Are you already familiar with these authors' main idea and their arguments? Do

   you need to know more? _____

_____

The following chart indicates the process a conscientious reader undertakes to gather information.

COMMUNICATING ABOUT A TOPIC

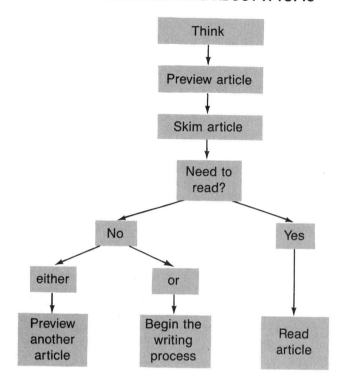

The Meaning of Work

Sara Levitan and Clifford M. Johnson

> Let us be grateful to Adam, our benefactor. He cut us out of the "blessing" of idleness and won us the "curse" of labor.
> —*Mark Twain*

1   Any attempt to discern future patterns of work must begin with a clear sense of why people work. The motivation to work is hardly self-evident—some people enjoy their jobs, while others relish only the paycheck. The diversity of reactions toward work is partly attributable to objective differences in the tasks which various jobs require, but more importantly it stems from the broad range of expectations which are brought to the workplace. In a world with many happy auto mechanics and disgruntled corporate executives, there can be no hierarchy of jobs or set of personal needs and interests which is applicable to all. The forces which are woven into work motivation are much more complex and difficult to predict.

2   Popular wisdom usually ties work motivation to some vague notion of the "work ethic," which in the extreme describes only a willingness to work while revealing nothing about one's reasons for working. Thus, even though a poet, a preacher and a plumber would likely offer very different explanations for why they "work," we count them all as staunch supporters of the "work ethic." Conversely, when we decry the disintegration of the "work ethic," we envision a world in which everyone refuses to work and civilizations crumble. It is a useful form of shorthand at times, but offers no guidance for assessments of work's future.

THEORIES OF WORK MOTIVATION

3   Recognizing that the rise and fall of the work ethic is linked only tenuously to work behavior and motivation, most analysts of this century have sought other explanations for our attachment to work. A variety of possibilities have been raised, most focusing on some concept of need fulfillment. Given the diversity of both work and individuals, no single concept can fully account for why people work, but the contributions of various disciplines form the basis for a relatively comprehensive portrait of work motivation in a modern era.

4   Perhaps the most basic theory of work motivation describes the desire to work as part of human nature. This simple view of work motivation posits the existence of a fundamental human urge to exert oneself, a drive to learn, to achieve, and to shape one's surroundings. The presence of a "work instinct" is impossible to prove, and its strength cannot be measured. Yet this perspective on work motivation does derive legitimacy from traits we commonly associate with human nature: a sense of curiosity, a responsiveness to challenge, a capacity for pursuing hopes and aspirations. Even as the debate over whether these qualities are acquired or whether they are innate continues, the desire of most to exert and achieve is difficult to dispute.

5   The economic explanations for work are familiar ones. Subsistence needs create pressures for work in all civilizations, and continue to fuel work motivation even in affluent welfare states. While the aggregate wealth of society may be sufficient to free substantial portions of the population from the necessity of work, distribution systems within the economy generally ensure that people work if they wish to enjoy anything more than the most meager of incomes and lifestyles. As the Industrial Workers of the World once chanted, "We go to work to get the dough to get the food to get the strength to go to work. . . ." A paycheck is no guarantee of an escape from poverty—millions of Americans earn too little for them to avoid this fate—but the economic advantages of working are almost always sufficient to give individuals powerful incentives to remain employed.

6   In themselves, these instinctual and economic views might be sufficient to explain why most people work. Still, the most intriguing (and in affluent societies perhaps the most powerful) accounts of work motivation have emerged from sociological and psychological perspectives. Arguing that work in modern societies is more than a means of subsistence or an avenue for fulfilling economic needs, sociologists have suggested that work is also essential in providing a sense of meaning, of community and self-esteem to the individual. Through work, we seek to justify our own existence, to develop a feeling of participation in a design which is grander than our personal lives. Through work, we join a community of individuals with common experiences, skills or goals. Through work, we derive feelings of competence and achievement, making contributions which enable us to believe in our own worth.

7   The impact of unemployment on the human psyche provides a dramatic illustration of the social and psychological needs which work fulfills. For those without jobs, the psychic scars can be great.

8   Deprived of a community of co-workers and unable to contribute to the support of family or society, the jobless quickly feel alienated and unproductive. The causes of this forced idleness are of secondary importance—even when wholly beyond the individual's control, the sense of dependency, of uselessness and isolation can be devastating.

9   Not surprisingly, research data suggest that unemployment and mental health are inversely related, with the strains of joblessness so severe as to be potentially life-threatening. M. Harvey Brenner of Johns Hopkins University has estimated that a 1 percent increase in the U.S. unemployment rate results in some 37,000 additional deaths, with more than half of those fatalities caused by in-

creased incidences of heart attacks and other cardiovascular diseases. Obviously most people denied work do not die. But unemployment has robbed them—if not of life, then of something else.

10   Thus, the forces which lead us to the workplace are much subtler than any proscriptions and religious moralisms of the work ethic. We work because it defines our place in the world, and creates a world in which we can feel both needed and useful.

A WORKER'S IDENTITY CRISIS?

11   "Who am I? . . . I'm a—." Almost regardless of how the response is completed—whether electrician, banker or teacher—the reply will conclude with a description of the individual's job. The sociological importance of work is epitomized by the widespread practice of defining people by their work roles, and often of characterizing ourselves in the same manner. A quick glance at the obituary page of the newspaper illustrates the point: the headlines do not announce the passing of a beloved husband, mother or neighbor, but rather of a former city councilman or social studies teacher. Terkel explored this theme repeatedly in interviews with a cross section of workers: "Your work is your identity"; it "tells you who you are"; "your occupation molds your personality"; and "my work and my life have become one" were typical replies. Even when people hated their work, Terkel concluded, it remained the reference point for identity.

12   It is important to note that the close connection between work and identity or self-esteem has had special meaning for women in American society. With dominant values still failing to acknowledge housekeeping activities as work, millions of women have been denied the recognition or status which virtually any other "job" would confer. Betty Friedan presented one of the many examples of how this lack of recognition has affected women who remain at home:

A young mother with a beautiful family, charm, talent and brains is apt to dismiss her role apologetically. "What do I do?" you hear her say. "Why nothing, I'm just a housewife." A good education it seems has given this paragon among women an understanding of the value of everything except her own worth.

Not surprisingly, women increasingly are working for wages outside the home, with dramatic implications for the composition of the labor force and the nature of work. The record number of women who are working may not be as single-minded in their attachment to jobs as their male counterparts, but they are clearly expressing a desire to define themselves in terms other than John Smith's wife or Bill Jones's mother.

13   Thus, among all of the groups which might be presumed to have the weakest attachment to the labor market—the unemployed, the poor, and women who previously have not entered the labor force—work continues to play a powerful role. Some of the pressures to work indeed may stem from the remnants of the Protestant ethic, placing a stigma on those choosing not to work. Yet these negative forces could not fully account for the continuing strength of work motivation in modern society. The desire to work reaches far beyond pious exhortations, and even beyond the pressures of economic necessity. We work because it offers one certain way of participating in the world around us, of developing a shared sense of community and of building a sense of identity and self-esteem which adds meaning to our lives.

WHO REALLY "WANTS" TO WORK?

14   The list of reasons why we may "need" to work—whether psychological, economic or sociological—provides ample ways of understanding the motivation

to work. Yet this discussion should not evoke images of workers springing cheerfully from their beds each morning, eager to reach their jobs. Just as work satisfaction is distinct from work motivation, *wanting* to work is quite different from *needing* to work. A fortunate few manage to hold jobs which they find challenging and exciting, but they are truly blessed. The struggle to cope with tedious and unpleasant work is far more common. Even if Americans do not shirk work in the coming decades, they may not rush to embrace it either.

15   It is perhaps most accurate to view people as of two minds, fundamentally ambivalent in their attitudes toward work. "The desire to work . . . is a powerful human need, an ego drive related to self-expression, power, creativity," concluded historian John Garraty, and yet "so . . . is the desire to be idle and free of responsibility." Freud articulated the same paradox fifty years earlier, suggesting that people depend on work and yet neither prize it as a path to happiness nor pursue it as a source of satisfaction, often working only under the stress of necessity. In the words of Eli Ginzberg, this "natural aversion to work" stems from the desire of workers to be "masters of their souls for as much of the day as possible."

16   Of course, these competing desires for freedom and social recognition, for pleasure and achievement, are not new additions to human nature. Yet the fundamental human ambivalence toward work may take on increasing importance in labor markets of the future as workers gain the ability to make more personalized choices between work and leisure. In pragmatic terms, work will remain an economic necessity for all but the very rich, and the noneconomic functions of work will ensure some attachment to work throughout society. Yet workers already are gaining the option to balance work and leisure time amidst growing affluence, and these work-leisure tradeoffs reflect their ambivalence toward work. The continuing motivation to work may not disappear, but workers are increasingly able to act on their own mixed emotions toward their labors.

ANALYZING

Before you begin reading an article thoroughly, you should recognize a few important aspects about the author's perspective.

- First, an essay, a short composition, discusses one topic. The essay usually presents the author's personal perspective on the topic; the author will not examine the topic in exhaustive detail since he or she does not have the space of an entire book. Whatever its length (from a few paragraphs to several pages), the essay should be clearly written and properly organized; therefore, it will probably have a recognizable structure. As you skim, you should be able to deduce that structure. Then, with this structural pattern in mind, you will be able to organize the author's points.

- Second, an essay presents a personal perspective. Although the author's point of view is subjective, he or she is writing to persuade you that this opinion is logically correct because it is based on reliable, objective evidence. Your preview of the material will identify any blatant prejudices; however, the author may reveal more subtle biases which can be discerned by a thorough reading. Carefully analyze the facts, statistics, and examples provided by the author. Decide whether they actually explain the main idea, provide additional details, and support the author's view.

- Third, an essay does not examine a topic completely. After all, an essay is not a book. Because of its comparatively short length, an essay must omit some information. Based on purpose, intended audience, and length of the essay, the author has included or excluded material. Consequently, some pertinent information may have not been given in the essay. In some cases, this information was excluded because it might have undermined or contradicted the author's main idea. Therefore, be aware that a completely different opinion might exist on the same topic.

By familiarizing yourself with additional evidence and opposing views, you can better evaluate the author's conclusions. In this way, you can judge for yourself whether the author presented his or her view honestly or whether the author omitted potentially contradictory information. To make these judgments, you must be well informed and familiar with your library and with research techniques.

EXERCISE 4 This exercise will guide you through the entire reading process. Return to the article on page 13 that you have previewed and skimmed. Treat it as if you were unfamiliar with it. Use this reading guide to help you process the article.

1. Based on the essay's title, what do you think the article will discuss?

   _____

2. Is there an ideological slant to the material? _____

   _____

3. How many subtopics are discussed? _____ Are they discussed in

   great detail? _____ How are they organized? _____

   _____

4. Skim the article.

5. Based on your skimming, write a short, preliminary summary of the authors' thesis

   and supports. _____

   _____

   _____

   _____

6. List below any words from the article with which you are not familiar. Look up their meanings in a dictionary and write their definition here.

   _____

   _____

   _____

   _____

   _____

7. Read the article thoroughly.

8. Based on your reading of the essay, revise your preliminary summary to include any important information that might not have been available to you when you skimmed.

   _____

_____

_____

_____

9. What is the authors' main idea? _____

_____

10. How do the authors support their main idea? _____

_____

11. Reread the conclusion carefully. What is the authors' final point?

_____

12. What do you know about this topic? What other information do you have to support

or reject the authors' main idea? _____

_____

13. Do you need to know more about this topic? _____

If you answered *yes* to the last question, then you need to research the topic more. A negative answer indicates that you have analyzed the material and are beginning to synthesize it with your own knowledge. This synthesis will make generating ideas for your own writing easier and make your communication more effective. The following chart identifies the stages of communication as a person assumes the varied roles of thinker, reader, and writer to become a more powerful communicator.

COMMUNICATING ABOUT A TOPIC

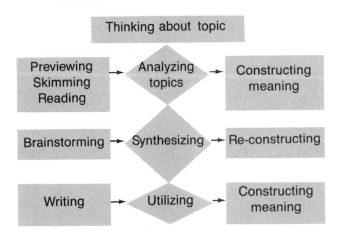

In the chapters that follow, you will increase your analytical ability as you learn how to identify the separate components of an essay or textbook:

Topics (Chapter Two in Part One)

Controlling Ideas, Facts and Opinions, and Topic Sentences (Chapter Three in Part One)

Supporting Details and Judgments (Chapter Four in Part One)

Transitional Words and Expressions (Chapter Six in Part One)

Connotations and Creating Tone (Chapter Seven in Part One)

Analyzing an Entire Essay (Chapter Nine in Part One)

As you increase your analytical ability, you will also strengthen your ability to compose effective paragraphs and essays. Your knowledge of combined reading and composing processes will make you a powerful communicator.

PART I

Composing Paragraphs and Essays

The Writing Process

OBJECTIVES:
1. To explore fallacies about writing.
2. To understand the writing commitment.
3. To explore the entire writing process, from generating ideas to revising papers.
4. To generate ideas through prewriting.

PREVIEW: Composing is a recursive activity; it does not end with a first, or even second, draft of a paper. Throughout the entire process of writing, you can discover and explore ideas as you compose. To generate ideas for paragraphs, you can use prewriting to explore your ideas before you begin to write.

All of us are writers. Certainly, the ability to write well contributes to your academic success. Through term papers, essay examinations, lab reports, book reviews, and short compositions, you demonstrate your ability to analyze and synthesize material from various sources and to utilize this material to support your ideas.

Composing, however, does not end when you receive your degree; writing belongs to the larger professional and social world we share with others. In an age when we seem to use the telephone and computer more frequently than the postal service, businesses still operate primarily through the written word. Your power to write for different audiences on a number of subjects will serve you well when you enter a career. Most employers readily admit that they prefer to hire graduates who write clearly and concisely; these employees will also be considered for promotions more quickly than those who fail to communicate effectively. On the job, your letters, memos, reports, proposals, and evaluations will be judged by all who read them. Therefore, the more effectively you communicate ideas to others, the more effectively you complete professional tasks. In addition, writing itself is a social activity; through our letters, reports, papers, and articles, we communicate and share ideas with our audiences. This interchange of thought demonstrates that composing is *not* an isolated activity practiced only by creative geniuses who live in attics.

Composing begins with an individual who, in response to personal observations and reading, wishes to transmit ideas to an audience who, in turn, will react to the written words. If we were to watch a writer at work, we would observe only the external process. We would see the writer bending over blank pages or a computer terminal, recording thoughts, adding and deleting sentences and words, rearranging the order of paragraphs or even crossing them out altogether, and possibly listening to the sound of words as the writer reads a sentence or paragraph aloud. But we do not see a number of other activities: the writer's thoughts, the knowledge drawn from personal experience and research, the facts selected, the organization chosen, the words employed to convey the writer's meaning best, the sense of audience and purpose the writer has established, the discussions about the piece the writer has had with others, and the constant revisions made. This mental process defines writing, which proves to be much more than the mechanical recording of black marks upon white paper.

As you improve your composing ability, you will notice the effect your ideas, conveyed through your choice of words and details, have upon an audience. To inform, entertain, or persuade your audience, you should employ the entire composing process to explore ideas, discover details, and organize papers effectively. Through successive drafts of papers, your analytical ability will enable you to revise conscientiously.

Within the next few pages, you can compare your thoughts about writing to a number of traditional beliefs, compare your own composing method to an overview of the writing process, and begin to explore ideas through prewriting exercises. This chapter will enable you to analyze your own composing method and learn about new techniques to aid you in writing better.

Fallacies About Writing

Too many of us believe that a writer sits down at a well-lighted desk, has a steady stream of ideas and paper, and simply constructs a unified piece within a few hours. We also believe that writing is a talent one either has or lacks. Moreover, we believe that certain conditions—such as environment, equipment, methods, time limits, or proficiency with grammar—guarantee a good product. However, each writer uses a personal method of constructing a text based upon individual experiences, knowledge, preferences, and abilities.

For example, each writer chooses a comfortable environment. Some professional writers, for instance, prefer to work at home in their libraries or workshops where they are not distracted by the bustling household. Other writers, particularly journalists, must work in an enormous room crowded with reporters, editors, and staff members also rushing to complete articles for the next edition of the paper. In this setting, with telephones ringing constantly, typewriters and video-display terminals clacking away, and conversations interrupting them, journalists must focus solely upon their own articles and not the movements of a busy city room. College students also select certain locations; many choose the quiet atmosphere of the college library while others compose in the chaotic setting of a dormitory room where the television and stereo constantly compete for their attention. Unfortunately, simply being in a comfortable environment does not guarantee that a writer can generate ideas each time he or she goes there. In fact, many writers always have pens and paper with them; they know that good ideas often come when they are engaged in activities other than writing.

We also believe that the tools we use will affect our ability to write. Some famous professional writers will not begin to work unless they have their favorite pen and paper with them. Using a basic writing implement—a pen or pencil—many writers scrawl ideas onto scraps of paper and then draw arrows to indicate additional sentences that will be incorporated into the final copy. Other writers compose at the typewriter because they believe that seeing their ideas in print is a more effective way of recognizing the worth of the ideas rather than trying to decipher their own handwriting. These writers wish to see how something will "look" when it is finished.

Modern technology has also given us options in the equipment we use. Many people, from professional writers to students, usually "write" on video-display terminals connected to a main computer or to a home unit. This method allows them to alter their text at any point, to rearrange paragraphs and sentences quickly, and to print a final edited copy rather than retyping each draft. This modern tool makes the task of writing easier, but it does not substitute for the content of the writing itself. Journalists or students who do not know what they want to say will be unable to compose even with the aid of a computer.

No matter what tools a writer uses, the methods of organizing material and the time to complete an assignment can vary greatly. For instance, a newspaper reporter who has a late-breaking story must write 800 to 1,000 words within an hour or two so that the front page is complete. The reporter will probably follow an age-old formula: he or she will answer the questions "what, when, how, where, who, and why." A good journalist's lead paragraph will inform the reader of what happened, when it occurred, how it happened, where it took place, who was involved, and why it happened. The rest of the column will expand upon this basic information. At other times, when a reporter is at the scene of the event, he or she may "write" the article by calling the newspaper and dictating the story to a rewrite person. On the other hand, a feature writer for the same paper may have weeks, even months, to research and write an article. Unlike reporters, however, a novelist does not have to work under the constraints of time and space. A novelist may literally take years to perfect a book. Unlike the reporter, who must be objective and concise, a novelist may wish to withhold information from readers in order to build suspense in a detective novel, to create a mood in a romantic scene, or to develop a character or setting thoroughly.

Students face other problems with time. Ideally, students will have a week or two to compose a single essay. Within this time limit, students can easily refine and revise the assignment several times. However, less-than-ideal situations also exist. Sometimes professors assign an essay for the next class meeting, or students may procrastinate. They are then forced to compose in an evening what had been assigned for a week. Certainly, the more time a writer has to compose, the better the piece should be, but the writer cannot use lack of time as an excuse. Imagine the embarrassment of a reporter who fails to submit copy on time; the final edition of the paper will have a gaping hole unless a substitute article can be found. Consider, too, the position of a business executive who promises to submit a proposal and a bid on a product to a client by a certain date. The executive's failure to complete the assignment will cost the company money and the executive his or her reputation.

Finally, too many writers believe that proficiency with grammar, punctuation, and spelling is the sole standard by which their writing should be judged. Because many inexperienced writers are intimidated by the red marks of a teacher's pen on their papers, they write only the types of sentences they can control and use only familiar words they can easily spell. Of course, correctness is important in writing; a writer's use of traditional grammar, punctuation, and spelling helps the reader understand the message quickly. However, during the initial process of composing, writers' insistence upon correctness frequently leads to a more serious problem: students often sacrifice their messages for correctness. When asked, for example, to analyze a particular short story, students may write only a summary of the events. Although their sentences may be correct, students do not address the assignment and instead repeat only what they already know well. Or when asked to describe a vacation, students may insist that it was interesting and exciting. But beginning writers usually do not make their descriptions of the events as interesting or exciting to the reader as they might have been to the authors. Fearing mistakes, they recite generalizations and clichés instead of making the piece original and lively. Correct grammar, punctuation, and spelling constitute a final portion of the composing process. However, writers cannot limit their messages because of their lack of knowledge in these areas. A paper that is correct grammatically but that says little new or interesting does not necessarily guarantee a good grade.

EXERCISE 1   Complete the following chart by identifying advantages and disadvantages of certain environments, tools, methods, and time limits. Also, fill in your own preferences for each item. Identify what you would use when you write different types of pieces, such as letters, class papers, research reports, or lab reports. In a group, compare your answers to your fellow students'. What changes would you like to make?

Conditions	Advantages	Disadvantages

1. Environment
 	
  a. a library
 	
  b. a dorm room
 	
  c. a room at your home
 	
  d. your preference
 	
  _____		

2. Tools
 	
  a. pen and paper
 	
  b. computer or word processor
 	
  c. tape recorder
 	
  d. your preference
 	
  _____		

3. Method
 	
  a. outline first
 	
  b. write several drafts
 	
  c. write one draft
 	
  d. discuss with others
 	
  e. your preference
 	
  _____		

4. Time
 	
  a. two or three hours
 	
  b. one week
 	
  c. two weeks
 	
  d. your preference
 	
  _____		

The Writing Commitment

Composing is a complex, individual activity. No particular method of composing ensures a successful paper, and writers find that, although one paper is easily written, another requires two or three times the number of hours. Our individual experiences, knowledge, preferences, and abilities determine how we compose each piece. However, composing effective prose to share with others requires time and honesty. To produce the best possible paragraph, essay, or report, a writer must be willing to invest time. A writer must generate and discover ideas, research facts, determine a purpose and audience, organize details, remove unnecessary items, verbalize complex ideas or descriptions, revise constantly, edit sentences and paragraphs, and, finally, proofread the finished piece for errors.

Composing also requires honesty. As writers, we must work until we are satisfied with the material and alter paragraphs or ideas we find weak, unnecessary, or uninteresting. Ernest Hemingway, the famous American author, once noted that the writer should begin with the truest thing he knows. Honesty with the topic and with ourselves forces us to refine our prose and to discover what we actually believe about a topic. Experienced writers often admit that they don't know what they mean to say about a topic, or what their views are, until they are forced to write about that topic.

Beginning writers, however, usually do not take the time to consider what they believe about a topic. When given an assignment, beginning writers often cling to the first idea that comes to them and do not carefully explore other possibilities, their own knowledge of the topic, or their ideas. Too often, they begin writing with seeming ease because they assume that they know what they want to say. However, in the middle of the paper, they run out of ideas and do not know how to conclude. They are then forced to write a paper which either relies upon generalizations or develops only part of the topic. In a more common situation, the students who carelessly complete writing assignments the night before a deadline know only too well that they have not done their best work. The marks upon the graded papers usually confirm the students' suspicions. In both cases, beginning writers have failed to devote their time to discovering what they want to say and to analyze the worth of their papers. Moreover, they have cheated themselves of one of the great rewards of writing—the discovery of their own ideas.

EXERCISE 2   Consider the techniques you use when you compose a piece. Use the questions below to identify your preferences about composing. Be honest; do not simply repeat what teachers have told you is the "correct" method. After answering these questions, describe your composing process in a paragraph or two. Finally, compare your responses, both in the list and in the paragraphs, to those of other students. What differences do you notice? What techniques do you share with others?

1. What types of prose do you write most frequently? (Do you write personal letters, business letters, papers and reports for school, or journal entries?) _____

_____

2. What do you usually do first when you approach a specific piece? _____

_____

3. How many drafts do you make for the piece? What do you do in each draft?

_____

4. What do you do if you get "stuck" in the piece? _____

_____

5. How do you organize ideas? _____

_____

6. How do you determine whether details fit your topic? _____

_____

7. When do you revise? How do you revise? _____

_____

8. Do you talk with others about the piece? When do you show others your paper? What do you ask them about the piece? _____

_____

9. How long do you usually spend on a piece? _____

_____

10. What determines when the piece is finished? _____

_____

11. What difficulties or rewards do you find when writing a piece? _____

_____

12. What is most important to you in your writing? _____

_____

13. What do you learn about yourself and others through your writing? _____

_____

14. How do you determine if your writing is effective? _____

_____

The Writing Process: An Overview

GENERATING IDEAS

Problems with composing usually can be avoided if you pay attention to the entire process of composing instead of only parts of it. If you take the time to generate ideas and consider them carefully, you will have a clearer idea of what you must do before you write. For example, you may be able to draw upon your own knowledge and experiences to create a sentimental description of a favorite family holiday and its rituals. Or you can use your own knowledge and interests as starting points. If you are interested in ecology, for instance, you can use your personal experience of camping in a national park as a beginning, but you must finally go to the library to research the topic more or interview authorities in the discipline. Usually, you generate these ideas before you organize details into a unified paper.

However, this process of invention also can continue while you are composing the piece. You may often find that your original ideas need refinement, that some facts are unnecessary, and that other facts must be included. In other words, you should not cling to your first impressions. You must remain flexible as you compose. You must be willing to view the topic in several ways and to discard your original ideas if they do not support your new attitudes and discoveries. This process of invention does not always require endless hours of thought and research. As you become more experienced, you can shorten this process. Usually, when experienced writers approach a topic, they quickly decide what to say and how to say it. Their familiarity with the topic, interest in it, and knowledge of writing help them to complete the piece more quickly than the writer who does not know where to begin.

AUDIENCE AND PURPOSE

After deciding upon a topic, experienced writers know that they must also identify their audience and purpose, for if writers fail to clarify these crucial elements, the final piece will not complete its function: to communicate and share ideas with others. Examples of writers who fail to consider their audiences and purposes abound in daily communication. Consider, for example, the instructions for operating a household appliance or the directions for assembling a child's toy. Many of these instructions, such as the directions for microwave ovens or the assembly directions for a bicycle, are so abstract, and the diagrams so complex, that only an engineer can comprehend them. However, these instructions are intended to help the consumer assemble and operate the appliance or toy. On the other hand, consider apartment rental contracts and insurance policies. Although many states now require that these documents be written in everyday English, many are still unintelligible and force consumers to ask for clarification of their rights and obligations. As a further example of writers' failure to address audiences and purpose, contrast the two following letters by college graduates applying for jobs.

1.   I hope that you won't mind my intrusion into your busy day, but I would be so grateful if you would spare a minute to consider my application for the entry-level position of junior accountant.

While at school, I did not learn everything possible about accounting, but I took as many courses as I could. I hope you will be kind enough to teach me more about the complexities of the accounting field.

Many people have told me that I am a diligent student, so I think I would be able to learn once I am on the job. I also humbly suggest that I get along well with others in a work environment.

I sure do want the opportunity to work with your excellent company, and I promise I'll give it my all. Please accept my apology for bothering you, but I really would be extremely appreciative if you'd call me anytime for an interview.

2.   Do you need an expert accountant? Then, I am your person. I just graduated from college with a degree in accounting.

I took every available course, so I know everything there is to know. I plan to start as a senior accountant. After all, if I am an expert, then why should I be forced to begin as a lowly junior accountant?

I'll call you within the next few days, when my schedule permits, so that I can set up an interview with you. I do want to know what you can offer me.

Neither letter will secure a position for its writer. Both authors do have a purpose in writing: they want to apply for positions with the company. However, both writers fail to identify the specific skills they could bring to the positions, and they do not provide the reader with any incentive to look further at their applications. For different reasons, both letters fail to address the intended audience: the prospective employer. In letter 1, the writer, perhaps unaware of his tone, indicates that he is insecure, subservient, and overly humble. He will not get the position because he is not confident about his own abilities. In letter 2, the writer suffers from the opposite problem: he is so overly confident that he demands a senior position in the firm. He, too, will not be hired, for several reasons. First, since he claims to know everything, he would be unwilling to learn the policies of a specific company. In addition, he lacks common courtesy; notice the way he demands an interview. He also fails to understand his potential relationship with an employer: he wants to know what the company can do for him, rather than what he can do for the company. Finally, his egotism may prove to be a source of conflict within the company. These examples clearly demonstrate the need for a writer to identify an audience and purpose.

ORGANIZING IDEAS

When writers finally commit ideas to paper, determine audience and purpose, organize facts, and construct paragraphs and sentences, they use any number of composing techniques. For example, some writers generate thousands of words before they begin to organize and revise their material. Thomas Wolfe, the 20th-century North Carolina author best known for his novel *Look Homeward, Angel,* would sometimes write 10,000 words a day. Stored in packing crates, his manuscripts could run to over 1,000,000 words, which his editor would shape into the final book. Other writers prefer to outline all of their thoughts and then perfect each paragraph before they write the next one. Because they spend long hours selecting, organizing, and outlining their ideas completely, the act of composing allows them to revise each section as they write. Since they already know what the next paragraph will discuss, they polish each paragraph as they write it. Occasionally, however, a writer may become overly conscious of style. Oscar Wilde, the controversial late-19th-century Irish playwright and novelist, was said to spend the morning putting a comma in and the afternoon taking it out. Some writers organize as they write. They begin with a general idea of their facts and write the entire piece first. They then return to the piece to revise and restructure their ideas. Finally, some professional writers complete a piece with one draft. Needless to say, their experience with writing and their knowledge make them rare exceptions, and even these writers will choose another composing process when they need to research a topic. Ideally, each writer chooses a composing process that best meets the needs of individual papers.

REVISING

Throughout the composing process, writers revise constantly. The act of revision requires that you, as a writer, rethink your original ideas. Because you must determine honestly when you are finished, it is difficult to say when you should stop working on a project. Some writers need only a few drafts; others need piles of paper scattered around their feet. After composing a paper, some writers discard their original topics and begin an entirely different paper. Other writers revise solely by correcting mistakes on the original draft of the paper. They incorrectly believe that "cleaning up" the first draft requires nothing more than checking spelling, punctuation, and grammar. They do not analyze what they have said and how they have said it, and they are unwilling to be honest about the worth of their writing. Hence, they fail to commit themselves to the writing process. Of course, there is a time to stop revising. Very often, the time you have for revision is determined by the due date of the assignment, yet, no matter what the time limit, you should be satisfied with what you submit.

A writer usually produces a number of drafts before the piece is finished. An analysis of these drafts offers the best understanding of the composing process. After generating ideas, you might use the first draft of a paper to explore your ideas. In this exploration, you will attempt to discover a topic, identify your interests, and play with ideas. Without regard for correctness in grammar and punctuation and without concern for organization, you will put everything down on paper; in fact, you may produce more than you will actually need later in the composing process. This freedom allows you to consider a topic from many vantage points. For example, if you wish to describe a basketball game, you might approach the topic from a number of viewpoints in the first draft: you might try to see the game as a coach, a parent, a member of the team, a cheerleader, an announcer, a scout from the National Basketball Association, or a substitute player does. While you do not need to consider every viewpoint, your consideration of a few of them will allow you to find what you believe to be the most interesting one.

In the second draft, you can begin to give direction to the paper by deciding upon a specific purpose and audience. After identifying these, you can choose those details and ideas from your first draft that support your purpose and correspond to your audience's needs. At this point, you might also make some decisions about an effective organization for the piece.

The third draft focuses upon organization of details selected in the second draft. You can now structure the paper into paragraphs that develop your purpose and central idea. You may also choose to revise your topic if you find that your original ideas no longer are effective, or to revise the order of paragraphs if they fail to produce the results you desire. Hence, you could construct a number of new paragraphs, alter their arrangement, or delete unnecessary paragraphs or sentences. Therefore, the third stage of drafts could actually contain any number of revisions as you work to make the piece more effective for your purpose and audience.

In the last drafts, you can edit sentences and paragraphs to ensure that they say what you want them to say, that your meaning is clear, that transitions help the reader understand the relationship between details and ideas, and that the paragraphs are unified. As a final check, you can proofread your piece for errors.

In each of these drafts, however, you must remain flexible and receptive to new ideas as you generate them, for it is the discovery of your own ideas that makes writing valuable for you. Certainly, too, there is not a "correct" way of constructing rough drafts; all writers create their own preferences and discover their abilities as they gain more experience through their writing.

Consider the following last drafts of a student's paper describing a softball game. Since the paper details the events of the game, the student was able to construct a time sequence for his topic. Hence, there are few changes in the placement of paragraphs, since each one describes in chronological order an aspect of the game. However, the writer does alter his material. Where does he make changes? Why might he revise words, sentences, and paragraphs?

Rough Draft:

Take Me Out of the Ballgame
~~The Big Swing~~

Softball is a dangerous sport. It lulls its participants into thinking that it's something enjoyable and easy to play. In this contest, men in the twilight of their youth, with receding hair and falling chest, savor every moment of both the game and the beer that inevitably follows. A *with substantially padded confidence, for example might* sprite teenager, ~~among the middle-aged, ought to be able~~ to clean up in *think it an easy task* such a league. But many take for granted, ~~as did I~~, that softball is safe *Unfortunately, this attitude before such a game is* for the inexperienced populace. ~~In truth, the game of softball can lead~~ *caused to* ~~to~~ fits of anxiety, obliteration of egos *during* and *afterwards* quite frankly, pain. For me, this realization came about in June of '85.

It all began at the ~~One summer, I~~ worked at Elkridge Country Club pool. One rainy day *where I worked as a lifeguard when* the pool was empty. The immature staff members, including myself, *illustrious* formed the ~~famed~~ Elkridge Baseball League (Generally, the scores were held to under a hundred runs) A home run in this demanding sport required hitting the side of a three-story barn with a tennis ball using a *commanded* metal pipe as a bat. At Elkridge, I ~~had~~ numerous home runs titles and was fondly referred to by my adoring fans as "Whipper Will" or simply "The Whip." ~~For some unexplainable reason~~, my confidence soared as *a good great several thousand feet,* each ball slammed into the metal pipe, flew ~~at least~~ twenty-five yards, *cruising at an altitude of* and bounced off the huge barn. With my ego ~~inflated~~, it came as no surprise to me when the manager of the pool asked if I could play softball *play* on Friday night. Knowing that I would ~~be playing~~ with slow thirty-five-*chuckled* year old men envious of my abilities, I ~~laughed~~ to myself and accepted.

preceded The week that ~~proceeded~~ the Friday night game overflowed with exaggerated stories of my baseball glory days. I could not help but let every-*I continued this streak of overconfidence even up to the day* one know that I was an official Rogers Forge Clinic All Star. I played *of the game* *deciding* an exhausting tennis match earlier that day, ~~figuring~~ that strength was *as the game neared* not a requirement for softball. But ~~as time passed~~, anxiety about proving my big words overtook me. By gametime I realized that my boasts were unattainable, and fits of nervousness possessed me. As if an omen, *drizzle* *diamond* the game began in a light ~~rain~~ on a muddy ~~field~~. During warmups I

[margin annotations:] pregame, game, postgame — catagorization — EBL — anxiety

couldn't relax ~~my tension~~, so the acting coach benched me for four in-

nings. Soaked by the rain, I ~~watched~~ peered from the cold bench ~~as the other~~ at the not-so-

old thirty-five year olds running, catching and ~~players ran, caught, and threw.~~ throwing

    In the top of the fifth inning, I got my chance to play. I was placed strategically

because-so I was told-.nobody hits it there

in right field. Of course the first ~~pitch yielded~~ batter hit a high fly ball to right

field, ~~the place where no one hits it.~~ I charged forward under the ball

preparing for my now-legendary play. In the last second, I realized the

ball was sailing way over my head (to my horror.) I applied the brakes

the probable   For one embarassing moment,

suddenly, forgetting ~~what~~ results on wet grass. A generous portion of

my body bounced across the grass as the softball rolled deep in the out-

strode

field. After the inning ended, I ~~walked~~ quickly back to the bench, on which

I sulked; in my empty glove I held my grounded ego.

    Learning I was the lead-off hitter, I concentrated my disappoint-

ment in determination at the bat. All I desired to do was swing at that

enormous ball with every ounce of strength that I could muster. I first

scanned the outfield, and decided to push the ball to right field in my

swing. With complete determination I dug each foot very securely in the

mud of the batter's box, and stared coldly back at the pitcher. The ball

trajectory

started its loping ~~course~~ towards the plate. My eyes focused only on that

journeying

gigantic softball ~~coming~~ towards me. With every ounce of muscle tensed,

I drew the bat from my shoulder and whipped it across the plate to-

wards the ball.

    Although the ball raced from my bat, I never moved more than two

feet from home plate. An excruciating pain ripped through my knee,

and forced me crippled to the ground. ~~The next thing I knew was the~~

envious

~~thirty-two year olds looked at the popped knee of the~~

~~Sprite teenager and shook their heads. The game was~~

~~called on account of too many paramedics on the field,~~

~~and the once cold beer now forgotten.~~ In the course

of this game's four and two-thirds innings I had

managed to invite an ulcer with my anxiousness,

crash in the outfield on my rear landing gear, and

dislocate my patella at home plate. So when the

grinning pool members exclaim, "You hurt your knee

playing softball?" I caution them. Softball is a dangerous

sport.

As the ~~thirty~~ thirty-five year olds surtly ~~gathered~~ gathered around the ~~figure~~ fallen ~~sport~~ teenager, I knew what had happened. My knee ~~had popped~~ had dislocated. Any movement on my part brought ~~instant~~ instant pain to my disarranged joint. ~~the game is so~~ The game was soon called on account of too many paramedics on the field and the once cold beer was forgotten. ~~any softball you want~~ My ordeal was finally over.

Maybe softball just isn't my game. Maybe I had a bad day. Whatever ~~the sou~~ may be the cause, The facts were ~~sure~~ evident. In the course of four and two-thirds innings I had managed to ~~too~~ lose all self-confidence through deep anxiety, crash in the outfield on my rear landing gear and dislocate my patella at home plate.

Final copy: Take Me Out of the Ballgame

Softball is a dangerous sport. It lulls its participants into thinking that it is something enjoyable and easy to play. In this contest, men in the twilight of their youth, with receding hair and falling chests, savor every moment of both the game and the beer that inevitably follows. But many take for granted that softball is safe for the inexperienced populace. A sprightly teenager with substantially padded confidence, for example, might think it an easy task to clean up in such a league. Unfortunately, this attitude is doomed to cause fits of anxiety before such a game, obliteration of egos during, and afterwards, quite frankly, pain. For me, this realization came about in June of '85.

It all began at the Elkridge Country Club pool where I worked as a lifeguard. One rainy day when the pool was empty, the immature staff members, including myself, formed the illustrious Elkridge Baseball League. A home run in this demanding sport required hitting the side of a three-story barn with a tennis ball using a metal pipe as a bat. Generally, the scores were held to under a hundred runs. At Elkridge, I commanded numerous home run titles and was fondly referred to by my adoring fans as "Whipper Will" or simply "The Whip." My confidence soared as each ball slammed into the metal pipe, flew a good twenty-five yards, and bounced off that huge barn. With my ego cruising at an altitude of several thousand feet, it came as no surprise when the manager of the pool asked if I could play softball on Friday night. Knowing that I would play with slow thirty-five-year-old men envious of my abilities, I chuckled to myself and accepted.

The week that preceded the Friday night game overflowed with exaggerated stories of my baseball glory days. I could not help but let everyone know that I was an official Rogers Forge Clinic All Star. I continued this streak of overconfidence even up to the day of the game. I played an exhausting tennis match earlier that day, deciding that strength was not a requirement for softball. But as the game neared, anxiety about proving my big words overtook me. By game time I recognized that my boasts were unattainable, and fits of nervousness possessed me. As if an omen, the game began in a light drizzle on a muddy diamond. During warmups I could not relax, so the acting coach benched me for four innings. Soaked by the rain, I peered from the cold bench at the not-so-old thirty-five-year-olds running, catching, and throwing.

In the top of the fifth inning, I got my chance to play. I was strategically placed in right field because—so I was told—nobody hits it there. Of course, the first batter hit a high fly ball to right field. I charged forward under the ball preparing for my now-legendary play. In the last second, to my horror, I realized the ball was sailing way over my head. I applied the brakes suddenly, forgetting the probable result on wet grass. For one brief, embarrassing moment, a generous portion of my body bounced across the grass as the softball rolled deep in the outfield. After the inning had ended, I <u>strode</u> quickly back to the bench <u>on which I sulked; in my empty glove I held my grounded ego.</u>

Learning I was the lead-off hitter, I concentrated my disappointment in determination at the bat. All I desired to do was swing at that enormous ball with every ounce of strength that I could muster. I first scanned the outfield, and decided to push the ball to right field in my swing. With complete determination I dug each foot very securely into the mud of the batter's box and stared coldly back at the pitcher. The ball started its loping <u>trajectory</u> towards the plate. My eyes focused only on that gigantic softball <u>journeying</u> towards me. With every ounce of muscle tensed, I drew the bat from my shoulder and whipped it across the plate towards the ball.

Although the ball raced from my bat, I never moved more than two feet from home plate. An excruciating pain ripped through my knee and forced me crippled to the ground. <u>As the thirty-five-year-olds swiftly gathered around the fallen teenager, I knew what had happened. My knee had dislocated. Any movement on my part brought intense pain to my quickly swelling knee. The game was soon called on account of too many paramedics on the field, and the once-cold beer was forgotten. The ordeal was finally over.</u>

<u>Maybe softball just is not my game. Maybe I had a bad day. Whatever the excuse may be, the facts are evident. In the course of four and two-third innings, I had managed to lose all self-confidence through deep anxiety, crash in the outfield on my rear landing gear, and dislocate my patella at home plate. So when the grinning pool members exclaimed, "You hurt your knee playing softball," I cautioned them. Softball is a dangerous sport.</u>

Notice the underlined passages in the final draft; these passages or words have been altered or added. While the overall structure of the essay does not change, the student does make substantial changes in the last two paragraphs, sentence structure, and wording. In particular, he incorporates changes that increase the dramatic action and irony. For instance, in the final two paragraphs, he completes the description of the end of the game and then turns to his conclusion; originally, he had covered both of these aspects in one paragraph. He incorporates humor into these final paragraphs by telling the reason the game ended suddenly: "too many paramedics on the field." His final paragraph summarizes his actions during the game ("lose all self-confidence through deep anxiety, crash in the outfield on my rear landing gear, and dislocate my patella at home plate") and returns to the statement beginning the essay ("Softball is a dangerous sport.").

In some paragraphs, the student consciously alters the placement of sentences or adds them to strengthen the paragraph's unity. In the first paragraph, for example, the student reverses the placement of sentences 4 and 5; this change stresses the movement from the fact that "many take for granted that softball is safe" to his own overconfidence as he anticipates the game against much older men. In addition, in paragraph 3, he adds one sentence ("I continued this streak of overconfidence even up to the day of the game"), which not only reinforces his topic sentence but also explains his reason for playing tennis the day of the game.

Finally, the writer combines a number of sentences to add sentence variety and pertinent information and chooses more descriptive words. In the second paragraph, for example, he combines the first sentence with an added sentence to form a more complete topic sentence. In his fourth paragraph, the final sentence is expanded to include more information about his actions; rather than saying he "walked" back to the bench, he "strode." The bench, which he had just left, becomes the place where he "sulked." He also adds a final touch of irony: although he had failed to catch the fly ball, the "empty glove" now holds his "grounded ego."

EXERCISE 3   Consider the changes the student could have made in the final draft. What changes would have made the final draft better? In a group, compare your answers to those of other students.

Prewriting

Prewriting, what writers do before they sit down to write an organized paper, can take many forms. You need this time to think about a topic, to consider it from several points of view, to examine it carefully, and to discuss it with others. Through these activities, you will begin to have a better sense of what you believe, what is important to say, and how you might say it. However, this invention—this thinking about writing—does not end when you pick up a pencil and paper. Even after committing ideas to paper, you can still add and delete facts or alter your original ideas or focus. Simply because you have constructed a certain sentence does not mean that you are required to keep it in the final draft. In other words, you should be flexible and willing to explore a topic throughout the entire writing process.

For many writers, including professionals, a blank piece of paper or a blank computer screen is intimidating because these writers believe that they must create a complete, unified piece immediately. They will often stare at the paper or screen for several hours as they wait for inspiration to strike; unfortunately, their wait often wastes time. Even if they manage to write a few sentences, they may find that they have little to say about the topic because they have not identified or discovered their thoughts and beliefs about it. Fortunately, two prewriting techniques, brainstorming and freewriting, help writers generate material quickly to give them a starting point.

BRAINSTORMING

Brainstorming, quickly identifying and listing ideas at random, provides a useful starting point in the composing process. During a brainstorming session, which could take as little as ten minutes, you should record all ideas and details you have about a general topic. When beginning a brainstorming session, think first of personal experiences and knowledge you have about a topic and list them. In addition, record any interests you have in the topic that you could later research. At the end of the session, you will have generated several potential starting points and have a number of ideas and points of view to consider. Examine the following results of a brainstorming session, completed in ten minutes, on the topic *baseball.*

Ideas generated for paper: types of fans at baseball games

types of pitches thrown

heroes from years past

famous games—the 1919 World Series, for example,

was rigged so that one team would win

famous clubs and their histories

changes in the game since its beginning

players' salaries and strikes

a team's commitment to a community

the revenue a franchise generates for the community

Little League games

the fun of a summer game with friends

parents and coaches at Little League games

the requirements for each position

the rewards of playing baseball

the scandals in baseball

different stadiums—the new domes or the old ballparks

the pleasure of watching a game

Of course, many other ideas could be generated for this paper, but this list gives the writer a starting point. Also, for most of these ideas, the writer can draw upon personal memories of attending baseball games to create a fresh and original piece about baseball. Because a brainstorming session allows you to identify a number of ideas, it can be used at any point in the composing process when you need to generate ideas quickly.

EXERCISE 4   Return to the essay "The Meaning of Work" on page 13, and quickly review it. In a brainstorming session, record ideas for a paper about the essay. Be sure to include your personal experiences and knowledge; also, identify areas you would like to research.

EXERCISE 5   Choose three of the categories below. Complete a brainstorming session on each topic chosen. At the end of each session, place a check by those ideas you believe could be developed into a paragraph.

1. School
2. Sports
3. Holidays
4. Dates
5. Family
6. Vacations
7. Jobs
8. Technology
9. Personal Heroes or Influential People
10. Parties

FREEWRITING

After you have used brainstorming to generate topics for a paper, you can be overwhelmed by the number and types of possible topics. Your greatest problem now is to decide which topic you can expand successfully. An efficient way to decide upon one or two possible topics is to use freewriting, since it will help you identify potential advantages and disadvantages of a topic. In addition, freewriting can generate details for a topic and allow you to explore a topic more fully than a brainstorming session would.

In a freewriting exercise, you force yourself to write continuously for ten to twenty minutes on a particular topic. Without concern for correct sentences, spelling, grammar, or punctuation, you must keep your pen moving for the required time as you record specific ideas about the topic. Sometimes, you may believe that you are moving away from the chosen topic; however, this is not the case. As its name implies, freewriting gives you freedom to explore and discover ideas. For example, if you begin a freewriting exercise on the topic *holidays,* you may begin by identifying specific holidays that are important to you. As you continue to write, however, you may find that the memory of a specific family holiday dominates your writing. Hence, you can use the details about one incident as a starting point in a paper about holidays or family celebrations. Occasionally, in a freewriting exercise, you might become "stuck" for ideas. At this point, you should repeat a key phrase or word until a new idea comes.

Writers are often pleasantly surprised when they read their finished freewriting exercises. They find that they do indeed have something to say about a particular topic. They may also find that ideas generated in the freewriting exercise are more interesting than their original topics. In either case, this method offers several advantages. First, it helps you decide whether a topic can be treated fully by using personal experience and knowledge or whether you need to research the topic before you commit ideas to paper. Second, freewriting helps generate ideas that can be used later for a more formally structured paper. Finally, freewriting can be used at any point in the composing process since it provides ideas quickly and yields supporting details for a topic.

EXERCISE 6 Select three subjects from Exercise 5, in which you employed brainstorming to identify topics for a paper. Use a set limit of fifteen to twenty minutes to complete a freewriting exercise on each one. Using the list of questions below, compare your responses with those of other students.

1. What ideas did you generate?

2. Which of these ideas can be used in a paper?

3. What differences do you note between your freewriting and that of others?

4. What different ideas did you generate?

5. Why might these differences occur?

2

Exploring Topics

PREVIEW: The topic of a paragraph is its main idea. The topic identifies the specific idea you will discuss and tells the reader your purpose for writing the paragraph.

Ranging in length from a journalist's one sentence to an essayist's twenty sentences, paragraphs share a common feature: they usually develop only one main idea. The main idea of a paragraph, the **topic** indicates the specific idea a writer will explore and alerts the reader to an author's purpose. Without a narrowed paragraph topic, writers only generalize for their readers, who will be unable to determine the purpose of the paragraph.

Identifying Topics

Identifying a topic gives an audience its first clue to the writer's purpose in the paragraph. Without an identifiable topic, a paragraph fails to communicate with its audience. Try to identify the topic of the following paragraph.

> As with many other things in life, this, too, is a process; it has a beginning, middle, and end. All of the steps must be followed in sequence, or the end product will be useless; it will not be a "finished" product, merely an end one. Obviously, such an outcome would be a disappointment. It would be a waste of time, effort, and energy, and it is something to be avoided at all costs.

This paragraph has no topic. It does not convey the writer's reason for discussing a process since the writer's audience has no idea what that process might be. If anything, the paragraph obscures the writer's meaning and indicates the writer's unwillingness to communicate with the audience.

A topic can be either **specific** (precise) or **general** (broad) depending upon the context into which it is placed. The topic *cars*, for example, could be specific if the writer described different means of transportation; on the other hand, the same topic could be general if the writer identified various makes and models of automobiles. The following ladder of abstraction represents this concept.

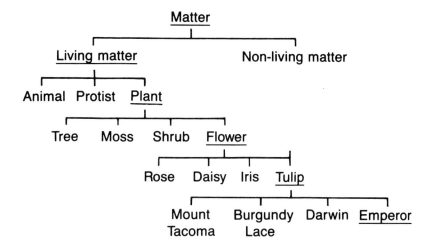

Follow the underlined topics through the chart; notice that the most general term is *matter*, and the most specific one is the *Emperor tulip*. However, items in the middle of the chart can be either specific or general, depending on their context. For example, the term *flower* can be specific when you compare it to the term *matter*.

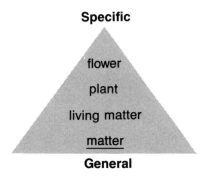

However, *flower* can be general if you compare it to a particular *type* of flower.

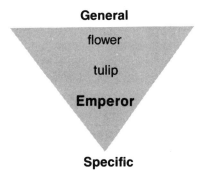

To identify a topic effectively, you should be able to recognize ideas as either general or specific.

EXERCISE 1 Read the following lists of topics closely, and decide whether the list is becoming more general or more specific. Complete the list by adding either specific details or general terms.

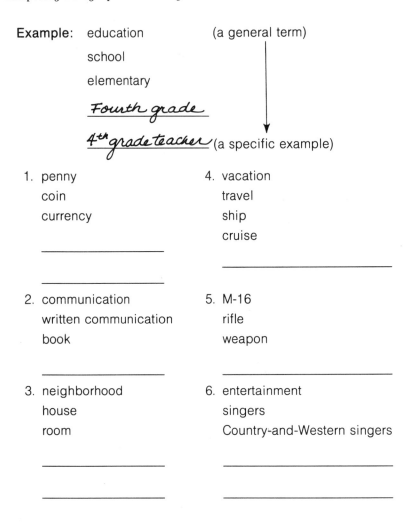

Example: education   (a general term)

school

elementary

Fourth grade

4ᵗʰ grade teacher (a specific example)

1. penny
   coin
   currency

   _____

   _____

2. communication
   written communication
   book

   _____

3. neighborhood
   house
   room

   _____

   _____

4. vacation
   travel
   ship
   cruise

   _____

5. M-16
   rifle
   weapon

   _____

6. entertainment
   singers
   Country-and-Western singers

   _____

   _____

Discovering Topics

Some writers prefer to discover what they might say about a *general* topic by writing first; they then analyze their details to determine a *specific* topic for the paragraph. Other writers use ideas generated in several journal entries to discover a paragraph topic. Since these two methods, as well as brainstorming for topics, require the classification of ideas into general and specific topics, writers should be able to identify paragraph topics from a list of details or from a paragraph itself. Identify the topic of the paragraph below by analyzing the specific details.

> Business people typically keep a close watch on *demographics*—the age, sex, income, education, and other key characteristics of the nation's people. The reason is that any significant change in demographics can dramatically alter consumer purchases. The rest of this century will see an increasingly larger middle-aged and elderly population as those who were born in the postwar "baby boom" in the late 1940s reach maturity. As you might expect, this demographic change will have a big effect on a number of different businesses, including the recording and motion picture industries, hospitals, apparel, and so forth. The expected slowdown in U.S. population until 2000 has caused Procter and Gamble to search for products besides those bought by consumers.

> (from William Rudelius and W. Bruce Erickson, *An Introduction to Contemporary Business*)

If you chose the topic *decrease in population,* your response is too specific. The probability of a decline in the U.S. population is mentioned in the paragraph, but only as one of many details. Therefore, as a topic, it represents too little information from the paragraph and is too specific to be the paragraph topic. Other topics also might be inappropriate. For example, the topic *demographics* would be too broad in the context of this paragraph. This topic includes too much information, more than is actually given in the paragraph itself. Because it raises readers' expectations of a more general discussion than actually occurs, it is too broad. (Consider, too, that a detailed treatment of demographics would require far more space than a paragraph allows.) However, the topic *businesses' interests in changing demographics* is appropriate since the paragraph discusses why business people are concerned with changing demographics. The following specific details from the paragraph support this topic: aging population affects businesses; changes in people's characteristics can alter their purchases, and overall decline in population requires that new products be created for consumers. Thus, by identifying and listing specific details, you can discover a paragraph's topic.

EXERCISE 2 Identify and list the specific details in the paragraphs below. From this list, determine a paragraph topic that identifies the main idea in the paragraph.

1.   Marketing people help create and bring about exchanges by performing certain functions. Some organizations may stress one function or another. Manufacturers take responsibility for transporting goods to convenient locations. Advertisers alert the public to the product's availability. Retailers are responsible for the details of the final exchange. Some functions—such as providing information, setting a price, and assuming risk—may be shared by many marketers. The point to keep in mind is that someone must perform these functions in order for an exchange to occur.

(from Daniel J. Rachman, *Marketing Today*)

Specific Details _____

_____

_____

Topic _____

2.   Many Europeans, from Karl Marx to Hitler, have been deluded by the so-called materialism of the Americans. It seems incomprehensible to them that in a country where there seems to be only a difference of appreciation between the methods of the robber barons and those of the gangsters, the faith of the people as a whole in the validity of democratic ideals should remain intact. It is a fact that in no other civilized nation—and up to a very recent past—has the power of money given more impunity and caused more injustice than in America. But it is also a fact that in no other nation have these abuses caused less moral damage to the nation as a whole.

(from Raoul de Roussy de Sales, "The Idea of Happiness," in *The Saturday Review Treasury*)

Specific Details _____

_____

_____

Topic _____

3. Prior to the Industrial Revolution in the early 1800s, American colonists depended on trade with England for everything from tea to textiles. After the Revolutionary War, the country was forced to become more self-sufficient. Soon mills and factories were being built, and a new era of production began. The Civil War spurred the growth of industry and mass production even further. When the war was over, factories turned from making armaments to producing consumer goods. With a seemingly limitless supply of customers and boundless natural resources, the first Industrial Age business philosophy was developed—the production concept.

(from Daniel J. Rachman, *Marketing Today*)

Specific Details _____

_____

_____

Topic _____

4. The great error in Rip's composition was an insuperable aversion to all kinds of profitable labor. It could not be from the want of assiduity or perseverance; for he would sit on a wet rock, with a rod as long and heavy as a Tartar lance, and fish all day without a murmur, even though he should not be encouraged by a single nibble. He would carry a fowling-piece on his shoulder for hours together, trudging through woods and swamps, and up hill and down dale, to shoot a few squirrels or wild pigeons. He would never refuse to assist a neighbor, even in the roughest toil, and was a foremost man at all country frolics for husking Indian corn, or building stone-fences; the women of the village, too, used to employ him to run their errands, and to do such little odd jobs as their less obliging husbands would not do for them. In a word, Rip was ready to attend to anybody's business but his own; but as to doing family duty, and keeping his farm in order, he found it impossible.

(from Washington Irving, "Rip Van Winkle")

Specific Details _____

_____

_____

Topic _____

5. What is in a handful of sand? poets have queried. The scientists have been able to answer that question with some assurance. These sand detectives can even tell a person where on the beach he picked up the sand in his shoes. No one should walk on the dunes of our beaches today—they are the natural guardians of our beach—but if anyone did, the sand between his toes could easily be identified under a microscope. Dune sand is smaller than the sand of the rest of the beach. If we study this closely, we shall find dune sand's surface and edge are rough because on the dunes they have been subjected to a fierce weathering of storms. We'll find salt too among the sand grains, in contrast to the uniform sand of the beach. Sand does not lie and, because it has such a high percentage of quartz, it is almost ineradicable. The pirates wind, water, and glaciers cannot destroy quartz. They can grind it smaller and smaller, but the quartz remains in sand.

(from Robert and Seon Manley, *Beaches*)

Specific Details _____

_____

_____

Topic _____

Generating Topics

Have you ever experienced the following situation? Toward the end of your English class, your instructor informs you that a paper on the topic of your choice is due in two days. In the middle row of the class, you immediately panic and think, "But I don't know what to write about." During the next day, you consider and discard many ideas because you believe that they are just not "right." Finally, late that evening, now desperate to produce a paper, you place a title on a blank piece of paper and stare out the window for the next hour. No ideas come to you as you constantly remind yourself that the finished paper is due the next day. As a last resort, you reach for another piece of paper and write down a topic you have used many times before—a student's responsibilities in school—even though you know you have no new insights to offer on this topic. Slinging words on paper, you decide that you will revise the paper before class. The next morning, however, you oversleep and rush to get to class on time. You grudgingly submit the paper to your instructor.

In a sense, you have cheated yourself of one of writing's great rewards: the discovery of new ideas. Because you believed that some ideas were not "right" since they did not fit a preconceived notion that a paragraph could be written easily in one draft, you failed to explore what were possibly more interesting topics for both you and your audience.

Few situations can intimidate writers as much as having a blank piece of paper on the desk, being alone in a room with only their own thoughts as guides, and knowing that they must write a paper. Where, then, do writers begin? Most writers admit that it is easier to write about themselves since they know the subject well and usually find their own experiences interesting. Nearly every subject imaginable can be a topic for a paragraph if writers carefully consider personal experiences, knowledge, and interests. Therefore, writers can begin with what they know—either from personal experience or study—or with a topic they wish to investigate more.

Certainly, the more interested you, as a writer, are in a subject, the more interesting you can make it for your audience. Writing about personal experiences makes the final piece an individual one and often gives you more control over the paragraph since you can visualize the event and draw upon memories of it for specific details. For example, if you were asked to describe a holiday, then you should consider the ones your family celebrates regularly. This process leads you to synthesize ideas from your background. The combination of ideas you know from your general background and from experience can be incorporated into your writing. For example, what makes the holiday important? Which family members visit only during the holiday season? How is the holiday celebrated? What rituals or customs does the family follow? Is the holiday celebrated at a particular place? Are certain foods and decorations used only at this time? Was one particular holiday more memorable than others? Has your attitude changed toward that holiday? All of these ideas will be interesting to others who either remember similar holidays or wish to learn about other cultures and ethnic groups. By asking questions like these in a brainstorming session, you can easily generate many ideas for a paragraph.

Some paragraphs, however, require more knowledge than you may already possess. Hence, you will not be able to synthesize ideas, since you lack background information. Therefore, you must research and analyze a topic by reading more about it in the library, interviewing authorities in the field, conducting experiments, or observing a particular event or location. However, even for a paragraph topic that demands research, you can synthesize personal experience into the piece by following your own interests. For instance, if you were asked to describe the effects of inflation upon the American economy, then you could research a recent period of inflation to obtain specific facts about unemployment and productivity. You also could interview people who were affected by the rise in prices. In addition, you could begin this paper with the story of a middle-class family that suffered greatly under inflation. By using a family's hardships as examples, you give life to otherwise dry statistics. In another type of writing situation, if you want to know more about the Great Depression in the 1930s, then you could begin your research by interviewing relatives who lived through that troubling decade. Whatever the assigned topic, you must begin with what you know and what you want to know. If you do this, then you will be interested in the topic and will convey your enthusiasm to your audience.

If you have difficulty generating paragraph topics, then use the questions reporters ask when they investigate a story: what, why, who, how, where, and when. These questions can guide you in your investigation of a topic.

1. What are your interests in the topic?

   What do you know from personal experience about the topic?

   What do you want to know about the topic?

   What is the history or development of the topic?

   What one item makes this topic interesting?

   What can you tell others about the topic?

2. Why is the topic important?

   Why should others know about this topic?

   Why did an event take place?

3. Who should know about this topic?

   Who are important people connected with this topic?

   Who helped discover, invent, or promote this topic?

4. How did an event take place?

   How has the topic had an impact on others?

   How is the topic related to everyday life?

5. Where did this event take place? (Is the location important?)

   Where does one find information about the topic?

6. When did an event occur? (What is its historical setting?)

   When is knowledge of this topic important?

EXERCISE 3   In a brainstorming session, use the questions above to generate five more specific topics for each of the following general topics. Compare the number and type of your responses with other students' topics. What does the variety of responses indicate about paragraph topics?

1. Family Life

2. Shopping Malls

3. Neighborhoods

4. Movies

5. Students

Narrowing Topics

Too often, writers choose paragraph topics that are too general; in other words, they choose topics that they cannot develop adequately in paragraphs because the topic is too broad. With a broad topic, writers are forced to make only general statements about the topic in their paragraphs. Contrast the two paragraphs below on *education*.

Education

1. Education is a necessity for all Americans. One must be able to deal with society, and education allows one to do this. In grade school, students are taught the basics of reading, writing, and mathematics. In high school, students develop their skills in these areas and gain additional knowledge. In college, students focus on one particular subject which will prepare them for careers. Therefore, education provides Americans with basic knowledge and prepares students for future employment.

Benefits of a Liberal-Arts Education

2. A liberal-arts education prepares college students for a career and for the rest of their lives. After graduates have entered the work force, they will call upon their liberal-arts education frequently. Their ability to analyze and synthesize information, gained from countless hours in history, literature, and sociology classes, will be valued in middle- and upper-management positions. Their flexibility in approaching problems, developed in various academic fields, will enable them to confront problems which resist traditional and time-worn solutions and to provide innovative answers. Their skill in communicating ideas, refined in writing and speech classes, will make them desirable candidates for a position. Moreover, knowledge acquired in liberal-arts courses will serve them well in life. Courses in psychology and sociology will give them insight into human behavior and needs. Courses in economics, political science and history will make them more informed citizens, with the ability to analyze political events. Courses in literature, art, and music will provide them with life-long interests. For these reasons, colleges should encourage students to enroll in liberal-arts classes.

In paragraph 1, the broad topic *education* forces the writer to make well-known statements about the value of education in American society and the types of knowledge students gain at each school level. The writer has not provided his readers with specific examples of the differences in levels of education and with specific examples of courses of study that will increase students' knowledge. For example, what does "gain additional knowledge" mean? Does it suggest that students will study subjects other than the basics of reading, writing, and mathematics? Or does it mean that students will be able to pursue individual interests through athletics, music, drama, or any other organizations the school might sponsor? The writer is too vague about the value of education, and his paragraph attempts to cover too many aspects of formal education in the United States. The topic *education* could generate thousands of ideas which could be developed in paragraphs, essays, journal pieces, and books. Hence, as this paragraph shows, the topic *education* is far too general to be covered adequately in a paragraph. In addition, this writer leaves his reader with questions about the topic. Certainly, there is no sense of the audience this paragraph is addressing; after all, most Americans do know these general statements about education. The paragraph also lacks a purpose; the writer does not indicate *why* education is a necessity for Americans. The writer implies that different school levels provide students with basic skills for everyday life and prepare them for careers; however, the writer fails to explain why this knowledge is important to Americans.

In contrast, paragraph 2 develops specific benefits of a liberal-arts education in college. The writer gives examples of how different liberal-arts courses connect with a student's career and personal interests. Hence, the writer has narrowed the original topic of *education* sufficiently so that he can explore ideas completely in the paragraph. Readers do not expect to read more about the topic, nor do they question the author's meaning. In addition, a specific audience is addressed in the paragraph. In his last sentence, the author urges college administrators and advisors to encourage students to enroll in liberal-arts classes for the reasons he has cited. The author's purpose is clear in his first sentence: liberal-arts classes benefit students. Therefore, the paragraph successfully develops the writer's purpose.

A paragraph topic is too general if you can think of several subtopics for it. Consider the following topics: *advertising, American politics, antiques,* and *national parks.* Each topic naturally leads to other, more specific, topics. For instance, *American politics* encourages readers first to question which century or decade the writer will focus on. Readers will also question which election—national, state, or local—the writer will discuss. Therefore, the topic is too general and must be narrowed before the writer develops a paragraph. However, a topic can be too specific if there is little for you to explore. For example, *the number of students who eat in the campus cafeteria* is too specific. One or two sentences listing the number of students would support this topic adequately. Hence, this topic cannot be developed in a paragraph. Yet you could easily turn this narrow topic into a possible paragraph topic if you consider other aspects of it. For example, the topic *student dissatisfaction with the food quality in the campus cafeteria* could provide material for a well-developed paragraph.

To narrow a topic successfully, you should be able to identify stages of subtopics. Consider the following example of how a topic is narrowed through various stages, each more specific than the last, until it is a suitable topic for a paragraph.

General Topic: *American History*

Specific Topic of American History: *The Civil War*

Specific Topic of The Civil War: *The Gettysburg Battlefield*

Specific Topic of The Gettysburg Battlefield: *Exhibits for Visitors at Gettysburg*

Specific Topic of Exhibits for Visitors at Gettysburg: *The Display of Equipment Used by Field Soldiers at Gettysburg*

For each specific topic, the writer chose one aspect of the preceding topic. From all of American history, the writer chose to discuss the Civil War. From this topic, she chose one particular battle. From her knowledge of the Gettysburg Battlefield, she selected the aspect of exhibits for twentieth-century visitors to Gettysburg. Of the many displays in the Visitors' Center and on the Battlefield, the writer concentrated on a single display.

Analyze the following reduction of a general topic. Is this topic narrowed in a logical manner? Or did the writer skip stages of reduction?

General Topic: Media

Reduction 1:   Radio

Reduction 2:   Advertising on radio

Reduction 3:   Advertising on television

Reduction 4:   Cost of advertising

Reduction 5:   Different advertisements for specific audiences

Actually, the writer has several topics to develop. However, his final topic is not part of a logical reduction because it is not clear which topic the writer will finally develop or how he narrowed the topic. In fact, the list approximates a brainstorming session more than it suggests a reduction of a general topic to a specific paragraph topic.

EXERCISE 4 Label each set ot topics from 1 for the most general to 5 for the most specific. Make sure that your stages of development are logical and that each topic really narrows the one before it.

Example: __4__ Training procedures for race horses

__2__ Horses

__1__ Animals

__3__ Race Horses

__5__ Training a race horse for its first race

1. __3__ Dramatic television programs

__2__ *St. Elsewhere*

__4__ Weekly plots on *St. Elsewhere*

__1__ Television

__5__ Diversity of plots each week on *St. Elsewhere*

2. __45__ Egyptians' contributions to geometry

__2__ Contributions of Egypt

__1__ Ancient civilizations

__3__ Egypt in the Pharaohs' times

__34__ Scientific contributions of Egyptians

3. __4__ Revival of musicals in the 1980s

__2__ Broadway plays

__1__ Theater

__3__ Musicals on Broadway

__5__ Reasons for the revival of older Broadway musicals in the 1980s

4. __4__ Effects of oil spills

__1__ Environment

__2__ Pollution in the environment

__3__ Effect of pollution

__5__ Effect of oil spills on aquatic life

5. __3__ Mark Twain's stories

_1_ American writers

_4_ Humor in Mark Twain's stories

_2_ Mark Twain

_5_ Humor in Mark Twain's *Tom Sawyer*

EXERCISE 5   For each general topic below, create a more specific topic that could be developed in a paragraph. Show the stages of your reduction.

1. **Athletes**

Reduction 1 _____

Reduction 2 _____

Reduction 3 _____

Reduction 4 _____

Reduction 5 _____

2. **Music**

Reduction 1 _Rock_____

Reduction 2 _types_____

Reduction 3 _heavy metal_____

Reduction 4 _Metallica_____

Reduction 5 _Success_____

3. **A town or city**

Reduction 1 _____

Reduction 2 _____

Reduction 3 _____

Reduction 4 _____

Reduction 5 _____

4. **A vacation spot**

Reduction 1 _____

Reduction 2 _____

Reduction 3 _____

Reduction 4 _____

Reduction 5 _____

5. **Part-time or summer jobs**

Reduction 1 _____

Reduction 2 _____

Reduction 3 _____

Reduction 4 _____

Reduction 5 _____

Identifying Audience and Purpose

The discovery of a paragraph topic does not end with selecting a reduced topic. What you write and how you present it depend on two conditions: audience and purpose. If you were to describe a recent trip to another college campus, then you would certainly choose the facts you present and alter the manner in which you present the facts to different audiences. Your parents, for example, would be interested in the size of the campus, its population, its academic facilities, and its reputation. Your best friend, however, might want more specific impressions about classes, programs in certain majors, the professors, and the social life on campus. Hence, in each situation, your letter would present different facts, have a different purpose, and vary greatly in the language used. We tend to tell people in authority fewer specific details than we tell close friends. In addition, our language becomes more formal when we speak with those in authority and more colloquial with peers. In most cases, your letter to your parents about the campus visit would be more formal and contain fewer details than the letter to your close friend. (You might, for instance, omit the details of a late-night dorm party or the antics of a professor in class in a letter to your parents.) When you write, you must use this natural ability to present a single topic in different ways to diverse audiences.

Consider the importance of audience and purpose in the types of writing all of us must do. When we write to communicate ideas, observations, experiences, and skills to others, we must consider that our audience may be people who differ greatly in the amount of education they have, their interest in the topic, the time they have to read our message, and their social and cultural experiences. Therefore, as much as possible, you must be able to visualize a specific audience and determine the purpose of your message to the audience. In each case, you must be able to explain, describe, and argue so that each member of a specific audience will comprehend your message fully.

In college, you constantly write lab reports, essays, and research papers. Each type of writing indicates to professors how well you have comprehended concepts, theories, or practices. However, each piece differs according to audience and purpose. For instance, a lab report should contain only objective information—information you gained through observation of a chemical process, the dissection of a frog, or any experiment. On the other hand, essays and research papers often require that you begin with your own ideas and support them with facts gathered from books, experiments, or individuals. In both cases, you must consider your audiences. If you were asked to write an analytical paper about Shakespeare's play *Hamlet,* then you cannot provide a summary of the play's events; the professor already knows the play well. Instead, the professor assumes that you can analyze particular passages and discuss themes or symbols that occur in the work.

Writing is not limited to college assignments, however. Even in this age of electronic communication—when the telephone and electronic mail seem to be more efficient and faster than letters—written communication is the means by which the business world operates. As a college graduate, you will begin your job search with a résumé and a cover letter of application mailed to a prospective employer. Your ability to write well will be judged long before an employer invites you for an interview. Once you begin work, you will write letters, memos, proposals, and reports to others. In each writing situation, your ability to communicate effectively will save the company time, money, and embarrassment. In addition, if you write well, then you will find that your chances for promotion are enhanced if you can address different audiences and convey your purpose.

Unfortunately, beginning writers often ignore their audiences and purposes. When they receive an assignment, they usually write the piece without sufficient reflection. The final product is sometimes flat, contains only generalizations, and lacks in direction; in fact the paper may bore both the writer and the reader. However, if these writers identify their audience and purpose, then their message will be focused, and the language and tone will be appropriate for the audience.

Consider the following topics designed for specific audiences and purposes. Note that one general topic can yield several specific topics for different audiences.

General Topic	Audience	Purpose
1. College Life	a. High-school Seniors	Discuss how to make the transition from high school to college
	b. Parents	Describe the college's facilities and housing for students
	c. Friends	Describe the campus's social activities.
2. Politics	a. College Students	Encourage students to support one candidate by voting
	b. Members of a Particular Political Party	Convince them to give money to the party's effort
	c. Supporters	Tell them how to promote their candidate
3. Law	a. Law Students	Explain the ethics of their profession
	b. Police Academy Students	Describe methods of enforcing laws
	c. Criminal Suspect	Define the suspect's rights under the law

To identify your audience and purpose, think first of a specific person to whom you would address a topic; consider also what you would want this writing to accomplish. If you cannot identify a specific member of an audience, then ask the following questions to create a potential audience.

1. Who would be most interested in the topic?
2. What might this person already know about the topic? (What pieces of information must be included? What items can be omitted?)
3. What is this person's educational background? What are his or her social and cultural interests?
4. How old is this person? What might be his or her political concerns?
5. Is this person sympathetic or hostile to the topic? (How would you handle each response?)

In addition to identifying an audience, you must decide what the purpose of the paper is. Do you want to explain, compare and contrast, define, classify, motivate, persuade, describe, narrate, or argue? Finally, how do you want your audience to respond? Do you want your readers to agree with your argument, enjoy the humor of a story, feel sympathy, follow your directions, understand a problem and possible solutions, or alter their behavior? Answers to these questions will provide you with a better sense of your audience and purpose in writing.

EXERCISE 6   For each topic below, several audiences are listed. Create and list a possible purpose for each audience.

1. Topic: **Drugs**

Audiences	Purpose
a. teenagers	_____
b. parents	_____
c. city police officers	_____

2. Topic: **Student Athletes**

Audiences	Purpose
a. college administrators	_____
b. high-school players	_____
c. college coaches	_____

3. Topic: **Urban Poverty**

Audiences	Purpose
a. city council members	_____
b. social workers	_____
c. someone on welfare	_____

EXERCISE 7   List two different audiences and purposes for each topic below.

General Topic	Audience	Purpose
1. Social Organizations	_____	_____
	_____	_____
2. Rural Areas	_____	_____
	_____	_____
3. Pets	_____	_____
	_____	_____
4. Peer Pressure	_____	_____
	_____	_____
5. Education	_____	_____
	_____	_____

Writing Strategy: NARRATION

In this section, you will have the opportunity to read and respond to three narrative pieces. A narration tells a story that is usually developed either by a chronological ordering of the story's events or by moving from the least important detail to the most important one. As you read these pieces, analyze the chronological method each author uses. These models will guide you later as you create a narrative paragraph.

means time

Incident on A Lake in Lausanne

Winston Churchill

My brother and I were sent this summer by our parents for a so-called walking-tour in Switzerland, with a tutor. I need hardly say we travelled by train so far as the money lasted. The tutor and I climbed mountains. We climbed the Wetterhorn and Monte Rosa. The spectacle of the sunrise striking the peaks of the Bernese Oberland is a marvel of light and colour unsurpassed in my experience. I longed to climb the Matterhorn, but this was not only too expensive but held by the tutor to be too dangerous. All this prudence however might easily have been upset by an incident which happened to me in the Lake of Lausanne. I record this incident that it may be a warning to others. I went for a row with another boy a little younger than myself. When we were more than a mile from the shore, we decided to have a swim, pulled off our clothes, jumped into the water and swam about in great delight. When we had had enough, the boat was perhaps 100 yards away. A breeze had begun to stir the waters. The boat had a small red awning over its stern seats. This awning acted as a sail by catching the breeze. As we swam towards the boat, it drifted farther off. After this had happened several times we had perhaps halved the distance. But meanwhile the breeze was freshening and we both, especially my companion, began to be tired. Up to this point no idea of danger had crossed my mind. The sun played upon the sparkling blue waters; the wonderful panorama of mountains and valleys, the gay hotels and villas still smiled. But I now saw Death as near as I believe I have ever seen Him. He was swimming in the water at our side, whispering from time to time in the rising wind which continued to carry the boat away from us about the same speed we could swim. No help was near. Unaided we could never reach the shore. I was not only an easy, but a fast swimmer, having represented my House at Harrow, when our team defeated all comers. I now swam for life. Twice I reached within a yard of the boat and each time a gust carried it just beyond my reach; but by a supreme effort I caught hold of its side in the nick of time before a still stronger gust bulged the red awning again. I scrambled in, and rowed back for my companion who, though tired, had not apparently realised the dull yellow glare of mortal peril that had so suddenly played around us. I said nothing to the tutor about this serious experience; but I have never forgotten it; and perhaps some of my readers will remember it too.

QUESTIONS 1. The title, "Incident on A Lake in Lausanne," is innocuous. What sentence tells you that the incident was a fateful one?

2. Why does Churchill describe the beautiful sights he sees from the lake?

3. Define the following words: *unsurpassed, prudence, panorama,* and *freshening.*

4. Why does Churchill mention his audience in the last sentence? What other indications do you have that Churchill is concerned about his audience?

5. How does Churchill develop this piece? Is there a single topic? Do the first few sentences perform a function other than narrating the story? Upon what incident does Churchill focus the piece? In what order does he present the events?

Theft and Flight
[from *Moll Flanders*]

Daniel Defoe

1   Wandering thus about, I knew not whither, I passed by an apothecary's shop in Leadenhall Street, where I saw lie on a stool just before the counter a little bundle wrapped in a white cloth; beyond it stood a maid-servant with her back to it, looking towards the top of the shop, where the apothecary's apprentice, as I suppose, was standing upon the counter, with his back to the door, and a candle in his hand, looking and reaching up to the upper shelf for something he wanted, so that both were engaged mighty earnestly, and nobody else in the shop.

2   This was the bait; and the devil, who I said laid the snare, as readily prompted me as if he had spoke, for I remember, and shall never forget it, 'twas like a voice spoken to me over my shoulder, "Take the bundle; be quick; do it this moment." It was no sooner said but I stepped into the shop, and with my back to the wench, as if I had stood up for a cart that was going by, I put my hand behind me and took the bundle, and went off with it, the maid or the fellow not perceiving me, or any one else.

3   It is impossible to express the horror of my soul all the while I did it. When I went away I had no heart to run, or scarce to mend my pace. I crossed the street indeed, and went down the first turning I came to, and I think it was a street that went through into Fenchurch Street. From thence I crossed and turned through so many ways and turnings, that I could never tell which way it was, nor where I went; for I felt not the ground I stepped on, and the farther I was out of danger, the faster I went, till, tired and out of breath, I was forced to sit down on a little bench at a door, and then I began to recover, and found I was got into Thames Street, near Billingsgate. I rested me a little and went on; my blood was all in a fire; my heart beat as if I was in a sudden fright. In short, I was under such a surprise that I still knew not whither I was going, or what to do.

4   After I had tired myself thus with walking a long way about, and so eagerly, I began to consider and make home to my lodging, where I came about nine o'clock at night.

QUESTIONS

1. Has Moll Flanders stolen before? Explain your answer.

2. Each paragraph delineates a specific aspect of the event. For each paragraph, label the part of the incident that is narrated.

3. The tone is informal and conversational. Indicate which elements contribute to this effect.

4. Does Moll know what is inside the package? If she does not, then why does she steal it?

The Calling

Russell Baker

1   The only thing that truly interested me was writing, and I knew that sixteen-year-olds did not come out of high school and become writers. I thought of writing as something to be done only by the rich. It was so obviously not real work, not a job at which you could earn a living. Still, I had begun to think of myself as a writer. It was the only thing for which I seemed to have the smallest talent, and, silly though it sounded when I told people I'd like to be a writer, it gave me a way of thinking about myself which satisfied my need to have an identity.

2   The notion of becoming a writer had flickered off and on in my head since the Belleville days, but it wasn't until my third year in high school that the possibility took hold. Until then I'd been bored by everything associated with English courses. I found English grammar dull and baffling. I hated the assignments to turn out "compositions," and went at them like heavy labor, turning out leaden, lackluster paragraphs that were agonies for teachers to read and for me to write. The classics thrust on me to read seemed as deadening as chloroform.

3   When our class was assigned to Mr. Fleagle for third-year English I anticipated another grim year in that dreariest of subjects. Mr. Fleagle was notorious among City [City College, a Baltimore high school] students for dullness and inability to inspire. He was said to be stuffy, dull, and hopelessly out of date. To me he looked to be sixty or seventy and prim to a fault. He wore primly severe eyeglasses, his wavy hair was primly cut and primly combed. He wore prim vested suits with neckties blocked primly against the collar buttons of his primly starched white shirts. He had a primly pointed jaw, a primly straight nose, and a prim manner of speaking that was so correct, so gentlemanly, that he seemed a comic antique.

4   I anticipated a listless, unfruitful year with Mr. Fleagle and for a long time was not disappointed. We read *Macbeth*. Mr. Fleagle loved *Macbeth* and wanted us to love it too, but he lacked the gift of infecting others with his own passion. He tried to convey the murderous ferocity of Lady Macbeth one day by reading aloud the passage that concludes

> . . . I have given suck, and know
> How tender 'tis to love the babe that milks me.
> I would, while it was smiling in my face,
> Have plucked my nipple from his boneless gums. . . .

The idea of prim Mr. Fleagle plucking his nipple from boneless gums was too much for the class. We burst into gasps of irrepressible snickering. Mr. Fleagle stopped.

5   "There is nothing funny, boys, about giving suck to a babe. It is the—the very essence of motherhood, don't you see."

6   He constantly sprinkled his sentences with "don't you see." It wasn't a question but an exclamation of mild surprise at our ignorance. "Your pronoun needs an antecedent, don't you see," he would say, very primly. "The purpose of the Porter's scene, boys, is to provide comic relief from the horror, don't you see."

7   Late in the year we tackled the informal essay. "The essay, don't you see, is the . . ." My mind went numb. Of all forms of writing, none seemed so boring as the essay. Naturally we would have to write informal essays. Mr. Fleagle distributed a homework sheet offering us a choice of topics. None was quite so simpleminded as "What I Did on My Summer Vacation," but most seemed to be almost as dull. I took the list home and dawdled until the night before the essay was due. Sprawled on the sofa, I finally faced up to the grim task, took the list out of my notebook, and scanned it. The topic on which my eye stopped was "The Art of Eating Spaghetti."

8   This title produced an extraordinary sequence of mental images. Surging up out of the depths of memory came a vivid recollection of a night in Belleville when all of us were seated around the supper table—Uncle Allen, my mother, Uncle Charlie, Doris, Uncle Hal—and Aunt Pat served spaghetti for supper. Spaghetti was an exotic treat in those days. Neither Doris nor I had ever eaten spaghetti, and none of the adults had enough experience to be good at it. All the good humor of Uncle Allen's house reawoke in my mind as I recalled the laughing arguments we had that night about the socially respectable method for moving spaghetti from plate to mouth.

9   Suddenly I wanted to write about that, about the warmth and good feeling of it, but I wanted to put it down simply for my own joy, not for Mr. Fleagle. It was a moment I wanted to recapture and hold for myself. I wanted to relive the pleasure of an evening at New Street. To write it as I wanted, however, would violate all the rules of formal composition I'd learned in school, and Mr. Fleagle would surely give it a failing grade. Never mind, I would write something else for Mr. Fleagle after I had written this thing for myself.

10   When I finished it the night was half gone and there was no time left to compose a proper, respectable essay for Mr. Fleagle. There was no choice next morning but to turn in my private reminiscence of Belleville. Two days passed before Mr. Fleagle returned the graded papers, and he returned everyone's but mine. I was bracing myself for a command to report to Mr. Fleagle immediately after school for discipline when I saw him lift my paper from his desk and rap for the class's attention.

11   "Now, boys," he said, "I want to read you an essay. This is titled 'The Art of Eating Spaghetti.' "

12   And he started to read. My words! He was reading *my words* out loud to the entire class. What's more, the entire class was listening. Listening attentively. Then someone laughed, then the entire class was laughing, and not in contempt and ridicule, but with openhearted enjoyment. Even Mr. Fleagle stopped two or three times to repress a small prim smile.

13   I did my best to avoid showing pleasure, but what I was feeling was pure ecstasy at this startling demonstration that my words had the power to make people laugh. In the eleventh grade, at the eleventh hour as it were, I had discovered a calling. It was the happiest moment of my entire school career. When Mr. Fleagle finished he put the final seal on my happiness by saying, "Now that, boys, is an essay, don't you see. It's—don't you see—it's of the very essence of the essay, don't you see. Congratulations, Mr. Baker."

14   For the first time, light shone on a possibility. It wasn't a very heartening possibility, to be sure. Writing couldn't lead to a job after high school, and it was hardly honest work, but Mr. Fleagle had opened a door for me. After that I ranked Mr. Fleagle among the finest teachers in the school.

QUESTIONS

1. Why does Baker finally want to write the piece? What difference does this motive make in his final paper? Why does Baker say that he "would write something else for Mr. Fleagle"?

2. Is Baker's description of Fleagle effective? Why does Baker repeat the word "prim" throughout the paragraph?

3. What effect does Baker's paper have upon other students?

4. Baker wrote this piece as an older man reflecting on his adolescence. What is his tone here? Would the tone have been the same if a sixteen-year-old boy had written this passage?

PARAGRAPH ASSIGNMENTS

1. Usually, the first week of a semester is an exhilarating, challenging time for students. Recount your experiences during the first week for a group of college-bound high-school seniors. In order to predict your audience's concerns and expectations, recall what you knew as a high-school senior. What would you have liked to know about the first week of the semester before you experienced it?

2. Doing something for the first time—whether it is skiing, taking a trip alone, or driving your own car—is unlike any repetition of the event. Narrate a personal first experience. Consider several different audiences before you begin. Finally, identify one audience and purpose.

3. Churchill indicates that he will never forget his "serious experience" on the lake and that he hopes "some of my readers will remember it too." Consider his purpose in making such a statement. Then, turn your attention to a dangerous or exciting experience of your own. What can you tell others about the experience? What makes that experience more important than others? Narrate your experience.

Creating Topic Sentences

1. To identify controlling ideas in topic sentences.
2. To identify facts and opinions.
3. To generate topic sentences.
4. To discover topic sentences in paragraphs.
5. To place topic sentences according to their functions in paragraphs.
6. To explore composing through description.

A topic sentence presents the main idea of a paragraph to your reader. The topic sentence defines your opinion, predicts your discussion, and controls the way in which you develop the paragraph. Each topic sentence has a controlling idea that offers an opinion about or limits the topic.

A **topic sentence** presents the main idea of a paragraph. It is the sentence in the paragraph that tells your audience the subject (topic) of the paragraph and the controlling idea (the statement you want to make about the topic). Therefore, the topic sentence *defines* your opinion, *predicts* what you will discuss in the paragraph, and *controls* the development of the paragraph.

Every paragraph you write should contain a topic sentence stating the main idea of the paragraph. Usually the first sentence of a paragraph, the topic sentence promises your reader that you will discuss a specific topic within the paragraph and thereby helps your readers to predict the outline of the discussion. In effect, the topic sentence limits what you can argue, explain, define, or describe within a certain paragraph and thereby controls the development of the paragraph.

Consider these paragraphs:

1. So Grant and Lee were in complete contrast, representing diametrically opposed elements in American life. Grant was the modern man emerging; beyond him, ready to come on the stage, was the great age of steel and machinery, of crowded cities and a restless burgeoning vitality. Lee might have ridden down from the old age of chivalry, lance in hand, silken banner fluttering over his head. Each man was the perfect champion of his cause, drawing both his strengths and his weaknesses from the people he led.

2. Each man had, to begin with, the great virtue of utter tenacity and fidelity. Grant fought his way down the Mississippi Valley in spite of acute personal discouragement and profound military handicaps. Lee hung on in the trenches at Petersburg after hope itself had died. In each man there was an indomitable quality . . . the born fighter's refusal to give up as long as he can still remain on his feet and lift his two fists.

(both from Bruce Catton, "Grant and Lee: A Study in Contrasts")

In the first paragraph, the topic sentence is the first one; it informs readers that the author intends to contrast two Civil War generals, Grant and Lee, as opposites in war and in character. The author also suggests that their differences were representative of separate elements in the America of the 1860s. The rest of the paragraph then describes each man's character.

In the second paragraph, the topic sentence, again the first one, notes a comparison between Grant and Lee: both men were loyal and dedicated. The author then supplies specific examples of separate campaigns to support his topic sentence.

Both of these paragraphs appear in a longer essay and develop only a small portion of the comparisons and contrasts between the men. However, notice that both topic sentences are more general than the sentences that follow. From these examples, you should conclude that, although a topic sentence narrows a limited topic for a paragraph-length discussion, the topic sentence is more general than the specific details that support it. Therefore, the topic sentence has two functions:

1. it unifies the paragraph, and
2. it organizes the ideas given in the paragraph.

The Controlling Idea

How does the topic sentence unify the paragraph? How does it organize the details in the paragraph? These functions are accomplished by the **controlling idea,** usually located in the sentence's predicate. The controlling idea offers an opinion or limits to the topic; it is the statement that the author wants to make about the topic. Because this idea states the point of the paragraph, it limits the discussion. Authors know that they must support that stated opinion or explain the given limit. Keeping that goal in mind, they choose only those details that will help them validate their opinion and thereby ensure a *unified* paragraph. They then present those facts in a logical manner and thereby organize their paragraph.

So, topic sentences contain two major parts: a subject that identifies the topic and a controlling idea, a word or phrase, that identifies the writer's opinions or limitations.

              subject   controlling idea

Example: Each new scientific *development* has *many benefits* for the average consumer.

In this sentence, *development* is the subject of the sentence; it is also a narrowed topic suitable for a paragraph. The controlling idea is *many benefits*. In the body of the paragraph, the writer will list and explain some major advantages of scientific discoveries.

How do you discover the controlling idea? That requires a two-step process.

1. Locate the topic. Look at the subject of the sentence and determine whether it is the concept under discussion.
2. Then, ask yourself, what statement is the author making about the topic? What is he or she trying to prove? You will probably find the answer in the verb part of the sentence. The answer is the controlling idea.

EXERCISE 1   Circle the controlling idea in each topic sentence below.

    1. Contemporary fads indicate a great deal about Americans' images of themselves.

    2. Training a pet requires time, patience, and determination.

    3. Urban crime has created many problems for residents of large cities.

4. Foreign travel increases one's knowledge of other cultures, languages, and customs.

5. Classical music offers several rewards to its listeners.

6. Television game shows promise their participants instant wealth and fame.

7. Americans' fascination with games has many far-reaching effects.

8. The senator listed five reasons for her popularity.

9. Stereo systems can be expensive to buy, complex to operate, and enjoyable to use.

10. Raising children is a difficult task.

Be careful when you choose a controlling idea. Some words may be inadequate because they are vague and open to interpretation by your reader. Analyze this topic sentence:

Gone with the Wind is the greatest movie ever made.

The controlling idea of this sentence is *greatest movie ever made*. What does *greatest* mean? Does the writer mean that he enjoyed the movie? Did he enjoy the movie for a particular reason, such as the acting, the dialogue, or the settings? Can he actually compare this movie, a historical romance, to every movie made? How, in fact, could he compare the value of *Gone with the Wind* to a movie like *Return of the Jedi* or *The Deer Hunter*? This controlling idea is inadequate because the reader will wonder what the writer means.

To correct an inadequate controlling idea, you could make one of the following revisions.

1. You could provide a more specific word or phrase to replace the vague controlling idea.

   Revision: For its theme of survival, *Gone with the Wind* is one of the best-remembered movies of all time.

2. You could qualify your statement by limiting your controlling idea.

   Revisions: *Gone with the Wind* captivates audiences with its characters and theme.

   Gone with the Wind creates an imperfect vision of the South before, during, and after the Civil War.

NOTE: Be particularly careful with words such as *good, bad,* or *interesting*. Each of these words is certainly open to a reader's interpretation of what may be good, bad, or interesting within a specific context.

EXERCISE 2 Identify the controlling idea in each topic sentence below. If the controlling idea is adequate, place an *A* in the blank next to the sentence. If the controlling idea is inadequate, place an *I* in the blank. Correct all inadequate controlling ideas by using one of the two methods discussed above.

_____ 1. In the past ten years, women have made outstanding contributions to businesses.

_____ 2. Unlike Europeans, Americans use the word *friend* to describe many types of acquaintances.

_____ 3. Jury selection is an arduous process.

_____ 4. Millions of Americans enjoy running because it promotes good muscle tone and cardiovascular fitness.

_____ 5. The Orient Express, the famous train which connected Paris and Istanbul, offered an interesting journey to its passengers.

_____ 6. Many advertising slogans have become part of our everyday speech.

_____ 7. The new XLT personal computer is a fascinating piece of equipment.

_____ 8. Americans are interested in purchasing good cars.

_____ 9. World War II brought many changes to Americans.

_____10. Most students prefer multiple-choice tests over essay tests.

In the following paragraphs, note how the controlling idea unifies and organizes the paragraph. Each paragraph works because the author was guided by the controlling idea and used only those details that directly contributed to the paragraph's message.

Paragraph 1: [In this paragraph, Henry David Thoreau describes the night he spent in a Concord, Massachusetts jail for failing to pay his poll tax.]

It was like travelling into a far country, such as I had never expected to behold, to lie there for one night. It seemed to me that I never had heard the town-clock strike before, nor the evening sounds of the village; for we slept with the windows open, which were inside the grating. It was to see my native village in the light of the Middle Ages, and our Concord was turned into a Rhine stream, and visions of knights and castles passed before me. They were the voices of old burghers that I heard in the streets. I was an involuntary spectator and auditor of whatever was done and said in the kitchen of the adjacent village-inn—a wholly new and rare experience to me. It was a closer view of my native town. I was fairly inside of it. I never had seen its institutions before. This is one of its peculiar institutions; for it is a shire town. I began to comprehend what its inhabitants were about.

(from Henry David Thoreau, "Civil Disobedience")

In the above paragraph, the topic sentence is the first one. *It* (Thoreau's night in jail) is the topic, and *travelling into a far country*, the idea of a new and unusual experience, is the controlling idea. For the paragraph to be unified, the details must demonstrate that spending his first night in jail was a remarkable experience for Thoreau. Notice how these details accomplish this task:

1. "heard town clock" and "evening sounds of the village"
2. medieval references (the Rhine, knights and castles, old burghers), and
3. "involuntary spectator" and "auditor"

Because the details support and enlarge upon the topic and because they explain the controlling idea, this paragraph is unified.

Paragraph 2: The return of Halley's Comet has caused quite a stir. The news media report on its progress daily and offer suggestions for the best viewing times and places. The sale of binoculars and telescopes has soared, all with the purpose of getting a better look at this once-in-a-lifetime visitor. Comet tee-shirts, coffee mugs, and key chains are being sold. Cruises to the southern hemisphere at prime viewing times have been organized. Scientists have cleaned all their instruments and devised various experiments in the hope of learning more about occasional celestial visitors. After all the commotion and promotion, not catching a glimpse of this astral pilgrim would be a great disappointment.

Again, the topic sentence is the first one: "The return of Halley's comet has caused quite a stir." The topic is the reappearance of the comet and the controlling idea is the sensation it is causing.

Supporting Details: 1. daily media reports

2. soaring sales of telescopes and binoculars and various souvenirs

3. cruises to likely viewing areas

Again, each of the details directly contributes to the controlling idea; consequently, the paragraph is unified.

EXERCISE 3   Underline the topic sentence in the following paragraphs. Then write the topic and the controlling idea. Finally, list the details that support the controlling idea.

1.   The rocket engine has overcome these disadvantages. Rockets do not depend upon the atmosphere to supply the oxygen they need for combustion. Instead, they carry their own supply. The liquid oxygen, or oxygen-rich compound, makes possible the combustion of the fuel. The liquid fuel and the liquid oxygen mix together in the combustion chamber to produce hot exhaust gases. These gases are hurled at very great speeds from the nozzle of the combustion, and the rocket engine moves by reaction.

(from *Foundations Physical Science*)

Topic _____

Controlling Idea _____

Supporting Details _____

_____

_____

_____

_____

2.   As the weeks went by, my [Dr. Watson's] interest in him [Sherlock Holmes] and my curiosity as to his aims in life gradually deepened and increased. His very person and appearance were such as to strike the attention of the most casual observer. In height he was rather over six feet, and so excessively lean that he seemed to be considerably taller. His eyes were sharp and piercing, save during those intervals of torpor to which I have alluded; and his thin, hawk-like nose gave his whole expression an air of alertness and decision. His chin, too, had the prominence and squareness which mark the man of determination. His hands were invariably blotted with ink and stained with chemicals, yet he was possessed of extraordinary delicacy of touch, as I frequently had occasion to observe when I watched him manipulating his fragile philosophical instruments.

(from Arthur Conan Doyle, "A Study in Scarlet")

Topic _____

Controlling Idea _____

Supporting Details _____

_____

_____

_____

_____

EXERCISE 4 The following sets of sentences are from paragraphs that have been rearranged and separated into individual sentences. From each set, select the sentence that controls and organizes the entire paragraph—in other words, select the main idea. This sentence is the topic sentence for the paragraph; circle its letter.

1. a. The city taxes tickets, parking, and concessions, and businesses close to the ball park—hotels, bars, and restaurants especially—note an increase in patronage.

   b. Also, citizens just seem to have more pride in their city—and perhaps about themselves—when there is a franchise, especially a successful one, performing at the ball park.

   c. A major-league sports franchise aids a city tremendously.

   d. Moreover, the city receives national coverage through the media as the city's name is mentioned in conjunction with that of its team.

   e. This franchise, for example, can generate a great deal of money.

2. a. For example, this exercise improves the body's cardiovascular system, for the heart and lungs come to operate more efficiently.

   b. Jogging proves beneficial in several ways.

   c. The jogger knows that he has gained control of his life and is doing what is best for him.

   d. Moreover, jogging increases the body's endurance; the legs, especially, grow stronger through repeated use.

   e. In addition, the discipline which jogging requires increases one's self-esteem.

3. a. With the aid of a catalogue and a course schedule, a student must first determine the courses she wishes to take and the times she wishes to take the courses.

   b. Next, the student must meet with her advisor to make sure that she has selected the courses that will fulfill college requirements.

   c. Finally, the student presents the amended schedule to the registrar only to be told that two of her five courses are already filled.

   d. The most difficult part of a freshman's first week at college may be the registration process.

   e. This process of creating a schedule can be especially exasperating if a student must also plan hours for a part-time job.

4. a. The oversized head measures one hundred and ten square inches and encloses a "sweet spot" three and a half times larger than traditional rackets.

   b. Before playing tennis, a person obtains the best equipment available on the market just as the professionals do.

   c. Framed in sixty-percent graphite and forty percent fiberglass for power and control, the high-performance instrument slices through the wind with its new aerodynamic design.

   d. Since the professional tennis player never appears in a tournament without a reserve racquet, the person has to buy several custom-made racquets costing two hundred dollars each.

   e. Padded with foam to prevent blisters, the handle is wrapped with genuine calfskin leather to assure a strong grip.

5. a. From the mirror-covered ceiling hung reflective balls reminiscent of 1970s discothèques.

   b. The inside of the tavern was something straight from an interior decorator's worst nightmare.

   c. Each table had four chairs made of aluminum frames with red vinyl cushions that almost, but not quite, matched the walls.

   d. The walls of the fifty foot by one hundred foot room were covered with maroon velvet and decorated with art work of dubious quality.

   e. Along one wall was the bar itself, and evenly distributed about the room were twenty-odd formica tables of differing shapes and sizes.

Identifying Facts and Opinions

As discussed earlier, the topic sentence states your opinion about the topic. Examine the following sentence. Does it offer an opinion?

> At Milbrook University, eighty percent of the full-time students commute to campus daily.

This topic sentence is not adequate. With such a sentence, the writer does not offer an opinion about the general topic of college students who commute to campus. Instead, the writer offers a fact. While facts are useful as supporting ideas, they do not create topic sentences, because there is nothing more that can be said about a factual statement.

A **fact** is a statement that can be definitively and objectively proven or disproven by using sensory evidence. An **opinion** is a personal belief concerning what one thinks is true or valid; it can never be absolutely proven or disproven. A factual statement can be shown to be false, but an opinion can be changed only because it is shown to be invalid. A fact is objective; an opinion is subjective.

Examine these sets of facts and opinions:

Fact: The Pacific Ocean is the largest body of water on the earth.

Opinion: The Indian Ocean is best for surfing.

Fact: Thomas A. Edison received the first patent for an incandescent light bulb.

Opinion: Thomas Edison's inventions propelled humankind into the modern era.

Fact: Whales are actually mammals, more closely related to humans than to sharks.

Opinion: Killing whales should be prohibited.

Each of the above facts can be proven true. All of the oceans can be measured to see which one is the largest. Patent Office records can be searched to see who patented the light bulb. Scientists can study the genetic make-up of whales, sharks, and humans to determine their genetic similarities. Because objective means have been used to prove or disprove those statements, they are facts.

Each of the opinion statements rests on a personal point of view. While one person may like surfing in the Indian Ocean, another may prefer the Mediterranean Sea. Similarly, although Mr. Edison's inventions changed America's lifestyles, not everyone would agree that they served as a catalyst for modernity. Finally, some nations need whale meat as a source of protein for their people, so they would resent any interdiction against whaling. Since neither side in the dispute can be absolutely proven true or false, right or wrong, these are opinion statements. An opinion should be supported by facts, but it is not itself a fact.

EXERCISE 5 Read each of the following statements carefully. If the statement can be proven or disproven by using objective evidence, write FACT in the blank to the left. If the statement reveals a personal viewpoint that cannot be absolutely proven or disproven, write OPINION in the blank.

_____ 1. New York City has the best Chinese restaurants.

_____ 2. NASA announced that it will redesign the space shuttle's booster rockets.

_____ 3. The first day of spring is the vernal equinox.

_____ 4. State law requires that all children, up to the age of six, use seat belts or safety seats while riding in cars.

_____ 5. If we rank the income of medical specialists, pediatricians are among the lowest-paid doctors.

_____ 6. Toddlers are contrary and fractious.

_____ 7. McDonald's is more popular than Roy Rogers.

_____ 8. A college degree has become worthless; one needs an MBA to get a good job.

_____ 9. Orchids are difficult plants to grow.

_____10. No one has yet patented a black tulip.

To correct a topic sentence that does not express an opinion, reconsider the original topic. Since most topics can be developed in several ways, you should be able to create another topic sentence that will include an opinion. Use the previous example, where the general topic was college students who commute to campus, to brainstorm quickly the topic. Here are a few possibilities:

commuter and travel time

advantages of living off-campus or at home

the school's responsibility to commuters

the economic responsibilities of the commuter

the disadvantages of commuting

Any of these ideas could be developed into a topic sentence:

1. During the day, Milbrook University must provide more activities for commuters.
2. Commuting to college has many advantages.
3. Commuters face many problems as they travel to and from school.

Note sentences two and three. Besides offering opinion statements (commuting is advantageous or commuting is problematical), these topic sentences also state limits: *many* advantages, *many* problems. So a topic sentence can limit the topic even as it offers an opinion, or it can simply limit the topic by listing causes, effects, steps in process, stages of development, or characteristics. Examine the following topic sentences. Do they offer opinion or limitation?

> Many college students choose to major in computer science for three reasons.

> To change a flat tire correctly and safely, you must complete four tasks.

Both topic sentences limit the writers' discussions to either the three reasons or the four tasks. Although the writers have not expressed an opinion, they have classified and enumerated essential elements and, thus, have limited the topics further.

EXERCISE 6   Identify the topic sentences that offer either an opinion or a limitation by placing a (√) next to them. Identify the factual statements by placing an (X) next to them. Consider ways that the factual statements can be made into topic sentences. For each factual statement, generate one topic sentence that offers an opinion and one that limits the topic.

_____ 1. Pollution can take many forms.

_____ 2. Americans watch an average of four hours of television each day.

_____ 3. Man O' War won the Preakness in 1920.

_____ 4. The new board game Trivial Pursuit requires many hours to play.

_____ 5. Mountain climbers must prepare themselves physically and mentally for each climb.

_____ 6. Candidates for the police academy must have a high school diploma and pass physical and aptitude tests.

_____ 7. Although retirement promises great rewards, many senior citizens face adversity, diminishing abilities, and financial hardships.

_____ 8. Many clothing fashions reappear every twenty years or so.

_____ 9. Because it has many untapped resources, Alaska offers great opportunities.

_____10. American government has become increasingly bureaucratic.

Generating Topic Sentences

As you learned earlier, one topic can often yield several topic sentences. You must choose the one you believe you can develop adequately in a paragraph. Generally it is best to choose the one you are most interested in, wish to research, or know about through personal experience or observation. For example, the general topic *agriculture* could be narrowed to the limited topic *farmers in the U.S.*

Here are several possible topic sentences:

1. To succeed financially, farmers must use modern technology, including computers.
2. Many environmental factors can cause financial ruin for American farmers.
3. To be a farmer, one must know the land, work hard, and know sound business practices.
4. Tobacco farmers in the South face three major problems each year.
5. For many reasons, thousands of farmers face bankruptcy each year.

EXERCISE 7 Limit each general topic below, and write *three* topic sentences for each limited topic. Try to write one opinion topic sentence and one limiting topic sentence in each category. Circle the controlling idea in each topic sentence and underline the topic.

1. General Topic: **Camping**

   Limited Topic: _____

   Topic Sentence 1. _____

   Topic Sentence 2. _____

   Topic Sentence 3. _____

2. General Topic: **Computers**

   Limited Topic: _____

   Topic Sentence 1. _____

   Topic Sentence 2. _____

   Topic Sentence 3. _____

3. General Topic: **Sports**

   Limited Topic: _____

   Topic Sentence 1. _____

   Topic Sentence 2. _____

   Topic Sentence 3. _____

4. General Topic: **Cities**

   Limited Topic: _____

   Topic Sentence 1. _____

   Topic Sentence 2. _____

   Topic Sentence 3. _____

Discovering Topic Sentences

Sometimes, as a result of your prewriting, you may develop an organized and unified paragraph that lacks a topic sentence. In other words, instead of writing the topic sentence first and then generating supporting ideas, you may have developed all the details but not have written a topic sentence. Obviously, comprehending the paragraph will be easier for your audience if you do provide a topic sentence. Here is an example:

> At first, the car proceeded down the road at 20 mph. Then, its speed increased suddenly to 55 mph, and it moved from the left lane into the middle one without signaling any intention to change. As the car's speed continued to increase, it moved erratically from the middle lane to the left lane and then quickly across the road to the right lane. At that point, the speed dropped dramatically to 15 mph, and the car began to drift slowly to the right. After its tires hit the curb, the car began to weave between the middle and right lanes until ultimately it was straddling the broken white line. There it came to a full stop.

There is no specific sentence in this paragraph that gives the reader the topic and the controlling idea. Since the topic sentence is not yet written you must, somehow, develop one. But how would you do it? The following process will help you organize the information you have generated so that you can formulate an appropriate topic sentence.

Developing a Topic Sentence from Detail Sentences

1. What is the whole paragraph about?

    a car

    (The answer is the paragraph's **topic.**)

2. What details about the topic have you stated?

    20mph - increase to 55

    lane change - no signals

    speed increase - erratic movement

    15mph drifting and weaving across lanes

    full stop in middle of road

    (The answer is the **significant details.**)

3. What do the details tell about the topic?
    What conclusion can be drawn?

    The driver can't control the car

    (The answer is the **controlling idea.**)

4. Formulate your conclusion into a topic sentence.

    The driver can be classified as Driving While Intoxicated

The last sentence is your first attempt at writing a topic sentence for that paragraph. The next step in the writing process is to reformulate the topic and controlling idea; try to generate a more sophisticated, less bare-boned opening sentence, one that will appeal more to your reader's interest.

EXERCISE 8   Use the above process to develop a topic sentence for the following paragraphs.

1.   "Run" can mean a fast means of personal locomotion; it can also refer to a flaw in a woman's stocking. In a more serious mood, a run on a bank can deplete its financial resources. To the baseball fan, a run can mean the difference between a win or a loss.

What is the whole paragraph about?

_____

(*topic*)

What information about the topic are you given?

_____

_____

_____

_____

(*significant details*)

What do the details tell you about the topic? What conclusion can be drawn?

_____

_____

(*controlling idea*)

Formulate your conclusion into a topic sentence.

_____

Rewrite the above topic sentence, making it more appealing to your audience.

_____

2.   George Washington was beloved by his troops and, living among them, shared their suffering at Valley Forge. The people's love for the man continued through his presidency. Andrew Jackson invited thousands of the "common folk" to his inaugural ball, and, although they destroyed the furniture in the White House, no one was injured. Ticker-tape parades for the president-elect were common, and President John F. Kennedy even strolled down Fifth Avenue. However, more recent presidents have been the victims of assassination attempts, and any venture off the White House grounds worries the Secret Service.

What is the whole paragraph about?

_____

(*topic*)

What information about the topic are you given?

_____

_____

_____

_____
(*details*)

What do the details tell you about the topic? What conclusion can you draw?

_____

_____
(*controlling idea*)

Formulate your conclusion into a topic sentence.

_____

Rewrite the above topic sentence; keep your audience in mind.

_____

Strategies for Placing the Topic Sentence

As you have probably noticed, the topic sentence is usually the first sentence in the paragraph. But it does not have to be. Take another look at the paragraph about Sherlock Holmes's appearance on page 66. Which sentence in that paragraph is the topic sentence? The second one is. If the topic sentence does not have to be first, then where else in the paragraph can it be? It can be anywhere: its placement depends on its purpose in the paragraph. You, the writer, must decide on the best placement based on what you want the topic sentence to accomplish.

PLACEMENT: FIRST SENTENCE

When the topic sentence is the first sentence in the paragraph, it *introduces* the details that support or explain the controlling idea. Such a paragraph could be diagrammed as an inverted triangle:

Topic Sentence
(general statement)

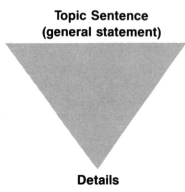

Details

The topic sentence serves as a broad statement, so the triangle narrows from it to the details. You are immediately telling your reader what the whole paragraph is about. You make it easy for the reader to skim your writing, and you forestall any possible misinterpretation of your message.

Practice this strategy by locating the topic sentence in the following paragraph. Write the sentence on the given line; then, underline the topic and circle the controlling idea. Then, in the column to the right, diagram the paragraph.

Registration is an impossible process. The first step requires a student to see his or her advisor for a heart-to-heart talk about career choices, academic options and schedules. Of course, all of that must be completed in the allotted ten minutes, or else the other one hundred student advisees become annoyed. Then, even if the student/advisor combination does manage to arrive at a mutually satisfactory arrangement, the odds are overwhelming that one, some, or all of the courses will be closed by the time the student actually arrives at the registration desk. That forces a reenactment of the whole scenario, beginning at the end of the line.

Topic Sentence: _____   Paragraph Diagram

_____

_____

PLACEMENT: LAST SENTENCE

Read this paragraph carefully and answer the questions that follow.

I should premise that I use this term [Struggle for Existence] in a large and metaphorical sense, including dependence of one being on another, and including (which is more important) not only the life of the individual, but success in leaving progeny. Two canine animals in a time of dearth may be truly said to struggle with each other which shall get food and live. But a plant on the edge of a desert is said to struggle for life against the drought, though more properly it should be said to be dependent on the moisture. A plant which annually produces a thousand seeds, of which on an average only one comes to maturity, may be more truly said to struggle with the plants of the same and other kinds which already clothe the ground. . . . In these several senses, which pass into each other, I use for convenience' sake the general term of Struggle for Existence.

(from Charles Darwin, "The Struggle for Existence"
in *The Origin of Species*)

1. What is the whole paragraph about?

_____

(topic)

2. What information about the topic does the author provide?

_____

_____

_____

_____

_____
(details)

3. You know the topic and details of the paragraph now. What is the author saying about the topic? What message is he trying to convey? (Look at what the details tell you about the topic.)

_____

_____
(controlling idea)

4. Which sentence in the paragraph conveys that same message?

_____
(topic sentence)

In this paragraph, the topic sentence is the last one in the paragraph. There, it can *summarize* all the details given in the paragraph. It should be diagrammed as an upright triangle, with the details at the top, and broadening to the base—the general statement.

Details

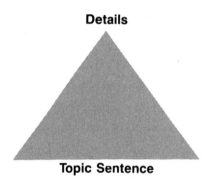

Topic Sentence

Practice this strategy by using the above example as a model to locate the topic sentence in the following paragraph, and then diagram the paragraph.

> Old people see their life's savings erode and fear that they will be reduced to penury. The middle-aged have trouble meeting their expenses, much less saving for retirement. Recent college graduates receive seemingly phenomenal salaries, but soon realize that they cannot afford to marry and form a family unit. In addition, businesses cannot accurately forecast their profits and expenses. Overall, inflation affects us, one and all.

1. What is the whole paragraph about?

_____
(topic)

2. What information about the topic does the author provide?

_____

_____

_____

_____

_____
(details)

3. What message is suggested?

_____

_____
(controlling idea)

4. State the topic sentence.

_____

5. Diagram the paragraph here.

PLACEMENT: FIRST AND LAST SENTENCES

In this strategy, the topic sentence appears in two places, usually at the beginning and end of the paragraph. When using this format, the writer *introduces* the reader to the general statement, supports and explains it, and then *summarizes* it. In effect, the author is trying to ensure that the reader gets the message. As a writer, you will probably use this placement when your audience is unfamiliar with the material and the material is difficult. By repeating the main idea, you reinforce the message for your readers and give them another opportunity to comprehend it. This type of paragraph is diagrammed in an unusual way:

Topic Sentence—Introduction

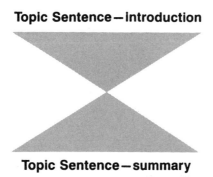

Topic Sentence—summary

Here is an example of this strategy in a paragraph:

> *"Body Language" can be used, both consciously and unconsciously, to project a message beyond the spoken word.* A mother wagging her finger at a child knowingly reinforces the serious intent of her words. Likewise, standing with arms akimbo projects power and stolidity. In contrast, standing with arms folded across the chest is a defensive posture; someone who stands that way unconsciously labels himself the weaker individual. Similarly, a slight frown implies impatience, no matter how honeyed the tone. *Therefore, be aware of the ways the body can be used to reinforce a spoken message; furthermore, be wary of the ways it can defuse the impact of verbal statements.*

The first and last sentences are the topic sentences.

Practice this strategy by locating the topic sentence in the following paragraph, and then diagram the paragraph.

> What then is the American, this new man? He is either a European, or the descendant of a European, hence that strange mixture of blood, which you will find in no other country. I could point out to you a family whose grandfather was an Englishman, whose wife was Dutch, whose son married a French woman, and whose present four sons have now four wives of different nations. He is an American, who, leaving behind him all his ancient prejudices and manners, receives new ones from the new mode of life he has embraced, the new government he obeys, and the new rank he holds. He becomes an American by being received in the broad lap of our great Alma Mater. Here individuals of all nations are melted into a new race of men, whose labours and posterity will one day cause great changes in the world. Americans are the western pilgrims, who are carrying along with them that great mass of arts, science, vigour, and industry which began long since in the east; they will finish the great circle. The Americans were once scattered all over Europe; here they are incorporated into one of the finest systems of population which has ever appeared, and which will hereafter become distinct by the power of the different climates they inhabit. The American ought therefore to love this country much better than that wherein either he or his forefathers were born. Here the rewards of his industry follow with equal steps the progress of his labour; his labour is founded on the basis of nature, self-interest, can it want a stronger allurement? Wives and children, who before in vain demanded of him a morsel of bread, now, fat and frolicsome, gladly help their father to clear those fields whence exuberant crops are to arise to feed and to clothe them all; without any part being claimed, either by a despotic prince, a rich abbot, or a mighty lord. Here religion demands but little of him; a small voluntary salary to the minister, and gratitude to God; can he refuse these? The American is a new man, who acts upon new principles; he must therefore entertain new ideas, and form new opinions. From involuntary idleness, servile dependence, penury, and useless labour, he has passed to toils of a very different nature, rewarded by ample subsistence.— This is an American.
>
> (from J. Hector St. John, "What is an American" in *Letters from an American Farmer*)

1. Topic:

   _____

2. Details:

   _____

_____

_____

_____

_____

3. Topic Sentence(s):

_____

_____

_____

_____

4. Location:

_____

5. Paragraph Diagram:

PLACEMENT: MIDDLE OF THE PARAGRAPH

Finally, you may place the topic sentence in the middle of the paragraph. There, it serves as a *transition* between the details given at the beginning and end of the paragraph. This placement is effective when the topic sentence has two parts to it, two controlling ideas. Here is an example:

> A mother wagging her finger at her child knowingly reinforces the serious intent of her words. Likewise, standing with arms akimbo projects power and stolidity. *As can be seen, "body language" can be used, both consciously and unconsciously, to project a message beyond the spoken word.* Standing with arms folded across the chest is a defensive posture; someone who stands that way unconsciously labels himself the weaker individual. Similarly, a slight frown implies impatience, no matter how honeyed the tone.

As you can see, this paragraph has been rearranged slightly by moving the topic sentence to the middle. Consequently, the diagram for this paragraph has changed; it is now a diamond.

details

details

When the topic sentence is in the middle of a paragraph, it is difficult to locate because it is hard to skim the paragraph for the topic sentence. Your reader might overlook your main idea because it is buried in a mountain of details. However, this placement strategy is especially useful with complex, two-part controlling ideas. When your message is complex and you want to assure that the reader organizes your facts and opinion, it is helpful to place the topic sentence in the middle of the paragraph.

To practice this strategy, read the following paragraph carefully. Underline the topic sentence and then diagram the paragraph.

> Houses are being burglarized even with the occupants at home. Purses and necklaces are snatched on the street with no hope of catching the thieves. Parked cars frequently "lose" their hubcaps and stereos. Because the populace feels unsafe in the neighborhood, auxiliary police forces are formed. Their function is to serve as the "eyes" and "ears" of the regular police force. Auxiliary officers do not attempt to stop crimes; they simply observe and report. They do not carry weapons, and they have no greater authority than any other civilian.

Diagram:

The chart below summarizes the placement strategies for the topic sentence, the purposes of those placements, and their effect on your audience.

Placement Strategy	Purpose	Effect
beginning	introduces supporting details	reader understands main idea immediately
end	summarizes supporting details	reader sees the proof for your position first
beginning and end	introduces and summarizes supporting details	reinforces difficult material for your reader
middle	provides transition from details that support one controlling idea to details that support the other controlling idea	supports and organizes a two-part controlling idea for your reader

EXERCISE 9   Refer to the topic sentences you wrote for Exercise 7. Beneath each one, indicate a possible purpose and placement for it in a paragraph.

EXERCISE 10   1. Choose a subject with which you are very familiar. Remembering that your reader is unfamiliar with the material and finds it difficult to understand, write a paragraph about that subject.

2. Write a paragraph expressing your point of view on a current controversy. Be sure to state your supporting details first, because your reader is skeptical and not likely to read material contrary to his or her opinion.

Writing Strategy: *DESCRIPTION*

Description is a frequently used strategy because it makes abstract statements concrete and general statements more specific. A generalization that "the conference was a complete success" becomes more comprehensible when specific details are provided and outcomes are described. When describing, authors must keep their audiences' viewpoints in mind; they should provide those details that will help readers to see things as the writers saw them. They must anticipate their audiences' familiarity with the subject matter and provide those details that will enable readers to understand the message, perhaps unspoken, of the authors. Notice how the authors of the following paragraphs use description.

Supper Time in a Jewish Kitchen

Alfred Kazin

Ripeness filled our kitchen even at supper time. The room was so wild with light, it made me tremble; I could not believe my eyes. In the sink a great sandy pile of radishes, lettuces, tomatoes, cucumbers and scallions broke upon their stark greens and reds the harshness of the world's daily monotony. The window shade by the sewing machine was drawn, its tab baking in the sun. Through the screen came the chant of the score being called up from the last baseball game below. Our front door was open, to let in air; you could hear the boys on the roof scuffing their shoes against the gravel. Then, my father home to the smell of paint in the hall, we sat down to chopped cucumbers floating in the ice-cold borscht, radishes, tomatoes and lettuce in sour cream, a mound of corn just out of the pot steaming on the table, the butter slowly melting in a cracked blue soup plate— breathing hard against the heat, we sat down together at last.

QUESTIONS   1. What sensory experience does Kazin describe?

2. The last sentence acts as an accumulation of information from the paragraph. Explain how Kazin does this.

3. Kazin states that the kitchen had "ripeness." What does he mean and how does he support his suggestion?

4. The author carefully provides details to support his suggested message. What is his message? What is his opinion of this household?

5. What probable details does Kazin omit because they did not contribute to his message? Why might he have omitted them?

A Building in Upper Harlem

Claude Brown

In his autobiography Manchild in the Promised Land, *Claude Brown describes a childhood filled with youth gangs, reformatories, and intermittent formal education; eventually, however, he graduated from Harvard University. In his book* The Children of Ham, *he writes about the experiences of black youth today.*

There is a building in upper Harlem on a shabby side street with several other buildings that resemble it in both appearance and condition. "This building" is in an advanced state of deterioration; only cold water runs through the water pipes, the rats here are as large as cats. The saving grace of this building might very well be the erratic patterns of the varied and brilliant colors of the graffiti which adorn it internally and externally from basement to roof. This building has no electricity in the apartments, but the electricity in the hallway lamp fixtures is still on. Some of the apartments have garbage piled up in them five feet high and that makes opening the door a very difficult task for those whose nasal passages are sufficiently insensitive to permit entry. In some of the apartments and on the rooftop, the garbage and assorted debris are piled only one or two feet high, and the trash has been there so long that plant life has generated. The most rapid tour possible through this building will necessitate boiling oneself in a hot tub of strong disinfectant for a couple of hours, and even then this astonishingly formidable breed of lice will continue to make its presence felt throughout a long itchy night. This building is adjacent to a fully occupied tenement whose inhabitants are families, some of which include several children. This building has a few steps missing from the staircase above the second floor and there are no lightbulbs in the hallway; it's a very unsafe place for trespassers, even during the day. This building's last family of tenants was emancipated several weeks ago; they hit the numbers and moved to the Bronx, shouting "Free at last, free at last; thank God for the number man." Prior to their liberation, the "last family" had lived a most unusual existence. Somebody had to be at home at all times to protect the family's second-hand-hot television from becoming a third-hand-hot television; there were too many junkies in and out who used the vacant apartments to stash their loot until they could "down" it and who also used some of the apartments for sleeping and as "shooting galleries." For protection, the last family had a large, vicious German shepherd. This dog was needed for the rats as well as the junkies. A cat would be no help at all. The sight of the rats in this building would give any cat smaller than a mountain lion instant heart failure. The last family considered itself fortunate, despite the many unpleasant, unhealthy and unsafe aspects of its residence. "We ain't paid no rent in two years. I guess the city just forgot that we was here or they was just too embarrassed to ask for it," said the head of the last family. This building has holes in the walls large enough for a man to walk through two adjacent apartments. This building has holes in the ceilings on the fourth and fifth floors, and when it rains, the rain settles on the floor of a fourth-story apartment. This building is not unique, there are many others like it in the ghettos of New York City; and like many others . . . this building is owned by the City of New York.

QUESTIONS
1. What is the overwhelming impression conveyed by this paragraph?
2. What details directly contribute to that impression?
3. Define *saving grace* and *formidable*.
4. Why would New York City be too "embarrassed" to demand rent payments?

The Turtle

John Steinbeck

The sun lay on the grass and warmed it, and in the shade under the grass the insects moved, ants and ant lions to set traps for them, grasshoppers to jump into the air and flick their yellow wings for a second, sow bugs like little armadillos, plodding restlessly on many tender feet. And over the grass at the roadside a land turtle crawled, turning aside for nothing, dragging his high-domed shell over the grass: His hard legs and yellow-nailed feet threshed slowly through the grass, not really walking, but boosting and dragging his shell along. The barley beards slid off his shell, and the clover burrs fell on him and rolled to the ground. His horny beak was partly open, and his fierce, humorous eyes, under brows like fingernails, stared straight ahead. He came over the grass leaving a beaten trail behind him, and the hill, which was the highway embankment, reared up ahead of him. For a moment he stopped, his head held high. He blinked and looked up and down. At last he started to climb the embankment. Front clawed feet reached forward but did not touch. The hind feet kicked his shell along, and it scraped on the grass, and on the gravel. As the embankment grew steeper and steeper, the more frantic were the efforts of the land turtle. Pushing hind legs strained and slipped, boosting the shell along, and the horny head protruded as far as the neck could stretch. Little by little the shell slid up the embankment until at last a parapet cut straight across its line of march, the shoulder of the road, a concrete wall four inches high. As though they worked independently the hind legs pushed the shell against the wall. The head upraised and peered over the wall to the broad smooth plain of cement. Now the hands, braced on top of the wall, strained and lifted, and the shell came slowly up and rested its front end on the wall. For a moment the turtle rested. A red ant ran into the shell, into the soft skin inside the shell, and suddenly head and legs snapped in, and the armored tail clamped in sideways. The red ant was crushed between body and legs. And one head of wild oats was clamped into the shell by a front leg. For a long moment the turtle lay still, and then the neck crept out and the old humorous frowning eyes looked about and the legs and tail came out. The back legs went to work, straining like elephant legs, and the shell tipped to an angle so that the front legs could not reach the level cement plain. But higher and higher the hind legs boosted it, until at last the center of balance was reached, the front tipped down, the front legs scratched at the pavement, and it was up. But the head of wild oats was held by its stem around the front legs.

QUESTIONS
1. What is the topic sentence? Where is it located?
2. What is Steinbeck's perspective? Does the scale change in the piece? If so, where?
3. What is Steinbeck's tone? What particular words suggest the tone?

PARAGRAPH ASSIGNMENTS

1. As Kazin does in his paragraph on the Jewish kitchen, choose one word and one time of the day to describe the central room within your house or apartment. Use specific sensory impressions to convey your attitude toward that time of day.

2. Steinbeck describes the turtle's actions as it moves across the road. In a similar fashion, describe one activity of a person or an animal in a particular location. For example, describe someone painting a room, washing dishes, or studying for a test, or describe an animal at play.

3. Describe a close friend's or relative's facial qualities, keeping in mind your audience and the impression you want to convey.

4. Think of tourists visiting your area for the first time. Besides the usual attractions, what would you like to suggest that they visit? Describe the site to demonstrate that it is a "must-see," even if usually overlooked, attraction.

4

Organizing Details

OBJECTIVES: 1. To recognize unified paragraphs.

2. To identify and create primary support sentences.

3. To identify and create secondary support sentences.

4. To draw conclusions and make judgments.

5. To explore composing through classification.

PREVIEW: A unified paragraph develops only one idea; it does not contain irrelevant or unnecessary information. Primary support sentences directly develop a topic sentence's controlling idea. Secondary support sentences provide specific examples, descriptions, or explanations for primary support sentences. Conclusions are opinions based on the information presented in the paragraph.

After exploring ideas and discovering a topic in early drafts, you should develop an organizational strategy for the generated material that will best suit your purpose and audience. Writers who record only their first impressions create disorganized paragraphs that ignore their audiences. Their readers are then forced to organize material as they read and to ignore statements that do not contribute to the paragraph's development. Such lack of courtesy reveals these writers' unwillingness to communicate with their audiences. This problem can be avoided, however, if you create unified paragraphs in which all of the supporting sentences develop the controlling idea of the topic sentence.

Using material generated by prewriting techniques and by initial drafts, you can select those items that best support your topic sentence. To make the material more accessible for an audience, you can organize details to reflect major ideas (primary support sentences) and minor ideas (secondary support sentences). **Primary support sentences** directly develop the controlling idea in the topic sentence. **Secondary support sentences** may contain a specific example or illustration, specific description, or explanation of the primary support sentences. Selected by the audience's needs and by your purpose, these details provide a well-organized paragraph that is accessible to your readers.

Unity

In a paragraph, you may explain, narrate, or describe a particular event or idea. However, you should develop only one idea in a paragraph. If, for example, you have promised the reader that you will discuss the importance of computers in high-school math classes, then you are committed to that idea only. Information describing the physical appearance of the computers, their operations, their use in other academic subjects, or personal experiences or ability with computers would be inappropriate in this paragraph. A reader could correctly question your inclusion of such details, since they do not develop the topic you promised: the importance of computers in high-school math classes.

If, in your paragraph, you present material you promised the reader in your controlling idea, then the paragraph will be unified. However, if you include random sentences that do not develop your topic sentence, then the paragraph is not unified and ignores its audience. To illustrate this point, consider the following example of a unified paragraph.

> In a slender, five-and-half-foot body, my forty-six-year-old uncle hoped for better conditions in the barrio. His eyes squinted in the bright sun like a hawk's eyes seeing prey from a distance. But unlike the hunter's eyes, my uncle's eyes were narrowed permanently because of insufficient light after dark; because electricity was scarce in the area, gasoline lamps were used. His back also curved slightly and forced his shoulders to be ahead of him when he walked, for lack of indoor plumbing had made him bend down to pump water from an outdoor well. Furthermore, standing on a dusty dirt road, he favored his left leg because long journeys on foot to other parts of the barrio left him with a bad leg. Although life in the barrio had left its physical marks upon him, my uncle continued to believe that life there could be better.

In this paragraph, the student describes his uncle's hope for better conditions by detailing the conditions that have affected him physically. Each physical problem, from the narrowed eyes to the bad leg, has its origin in the barrio, which has not benefitted from advances in technology.

Contrast the next student's paragraph with the one above.

> The best strategy of dieting is not to decrease weight in a short period of time, as in a fad diet, but to commit oneself to a program of food reduction and exercise. To lose weight and keep it off, one has to exercise while dieting. The dieter must also watch his intake of calories. However, this type of weight loss requires more time than a fad diet. At a certain point, weight loss levels off, and one remains at a constant weight for a brief period of time. This is called a plateau in weight loss, but eventually one begins to lose weight again. As soon as the dieter acquires the habit of eating correctly and exercising while dieting, then the dieter can maintain a constant weight.

This student's paragraph is not unified because the student includes a definition of *plateau* used in the specific context of dieting. However, the paragraph has promised the reader a description of the proper way to diet. Moreover, the writer fails to include sufficient information about the process of losing weight. The reader does not know the quantity or types of food a dieter should eat, nor does the reader know what types of exercise are most beneficial to dieters. Therefore, the information given in the paragraph is too general to be of use to the reader.

EXERCISE 1 In each of the paragraphs below, locate the topic sentence, and then identify the sentence or sentences that do *not* support the topic sentence. Write their numbers in the blanks provided.

_____ 1. (1) Although weddings are for the bride and groom, parents and other relatives often determine the formality and size of the wedding. (2) If the bride and groom want a small, simple wedding, they frequently find that their parents insist upon inviting all of the relatives down to third cousins twice removed and friends from decades ago. (3) The guest list, once set at thirty, has now grown to over three hundred. (4) In addition, the simple ceremony, with the bride in a plain white dress and the groom in a suit, has now been transformed into a formal occasion. (5) The bride now wears a long white gown with a ten-foot train, and the groom sports a tuxedo. (6) Many conflicts can occur when the bride and groom want one type of ceremony and the parents want another. (7) Many parents want to use the occasion to repay old social obligations and to insure that their offspring receive many gifts. (8) The wedding party now includes seven bridesmaids, seven ushers, a ring bearer, and a flower girl. (9) The informal reception now takes place in a rented hall with a caterer and an orchestra. (1) Perhaps parents feel obligated to provide the best for their children on their wedding days; however, the wishes of the bride and groom should be respected. (11) It's their wedding.

_____ 2. (1) Being an only child has several advantages. (2) The child receives the full attention of both parents. (3) Certainly, this attention can benefit the child as she goes through school; both parents support her efforts completely. (4) At holidays, the only child is showered with gifts from both parents and grandparents. (5) Often, the parents will include the child in their social plans, so the child becomes adept at handling social situations at an early age. (6) Also, the child is taken to "adult" places: restaurants, museums, movies, and plays. (7) Many only children are overachievers; they must be the best at everything they do, so they become overly ambitious and studious. (8) Being around adults so often, the child actually is never given a chance to be a child. (9) Moreover, an only child must learn to be self-reliant and creative. (10) Unless there are neighborhood children her age, the only child relies upon her own imagination for games and activities. (11) As the child becomes more self-reliant, she is given more responsibility and freedom. (12) Therefore, the only child benefits from the attention her parents give her.

_____ 3. (1) Football's advantages outweigh its disadvantages. (2) As the sport's detractors like to point out, and as all athletic directors clearly know, football is expensive. (3) To outfit a player for practice costs over $200, with the helmet and face mask requiring the largest investment. (4) Game uniforms add an additional expense, as do such items as two- and seven-man sleds and blocking dummies. (5) Football's critics also dwell upon the possibility of serious injury by stressing the vulnerability of the head and neck. (6) Only boys who stand six feet tall and weigh over 180 pounds should play football. (7) While both arguments contain elements of truth, they do not prove conclusive. (8) Careful maintenance and judicious purchasing can decrease equipment costs. (9) Moreover, successful football programs can often generate more money than they spend. (10) Many college coaches are paid more than the presidents of the universities. (11) Also, while it is impossible to remove completely the risk of injury—from football or from any other contact sport—the incidence of injury can be reduced through the teaching of safe blocking and tackling techniques. (12) Football's detractors—and a number of them seem never to have played the game—fail to appreciate the mental discipline which the sport requires. (13) Even Howard Cosell's newest book on his adventures with football is entitled *I Never Played the Game.* (14) Played properly, football in no way proves to be a contest between Neanderthals but rather a sport that requires a mixture of strength, speed and mental acuity. (15) As the players know, the camaraderie raised through mutual hard work makes the sport a most rewarding one. (16) The following scene is a familiar one: on a crisp, fall afternoon, before a brightly dressed, noisy, and appreciative crowd, the coach calls the correct play; the defenders are knocked to the ground, and the back speeds into the end zone as the referee raises his hands signalling a touchdown. (17) At times such as these, the expense, self-denial, and possibility of injury matter little, if at all.

_____ 4. (1) America's geographical diversity has encouraged many American writers to celebrate their regional cultures. (2) In New England, Henry D. Thoreau recorded life in Concord, Massachusetts and described his travels in Maine and on Cape Cod. (3) Louisa May Alcott also depicted the village of Concord in her classic *Little Women.* (4) The lives of New England farmers were immortalized in Robert Frost's poems. (5) Alexander Solzhenitsyn, the Russian novelist, now lives in Vermont. (6) In the South, William Faulkner and Thomas Wolfe captured the essence of small southern towns like Oxford, Mississippi and Asheville, North Carolina. (7) Faulkner also travelled to Los Angeles during the 1930s to write screen plays for the movies. (8) In the Midwest, Sherwood Anderson and Willa Cather described the loneliness of rural communities. (9) In the West, Jack London and John Steinbeck provided an accurate portrayal of California. (10) Jack London also wrote *Call of the Wild,* a story based in Alaska. (11) America has, indeed, proven to be a fertile ground for its native writers.

_____ 5. (1) Movies often reflect attitudes Americans hold. (2) For example, in the 1950s, when Americans enjoyed immense economic prosperity and domestic tranquility, many Westerns were made. (3) John Wayne, the archetypal western hero, portrayed a strong, moral, silent man who always held high principles. (4) In his films, Wayne usually won the love of a beautiful girl, but she was not his goal throughout the movie. (5) Instead, he saved ranchers from evil bankers who threatened to foreclose and settlers from marauding bands of belligerent Indians. (6) In sharp contrast, films from the mid-Sixties to the late Seventies offered heroes who seemed tortured by the political turmoil of the times. (7) This was not seen in the 1942 film *Casablanca.* (8) In the film *The Deer Hunter,* the protagonist Nick enlisted in the Army to fight in Vietnam. (9) Instead of the glorious military victory he anticipated, he found that the war, filled with death and destruction, lingered on long after the last American assault. (10) War films in the 1940s always showed the Americans as victors. (11) In the 1980s, however, America has returned to a stronger economy and is led by a president who advocates self-reliance and strength. (12) Ronald Reagan won by a landslide in the 1984 election. (13) These beliefs are evident in our movies. (14) For instance, in the *Rocky* series, Rocky Balboa moves from the underdog in a championship fight to the heavyweight champion of the world through his determination and perseverance. (15) In the *Rambo* movies, Sylvester Stallone creates a Vietnam vet, trained in guerrilla warfare, who single-handedly destroys a town in *First Blood* and who rescues American prisoners of war from Southeast Asian communists in the second *Rambo* film. (16) Hence, American attitudes toward ourselves and our country are often apparent in our films.

Primary Support Sentences

After generating ideas by brainstorming, freewriting, or composing a first draft, you need to select and organize those ideas that best develop your purpose, stated in the topic sentence, and that best address your audience's background, knowledge, and need for information.

An effective method of organizing is to identify major details, or primary support sentences.

Primary support sentences directly develop the controlling idea in a topic sentence. To develop the controlling idea, primary support sentences might provide explanations, descriptions, definitions, illustrations and examples, causes or effects, points of comparison and contrast, or reasons for an argument. Consider the following topic sentence:

As a hobby, photography provides many benefits for the amateur.

The controlling idea is "many benefits." Therefore, the primary support sentences should enumerate the types of benefits photography offers. Now, examine these three primary support sentences:

1. Photography helps record many family events.
2. Photography allows individual artistic expression.
3. Photography can become a lucrative hobby.

Each of these sentences identifies a specific benefit of photography as a hobby. Certainly, each sentence needs further explanation—about the types of family events one might record, about the methods of artistic expression, and about the monetary reward of the hobby—but these primary support sentences give readers a clear indication of the types of benefits the hobby provides.

Analyze the following paragraph about a model office for a high-school yearbook staff. Identify the topic sentence, its controlling idea, and the primary supports.

> The model yearbook staff works in a spacious, well-equipped office. Within this large office, several long tables line the walls to provide ample work space. In addition to plenty of work space, the ideal yearbook office has ample room for storage in the form of both numerous filing cabinets and a walk-in closet. This spacious office houses outstanding modern equipment. On one long table, there rest both several electronic typewriters and a state-of-the-art computer and printer. To one side of the office, a door leads to the yearbook staff's newly equipped darkroom.

- The topic sentence is *The model yearbook staff works in a spacious, well-equipped office.*
- The controlling idea is *spacious, well-equipped office.*
- The primary support sentences are (1) *Within this large office, several long tables line the walls to provide ample work space.* (2) *In addition to plenty of work space, the ideal yearbook office has ample room for storage in the form of both numerous filing cabinets and a walk-in closet.* (3) *This spacious office houses outstanding modern equipment.*

Each primary support sentence describes what a "spacious, well-equipped office" should have. The first two primary support sentences give examples of the spacious office by describing ample work and storage space. The third primary support sentence defines the "well-equipped office" as having "outstanding modern equipment." The writer then gives specific examples—the typewriters, computer and printer, and the darkroom—of the modern equipment the office has. Thus, each primary support sentence helps develop the controlling idea in the topic sentence.

EXERCISE 2   In the following paragraphs, underline the topic sentence, circle the controlling idea, and number the primary supports.

1.   While in high school, the lazy student reflects his attitude by the way he studies, acts, and dresses. I know a student, for example, who does no homework

at all; he foolishly wastes his free study periods in the cafeteria with others like himself. His actions also reflect his slothful attitudes. When walking between classes, he moves slowly and speaks with everyone; as a result, he is always late for his next class. After his last class, he jumps into his car and rushes out of the parking lot with the car radio blaring; his only desire is to leave school quickly. He cares neither about what he gets on his report card nor about his appearance during school hours. His shirttail always hangs out, and he has no problem wearing stripes with plaids. His hair is rarely combed, and his shoelaces are untied.

2.   Besides being destructive to one's health, smoking can also be destructive to one's property. Over the years, smoking can result in property damage that will cost several thousands of dollars. For example, the carelessly dropped hot ash or spark, as well as the burning cigarette left on the edge of an ash tray, can do considerable damage to both furnishings and clothing. Furniture may be marred by a burn, and clothing can be spotted with holes from ashes or sparks. Moreover, the destructive effect smoking has on property inadvertently can affect one's health and life. For instance, a smoldering mattress, the result of a careless smoker's unnoticed spark, can itself produce enough smoke to cause the death of the bed's occupant through smoke inhalation. A house fire, the result of a carelessly extinguished cigarette, can lead to serious burns or death of the occupants of the house. Also, a carelessly dropped cigarette can destroy an entire ecological system and its wildlife. If one thinks the effects of smoking on property are minimal, then think again.

3.   When I moved into my apartment, I had to assume the household chores my parents had previously done for me. One of my first tasks was learning to push a vacuum cleaner. But about six weeks ago, the motor in my vacuum died. During this month and a half, the carpet went uncleaned. The carpet got so dirty that I was forced to make a decision: either borrow a vacuum cleaner or allow the carpet to walk out the door on its own. So recently, I decided to pay my parents a visit and borrow their cleaner. I am sure I made the right decision; this fifteen-minute cleaning job made a noticeable difference in my carpet's appearance. I have also learned to clean the bathroom, mop the floor, and wash the windows. Although none of these chores are enjoyable, they are all done at regular intervals. For example, the bathroom fixtures are cleaned every two weeks, and the kitchen floor is mopped once a month. Finally, the windows are cleaned once every six months. Living on my own has taught me new responsibilities.

4.   The role-playing game Dungeons and Dragons has been blamed by some for causing violent behavior, devil worship, and even suicide among its players. Critics claim that the game's violent nature—players imagine that they are medieval heroes who confront and destroy various monsters—encourages players to be more aggressive in real life. Opponents of the game also assert that the game, rather than being mere entertainment, is actually a form of mind control that alters the player's personality; they believe that the game's "occult" nature leads some players to devil worship. Moreover, critics claim that the game has led some players to commit suicide. Supposedly, the player becomes so involved with the game that he can no longer distinguish between fantasy and reality. According to the game's critics, a participant, believing that he will be brought back to life in the game, may kill himself. However, such claims are poorly supported by facts.

5.   Other people support the position that Dungeons and Dragons is actually beneficial to players. According to its advocates, the game encourages players to use their imaginations and logic while they are finding solutions to problems they encounter during the course of the game. Proponents argue that this imaginative role-playing helps players to develop more mental flexibility and that the players, consequently, are more able to find solutions to real-life problems.

Also, since the game relies upon a numerical rating system for combat, magic, characters, and other aspects, the players develop their mathematical skills and their abilities to work with and understand numbers. Hence, two distinct skills are developed by the game: inventive problem-solving and mathematical ability.

EXERCISE 3 To understand the relationship between a topic sentence and its primary supports, read each pair of topic sentences below. Then read the list of primary supports. In the blank to the left of each primary support, write the letter of the topic sentence to which the support is more closely related.

1.

A	B
The use of corporal punishment must be curbed.	Spanking is still a time-honored form of discipline.

_____a. Physical abuse by anyone against anyone cannot be tolerated.

_____b. Children have been spanked for years, and no one is harmed by it.

_____c. Some children need quick reminders of who is in charge.

_____d. Corporal punishment merely condones the use of violence to solve problems.

_____e. It is better to punish physically and quickly than to withdraw love and affection.

2.

A	B
Properly used, the grading system benefits students.	Improperly used, grades can harm students.

_____a. Grades rank a student against his or her peers and thereby foster competition.

_____b. Tests measure the ability to take tests, not knowledge gained or information acquired.

_____c. A poor grade can indicate which areas need to be studied.

_____d. Grades are an indication of progress and improvement.

_____e. Grades can't predict success or failure because they do not measure motivation and interest.

3.

A	B
The concept of comparable worth has generated a great deal of controversy.	Feminists believe "equal pay" for work of comparable value is an idea whose time has come.

_____a. Many business and manufacturing associations have voiced opposition to it.

_____b. Opponents argue that it will build another layer of bureaucracy.

_____c. Even the federal judiciary is divided: some judges have mandated it, others have thrown the suits out of court.

_____d. Why should nurses be paid less than truck drivers when nurses have even greater responsibilities?

_____e. The marketplace has traditionally been dominated by men who tend to see their occupations as more valuable.

_____ f. The issue will not be settled easily or quickly.

4.

A	*B*
Many researchers believe that cancer is a self-induced disease.	Cancer does not have to be a death sentence.

_____a. Skin cancer is almost 100% curable if caught in its early stages.

_____b. Leukemia victims now live many years with their disease in remission.

_____c. Stress definitely puts an extra load on the body by decreasing its chances of repelling harmful agents.

_____d. Known carcinogens such as tobacco can and should be eliminated from one's lifestyle.

_____e. Gene splicing offers the hope of eliminating many causes of cancer.

_____ f. Poor or inappropriate diet contributes to specific kinds of cancer.

_____g. Radiation therapy and chemotherapy can now eradicate the disease, not just prevent its spread.

5.

A	*B*
Some students believe that they should take only courses in their majors during college.	Educators encourage students to take courses in a number of disciplines.

_____a. In highly technical fields, such as computer science and engineering, students should concentrate on acquiring knowledge they will need later on the job.

_____b. Since many students attend college to learn a profession, additional courses not related to their majors are unnecessary.

_____c. Many business executives value the graduate who took a number of different types of courses in college, since this graduate can approach problems in various ways.

_____d. Courses in psychology, English, sociology, and history can prepare a student for a number of professional fields.

_____e. The student who learns about different fields is better prepared to change careers if he or she wishes.

_____ f. In some majors, taking courses in a number of disciplines can add extra semesters to a student's college education.

When you want to create primary support sentences, try brainstorming for ideas about your topic sentence and its controlling idea. This method will give you ideas for several primary support sentences, probably more than you will need for the adequate development of the controlling idea. Choose the best primary support sentences for your paragraph; for example, you might choose the most important examples from a list to support a topic sentence. Consider the following example.

Topic Sentence: Many first-semester college students are not prepared for the rigors of college life.

Brainstorming: poor study habits
lack of self-discipline
lack of academic preparation in high school
lack of a workable schedule
lack of a place to study
can't handle complete freedom away from parent's watchful eyes
unprepared to live with a roommate
failure to take responsibility for themselves
unable to deal with different types of people
too many temptations in the form of parties or sports
first time away from home

Primary Supports:
1. Many students are not prepared academically for the demands of college courses.
2. Many students did not develop good study habits in high school.
3. Some students are tempted by the social life on a college campus rather than by the intellectual activities.
4. Some students have never before had complete responsibility for themselves.

These four primary support sentences will develop the paragraph adequately. In addition, the ideas are broad enough so that the writer will be able to incorporate other pieces of information from the brainstorming session. For example, the last primary support about the lack of complete responsibility could also include the idea about the lack of self-discipline. Moreover, these four primary support sentences list major reasons why first-semester college students might not be prepared to do well in college.

Would the writer want to use all of these ideas from his brainstorming session? More than likely, he would not. If the writer tried to include all of the ideas he developed during the brainstorming session, then his paragraph would be extremely long, and he probably would not develop each idea thoroughly.

To create a unified paragraph, you must also make sure that the primary support sentences develop only the topic sentence you have chosen. In other words, if you commit to one idea in the topic sentence, then you cannot include tangential, but related, material. You have promised to discuss one topic; you must adhere to the promise you made to the reader in the topic sentence. Consider the following example.

Topic Sentence: Before purchasing a dog, one should consider several matters carefully.

Primary
Supports:

1. The amount of space in an apartment or house is important.
2. The buyer must consider the animal's purpose in the household.
3. The buyer should also consider the breed, its size, and its temperament.
4. Great Danes are often cute puppies but become large dogs.

Do all of these primary supports develop the topic sentence? Which one does not? Why?

EXERCISE 4   Carefully read each topic sentence and the primary support sentences below it. Place an *X* by those primary support sentences that do not develop the topic sentence. Replace the faulty primary supports with ones of your own.

1. **Topic Sentence:**   Recent high-school graduates should not rush to enroll in college immediately.

   Primary Support 1:   Working for a year or two gives a teenager time to experience the business world.

   Primary Support 2:   Colleges are anxious to reverse a trend toward declining enrollments.

   Primary Support 3:   Working awhile and saving money enable the student to choose a more expensive college; the choice of schools is not limited by finances.

   Primary Support 4:   A "young adult" of twenty is much more likely to appreciate the benefits of a college education than is a "teenager."

2. **Topic Sentence:**   Board games for adults have risen in popularity lately.

   Primary Support 1:   Grown-ups prefer to beat a peer rather than a computer.

   Primary Support 2:   Board games are a social activity; couples can compete with one another.

   Primary Support 3:   Because they require strategy and knowledge rather than eye-hand coordination, such games are more suited to the over-30 age group.

   Primary Support 4:   Trivial Pursuit has started a new craze.

3. **Topic Sentence:**   House plants add beauty to a house and provide a hobby for the grower.

   Primary Support 1:   House plants can be used effectively to decorate a home or apartment.

   Primary Support 2:   Cacti do not always grow well in humid environments.

   Primary Support 3:   Growing plants is a relaxing hobby.

4. **Topic Sentence:**   A child should have a pet.

   Primary Support 1:   By caring for a pet, a child learns responsibility.

   Primary Support 2:   A child gains companionship and affection from the pet.

   Primary Support 3:   Pets can be expensive.

5. **Topic Sentence:**   Good study skills are important for success in college.

   Primary Support 1:   Good students know the value of taking good lecture notes.

   Primary Support 2:   Conscientious students read their textbooks carefully, underline important concepts, and outline the chapter.

   Primary Support 3:   Students do not need to read everything an instructor assigns.

EXERCISE 5 For each topic sentence below, use brainstorming to create as many supporting details as you can. Identify a specific audience and purpose for each topic sentence. Finally, select from your list of details those that best support the topic sentence according to the audience and purpose you named.

1. College students should/should not be required to take at least a basic course on computers.

   _____

   _____

   _____

   Audience _____ Purpose _____

2. Owning a car can be expensive.

   _____

   _____

   _____

   Audience _____ Purpose _____

3. Selecting a college requires careful consideration of many aspects.

   _____

   _____

   _____

   Audience _____ Purpose _____

4. Sex education courses should/should not be required in high schools.

   _____

   _____

   _____

   Audience _____ Purpose _____

5. High-school students should/should not be required to pass competency tests in writing, reading, and mathematics before they graduate from high school.

   _____

   _____

   _____

   Audience _____ Purpose _____

Secondary Support Sentences

Secondary support sentences explain and illustrate the primary support sentences by giving examples or descriptions. Consider the following paragraph.

> As a hobby, photography provides many benefits for the amateur. First, photography helps the amateur record many family events. Next, photography allows artistic expression. Finally, photography can become a lucrative hobby for the amateur.

Is this paragraph adequately developed? No, it is not. Although the paragraph contains a topic sentence with a controlling idea and three primary supports, it does not answer all of the questions readers might have if they are considering photography as a hobby. For example, the first primary support might be clear to readers; most readers could easily think of examples of family events that would be captured on film. However, the second primary support, "allows artistic expression," and the third, "can become a lucrative hobby," need far more explanation than the writer provides. Certainly readers would want to know more. What might be an example of artistic expression in film? How does one begin to use photography artistically? How can photography be lucrative? What steps should the amateur take to make money with this hobby? Since the paragraph fails to answer the readers' questions, it fails to fulfill the promise made to readers in the topic sentence: to explain the benefits of the hobby. The paragraph merely *lists* the benefits.

Analyze the following paragraph. How does it differ from the first one? Does it answer some questions a reader might have?

> As a hobby, photography provides many benefits for the amateur. First, photography helps the amateur record many family events. For example, photographs capture important family celebrations, such as a wedding, the birth of a baby, a family reunion, or a family member's graduation. Snapshots also record daily events, such as a baby's first steps, the antics of children or pets, or a child's growth. Moreover, these pieces of film give us a glimpse into family history; pictures of grandparents and great-grandparents remind us of our heritage. Next, photography allows artistic expression. Because photography is more than the mere capturing of a moment of time, the photographer can use many devices to create the mood or emotion he or she wants to convey. The amateur photographer begins to learn more about composition of elements in the photograph, light, and color to create the effect he or she seeks. For example, with black and white film, the photographer can create dramatic juxtapositions of shadow and light. The photographer also begins to recognize that the same setting, taken from different angles, yields many different interpretations. Finally, photography can become a lucrative hobby for the amateur. The amateur who develops skill with the camera can submit photos for contests to gain either monetary prizes or public recognition of this ability. The amateur may wish to publish some shots in a local newspaper; for example, these shots may accompany a travel article about a local historical landmark. By photographing weddings or portraits of friends and associates, the amateur can also expand this hobby into a part-time business. These benefits make photography more than just owning a camera.

The additional sentences illustrating the primary supports are secondary support sentences. The paragraph now offers more development of the controlling idea, and it answers many questions that readers might have.

By creating primary and secondary supports, the writer has actually developed a basic outline for the paragraph. This outline ensures that the writer will fulfill his or her promise to the reader to develop the paragraph completely. Were you to outline the paragraph above, it would appear as the one on p. 98.

Topic Sentence: As a hobby, photography provides many benefits for the amateur.

I. Primary Support 1: First, photography helps the amateur record many family events.

   A. Secondary Support 1A: For example, photographs capture important family celebrations, such as a wedding, the birth of a baby, a family reunion, or a family member's graduation.

   B. Secondary Support 1B: Snapshots also record daily events, such as a baby's first steps, the antics of children or pets, or a child's growth.

   C. Secondary Support 1C: Moreover, these pieces of film give us a glimpse into family history; pictures of grandparents and great-grandparents remind us of our heritage.

II. Primary Support 2: Next, photography allows artistic expression.

   A. Secondary Support 2A: Because photography is more than the mere capturing of a moment of time, the photographer can use many devices to create the mood or emotion he or she wants to convey.

   B. Secondary Support 2B: The amateur photographer begins to learn more about composition of elements in the photograph, light, and color to create the effect he or she seeks.

   C. Secondary Support 2C: For example, with black and white film, the photographer can create dramatic juxtapositions of shadow and light.

   D. Secondary Support 2D: The photographer also begins to recognize that the same setting, taken from different angles, yields many different interpretations.

III. Primary Support 3: Finally, photography can become a lucrative hobby for the amateur.

   A. Secondary Support 3A: The amateur who develops skill with the camera can submit photos for contests to gain either a monetary prize or public recognition of this ability.

   B. Secondary Support 3B: The amateur may wish to publish some shots in a local newspaper; for example, these shots may accompany a travel article about a local historical landmark.

   C. Secondary Support 3C: By photographing weddings or portraits of friends and associates, the amateur can also expand this hobby into a part-time business.

Concluding
Sentence: These benefits make photography more than just owning a camera.

Each primary support is followed by secondary supports, which further illustrate and explain the primary support. If you examine primary support 2 and its secondary supports, then you will see that, in addition to supports that directly develop the primary support, some sentences actually develop each other more specifically. For example, secondary support 2B lists the types of devices to create a mood; moreover, secondary supports 2C and 2D further explain how light and composition might be used artistically. Each secondary support, however, does develop its corresponding primary support sentence.

As you can see, outlines are extremely helpful at this point in the writing process. First, they allow you to determine if you have adequate support for your ideas. If you create only primary supports, then you should recognize your lack of specific details in the outline. Second, outlines allow you to determine if every sentence performs its function. For example, after you have identified the controlling idea, then you can quickly check your primary supports to ensure that they develop only the controlling idea of your topic sentence. Also, you can ensure that your secondary supports are more specific than your primary supports and that the secondary supports do further illustrate the primary supports. Finally, outlines allow you to identify sentences that do not contribute to the paragraph's unity. Therefore, you can replace these irrelevant sentences with others that adhere to your controlling idea.

As you outline your ideas, you may find that a particular idea does not require a specific number of primary supports. In the same manner, every primary support does not have to be followed by a particular number of secondary supports. Therefore, you retain some flexibility in the organization you choose. Of utmost importance to you is the ability to address a specific audience and to develop a paragraph so that it presents your purpose in writing. Hence, only those details, both primary and secondary, that best support your main idea, develop your purpose, and address your audience should be used.

EXERCISE 6   In each paragraph below, identify the topic sentence (TS), the controlling idea (CI), the primary supports (PS), the secondary supports (SS), and the concluding sentence (CS).

1. ____(1) Although American society provides no formal rite of passage from childhood to adulthood, several informal rites exist. ____(2) An adolescent's first date, for example, is one such informal initiation into the adult world. ____(3) The first date is usually filled with expectation, excitement, and anxiety as both parties adopt more mature attitudes and prepare for the date. ____(4) Getting a driver's license also proves that a teenager is almost an adult. ____(5) To new drivers, licenses represent the freedom to go places on their own without a chaperon. ____(6) For parents, the license represents the teenager's acceptance of responsibility and independence. ____(7) Also, a teenager's first job indicates a willingness to develop new skills and assume new responsibilities. ____(8) The teenager must make sure to arrive on time and be prepared to work; he or she also will learn how to budget money from the job. ____(9) Although there are few formal celebrations for these activities, each informal rite marks the teenager's movement into the adult world.

2. ____(1) Of the many differences between college and high school, perhaps the most important is the students' degree of independence. ____(2) While students are in high school, parents often assume more responsibility than students for their performance, motivation, and attendance at school. ____(3) For example, parents provide a comfortable environment in which students can relax; students, in fact, may do little to clean their rooms or the house. ____(4) Parents may provide the extra money that students need. ____(5) Parents encourage students by asking about the school day and grades. ____(6) Parents may also discuss

with teachers the students' abilities and progress to ensure that they are receiving the correct support at home. _____(7) However, in college, all of this changes for students. _____(8) Students must force themselves to rise at 7:00 a.m. for that 8:00 a.m. class. _____(9) They must also prepare their own breakfasts, wash their clothes, and clean their dorm rooms. _____(10) College students must determine a schedule for study time. _____(11) With no one to remind them of homework and assignments, students must assume the responsibility themselves. _____(12) They must take the responsibility of discussing any academic difficulties with their instructors. _____(13) In other words, college students are on their own while high-school students have others to monitor them.

3. _____(1) Most of us believe that only housewives watch soap operas; however, many other types of people comprise the legions who watch the daytime and nighttime dramas. _____(2) Many students enjoy soap operas. _____(3) The proof of their loyalty is readily available; one need only look into television rooms in student centers and dorms each day between noon and 4 o'clock. _____(4) In addition, many executives are rumored to be faithful fans. _____(5) Perhaps their interest lies in the advertisement of their products during this prime viewing time. _____(6) Certainly, too, millions of Americans who watch the nighttime soaps break the stereotype of soap-opera watchers. _____(7) For example, during that memorable summer when J. R. Ewing's life was in danger on *Dallas,* many sophisticated adults speculated about the identity of J. R.'s attacker. _____(8) With their intrigue, sophisticated fashions, and melodramatic plots, soap operas are no longer aimed at only one segment of the population.

4. _____(1) Many of the books children enjoy are actually not children's books at all. _____(2) *The Adventures of Huckleberry Finn,* long considered to be a companion book to *The Adventures of Tom Sawyer,* is far more than the adventures of the orphan Huck and his friend Jim on the Mississippi River. _____(3) The book actually exposes the insidious way that Southern society defended slavery as a

legal and moral obligation. ____(4) However, young readers too often comprehend only the great adventures described in the book; they rarely understand Mark Twain's attacks upon the institution of slavery. ____(5) Another children's classic, *Gulliver's Travels,* has been made into a cartoon that regularly appears on Saturday morning television. ____(6) The book really provides a biting social and political satire of England in the eighteenth century; however, few children recognize this message. ____(7) Moreover, *Robinson Crusoe,* the tale of a man on a deserted island, imparts religious and economic comments about humankind and our universe. ____(8) Unfortunately, many people read these books only once—when they are young—and fail to appreciate the books' true messages and worth.

5. ____(1) Christmas has become too commercialized within the past two decades. ____(2) First, we begin to anticipate the holiday months before its arrival. ____(3) Stores now decorate their spaces with elves and reindeer just after Halloween. ____(4) Before Thanksgiving, Santas arrive at department stores, not in sleighs, but in helicopters. ____(5) Television and magazine advertisements with Christmas themes begin at least six to eight weeks before December 25. ____(6) Second, Christmas is celebrated with gifts and material possessions, not family gatherings and religious feeling. ____(7) We are all encouraged to purchase presents for everyone—from Johnny's grade-school teacher to the box boy at the local supermarket. ____(8) Children, for whom the holiday remains a magical time, count their blessings in the number of gifts they receive, not in the messages of peace and good will. ____(9) Retailers, moreover, make sure that we spend plenty of money; early in December, dire predictions of a poor retail year suggest that everyone will suffer economically unless we hurry to spend money during the last few weeks of the year. ____(10) Perhaps a solution to all of this commercialization would be to ban the purchase of presents; instead, only homemade presents would be given, and families would focus on their own happiness together rather than on material blessings.

EXERCISE 7   Each set of sentences below forms a unified paragraph. Identify the correct order of the sentences, and label the topic sentence (TS), the primary supports (PS), and the secondary supports (SS).

1. _____ 1. The same is true for typhoons and monsoons.

   _____ 2. Blowing hot and dry as it sweeps down the side of a mountain, it can quickly wither lush crops and destroy a farmer's dreams.

   _____ 3. A cool, light breeze can bring welcome relief from summer's heat and humidity.

   _____ 4. Some types of wind are harmful because of their speed and strength.

   _____ 5. The wind, an infrequently researched aspect of our environment, is a friend to man, but it can also be his enemy.

   _____ 6. Hurricanes cause millions of dollars worth of damage each year and sometimes take lives.

   _____ 7. One of the signs of approaching autumn is the wind rustling through the leaves high on a tree.

   _____ 8. Twisters or tornadoes bring fear to the hearts of the plainsmen.

   _____ 9. The foehn is one such wind.

   _____ 10. Sailors fear the absence of wind; they know the dangers of being becalmed.

   _____ 11. Other winds are hated because they are lifeless; all they carry is hot air.

2. _____ 1. This requires paper, paper, and more paper.

   _____ 2. The world is drowning in paper—not people, not pests, but paper.

   _____ 3. In school, students make copies of notes, rather than take their own.

   _____ 4. The demand for "copies" has outstripped the need for those reprints a thousandfold.

   _____ 5. Reports devour paper, too.

   _____ 6. Everyone wants a copy of whatever has been deemed important, necessary, useful, or top secret.

   _____ 7. Superiors demand reports.

   _____ 8. They no longer want to be "kept informed"; they want twenty typed pages of details, statistics, and examples.

   _____ 9. In government, the IRS requires triplicates.

   _____ 10. In business, memos circulate widely, and each recipient makes a personal copy "for the files."

3. _____ 1. Public opinion surveys seem to indicate that Americans are quickly becoming a semi-literate people.

_____ 2. While that statement may be true, it can quickly be rendered harmless by pointing to the large numbers of periodicals and newspapers published in the United States.

_____ 3. That is an acceptable percentage.

_____ 4. Some one must read them.

_____ 5. Much publicity has been given to statistics that proclaim that almost one quarter of the population is functionally illiterate—i.e., unable to read a newspaper or comprehend a job application.

_____ 6. Another nail in the coffin of the literate American is the statement that "fewer than twenty percent of Americans read at least three books last year."

_____ 7. Of course, no attention is paid to the flip side of those statistics: seventy-five percent of Americans can read and write.

4. _____ 1. Finally, there must be jobs.

_____ 2. With an adequate academic background (it does not have to be brilliant or even outstanding), a poor person can step onto the ladder of success.

_____ 3. Self-respect is of primary importance.

_____ 4. Without it, there is no hope, no goal, no purpose.

_____ 5. The cycle of poverty must be broken, and it can be done.

_____ 6. He can begin the climb.

_____ 7. A finely-honed mind and a willing spirit need a work area.

_____ 8. Without academic skills, he is doomed to rely on his brawn, not his brain, and a life of poverty quickly robs the body of its strength.

_____ 9. Education, jobs, and self-respect will enable the poor to cast aside their chains and rise from the bottom of society.

_____10. There can be belief in a better future.

_____11. They must not be stifled but should be encouraged to create and grow.

_____12. Of course, incentive and motivation are useless without the proper tools.

_____13. Their creativity and development will benefit all of society, not just the poor.

_____14. With it, there is a reason to strive and to seek improvements.

_____15. Self-respect provides incentive and motivation.

5. _____ 1. Best of all, the window allowed the soft morning sunlight to shine through; the sunshine matched the pale yellow walls.

_____ 2. A ceramic lamp sat on the desk; its base was a baseball player who was the embodiment of a young Little Leaguer like me—oversized uniform, wide-eyed stare, and a boyish grin.

_____ 3. A double window faced the front lawn and offered a spacious view of full-bodied spruces and spindly white pines.

_____ 4. At first glance, the bedroom I shared as a child with my brother seems too small to hold two growing boys; however, the room suited me fine, and it had the right features.

_____ 5. The bed consisted of four carved posts, two mattresses—one four feet above the other—and a simple three-step ladder that I used to reach the top bunk.

_____ 6. Beneath the window was a three-drawer desk marked with wounds inflicted by my pocket knife.

_____ 7. Then there was the bunk bed, a space-saving monstrosity that occupied a prominent position against the wall across from the desk.

_____ 8. These features created a sanctuary for a young boy.

EXERCISE 8   Choose one of the topics below for a paragraph topic. Brainstorm for ideas, and then write a first draft to explore the topic. After you have identified your topic, audience, and purpose, select details that would best support your topic sentence. Finally, compose your paragraph. To check your ability to organize effectively, share your paper with two or three other students in a group. For each paper, identify the supports in the paragraph and discuss their relationships to the topic sentence.

1. a movie you saw recently

2. a nearby recreational spot or amusement park

3. parents and discipline

4. problems of working and going to school simultaneously

5. a problem that needs to be solved in your community or at your school

Conclusions

CONCLUDING SENTENCES

Since each paragraph acts as a complete unit and is self-contained, the last sentence in the paragraph should offer some conclusion to the reader. If the last sentence does not conclude the paragraph, then conceivably the paragraph remains open, and more information could be added. Therefore, paragraphs should have concluding sentences. The concluding sentence can perform one of three functions:

1. It can restate the topic sentence.
2. It can restate the topic sentence and summarize the primary supports.

3. It can offer a logical conclusion based upon information provided in the paragraph. (This type of concluding sentence can be introduced by one of the following words or phrases: *therefore, as a result, as a consequence, thus,* or *consequently.*)

Any one of these methods will work well as a final sentence in a paragraph.

However, students often use another method which does not work: a concluding sentence that introduces new material. If you conclude with new information—information that you did not cover in the paragraph and information that you will not have time or space to develop—then you have broken your promise to discuss only one topic in the paragraph. In this situation, you have not completed the paragraph, and the reader is left to wonder what importance the new material might have to the paragraph. Consider the following paragraph, and analyze the concluding sentence.

> Because corporal punishment might leave psychological scars, parents should be very wary about using spanking or slapping as a means of correcting a child's behavior. First, a child often becomes resentful of the parent who administers the punishment. Very often, the child will seek revenge upon the offending parent by withholding affection or by refusing to speak to that parent. Second, a child who is punished physically may become anxious around other adults because he fears that they too will inflict pain if he misbehaves. In this case, a child may become distrustful of all adults and become withdrawn. Certainly, this child will not mature emotionally as he should. Third, a child may believe that inflicting physical pain is an acceptable way of dealing with situations and people he doesn't like. The child might become belligerent towards his peers and turn into a bully who intimidates those who are weaker. *Therefore, parents should consider other means of disciplining a child.*

The concluding sentence in this paragraph tells parents to consider other means of disciplining a child; however, it does not discuss those means. While readers might understand the possible consequences of corporal punishment, they would need more information about different ways to discipline a child. Because this concluding sentence actually offers new information, but no discussion of the information, it is inadequate. However, here are three sentences that could conclude the paragraph:

1. A **restatement** of the topic sentence:

   Parents should be careful about administering corporal punishment because it may damage the child psychologically.

2. A **summary** of the topic sentence and the primary supports:

   Because physical punishment can cause a child to grow resentful, anxious, or belligerent, parents should be cautious about administering corporal punishment.

3. A **logical conclusion** of the paragraph:

   Therefore, parents should consider the consequences of physical punishment before they discipline a child who misbehaves.

EXERCISE 9   Create each of the three types of concluding sentences for each of the following paragraphs. Identify the audience that would best appreciate each of the three conclusions. Also, check the conclusion you believe is most effective. Be prepared to explain its effectiveness.

1. Founded in 1910, the organization of Boy Scouts gives valuable benefits to its members. The typical Scout learns lasting values. For example, many former Scouts still remember the Scout's code well: "A Scout is trustworthy, loyal, helpful, friendly, courteous, kind, obedient, cheerful, thrifty, brave, clean and reverent." Certainly, these are admirable virtues upon which a young man builds character. In addition, the organization provides its members with companionship. Many young boys learn how to deal with others through competition and through united efforts. Finally, a boy learns about the world around him. While tying knots seems to be the staple knowledge of Boy Scouts, many learn about science, the environment, citizenship, and survival.

Restatement: _____

_____ Audience _____

Summary: _____

_____ Audience _____

Logical Conclusion: _____

_____ Audience _____

2. Although cowboys have long since disappeared from the American West, a new breed of men has taken their place in contemporary America—the truck driver. Like the cowboy, the trucker is always on the move and usually far from home. The typical trucker will cover thousands of miles and cross several states as he delivers goods throughout the country, and he will do this in a week's time. Because his business requires constant motion, a trucker usually drives twelve to fourteen hours a day for ten out of fourteen days. Truckers share another characteristic with cowboys; they are fiercely independent. Many truckers prefer to own their own rigs, select their shipping contracts, and rely upon their own initiative to make a living rather than work for a company. Their independence is easily proven: truckers resist an easy stereotype. Some truckers have little formal education; others have doctorates. Some truckers are from blue-collar working families; others are from white-collar, upper-income families. Look at their trucks also. Even trucks which were identical on the assembly line are not identical by the time their owners equip them.

Restatement: _____

_____ Audience _____

Summary: _____

_____ Audience _____

Logical Conclusion: _____

_____ Audience _____

3. During the 1920s, many American writers chose to live in Europe for various reasons. First, European countries, particularly France, offered more artistic freedom and a larger intellectual community than the United States did. Regularly enforced in the United States, censorship was rarely in evidence in Europe. In

addition, the large colony of expatriates in France offered a congenial intellectual atmosphere to many Americans, such as F. Scott Fitzgerald and Ernest Hemingway. Second, Europe was exciting and inexpensive. For those writers too young to have served in the Great War, Europe was filled with adventure. Writers could easily travel to many countries and experience new cultures. Because the American dollar was strong after World War I, a poor writer who would have lived meagerly in New York or Chicago could live comfortably in France or Spain. In addition, many small literary magazines could be published for much less in Europe than in the United States. Third, European countries allowed more personal liberty than the America of the 1920s. While Americans could not drink alcohol because the Eighteenth Amendment prohibited the sale and consumption of alcoholic beverages, Americans in Paris could enjoy whatever they wanted to drink. The rules of personal conduct, so rigid in the United States, were more relaxed in Europe.

Restatement: _____

_____ Audience _____

Summary: _____

_____ Audience _____

Logical Conclusion: _____

_____ Audience _____

4.   Completed in 1809, Monticello reflects many of Thomas Jefferson's interests. Architecturally, the house is a masterpiece. It is topped with a dome—one of the first American houses to have one—and has skylights. Because Jefferson did not want the view of his lawn spoiled, many of the dependencies—the kitchen, the stables, the ice house, and other sections—were built into the sides of hills and connected to the main house by a series of corridors. Jefferson's inventiveness can easily be seen inside the house. Above the front door hangs a seven-day clock, driven by weights and pulleys, that still keeps time. Dumbwaiters helped carry wine from the cellar to the dining room and saved the servants from climbing many flights of stairs. Finally, the contents of the rooms tell us about the man himself. In his library are over 6,000 books, many in other languages. (Jefferson could read six languages.) Also, bookstands are located in every room of the house so that Jefferson could read during each spare moment.

Restatement: _____

_____ Audience _____

Summary: _____

_____ Audience _____

Logical Conclusion: _____

_____ Audience _____

5.   The country homes of the British aristocracy offer more than retreats from urban living; they display centuries of art and history. Many of the gentry collected

paintings and sculpture; aristocrats in past centuries were patrons of the arts. Therefore, the private collections of paintings and sculpture are some of the best in the world. Landscapes by Constable and portraits by Gainsborough grace the halls and drawing rooms of some country homes. In addition, because families lived in the houses for generations, attics and even kitchens and dining rooms contain priceless examples of past centuries. Attic trunks with Victorian clothing and central halls guarded by empty suits of armor give specific examples of the treasures these houses hold.

Restatement: _____

_____ Audience _____

Summary: _____

_____ Audience _____

Logical Conclusion: _____

_____ Audience _____

DRAWING VALID CONCLUSIONS

When writing a final sentence that offers a conclusion, you must be sure that the last sentence is based on the facts given in the paragraph. After all, a conclusion is an opinion formed after thought and investigation. As the final, logical result of the reasoning process, a conclusion ends all further reasoning; therefore, the conclusion must pull together all available facts and then state where those facts have led the audience. When it does all that, the conclusion is considered **valid.** The conclusion is **invalid** when it merely offers another fact or when it is not based on the given information. Examine these examples:

1.   Susie has two dogs, a cat, two doves, and a rabbit for pets. When she was only seven years old, she found a sick duck, nursed him back to health, and then released him. Since then, she has doctored snakes, turtles, and hamsters. From the age of twelve, she has spent most of her free time at the racetrack, not in the grandstands, but in the stables, and has befriended the horses and cared for them.

Invalid Conclusion: Her dogs are called Zeb and Zack. (This simply provides another fact; it does not offer a result.)

Valid Conclusion: Susie likes animals. (Nowhere in the paragraph is that statement made, but it is the logical result of all the information given.)

2.   No neurosurgeon has ever seen or touched a mind, yet when certain parts of the human brain are injured or destroyed, certain aspects of the mind are also damaged or annihilated.

Invalid Conclusion: Most neurosurgeons are males. (This may or may not be true, but the sex of the doctor has nothing to do with the point of the sentence.)

Valid Conclusion: The mind is located within the skull cavity. (That the mind is situated in the brain is the only logical conclusion to be drawn from these facts.)

Therefore, you as the writer must remember to edit your paragraphs and check your concluding sentences carefully. If you want to offer a conclusion, make sure the sentence states a logical result and not just another fact.

EXERCISE 10   Carefully read each of the following paragraphs and the pair of sentences that follow. Write (C) next to the sentence that is a valid conclusion based on the evidence given. Write (F) next to the factual statement. Then check the one that would be more appropriate as the last sentence in the paragraph.

1.   The movie *Bad Days* uses stock characters: the shy, bumbling bank clerk and the prostitute with a heart of gold. The typical improbable situation develops; he falls in love with her and wants to bring her home to meet his parents. What this movie lacks in plot and character it does not make up for in special effects or action. Both seem to be based on C-grade movies from the 1950s. In addition, *Bad Days* was obviously shot on a studio's back lot, one that had been allowed to fall into disrepair.

_____ This movie will not win an Oscar for anything.

_____ The plot is the standard "boy-meets-girl-and-falls-in-love."

2.   Within two hours the patient's temperature rose to 104°F and stayed there; nothing brought it down. Body fluids were lost in great quantities and were not replaced because of severe vomiting and diarrhea. Then the patient became lethargic and unconcerned about his illness; he was content to just lie in bed. Finally, he even stopped asking for water.

_____ The patient had a high fever.

_____ The patient required immediate medical care and should have been rushed to an emergency room.

3.   The nature of the refugee issue has been transformed in very fundamental ways over four decades. It has grown from a continental to a global problem, from one that could be kept at a distance to one that may be very near. The world's refugee population has expanded manyfold. It has changed from a transient to a semi-static population. Assistance requirements have multiplied. Any crisis anywhere can now produce refugees everywhere. The resulting problems now need close and urgent attention.

(from W. R. Smyser, "Refugees: A Never-Ending Story," *Foreign Affairs*)

_____ There are more refugees today than there were forty years ago, and they are displaced for a greater variety of reasons.

_____ Americans must be awakened to the dangers inherent in the world-wide refugee problem.

4.   House hunting is an arduous task. Everyone begins the assignment with a mental image of the "perfect house." Slowly, parts of that image are gnawed away by the realities of money, location, availability, and luck. Too often, after combing the real estate ads and arriving on the doorstep of the fourth open house for that day, one learns that a bid on the "almost-perfect" house was accepted fifteen minutes ago.

_____ Cost and neighborhood affect the purchase of a house.

_____ People rarely buy their dream house.

5. Despite many suggestions to the contrary, few students study in a quiet atmosphere. Although they may have been told that quiet enhances concentration and prevents distraction, students seem to feel that quiet is unnatural and enervating. Consequently, they study in groups, with music blaring in the background, while munching on popcorn and peanuts.

_____ Many students have poor study habits.

_____ Listening to music distracts a student from studying.

MAKING JUDGMENTS

Closely related to conclusions are judgments. Just as you must review the given information and decide whether a conclusion is valid, so you must examine facts, make comparisons and contrasts, and think critically about any stated opinions when you make a judgment. A **judgment** is an evaluation; it is a decision about the merits of a given situation. When you write, you must be careful to use facts, not judgments, to support your controlling idea. It is very easy to include judgments rather than facts in your paragraph as secondary supports; therefore, you must read and reread carefully to ensure that your audience is not being misled by your statements. Analyze the difference between these two statements:

Fact: Hemingway won the Nobel Prize for Literature.

Judgment: Hemingway deserved to win the Nobel Prize.

That Hemingway won the Nobel Prize is a fact—it can be checked. That he was a worthy recipient of the prize is a judgment made after one has evaluated Hemingway's writing and the writings of his contemporaries. The statement that he deserved to win is a judgment. What is the difference between these next two sentences?

Fact: Koko the gorilla was taught to use sign language.

Judgment: Primates have the capacity for meaningful nonverbal communication.

No one denies that Koko was able to manipulate her fingers to form the symbols used in sign language; that is a fact. Whether that finger play represented meaningful nonverbal communication is a judgment, based on a review of this experiment, interviews with Koko's trainer, and an evaluation of the evidence.

EXERCISE 11   Read each pair of sentences below. Write (F) next to the factual statement and (J) next to the judgment.

1. a. _____ New York City has more Chinese restaurants per capita than any other American city.

   b. _____ Little Lotus in Chinatown is the best Chinese restaurant.

2. a. _____ The Sanitation Department has hired 1,000 additional workers.

b. _____ The "Clean Streets" campaign is a failure.

3. a. _____ A college education is an absolute necessity in today's society.

b. _____ Less than twenty-five percent of the population has a college degree.

4. a. _____ Teenagers believe that an MBA is a guaranteed ticket to success.

b. _____ Enrollment in graduate business programs has increased by eight percent in each of the last three years.

5. a. _____ Whales are the largest species of mammal still extant.

b. _____ Whaling must be prohibited; it is an abomination.

There are two situations in which judgment statements may be made: (1) your audience may render a judgment concerning the validity of your opinion (in this case, you will probably never know how you rated), or (2) you may present an evaluation of the preceding topic in the final sentence.

EXERCISE 12 Read each of the following paragraphs carefully. Then, write (J) next to the judgment statement and (F) next to the factual one and circle the better choice for a concluding sentence.

1. The coach had three rows of seats, each calculated to hold three persons, and as we were only six, we had, in the phrase of Milton, to "enhabit lax" this exalted abode, and, accordingly, we were for some miles tossed about like a few potatoes in a wheelbarrow. Our knees, elbows, and heads required too much care for their protection to allow us leisure to look out of the windows; but at length the road became smoother, and we became more skillful in the art of balancing ourselves, so as to meet the concussion with less danger of dislocation.

(from Frances Trollope, *Domestic Manners of the Americans*)

a. _____ The stage coach traveled on rough roads.

b. _____ The stage coach was an uncomfortable means of transportation.

2. The cars were very full, and were not able to seat all the passengers. Consequently, according to the usages of American etiquette, the gentlemen vacated the seats in favour of the ladies, who took possession of them in a very ungracious manner as I thought. The gentlemen stood in the passage down the centre. At last all but one had given up their seats, and while stopping at a station another lady entered.

(from Isabella Lucy Bird, *The Englishwoman in America*)

a. _____ Good manners required a gentleman to relinquish his seat to a lady.

b. _____ The men of the nineteenth century were more courteous towards and considerate of women than are their twentieth-century counterparts.

3. On board this steamboat, there were two young gentlemen, with shirt collars reversed as usual, and armed with very big walking sticks; who planted two seats

in the middle of the deck, at a distance of four paces apart; took out their tobacco boxes; and sat down opposite each other, to chew. In less than a quarter of an hour's time, these hopeful youths had shed about them on the clean boards, a copious shower of yellow rain; clearing, by that means, a kind of magic circle, within whose limits no intruder dared to come, and which they never failed to refresh and re-refresh before a spot was dry. This being before breakfast, rather disposed me, I confess, to nausea; but looking attentively at one of the expectorators, I plainly saw that he was young in chewing, and felt inwardly uneasy, himself. A glow of delight came over me at this discovery; and as I marked his face turned paler and paler, and saw the ball of tobacco in his left cheek quiver with his suppressed agony, while yet he spat, and chewed, and spat again, in emulation of his older friend, I could have fallen on his neck and implored him to go on for hours.

(from Charles Dickens, *American Notes and Pictures From Italy*)

a. _____ Tobacco-chewing is an offensive and vulgar habit.

b. _____ One of the tobacco-chewers was inexperienced at chewing.

4.   Lawyers are so numerous in all our populous towns, that I am surprised they never thought before of establishing themselves here: they are plants that will grow in any soil that is cultivated by the hands of others; and when once they have taken root they will extinguish every other vegetable that grows around them. The fortunes they daily acquire in every province, from the misfortunes of their fellow-citizens, are surprising! The most ignorant, the most bungling member of that profession, will, if placed in the most obscure part of the country, promote litigiousness, and amass more wealth without labour, than the most opulent farmer, with all his toils. They have so dexterously interwoven their doctrines and quirks with the laws of the land, or rather they are become so necessary an evil in our present constitutions, that it seems unavoidable and past all remedy. What a pity that our forefathers, who happily extinguished so many fatal customs, and expunged from their new government so many errors and abuses, both religious and civil, did not also prevent the introduction of a set of men so dangerous! In some provinces, where every inhabitant is constantly employed in tilling and cultivating the earth, they are the only members of society who have any knowledge; let these provinces attest what iniquitous use they have made of that knowledge.

(from J. Hector St. John, *Letters from an American Farmer*)

a. _____ Men could live together in harmony if there were no lawyers.

b. _____ Lawyers are educated people.

5.   Singular as it may appear to you, there are but two medical professors on the island [of Nantucket]; for of what service can physic be in a primitive society, where the excesses of inebriation are so rare? What need of galenical medicines, where fevers, and stomachs loaded by the loss of the digestive powers, are so few? Temperance, the calm of passions, frugality, and continual exercise, keep them healthy, and preserve unimpaired that constitution which they have received from parents as healthy as themselves; who in the unpolluted embraces of the earliest and chastest love, conveyed to them the soundest bodily frame which

nature could give. But as no habitable part of this globe is exempt from some diseases, proceeding either from climate or modes of living; here they are sometimes subject to consumptions and to fevers. Since the foundation of that town no epidemical distempers have appeared, which at times cause such depopulations in other countries; many of them are extremely well acquainted with the Indian methods of curing simple diseases, and practice them with success. You will hardly find anywhere a community, composed of the same number of individuals, possessing such uninterrupted health, and exhibiting so many green old men, who show their advanced age by the maturity of their wisdom, rather than by the wrinkles of their faces; and this is indeed one of the principal blessings of the island, which richly compensates their want of the richer soils of the south; where iliac complaints and bilious fevers grow by the side of the sugar cane, the ambrosial ananas, etc. The situation of this island, the purity of the air, the nature of their marine occupation, their virtue and moderation, are the causes of that vigour and health which they possess.

(from J. Hector St. John, *Letters from an American Farmer*)

a. _____ Only two doctors practiced medicine on Nantucket Island during the late eighteenth century.

b. _____ Nantucket was a healthy place to live during the 1700s.

Writing Strategy: CLASSIFICATION

Classification is an everyday activity. Consider the way that most individuals shop for groceries: first, they determine their needs and then group items under categories such as meats, vegetables, and household supplies. They may even arrange their shopping lists to reflect the organization of their favorite supermarket. Without this classification of items, shoppers could wander down aisles for hours as they determine what to purchase and its location. Classification of items requires that items be separated into broad categories; then, specific items are assigned, according to their inherent characteristics, to these broad categories. In brainstorming sessions, you begin to classify ideas and details into categories that will help you develop a paragraph. You might also divide details into groups according to their connections with the topic sentence. Hence, you classify items that support a topic sentence and items that explain the main supports in more detail.

Classification requires that your categories do not overlap. For example, if you classify students by their majors, then you should not include a category identifying their political interests. In addition, because a classification seeks to divide items into meaningful groups, try to avoid stereotypes and generalizations. In a survey of students' political preferences at your school, for instance, it would be inappropriate to suggest that all students share the same political preferences.

As you read the selections that follow, consider the ways in which the writer uses classification. For example, in "Three New Yorks," E. B. White identifies three different views of the same city; each view is represented by a different group of people, such as suburban commuters or city dwellers, who understand the city only in terms of their immediate relationship to it.

Three New Yorks

E. B. White

There are roughly three New Yorks. There is, first, the New York of the man or woman who was born here, who takes the city for granted and accepts its size and its turbulence as natural and inevitable. Second, there is the New York of the commuter—the city that is devoured by locusts each day and spat out each night. Third, there is the New York of the person who was born somewhere else and came to New York in quest of something. Of these three trembling cities the greatest is the last—the city of final destination, the city that is a goal. It is this third city that accounts for New York's high-strung disposition, its poetical deportment, its dedication to the arts, and its incomparable achievements. Commuters give the city its tidal restlessness, natives give it solidity and continuity, but the settlers give it passion. And whether it is a farmer arriving from Italy to set up a small grocery store in a slum, or a young girl arriving from a small town in Mississippi to escape the indignity of being observed by her neighbors, or a boy arriving from the Corn Belt with a manuscript in his suitcase and a pain in his heart, it makes no difference: each embraces New York with the intense excitement of first love, each absorbs New York with the fresh eyes of an adventurer, each generates heat and light to dwarf the Consolidated Edison Company.

QUESTIONS

1. The topic sentence is the first sentence. Does the author provide sufficient support for it? Explain.

2. The author structures this paragraph by using three groups of elements. Locate the groups and explain his organization.

3. What is the tone of the paragraph?

Whales

Rachel Carson

Eventually the whales, as though to divide the sea's food resources among them, became separated into three groups: the plankton-eaters, the fish-eaters, and the squid-eaters. The plankton-eating whales can exist only where there are dense masses of small shrimp or copepods to supply their enormous food requirements. This limits them, except for scattered areas, to arctic and antarctic waters and the high temperate latitudes. Fish-eating whales may find food over a somewhat wider range of ocean, but they are restricted to places where there are enormous populations of schooling fish. The blue water of the tropics and of the open ocean basins offers little to either of these groups. But that immense, square-headed, formidably toothed whale known as the cachalot or sperm whale discovered long ago what men have known for only a short time—that hundreds of fathoms below the almost untenanted surface waters of these regions there is an abundant animal life. The sperm whale has taken these deep waters for his hunting grounds; his quarry is the deep-water population of squids, including the giant squid Architeuthis, which lives pelagically at depths of 1500 feet or more. The head of the sperm whale is often marked with long stripes, which consist of a great number of circular scars made by the suckers of the squid. From this evidence we can imagine the battles that go on, in the darkness of the deep water, between these two huge creatures—the sperm whale with its 70-ton bulk, the squid with a body as long as 30 feet, and writhing, grasping arms extending the total length of the animal to perhaps 50 feet.

QUESTIONS 1. What is the basis for Carson's classification of whales?

2. Which of the three types of whales suffers most for its food? Give specific examples of the struggle.

3. Define the following words: *untenanted, writhing, temperate,* and *formidably.*

Types of College Students

Theodore H. White

1 Students divide themselves by their own discriminations in every generation, and the group I ran with had a neat system of classification. Harvard, my own group held, was divided into three groups—white men, gray men and meatballs. I belonged to the meatballs, by self-classification. White men were youngsters of great name; my own class held a Boston Saltonstall, a New York Straus, a Chicago Marshall Field, two Roosevelts (John and Kermit), a Joseph P. Kennedy, Jr. The upper classes had another Roosevelt (Franklin, Jr.), a Rockefeller (David, with whom I shared a tutor in my sophomore year), a Morgan, and New York and Boston names of a dozen different fashionable pedigrees. Students of such names had automobiles; they went to Boston deb parties, football games, the June crew race against Yale; they belonged to clubs. At Harvard today, they are called "preppies," the private-school boys of mythical "St. Grottlesex."

2 Between white men above and meatballs at the bottom came the gray men. The gray men were mostly public-high-school boys, sturdy sons of America's middle class. They went out for football and baseball, manned the *Crimson* and *Lampoon,* ran for class committees and, later in life, for school committees and political office. They came neither of the aristocracy nor of the deserving poor, as did most meatballs and scholarship boys. Caspar Weinberger, of my class of 1938, for example, was president of the *Crimson* and graduated magna cum laude; he later became Secretary of Health, Education and Welfare, but as an undergraduate was a gray man from California. John King, of the same class of 1938, was another gray man; he became governor of New Hampshire. Wiley Mayne, an earnest student of history, who graduated with us, was a gray man from Iowa, later becoming congressman from Sioux City. He served on the House Judiciary Committee that voted to impeach Richard Nixon—with Wiley Mayne voting to support the President. The most brilliant member of the class was probably Arthur M. Schlesinger, Jr., who defied categorization. Definitely no meatball, Schlesinger lacked then either the wealth or the savoir-faire of the white men. Indeed, Schlesinger, who was to go on to a fame surpassing that of his scholar father, was one who could apparently mingle with both white men and meatballs. In his youth, Schlesinger was a boy of extraordinary sweetness and generosity, one of the few on campus who would be friendly to a Jewish meatball, not only a liberal by heredity, but a liberal in practice. Since Wiley Mayne, Arthur Schlesinger and I were all rivals, in an indistinct way, in the undergraduate rivalry of the History Department, I followed their careers with some interest. Mayne was a conservative, tart-tongued and stiff. I remember on the night of our Class Day dance, as we were all about to leave, he unburdened himself to me on "Eastern liberals who look down their long snob noses on people like me from the Midwest." Over the years Mayne grew into a milder, gentler, warmer person until in his agony over Nixon, wrestling with his conscience on whether to impeach or not, he seemed to be perhaps the most sensitive and human member of the Judiciary Committee. Schlesinger, by contrast, developed a certainty about affairs, a public tartness of manner associated with the general liberal rigidity of the late sixties that offended many—and yet, for all that, he remained as kind and gentle to old friends like

myself, with whose politics he came profoundly to disagree, as he had been in boyhood. Both Schlesinger and Mayne, the liberal and the conservative, were always absolutely firm in their opinions. I, in the years starting at Harvard, and continuing in later life, wandered all through the political spectrum, and envied them both for their certainties.

3   I find some difficulty in describing what a "meatball" was. Meatballs were usually day students or scholarship students. We were at Harvard not to enjoy the games, the girls, the burlesque shows of the Old Howard, the companionship, the elms, the turning leaves of fall, the grassy banks of the Charles. We had come to get the Harvard badge, which says "Veritas," but really means a job somewhere in the future, in some bureaucracy, in some institution, in some school, laboratory, university or law firm.

QUESTIONS

1. Identify the three groups of college students White describes. What individual characteristics do the groups possess?

2. Each of the groups was at Harvard for different reasons. List each group's reasons for attending that university.

3. Which group is given the greatest number of specific examples? What does White suggest about this group?

PARAGRAPH ASSIGNMENTS

1. As E. B. White did, classify the different ways people might view your city or town. Present this information to someone who is moving into the area so that he or she can understand the variety your city has to offer.

2. For your own information, and for presentation to a group of students who share your major course of study, identify the various types of entry-level positions you could obtain with your college degree. You may want to research this topic more thoroughly by completing readings at the library and interviewing people in the field.

3. Arrange an interview with someone who has recently moved to your city or town or with someone from a foreign country. In the interview, ask the person to identify specific characteristics of people in your town or of Americans in general. Report your findings in an article for the school newspaper.

4. As a means of describing your campus to a friend at another college or to high-school students, identify at least three types of college students. You should identify your basis of classification (for example, by interests, styles, majors, ages, or college status). You might consider also classifying members of a particular group; for example, you could detail characteristics of types of college athletes. Include as many specific traits about each group as possible.

5

Revising

OBJECTIVES:
1. To revise a paragraph effectively.
2. To edit a paragraph effectively.
3. To proofread a paragraph effectively.
4. To explore composing through illustration by example and process analysis.

PREVIEW: When you revise, you re-examine the purpose, audience, topic sentence, and organization in your paragraph. When you edit, you reread your paragraph to polish your sentences for a final draft of the paragraph. Through proofreading, you carefully review the final draft to correct minor errors.

Throughout the composing process, writers constantly revise their ideas, tone, purpose, and organization. Through revision, they explore ideas, discover insights, and gain more control over their paragraphs. This chapter presents many strategies you can use to revise your work.

Revision Checklist

Too often, beginning writers consider the process of writing completed once they produce a first draft of a paragraph; they do not take the time to analyze what they have written or how they have stated ideas. If they do revise, then they tend to look only for obvious grammatical and mechanical errors; they do not examine the content and the organization of the paper. However, by revising, writers can develop a paragraph more and make it more effective.

Revision can take many forms. You can produce three or four drafts of a paper, each with a different goal, before the paper is completed. (See "The Writing Process: An Overview" in Chapter One for information on stages of drafts.) You can also choose to analyze your first or second draft for specific weaknesses in organization, details, and transitions. In each case, because there are too many areas to check and analyze at one time, you should revise in stages. The following checklist will guide you in the revision process.

I. *Purpose* (See "Identifying Audience and Purpose" in Chapter 2 of Part One.)
   A. What is your purpose in writing? Do you wish to explain, narrate, describe, or persuade?
   B. Is your purpose clearly evident to your readers?
   C. What identifies the purpose in your paragraph?

D. Does the entire paragraph support your purpose? How does it accomplish this support?

II. *Audience*

A. Who is your intended audience?

B. What are some characteristics of this audience?

C. What in the paragraph identifies your audience?

D. How do you want your audience to respond to the paragraph? What in the paragraph will lead the audience to this response?

III. *Topic Sentence* (See Chapter 3.)

A. Does the paragraph have a topic sentence? Where is it?

B. Does the topic sentence predict, control, and obligate?

C. Does the topic sentence have a controlling idea?

D. Is the controlling idea specific? Does it avoid vague words?

IV. *Organization* (See Chapter 4 of Part One.)

A. How is the paragraph organized? Does this organization support your purpose?

B. Does the paragraph have primary support sentences? Do the primary support sentences directly develop the topic sentence?

C. Are the primary support sentences arranged in the most effective order? Should they be arranged in another manner?

D. Did you choose primary support sentences that will best address your audience's needs and knowledge? Do these primary support sentences represent the best examples, descriptions, or arguments to develop the topic sentence? Or can you think of other supports now?

E. Does the paragraph contain secondary support sentences? Do these secondary support sentences provide additional information about the primary support sentences? Are the secondary support sentences specific?

F. Do these secondary support sentences represent the best examples and explanations possible for the primary support sentences? If they do not, then can you now think of more effective ones?

V. *Transitions* (See "Transitional Words and Expressions" in Chapter 6 of Part One.)

A. Are there transitions between sentences and ideas?

B. Are these transitions appropriate? Do they represent the types of relationships you wish to stress?

C. Can the reader easily follow the ideas presented in the paragraph?

EXERCISE 1 Russell Baker, a Pulitzer Prize winner in journalism, wrote the following essay. You should recognize the story as an old favorite. However, Baker has taken some liberties with the language of the original story; he has rewritten the story for a contemporary audience. Identify the contemporary language and types of characters Baker has created. After you have finished reading the story, create a different purpose in telling the story, and rewrite it to address a different audience. State your audience and purpose; also, identify the language you will use to reach this audience. (You might consider rewriting the piece for an audience of business executives, college professors, teenagers, advertising executives, or computer specialists, or you might consider creating your own audience.) This exercise will help you identify and address specific audiences by altering the details you present and the level of language you use.

Little Red Riding Hood Revisited

In an effort to make the classics accessible to contemporary readers, I am translating them into the modern American language. Here is the translation of "Little Red Riding Hood":

Once upon a point in time, a small person named Little Red Riding Hood initiated plans for the preparation, delivery and transportation of foodstuffs to her grandmother, a senior citizen residing at a place of residence in a forest of indeterminate dimension.

In the process of implementing this program, her incursion into the forest was in mid-transportation process when it attained interface with an alleged perpetrator. This individual, a wolf, made inquiry as to the whereabouts of Little Red Riding Hood's goal as well as inferring that he was desirous of ascertaining the contents of Little Red Riding Hood's foodstuffs basket, and all that.

"It would be inappropriate to lie to me," the wolf said, displaying his huge jaw capability. Sensing that he was a mass of repressed hostility intertwined with acute alienation, she indicated.

"I see you indicating," the wolf said, "but what I don't see is whatever it is you're indicating at, you dig?"

Little Red Riding Hood indicated more fully, making one thing perfectly clear—to wit, that it was to her grandmother's residence and with a consignment of foodstuffs that her mission consisted of taking her to and with.

At this point in time the wolf moderated his rhetoric and proceeded to grandmother's residence. The elderly person was then subjected to the disadvantages of total consumption and transferred to residence in the perpetrator's stomach.

"That will raise the old woman's consciousness," the wolf said to himself. He was not a bad wolf, but only a victim of an oppressive society, a society that not only denied wolves' rights, but actually boasted of its capacity for keeping the wolf from the door. An interior malaise made itself manifest inside the wolf.

"Is that the national malaise I sense within my digestive tract?" wondered the wolf. "Or is it the old person seeking to retaliate for her consumption by telling wolf jokes to my duodenum?" It was time to make a judgment. The time was now, the hour had struck, the body lupine cried out for decision. The wolf was up to the challenge. He took two stomach powders right away and got into bed.

The wolf had adopted the abdominal-distress recovery posture when Little Red Riding Hood achieved his presence.

"Grandmother," she said, "your ocular implements are of an extraordinary order of magnitude."

"The purpose of this enlarged viewing capability," said the wolf "is to enable your image to register a more precise impression upon my sight systems."

"In reference to your ears," said Little Red Riding Hood, "it is noted with the deepest respect that far from being underprivileged, their elongation and enlargement appear to qualify you for unparalleled distinction."

"I hear you loud and clear, kid," said the wolf, "but what about these new choppers?"

"If it is not inappropriate," said Little Red Riding Hood, "it might be observed that with your new miracle masticating products you may even be able to chew taffy again."

This observation was followed by the adoption of an aggressive posture on the part of the wolf and the assertion that it was also possible for him, due to the high efficiency ratio of his jaw, to consume little persons, plus, as he stated, his firm determination to do so at once without delay and with all due process and propriety, notwithstanding the fact that the ingestion of one entire grandmother had already provided twice his daily recommended cholesterol intake.

There ensued flight by Little Red Riding Hood accompanied by pursuit in respect to the wolf and a subsequent intervention on the part of a third party, heretofore unnoted in the record.

Due to the firmness of the intervention, the wolf's stomach underwent ax-assisted aperture with the result that Red Riding Hood's grandmother was enabled to be removed with only minor discomfort.

The wolf's indigestion was immediately alleviated with such effectiveness that he signed a contract with the intervening third party to perform with grandmother in a television commercial demonstrating the swiftness of this dramatic relief for stomach discontent.

"I'm going to be on television," cried grandmother.

And they all joined her happily in crying, "What a phenomena!"

EXERCISE 2   Use the questions in the revision checklist to analyze the following student paragraph. At what points should there be revision? Make specific suggestions about the types of revision the writer should make. Compare your answers to those of other students. Finally, revise the paragraph yourself.

Some people who enjoy skiing go to extremes and buy all kinds of expensive equipment to make themselves look professional. The skier starts with buying an expensive pair of skis, bindings, boots, and poles. He buys Rossignol skis with the best pair of Marker bindings. Next, the skier purchases Scott poles and Nordica rear-entry boots making sure that the entire package is color coordinated. This package runs anywhere from six hundred to seven hundred dollars. Furthermore, his looks are taken too seriously. The person purchases a Rossignol hat, Smith double-lens goggles, a Roffe powder jacket with matching Roffe stretch pants, and the appropriate color of Rossignol gloves. Also, the skier must buy a slalom ski sweater which has padded shoulders and elbows. His entire wardrobe totals approximately six hundred dollars. If he were not so serious about skiing, he would wear blue jeans, any winter coat, and rent skis, boots and poles.

EXERCISE 3   Choose a paragraph of your own to revise. With the assistance of other students and the revision checklist, decide what revisions would make the paragraph more effective. List the necessary revisions, and then revise the paragraph.

Editing Checklist

In editing a paragraph, you must concentrate upon the individual sentences to ensure that they are concise, effective, and correct. Like revision, editing can best be accomplished in stages. You should begin by reading the paragraph aloud. Often this act of reading aloud will alert you to potential problems. If some sentences are not easily understood when the paragraph is read aloud, then you will know that you must edit those particular sentences. Below are several stages by which you can easily edit a paper.

I. *Clarity*

    A. Do sentences mean what they say? Or are they ambiguous?

    B. Have you used the correct words to describe your meaning? Check unfamiliar words in the dictionary.

II. *Coherence* (See Chapter 6 in Part One.)

    A. Do you use pronouns to achieve coherence? Are any pronouns ambiguous in their reference?

    B. Do you use synonyms? Are the synonyms accurate?

    C. Do you use limited repetition to achieve coherence?

    D. Do you use sentence combining to achieve coherence?

III. *Diction* (See Chapter 7 in Part One.)

    A. Do you avoid vague words and use specific ones instead?

    B. Do you avoid slang, jargon, and regional expressions?

    C. Do you use clichés? If you did, can you think of another way to phrase the meaning?

    D. Do you create a specific, identifiable tone through word choice?

    E. Are key terms clearly defined? Is this tone appropriate for your intended audience?

IV. *Style* (See Chapter 8 in Part One.)

    A. Are sentences wordy?

    B. Do you use active voice and descriptive verbs?

    C. Do you subordinate ideas effectively?

    D. Are sentences varied in structure? Or are they all the same type?

V. *Correctness*

    A. Are there any fragments, run-ons, or comma splices? (See Chapters 6, 7, and 8 in Part Two.)

    B. Do subjects and verbs agree in number? (See Chapter 9 in Part Two.)

    C. Are there any unnecessary shifts in verb tense? (See Chapters 1, 2, and 3 in Part Two.)

    D. Are there any unnecessary shifts in point of view?

    E. Are your pronouns correct in case, number, and gender? (See Chapter 10 in Part Two.)

    F. Have you checked marks of punctuation? Are commas, semicolons, colons, and other marks of punctuation used correctly? (See Chapters 11, 12, and 13 in Part Two.)

    G. Are words properly spelled? (See any good dictionary.)

EXERCISE 4   Edit the following two student paragraphs for sentence problems. Use the editing checklist as a guide in your editing. Compare your responses with those of other students. Did you identify the same problems? Did you make the same alterations? With your classmates, discuss which changes are the most effective.

    1.   Having lived my entire life in a house located at the western part of Maryland, I adapted to the weather and the lifestyle of the residents. However, when I graduated from high school, I decided to spend my summer

with friends working at Ocean City. For the first time I was living on my own in an apartment without my parents, older brothers, and sisters. So, spending a summer working at Ocean City caused my lifestyle and responsibilities to change. Going from a dependent life to an independent one at age eighteen caused my lifestyle to change. First, I went from going to school and working part-time in a small bakery in the mall to a full-time waitress at Lombardi's Italian Restaurant. Now, I was working from five in the afternoon until two in the morning everyday or from twelve in the afternoon to ten at night. Also, one would think that an Italian restaurant at the ocean would not be busy, however, this was not the case. Furthermore, I started to enjoy lying on the beach in the sun as much as I like skiing down a mountain. Another part of my lifestyle freedom affected. First of all, I was able to come and go as I pleased since I did not have my parents around to watch over me. Since I did not have a curfew I arrived at my apartment anywhere from one o'clock A.M. to seven o'clock A.M. Also, being on my own enabled me to invite friends over anytime I wanted for example if I had the night off I would call up some people to come over and have a party. Along with these freedoms I could dress anyway I wanted without my parents, brothers, or sisters telling me to change. My living conditions were affected by my move to the ocean. I went from my two-bed, two-closet bedroom to sharing a two bed, two closet bedroom with three girls. Having no parents to pick up after me, I realised it would not get done unless I did it. Hence I learned how to do laundry, clean the bathroom, and vacuum however these chores did not get done as often as I would have liked them to because of working late, partying late, and being too tired. I also had to learn how to cook. A summer away from parents and pressures gave me a chance to see how I was going to handle moving away to college. I believe without this summer at the beach I would have had a hard time adjusting to college life.

2.   San Diego California and Rockville, Maryland are two cities that are separated by many miles and differ in several ways. One difference between these two cities is their variety of seasons. Summer and Fall are the only

two seasons a year San Diego really has. The summers last through early March to late November with the temperature fluctuating between 80 degrees and 101 degrees fahrenheit. The Fall season lasts from early December to late February with large amounts of rainfall. During this dreary season, the temperature does not reach below 30 degrees. However, Rockville has four distinct seasons: Spring, Summer, Winter, and Fall. Spring, the most beautiful season of all, last from March to late May. During the summer season, which lasts from June to August, the humidity ranges from 70-80%. The Fall season lasts from late August to late November, with pleasantly cool winds. Winter, the snow-filled season, is cold but gratifying. In addition the distance traveled for entertainment is another difference. In San Diego, the distance to and from entertainment is much less that that of Rockville. LaJolla Shores Beach located twenty minutes away from downtown San Diego. McDonalds, the favorite hangout of high school students, is five minutes away from Mt. Carmel High School, which I attended, also the worldwide known San Diego Zoo is only an half hour away from the vacinity of Mt. Carmel High. On the other hand, Rockville is three hours away from Ocean City beach. The regular high school hangout, McDonalds, is fifteen minutes from Magruder High School, and at times it seems like forever to get there. Furthermore, the National Zoo is an hour and a half away, a considerable distance to drive. Besides the seasons and distances, the attitudes of people differ immensely between San Diego and Rockville the people of San Diego posses a very "laid-back" attitude. They go about their daily lives in an unrushed manner. Work projects and punctuality are second priority to recreation and social activities. On the contrary, people of Rockville are much more rushed and tend to put work as their number one priority. Trivial incidences upset and aggrevate Rockville inhabitants, which create a very tense atmosphere. The seasons, distances, and attitudes are just some of the differences between the two cities one should always keep in mind.

EXERCISE 5 Return to your paragraph that you revised in Exercise 3, and edit it now for sentence-level problems. Ask others to assist you, and compare your answers with theirs.

Proofreading Checklist

After writers have revised and edited a paragraph, they should produce a clean copy for submission. Since students tend to be rushed in this last stage, they often overlook typing errors (such as transposed letters in words), the omission of words, and stray marks of punctuation. Therefore, you should proofread the final copy for these errors. Corrections can easily be made in pen, and words can be inserted neatly. (Most instructors will accept final copies with some corrections on them.) Use the following guidelines for proofreading the final copy.

I. Is each word spelled correctly? (Very often when writers proofread quickly, they antici-pate what they will see and miss simple spelling or typing errors. To break this pattern of anticipation, read the paper backwards. In this way, you can isolate each word and easily check its spelling.)

II. Are any words omitted or repeated? (Again, writers anticipate what they meant to say and misread what is on the paper. Read each sentence aloud slowly and carefully. Listen closely to the words. Are there any omissions or repetitions?)

III. Are there stray marks of punctuation? (Isolate each sentence by placing pieces of paper around it; then, read the sentence carefully.)

EXERCISE 6   Read the following student paragraph carefully. Proofread it and make any necessary corrections here.

Competitiveness is very influential to students because it encourages the student and it improves the quality of the student's work. Most impor-tantly, the competitive spirit encourages the student to work. Though the years, humans have always tried to do better than their peers. Hunters competed with each other to see who shoots the greatest number of deer or catches the most fish, so everyone has this natural instinct of competition between other individuals. This natural instinct is the whole idea for using competition in schools. Students are constantly trying to do better then each other, and teachers encourage this so that everyone tries to improve his standing in the class. As a result, students who work at their grades will improve. In addition, as a consequence of being challenged, quality in the work becomes an important issue. To insure a high grade, students want their work to be the best it can be. The student may spend hours and hours reading English papers to insure perfection. Furthermore, neatness is very important because it makes the instructor's job easier and, thus, gives the student an advantage over students who are sloppy writers. With this drive for perfection, a sense of pride in accomplishments accurs. Receiving a paper back from a teacher with no mistakes makes the student feel that the few extra hours of work payed off. In the long run, students are better off when they are challenged to suceed.

EXERCISE 7   Make a final copy of your edited paragraph from Exercise 5. Using the questions to guide you, proofread the copy carefully and make any necessary corrections.

Writing Strategies: ILLUSTRATION BY EXAMPLE and PROCESS ANALYSIS

In this section, you will have the opportunity to analyze two different organizational strategies. In addition to the reading selections that demonstrate these techniques and the writing assignments that will guide your exploration of these strategies, you will be asked to use the revision techniques in this chapter to revise and edit two student paragraphs. Your revision of the two student paragraphs will help you to revise more effectively when you develop your own paragraphs.

Illustration by Example

Illustration by example means exactly that: the supporting sentences provide examples for the main idea of the paragraph. For instance, if you wished to explain that the registration process at college is complex and frustrating, then your supports would identify examples of frustrating and complex situations. Or, if you wished to explain that living on campus has several advantages, then you would list the advantages for your reader. You determine how the paragraph will be structured. You can move from the least important example to the most important one, or you can reverse this order. In addition, you could move in a chronological order or even in an order determined by geographical distance or area. In other words, the structure of the piece is determined by the purpose and audience *you* select.

The Commuter

E. B. White

The commuter is the queerest bird of all. The suburb he inhabits has no essential vitality of its own and is a mere roost where he comes at day's end to go to sleep. Except in rare cases, the man who lives in Mamaroneck or Little Neck or Teaneck and works in New York, discovers nothing much about the city except the time of arrival and departure of trains and buses, and the path to a quick lunch. He is desk-bound, and has never, idly roaming in the gloaming, stumbled suddenly on Belvedere Tower in the Park, seen the ramparts rise sheer from the water of the pond, and the boys along the shore fishing for minnows, girls stretched out negligently on the shelves of the rocks; he has never come suddenly on anything at all in New York as a loiterer, because he has had no time between trains. He has fished in Manhattan's wallet and dug out coins but has never listened to Manhattan's breathing, never awakened to its morning, never dropped off to sleep in its night. About 400,000 men and women come charging onto the island each weekday morning, out of the mouths of tubes and tunnels. Not many among them have ever spent a drowsy afternoon in the great rustling oaken silence of the reading room of the Public Library, with the book elevator (like an old water wheel) spewing out books onto the trays. They tend their furnaces in Westchester and in Jersey but have never seen the furnaces of the Bowery, the fires that burn in oil drums on zero winter nights. They may work in the financial district downtown and never see the extravagant plantings of Rockefeller Center—the daffodils and grape hyacinths and birches and the flags trimmed to the wind on a fine morning in spring. Or they may work in a midtown office and may let a whole year swing round without sighting Governors Island from the sea wall. The commuter dies with tremendous mileage to his credit, but he is no rover. His entrances and exits are more devious than those in a prairie-dog village, and he calmly plays bridge while buried in the mud at the bottom of the East River. The Long Island Rail Road alone carried forty million commuters last year, but many of them were the same fellow retracing his steps.

QUESTIONS

1. What does White suggest commuters miss by not living in the city?

2. What is the tone of the piece?

3. In the first sentence, White likens a commuter to a bird. Where is this metaphor continued? What other metaphors does White include in the piece?

4. Define the following words: *gloaming, spewing, devious,* and *ramparts.*

Queen Victoria's Legacy

Lytton Strachey

Queen Victoria ruled England from 1837 to 1901. In this passage, Lytton Strachey identifies one of Victoria's characteristics: an unwillingness to admit change. To preserve her memories, Victoria insisted that nothing should be changed in the family rooms she shared with her husband Albert and her children.

She gave orders that nothing should be thrown away—and nothing was. There, in drawer after drawer, in wardrobe after wardrobe, reposed the dresses of seventy years. But not only the dresses—the furs and the mantles and subsidiary frills and the muffs and the parasols and the bonnets—all were ranged in chronological order, dated and complete. A great cupboard was devoted to the dolls; in the china room at Windsor a special table held the mugs of her childhood, and her children's mugs as well. Mementoes of the past surrounded her in serried accumulations. In every room the tables were powdered thick with the photographs of relatives; their portraits, revealing them at all ages, covered the walls; their figures, in solid marble, rose up from pedestals, or gleamed from brackets in the form of gold and silver statuettes. The dead, in every shape—in miniatures, in porcelain, in enormous life-size oil-paintings—were perpetually about her. John Brown stood upon her writing-table in solid gold. Her favorite horses and dogs, endowed with a new durability, crowded round her footsteps. Sharp, in silver gilt, dominated the dinner table; Boy and Boz lay together among unfading flowers, in bronze. And it was not enough that each particle of the past should be given the stability of metal or of marble: the whole collection, in its arrangement, no less than its entity, should be immutably fixed. There might be additions, but there might never be alterations. No chintz might change, no carpet, no curtain, be replaced by another; or, if long use at last made it necessary, the stuffs and the patterns must be so identically reproduced that the keenest eye might not detect the difference. No new picture could be hung upon the walls at Windsor, for those already there had been put in their places by Albert, whose decisions were eternal. So, indeed, were Victoria's. To ensure that they should be the aid of the camera was called in. Every single article in the Queen's possession was photographed from several points of view. These photographs were submitted to Her Majesty, and when, after careful inspection, she had approved of them, they were placed in a series of albums, richly bound. Then, opposite each photograph, an entry was made, indicating the number of the article, the number of the room in which it was kept, its exact position in the room and all its principal characteristics. The fate of every object which had undergone this process was henceforth irrevocably sealed. The whole multitude, once and for all, took up its steadfast station. And Victoria, with a gigantic volume or two of the endless catalogue always beside her, to look through, to ponder upon, to expatiate over, could feel, with a double contentment, that the transitoriness of this world had been arrested by the amplitude of her might.

QUESTIONS

1. Enumerate the major supports within the paragraph.

2. Why were the horses and dogs cast in bronze and silver gilt?

3. Define the following words: *durability, immutably, irrevocably,* and *transitoriness.*

4. What is Strachey's tone? Why does he accumulate details as the paragraph moves along?

5. What does Strachey imply about Victoria's character?

Sharks

Philippe Cousteau

In the Mediterranean, sharks are rare and cause few accidents. But their very rarity confers a peculiar solemnity on each encounter. My "first" sharks, at Djerba, were Mediterranean and impressed me unduly, because I had not expected to see them. On the other hand, in the Red Sea, where it is practically impossible to dive among the reefs of the open sea without being surrounded by sharks, coexistence was inevitable and my companions and I very soon became imprudent, almost unaware of their presence. I even sensed in our team the beginnings of a certain affectation of disdain for these inoffensive prowlers, a tendency to feign ignorance of them, to speak of them only in jest. I argued against this form of snobbishness because it could become dangerous, but I was vulnerable to it myself. It is intoxicating for an awkward and vulnerable creature, such as a diver becomes the instant he drops beneath the surface of the water, to imagine himself stronger than a creature far better armed than he. It was in this climate of excessive vanity and confidence in the early years that I dived myself and allowed others to dive, without protection, in the most dangerous waters. On the reef of João Valente, in the Cape Verde Islands, we jostled or pulled on the tails of animals over twelve feet in length, incomparably more powerful and competent than we awkward intruders with steel bottles on our backs, our field of vision limited by the masks we wore, and caricatures of fins on our feet. The day at João Valente when Dumas and I glimpsed in the distance the pale silhouette of a great white shark (the species that all specialists qualify as a man-eater), we were frozen with terror and instinctively drew closer together. We had seen him before he saw us. But as soon as he became aware of our presence, it was he who was seized with panic; emptying out his intestines, he disappeared with a single flick of his tail. Later, in the Indian Ocean, the same incident occurred on two separate occasions. And each time, the violent emotion brought on in us by the appearance of the great white shark gave way to an unjustified sensation of triumph when he fled at the mere sight of us. Each of these unusual encounters provoked great excitement among us, and with it an excessive confidence in ourselves and a consequent relaxation of security measures.

QUESTIONS

1. What is the topic sentence of the paragraph? Why is it placed there?

2. How does Cousteau compare divers to sharks?

3. The initial reaction of Cousteau and Dumas to sharks is replaced by another emotion. Identify both reactions, and explain their significance.

4. What does Cousteau reveal about himself as he details the encounters with sharks?

REVISION PRACTICE

Using the techniques discussed in this chapter, revise the following draft of a student's paragraph. Apply all of the questions about revising, editing, and proofreading to the paragraph; then write a final draft.

The serious amatear tennis player must look like a tennis player and wear the identical garmets the proffessionals wear in tournaments. Because they have a place to carry tennis balls. The white shorts with oversized pockets are an integral part of the players game. A tennis bag is also necessary to carry the equipment the player brings. Made of waterproof canvas the bag has to be large enough to hold all the gear and more important, it has to have a sporty design and the name of a well known racket manufacturer on it. The serious amateur tennis player acquired the "tennis look" before they step onto the court. The two balls fit snuggly in each front pocket a person possesses a total of five balls including the one in his hand. He appears deformed because of the protusions created by the balls, so that number of balls allow the game to be played continually. The players don't have to chase every ball they smash over the fence. Another important piece of clothing is the white collered shirt with colorful design stretched across the chest. Somehow, the amateurs wearing the same kind of shirt that John McEnroe wore when he won the Wimbledon title transfers John's abilities to the neophyte. The shirt gives the person an inflated sense of confidence: he feels that he can beat Jimmy Connors with his eyes closed. A last important garmet is the terrycloth headband. The headband gives the impression that the player has been sweating from running back and forth over the court. Although he has yet to hit the ball over the net. The headband also keeps his hair from interferring with his eyesight when he searches for the balls that flew over the fence. Although clothes do not make the tennis player, many amateurs must believe they do.

PARAGRAPH ASSIGNMENTS

1. E. B. White is critical of the commuter, for he seems to believe that commuters leave little for a city and instead take from the city. In this paragraph, White does not write from a commuter's viewpoint. Respond to White by identifying in a paragraph the advantages of commuting to a large urban area. Be specific about the commuter's location, lifestyle, and the city to which he or she commutes.

2. If you agree with White, who was a city dweller when he wrote this piece, then identify the advantages of living in a large city. In a paragraph, be specific about the city and its resources; also, identify a clear purpose and audience for the piece.

3. Does it make a difference where one lives while attending college? For a group of high-school seniors, identify in a paragraph the advantages of living at home or the advantages of living on campus.

4. People choose colleges for a number of reasons. Explain your decision to attend a college close to home, in a different part of the state, or out of state. In a paragraph, address your comments to either a group of parents of college-age students or to a group of high-school students preparing to attend college.

5. Very often others see us more clearly than we see ourselves. Our emotions affect our ability to describe our characteristics objectively. Choose an outstanding trait of an individual, perhaps a close friend or family member, and describe the trait so the person can view it objectively. Support your description with ample details. Determine a specific purpose for your paragraph.

6. Cousteau explains that he often took unnecessary chances while diving in shark-infested waters. Although he was aware of the potential danger, he felt confident that he would not be attacked. Describe a similar situation that you have faced. When did you take unnecessary risks? Why did you take them? What was the outcome? Would you repeat the incident now? Specify an audience who could profit from your experience, and determine a specific purpose for your paragraph.

Process Analysis

A process analysis explains to a reader how to do a task, or it may illustrate how something works. Hence, two types of process analyses are used as organizational strategies: a **directional** process analysis provides a set of instructions for the reader, and an **informational** process analysis explains the steps in an operation. For example, in a directional process analysis, a writer may describe how to operate a computer or calculator, how to serve a tennis ball, how to apply to college, or how to build a deck for a house. An informational process analysis, however, will explain in a sequence of steps how a telephone works, how the heart pumps blood throughout the body, or how a microwave oven cooks food.

To provide either type of process analysis, you must consider the audience's knowledge of the process and tailor the analysis to meet the audience's needs. It would be inappropriate, for instance, for a computer expert to explain to novices, in computer jargon, how a word-processing system works. In the same fashion, it would be inappropriate for the computer expert to explain in layman's language how an advanced computer works to those who are familiar with computers. In addition, you must set forth *in chronological fashion* the steps of the process or the instructions. While this may be obvious, many of us forget the difficulties we had when we first learned to water ski or to ride a bike. Hence, we often omit necessary steps or stages simply because they seem so obvious to us. These steps, however, are *not* obvious to anyone who is just learning. Therefore, be sure that you include all the information someone needs to perform the task.

The Birth of an Island

James Michener

1   For eons of time the two massive volcano systems stood in the sea in fiery competition, and then, inevitably, the first began to die back, its fire extinguished, while the second continued to pour millions of tons of lava down its own steep flanks. Hissing, exploding, crackling, the rocks fell into the sea in boundless accumulations, building the later volcano ever more solidly, ever more thickly at its base on the remote floor of the ocean.

2   In time, sinking lava from the second master builder began to creep across the feet of the first, and then to climb its sides and finally to throw itself across the exposed lava flows that had constituted the earlier island. Now the void in the sea that had separated the two was filled, and they became one. Locked in fiery arms, joined by intertwining ejaculations of molten rock, the two volcanoes stood in matrimony, their union a single fruitful and growing island.

3   Its soil was later made from dozens of smaller volcanoes that erupted for a few hundred thousand years, then passed into death and silence. One exploded in dazzling glory and left a crater looking like a punch bowl. Another, at the very edge of the island, from where it could control the sea approaches, left as its memory a gaunt headland shaped like a diamond.

QUESTIONS   1. List the steps in the birth of an island by volcanic action.

2. Explain the final form of the volcanos.

3. Define the following words: *eons, void, ejaculations,* and *intertwining.*

How Dictionaries Are Made

S. I. Hayakawa

1   It is widely believed that every word has a correct meaning, that we learn these meanings principally from teachers and grammarians (except that most of the time we don't bother to, so that we ordinarily speak "sloppy English"), and that dictionaries and grammars are the supreme authority in matters of meaning and usage. Few people ask by what authority the writers of dictionaries and grammars say what they say. I once got into a dispute with an English woman over the pronunciation of a word and offered to look it up in the dictionary. The English woman said firmly, "What for? I am English. I was born and brought up in England. The way I speak *is* English." Such self-assurance about one's own language is not uncommon among the English. In the United States, however,

anyone who is willing to quarrel with the dictionary is regarded as either eccentric or mad.

2   Let us see how dictionaries are made and how the editors arrive at definitions. What follows applies, incidentally, only to those dictionary offices where first-hand, original research goes on—not those in which editors simply copy existing dictionaries. The task of writing a dictionary begins with the reading of vast amounts of the literature of the period or subject that the dictionary is to cover. As the editors read, they copy on cards every interesting or rare word, every unusual or peculiar occurrence of a common word, a large number of common words in their ordinary uses, and also the sentences in which each of these words appears, thus:

> pail
> The dairy *pails* bring home increase of milk
> Keats, *Endymion*
> I, 44–45

3   That is to say, the context of each word is collected, along with the word itself. For a really big job of dictionary writing, such as the *Oxford English Dictionary* (usually bound in about twenty-five volumes), millions of such cards are collected, and the task of editing occupies decades. As the cards are collected, they are alphabetized and sorted. When the sorting is completed, there will be for each word anywhere from two or three to several hundred illustrative quotations, each on its card.

4   To define a word, then, the dictionary editor places before him the stack of cards illustrating that word; each of the cards represents an actual use of the word by a writer of some literary or historical importance. He reads the cards carefully, discards some, re-reads the rest, and divides up the stack according to what he thinks are the several senses of the word. Finally, he writes his definitions, following the hard-and-fast rule that each definition *must* be based on what the quotations in front of him reveal about the meaning of the word. The editor cannot be influenced by what *he* thinks a given word *ought* to mean. He must work according to the cards, or not at all.

5   The writing of a dictionary, therefore, is not a task of setting up authoritative statements about the "true meanings" of words, but a task of *recording,* to the best of one's ability, what various words have *meant* to authors in the distant or immediate past. *The writer of a dictionary is a historian, not a lawgiver.* If, for example, we had been writing a dictionary in 1890, or even as late as 1919, we could have said that the word "broadcast" means "to scatter" (seed, for example), but we could not have decreed that from 1921 on, the most common meaning of the word should become "to disseminate audible messages, etc., by radio transmission." To regard the dictionary as an "authority," therefore, is to credit the dictionary writer with gifts of prophecy which neither he nor anyone else possesses. In choosing our words when we speak or write, we can be *guided* by the historical record afforded us by the dictionary, but we cannot be *bound* by it, because new situations, new experiences, new inventions, new feelings, are always compelling us to give new uses to old words. Looking under a "hood," we should ordinarily have found, five hundred years ago, a monk; today, we find a motorcar engine.

QUESTIONS

1. What is Hayakawa's thesis? Where is it located?

2. Why does Hayakawa believe that it is important that we understand how dictionaries are made? What assumptions do we make about dictionaries? Are these assumptions accurate?

3. Why must writers of dictionaries use words only within the contexts of sentences? What does this suggest about language?

Teach Bike Riding in One Hour

Michael H. Kelly

1   That Great American Pastime known as "teaching your kid to ride a bike" ranks right up there on the parent-unpleasantness scale with telling your kid about sex—only worse. You don't tell your kid about sex with all the neighbors standing around thinking, if not saying, "He's doing it all wrong."

2   It never fails. No matter how carefully you watch and wait until there's no one on the street, as soon as you step out the door with your child and his new bike, your neighbors suddenly appear. *All* your neighbors suddenly appear. Neighbors you've never seen before. Neighbors with relatives. Neighbors with people they've met in malls, bars, bus stops. Neighbors with bag ladies. Bedouin nomads, the Altar and Rosary Society from Saint Hyacinth's. Hundreds, thousands of neighborly people line the street.

3   Or so it seems.

4   And you puff and wheeze and run yourself silly up and down that narrow, endless ribbon of sidewalk while these neighbors offer can't-fail suggestions: "It's all in his butt. Tell him he's gotta feel it in his butt."

5   You swear, redden, and smile, then run the gauntlet again and tell yourself this is quality time you're spending with your child.

6   That's the way it was for me anyway. But after several weekends of turfed lawns, trashed tulip beds, a battered bike, a bruised kid, and a near-terminal loss of human dignity, I figured it was time to engage in another Great American Pastime known as "inventing a better way." Here it is: how to teach bike riding in one hour *without* running yourself silly. It's easy. And it's kid-tested.

1

7   How long would it have taken us to learn to walk as babies if we had had to learn by walking on the side of a two-by-four? We'd still be crawling on our hands and knees, ruining expensive clothes, and having a tough time on the dance floor. Learning to ride a bike on a sidewalk is a little like learning to walk on a two-by-four.

8   Your kid can't even sit on a bike yet and you're asking him to master the complex art of steering down a narrow strip of cement between the terrifying, forbidden zones of neighbors' lawns. Put the bike in the car. Take it and your kid to a school playground or empty church parking lot—someplace where he won't have to worry about steering until he learns how to stay up.

2

9   Most of us "just learn" how to ride a bike in a single, blazing, inspired moment after a suitable period of bashing our knees on the ground—sometimes for as long as two summers. One moment we can't ride to save our lives. The next moment we can. We know how. But we don't know *the how*.

10   The fact is, there is a real *method* to riding a bike and the secret is all in the front wheel. Simply put, when you start to fall right, turn the front wheel right and when you start to fall left, turn the front wheel left.

11   This is the *technique* we master in our "inspired moment." We think we learned the balance, the feel, of bike riding. What we really learned was a way to stop the tilt of a falling bike by turning the wheel (think of it as sticking your leg out) while at the same time redirecting the momentum of the bike, allowing it to right itself. Of course, in actual practice, we constantly make these small, front-wheel adjustments—adjustments so small we don't even notice them.

3

12   You're in an empty church parking lot. Your kid is on his bike, feet on the pedals, hands on the handlebars. You're holding him up by the back of his bike seat. Next move is don't move—not one puffing, wheezing, sweating inch. Here's where you teach *the how*.

13   Tilt the bike to the right and to the left. Tell your child, "When you start feeling yourself fall this way (right), turn your front wheel this way (right). When you start feeling yourself fall this way (left), turn your front wheel this way (left)." Stand there, without moving, for five or ten minutes practicing with your child. Tilt the bike unexpectedly one way and then the other until your child gets the hang of turning the front wheel into tilts.

4

14   Walk, don't run, with your child. Move slowly. Hold lightly on to the back of his bike seat. The concept of turning the front wheel into a fall is easy to understand. But, there are two things your child will probably do that you should practice here: he will wait until he's tilting too far into the fall before correcting with the front wheel, or he will overcorrect and go right into a fall/correct situation in the opposite direction.

15   Explain to your child that he wants to correct early. Tilt him very slightly and show him how far to correct with the front wheel. Tilt him a little more and show him how much he'll have to turn the wheel to correct. Show him that if he waits too long, he'll either crash or start losing control in the other direction.

5

16   You will have to run a little now. But you won't have to do it for long, and, even better, you won't have to do it in front of the neighbors.

17   Run slowly at first. Let your child set the pace. Stay a little back, just out of your child's field of peripheral vision. Hold lightly on to the back of the bike seat. Let go of the seat as soon as possible for as long as possible. Don't let your child know when you're holding and when you're not. Saying "I'm letting go now" is like saying "Look over your shoulder, son. Panic. And run your bike into that wire fence over there."

18   Now you'll see why the wide-open spaces are important. Your young novice bicyclist will dip, loop, zigzag, ride in crazy circles. At times it will seem as if your child is in a slow-motion death spiral, when suddenly some invisible hand will push him upright. You'll die a thousand times in the next fifteen minutes. And, of course, there will be a few crashes, but it won't be long now.

19   Your child will still be waiting too long before correcting with the front wheel. He'll still overcorrect, too. When the ride gets too crazy, stop him. Give him a breather. Remind him to correct sooner with the front wheel. Then go at it again.

20   At some point (you'll know when), stop running alongside your youngster and let him go. After 50 or 60 yards he'll realize you're not there. He'll look around—probably crash—but when he sees how far back you are, he'll know he can ride. There's no stopping him after that.

6

21   Once he's riding, let him ride. He's proud of himself. He still can't believe it. Let him ride, build confidence, and have fun. Help him get on and off the bike. Help him stop. Let him go.

22   Before you leave, you can show him how to get on the bike—at a stoop or stair if necessary—and how to brake. But don't practice these things now—unless he wants to. He'll pick them up quickly on his own.

23   In fact, in a day or two, he'll be riding as if he were born with wheels instead of legs. A day or two after that he'll be asking for a bigger, faster, spiffier bike. And not long after that, you'll be reading another article similar to this: "How to tell your kid about sex without breaking out in hives and swallowing your tongue."

QUESTIONS

1. What is the tone of this article? Does the tone change? If so, why might it change? Is the change effective?

2. In the beginning of the article, Kelly compares teaching a child to ride a bike to what other lesson? Does he repeat this other lesson? If he does repeat this similarity, where and why does it appear?

3. What are some problems inherent in teaching a child to ride a bike?

4. How many steps does Kelly identify in this process?

5. What is Kelly's purpose in listing the numbers and types of neighbors who watch the lesson?

REVISION PRACTICE

Using the revision techniques discussed in this chapter, revise the following draft of a student paragraph. Apply all of the questions about revising, editing, and proofreading to the paragraph until you complete a final draft.

Building a fire properly require a good deal of preparation and a lesser amount of expertise. Above all, make certain that the flue in your fireplace or wood stove is clear and is drafting well. if this flue is blocked, then the smoke from the fire will fill your room with acrid fumes. It is recommended that your chimney be cleaned once a year by a sweep, simply check the classified ads for the name of a professional. Next, try to make certain that your wood is seasoned and dry for the best burning. This wood can be purchased—prices vary across America—or you can cut it yourself. As Henry David Thoreau remarked, you get warm twice when you chop your own wood. Now, consider your kindling: twigs of any sort of dry wood which has been gathered from your own yard, bark fallen from your logs, or uniform, small sticks that can be purchased commercially. Finally, keep a pile of old newspapers, preferably those with no color photographs, for they produce noxious fumes when burning. Once you have gathered this material, you are ready to build your fire. Ball up several newspapers and shove them under the grate then begin to layer your kindling, papers and logs. On the grate first place your kindling, preferably in a crisscross pattern. Place two or three logs vertically on the kindling, and stuff the space between the logs with more newspaper. This is your first layer, reverse the procedure for your second: that is, the next set of logs should be layed horizontally, and then vertically again. Above all, make certain that the spacing of the logs provides air pockets for the fire to draft. If the fire has been laid properly, you need only to touch a match to the newspaper on the bottom to start a roaring blaze. You need none of the other pathetic devices I have witnessed: a frantic householder dangerously squirting lighter fluid into the fireplace, the strongest son pumping bellows, or a family praying in unison to Vulcan, the god of fire. At a cost lower than either gas or oil, you now have an attractive source of heat, the spot, above all others, for the family to gather, the dog to lie, or for the solitary person to commune with a good book.

PARAGRAPH ASSIGNMENTS

For each assignment below, identify a specific audience that will perform a task or understand a process. Identify, also, the skills that the audience will need to perform this task or understand this process. Finally, create a purpose for the readers. Why should they know how to complete the task or understand how this process is performed?

1. Provide a directional process analysis for one of the following tasks:

    planning a large party

    eating an ice cream cone (or any other food, such as tacos, spaghetti, or barbequed ribs)

    enrolling in college

    applying for a part-time job

2. Provide an informational process analysis for one of the following items:

    how a car's engine works

    how television signals are relayed

    how a camera takes pictures

    how an assembly line works

Typed
1 pg

Achieving Coherence

1. To write a coherent paragraph by using pronouns, synonyms, limited repetition, sentence combining, and transitional words and expressions.

2. To explore composing through comparison/contrast and cause/effect.

PREVIEW: Coherence is the logical connecting of ideas. You may use a number of techniques to link your ideas smoothly and logically.

Paragraphs require **coherence,** the logical connection of ideas, so that the reader can easily perceive the connections between sentences and ideas. Writers achieve coherence by using pronouns, synonyms, limited repetition, sentence combining, and transitional words and expressions.

Coherence allows a writer to show the relationship between ideas and sentences, to avoid needless repetition of the same words, to reinforce certain key concepts, and to avoid simplistic and wordy sentences. A paragraph without coherence tends to be somewhat boring and difficult to read; in effect, its readers must connect ideas and sentences themselves, since the writer has failed to do so. Consider the following paragraph, which lacks coherence.

Henry Louis Mencken was born in Baltimore. He had a long, tumultuous and eclectic career. He played a variety of roles. Edgar Allan Poe was a great literary critic. Mencken also was a truly American literary critic. Mencken struggled for freedom of expression. This helped change the course of American literary history. Mencken was a newspaperman. He wrote literally thousands of columns for the Baltimore *Herald* and the Baltimore *Sun*. His newspaper work was also syndicated in papers around the country. He covered everything in his columns. He wrote about art, economics, politics, food, heavyweight championship fights, and the Scopes trial in Tennessee. From 1914 to 1933, Mencken edited two monthly magazines. They were the *Smart Set* and the *American Mercury*. He wrote about language in his study *The American Language*. The philological work ran to four editions and two supplements. His autobiographical trilogy, the *Days* books, sold well and entertained generations of readers. Mencken estimated that he wrote ten million words for publications over his career. His career lasted for half a century. His writing generated a critical response of more than one million words. He declared joyfully that most of these words were derogatory. Few, if any, American authors have proven as prolific or as colorful as this Baltimorean. He never went to school a day beyond the age of fifteen.

The paragraph has rather basic sentence structure: most of its sentences are simple or compound. (Simple sentences have one independent clause; compound sentences have two or more independent clauses. See "Sentence Types" in Chapter 8, Part One, and see also Chapter 5 in Part Two. Moreover, the author needlessly repeats names and words, makes no connection between sentences, and fails to reinforce key concepts. Below, analyze the same paragraph, now rewritten, in which several methods were used to achieve coherence.

> Throughout his long, tumultuous and eclectic career, Henry Louis Mencken, a Baltimorean, played a variety of literary roles. After Edgar Allan Poe, Mencken proved to be the next truly American literary critic. As a critic, Mencken's struggle for freedom of expression helped to change the course of American literary history. Mencken the newspaperman wrote literally thousands of columns in which he covered everything from art to economics, from politics to food, from a heavyweight championship fight to the Scopes trial in Tennessee. In addition to his newspaper work, Mencken edited two monthly magazines, the *Smart Set* and the *American Mercury*, from 1914 to 1933. Moreover, Mencken was a philologist; his highly respected philological study, *The American Language*, ran to four editions and two supplements. His efforts as a writer did not end there; his winsome autobiographical trilogy, the *Days* books, sold well and entertained generations of readers. Mencken once estimated that, over a career that lasted half a century, he wrote ten million words for publication. These words generated a critical response of more than one million words, the majority of which, he joyfully declared, were highly derogatory. Few, if any, American authors have proven as prolific or as colorful as this Baltimorean who never went to school a day beyond the age of fifteen.

The revised paragraph, with ten sentences, is far more interesting and lively. In addition, readers can easily understand the relationship between ideas. Compare the two paragraphs to identify the writer's revisions. The writer used five techniques to achieve coherence in his revision: pronouns, synonyms, limited repetition of key ideas, transitional words and expressions, and sentence combining.

Pronouns

The constant repetition of nouns in the same sentence or paragraph can become monotonous. However, a writer can easily improve the coherence in a sentence or paragraph by using pronouns, words that replace nouns. Consider this example:

> New York is a marvelous city because New York offers many different types of attractions for tourists.

Now consider this revision of the same sentence.

> New York is a marvelous city because it offers many types of attractions for tourists.

The pronoun *it* has replaced the noun *city* which, in turn, has been identified as New York. The pronoun eliminates the unnecessary repetition of the name of the city.

While this method of achieving coherence is relatively easy, be sure to follow these rules governing pronouns:

1. A pronoun can replace a noun if the noun has been named or identified previously. A pronoun must refer to a specific **antecedent,** the noun the pronoun will replace. If the

antecedent is missing, then the reader will be unable to identify the word the pronoun has replaced. Consider this example:

It was too large.

What word does the pronoun *it* replace? What could the sentence possibly describe? There are literally thousands of nouns that could be the antecedent. If this sentence were placed in the middle of a paragraph, then perhaps the reader could identify the antecedent. However, as an opening sentence in a paragraph, it would be inappropriate unless the writer were attempting to build suspense or had identified the antecedent in the title of the paragraph.

2. The antecedent of the pronoun cannot be ambiguous. Consider the following example:

Hannah told Liza that she should have completed her assignment.

In this sentence, it is unclear whether the pronouns *she* and *her* replace the noun *Hannah* or the noun *Liza*. The sentence could have one of two meanings:

Hannah told Liza, "I should have completed my assignment."

(The pronouns *I* and *my* replace the noun *Hannah*.)

Hannah told Liza, "You should have completed your assignment."

(The pronouns *You* and *your* refer to the noun *Liza*.)

Because the sentence has two possible meanings, the antecedent is unclear or ambiguous. Therefore, make sure that the pronoun has a direct antecedent.

3. Pronouns must agree in gender, number, and case with the nouns they replace. It is usually easy to identify the correct gender and number that the pronoun must follow. For example, the pronoun *he* is obviously inappropriate as a replacement for the noun *Elizabeth*. Also, the pronoun *they* could not be a substitute for the noun *car*. It is more difficult, however, to determine the correct case for the pronoun. Consider this example:

Helen told Sam a secret that must be confidential between she and him.

In this sentence, the pronouns *she* and *him* act as objects of the preposition *between* and should be in the objective case. However, the pronoun *she* is not in the objective case; it is in the nominative case. Therefore, the pronoun *she* is incorrectly used. The sentence should be revised to say *between her and him*.

Pronouns and nouns are used in three cases: the nominative, the objective, and the possessive. First, the **nominative case** is used for subjects (the actors in a sentence) and predicate nominatives (the nouns or pronouns following linking verbs). For instance, in the following sentences, pronouns in the nominative case act as subject in the first set of examples and as predicate nominatives in the second set of examples.

Marsha wrote a paper.
She received an "A" from her teacher.

In the above sentences, Marsha is the antecedent for the pronoun *she*; the pronoun is in the nominative case, since it is the subject of the second sentence.

The speaker is *Tom*.
The speaker is *he*.

In these sentences, the pronoun *he* replaces its antecedent *Tom*. The pronoun is in the nominative case because it is a predicate nominative. The linking verb *is* (present tense of *to be*) makes the noun after the verb equivalent to the subject; therefore, the noun must be in the same case as the subject.

Second, the **objective case** is used for direct and indirect objects and for objects of prepositions. A direct object receives the action of the verb; an indirect object tells to whom or for whom an action is done. For example, in the following sets of sentences, pronouns in the objective case act as direct object in the first example and indirect object in the second example.

> Harris brought the *roses*.
> Harris brought *them*.

In these sentences, the pronoun *them* replaces the antecedent *roses*. The pronoun *them* is the direct object of the verb *brought*; it tells what Harris brought.

> Jerry gave his *mother* a birthday present.
> Jerry gave *her* a birthday present.

In these sentences, the pronoun *her* replaces its antecedent *mother*. The pronoun *her* is the indirect object in the sentence; it tells to whom Jerry gave a present. In addition, the objective case is used for objects of the preposition, nouns that follow prepositions, such as *by, to, from,* or *around.* In the following sentences, a pronoun in the objective case acts as the object of the preposition.

> Jason gave a travel brochure to *Alex*.
> Jason gave a travel brochure to *him*.

In these sentences, the pronoun *him* replaces its antecedent *Alex*. The pronoun *him* is the object of the preposition *to*.

Third, the **possessive case** is used to show ownership. The following chart will help you determine which pronouns are appropriate in each case.

PERSON	Nominative Case		Objective Case		Possessive Case	
	SINGULAR	PLURAL	SINGULAR	PLURAL	SINGULAR	PLURAL
First	I	we	me	us	my, mine	our, ours
Second	you	you	you	you	you, yours	you, yours
Third	he she it	they	him her it	them	his her, hers its	their, theirs

One problem you may face with pronouns is the traditional use of a masculine, singular pronoun to substitute for an indefinite pronoun, such as *each, everyone, someone, somebody,* and *anybody,* or for a noun that does not identify gender, such as *student, driver, employee,* and *lawyer.* Certainly, this usage ignores women in the audience, as the following sentence demonstrates:

> Once the *student* has completed the registration process, *he* should report to *his* academic advisor.

This sentence, which could be found in a college catalog, would be appropriate only at an all-male institution. It is not appropriate in a catalog that addresses both men and women. There are a number of methods you can use to avoid sexist language; each has its own advantages and disadvantages.

1. Use both masculine and feminine pronouns when you refer to both men and women:

> Once the student has completed the registration process, *he or she* should report to *his or her* academic advisor.

This usage, however, can be awkward if you incorporate it in a lengthy passage. In addition, this usage calls attention to itself throughout the passage and may interrupt your readers needlessly.

2. Alternate masculine and feminine pronouns throughout a passage:

> Once the student has completed the registration process, *he* should report to *his* academic advisor. Finally, *she* should return to the bursar's office to pay *her* bill.

This usage, however, can be, at best, confusing to readers.

3. Use only nouns, rather than pronouns, in a passage:

> Once *the student* has completed the registration process, *the student* should report to *the student's* academic advisor.

This method can become repetitive for your reader.

4. Use plural pronouns and plural nouns:

> Once the *students* have completed the registration process, *they* should report to *their* academic *advisors.*

This method allows you to include everyone in your discussion and avoids the problem of being repetitive and confusing for your reader.

5. Finally, choose alternative terms for words that specifically identify men or women:

Rather than:		Choose:	
	mailman		mail carrier
	postman		postal clerk
	chairman		chairperson
	fireman		firefighter
	policeman		police officer

This method is also effective if you have to write a letter to someone you do not know. For example, rather than saying "Dear Sir," you could address the person by title, "Dear Personnel Manager."

EXERCISE 1   Supply the correct pronoun to replace the noun in parentheses.

Example: The car needs a tune-up; _*its*_ (the car's) engine isn't operating properly.

1. Tony ran to catch the bus, but _____ (Tony) was too late.

2. Faith explained to _____ (Faith's) sister that _____ (Faith and the sister) could not go to the movies.

3. Mark Twain earned a great deal of money from his writing; however, because _____ (Twain) made poor investments, _____ (Twain) was forced to give lectures at the end of his career in order to make money.

4. The professor returned the students' papers; _____ (the professor) was pleased that the class had worked diligently on the assignment.

5. Thomas Jefferson is well known as the author of the Declaration of Independence; however, many people do not recognize the extent of _____ (Jefferson's) talents. _____ (Many people) do not know _____ (Jefferson) as an inventor, scientist, architect, and educator.

6. Everyone must complete _____ (everyone's) own work.

7. The house was in terrible condition: _____ (the house) needed a new roof, new floors, and a fresh coat of paint. _____ (The house's) previous owners had not maintained _____ (the house) properly.

8. The dog waited patiently by the entrance of the building for _____ (the dog's) master, but it was over an hour before _____ (the master) returned.

9. The jury made _____ (the jury's) decision about the case after long days of debate among _____ (the jury's) members.

10. The basketball team was ready for the championship game; the players knew what parts _____ (the players) were to play in this effort.

Synonyms

If an author uses the same word constantly, then readers will lose interest. Analyze the effect the repetition of the word *jogging* has in this example:

> Jogging can be beneficial to one's health. Jogging helps to reduce tension and can aid in weight reduction. Jogging also helps strengthen the cardiovascular system. Jogging, moreover, can help develop muscle tone. Therefore, jogging provides excellent benefits.

The repetition of *jogging* as the subject of each sentence is monotonous. Consider some of the synonyms for this word: *light running, this exercise,* and *this sport.* Analyze the effect of these synonyms in the revised paragraph on p. 144:

Jogging can be beneficial to one's health. This sport helps to reduce tension and can aid in weight reduction. The exercise also helps strengthen the cardiovascular system. Moreover, this activity can help develop muscle tone. Therefore, jogging provides excellent rewards.

Notice how the synonyms easily replace the repetitious word *jogging*. In addition, the demonstrative pronoun *this* refers to jogging and increases the coherence of the paragraph. Certainly, the use of synonyms can keep sentences more lively than does the repetition of one word.

Synonyms replace not only single nouns but also long phrases and sentences. Consider this example:

The cast and crew of the play worked throughout the night to prepare for the opening night. Because of their diligence and perseverance, the first night was a success.

In the second sentence, the words *their diligence and perseverance* replace the entire first sentence.

In addition to synonyms, the words *there* and *here* can provide quick replacements for the names of places that have already been identified. Analyze the following example:

In London, the group visited many historical places. There, the members of the group enjoyed the fine theatres and restaurants, too.

The word *There* refers to London and provides coherence without the unnecessary repetition of the city's name.

EXERCISE 2   Provide synonyms for the italicized words in each sentence below.

Example: After long hours of waiting, we finally entered the *National Gallery of Art*. *Here*, we would view the exhibit of Ansel Adams's photographs and the exhibit on the treasure houses of Britain.

1. Although we tend to group all of the *painters* in the French Impressionist school together, these _____ had quite different styles.

2. Each *teacher* had an individual approach to education, but each _____ was successful at conveying knowledge to her students.

3. The *ground hog* is supposed to forecast the last six weeks of winter. If _____ sees his shadow, then we can expect another six weeks of cold weather. If _____ does not, then spring will arrive soon.

4. My *car* seems to have a personality of its own. _____ will not start if the temperature drops below 30 degrees, and its engine produces various groans if it is called upon to climb steep hills.

5. The ski patrol planned to meet at *Bear Mountain* for its annual convention. _____, the members would review first-aid procedures, discuss safety measures for skiers, and practice emergency drills.

6. The *interstate highway system* connects many states; because of _____, we can travel from coast to coast in only several days.

7. The young soldier *could not clean his rifle properly, complete the obstacle course, or stay in line for marches;* because of his _____, he was transferred to permanent kitchen duty.

8. Hank *studied for five days for his chemistry examination.* His _____ was rewarded; he earned an "A" on the examination.

9. Lee and Grant met at *Appomattox Court House.* _____, the Civil War ended.

10. The first settlers in the New World were *extremely brave* to face an entire continent alone. Their _____ helped to create a new country.

Limited Repetition

For short pieces of three or four sentences, repetition of key terms or phrases is inappropriate. Because the piece is so brief, the repetition would add monotony, not coherence. However, for longer paragraphs, repetition, used wisely, can very effectively reinforce main concepts. Several methods of repetition can be used: repeating major words or phrases, repeating specific structures, and repeating metaphors. (Because repetition of metaphors requires space, this last method is more effective in essays than in paragraphs.)

Repetition of key words or phrases is most effective when the writer has a specific purpose in mind. For example, in a paragraph on the rights and privileges of Americans, the repetition of the word *freedom* could reinforce the concept that these rights and privileges are a result of the guaranteed freedom Americans enjoy.

Finally, repetition of specific structures not only reinforces primary ides, but also provides transitions in a paragraph. For example, in the revised sample paragraph on the literary roles H. L. Mencken played, the prepositional phrases beginning with the word *as—as a critic* and *as a writer*—name the different roles Mencken played; moreover, these phrases, placed at the beginning of the sentences, provide transitions for the reader.

EXERCISE 3   Underline the key words or phrases and specific structures that are repeated in the paragraphs below.

1.   To those old allies whose cultural and spiritual origins we share, we pledge the loyalty of faithful friends. United, there is little we cannot do in a host of new cooperative ventures. Divided, there is little we can do—for we dare not meet a powerful challenge at odds and split asunder.

To those new states whom we welcome to the ranks of the free, we pledge our word that one form of colonial control shall not have passed away merely to be replaced by a far more iron tyranny. We shall not always expect to find them supporting our view. But we shall always hope to find them strongly supporting their own freedom—and to remember that, in the past, those who foolishly sought power by riding the back of the tiger ended up inside.

To those peoples in the huts and villages of half the globe struggling to break the bonds of mass misery, we pledge our best efforts to help them help themselves, for whatever period is required—not because the Communists may be doing it, not because we seek their votes, but because it is right. If a free society cannot help the many who are poor, it cannot save the few who are rich.

(John F. Kennedy, *Inaugural Address*)

2.   "Call this a govment! why, just look at it and see what it's like. Here's the law a-standing ready to take a man's son away from him—a man's own son, which he has had all the trouble and all the anxiety and all the expense of raising. Yes, just as that man has got that son raised at last, and ready to go to work, and begin to do suthin' for *him* and give him a rest, the law up and goes for him. And they call *that* govment! That ain't all nuther. The law backs that old Judge Thatcher up and helps him to keep me out o' my property. Here's what the law does. The law takes a man worth six thousand dollars and upards, and jams him into an old trap of a cabin like this, and lets him go around in clothes that ain't fitted for a hog. They call that govment! A man can't get his rights in a govment like this. Sometimes I've a mighty notion to just leave the country for good and all. Yes, and I *told* 'em so; I told old Thatcher so to his face. Lots of 'em heard me, and can tell what I said. Says I, for two cents I'd leave the blamed country and never come anear it agin. Them's the very words. I says, look at my hat—if you call it a hat—but the lid raises up and the rest of it goes down till it's below my chin, and then it ain't rightly a hat at all, but more likely my head was shoved up through a jint o' stove-pipe. Look at it, says I—such a hat for me to wear—one of the wealthiest men in this town if I could git my rights."

(from Mark Twain, *The Adventures of Huckleberry Finn*)

3.   Four score and seven years ago, our fathers brought forth on this continent, a new nation, conceived in Liberty, and dedicated to the proposition that all men are created equal.

Now we are engaged in a great civil war; testing whether that nation, or any nation so conceived and so dedicated, can long endure. We are met on a great battlefield of that war. We have come to dedicate a portion of that field as a final resting-place for those who here gave their lives that that nation might live. It is altogether fitting and proper that we should do this.

But, in a larger sense, we cannot dedicate—we cannot consecrate—we cannot hallow—this ground. The brave men, living and dead, who struggled here have consecrated it, far above our poor power to add or detract. The world will little note, nor long remember, what we say here, but it can never forget what they did here. It is for us the living, rather, to be dedicated here to the unfinished work which they who fought here have thus far so nobly advanced. It is rather for us to be here dedicated to the great task remaining before us—that from these honored dead we take increased devotion to that cause for which they gave the last full measure of devotion; that we here highly resolve that these dead shall not have died in vain; that this nation, under God, shall have a new birth of freedom; and that government of the people, by the people, for the people, shall not perish from the earth.

(Abraham Lincoln, *The Gettysburg Address*)

Sentence Combining

Beginning writers sometimes believe that a sentence can contain only one piece of information. They produce sentences like the following ones:

> Inez is an exceptional child. She has many talents. She can dance and sing. She loves to tell jokes.

Notice how each sentence adds one more piece of information. This method results in a number of simple sentences that lack coherence. The following revisions use sentence combining to provide coherence:

> With her many talents—singing, dancing, and telling jokes—Inez is an exceptional child.

> Inez is an exceptional child because she has many talents, such as singing, dancing, and telling jokes.

Both revisions are far more effective than the initial sentences because they are coherent and because they indicate the relationships of ideas to each other.

There are six easy ways to combine sentences: joining adjectives and other modifiers, appositives, relative-pronoun clauses, participles, coordination, and subordination.

I. Adjectives and other modifiers can be joined in one of two ways.

  A. Create a list of adjectives joined by commas.

      Example: Harriet is kind. She is also considerate and amenable.

    Combination: Harriet is kind, considerate, and amenable.

  B. Place two adjectives after a noun to modify it, and enclose the adjectives within commas.

      Example: The teenager approached the microphone. He was lanky and nervous.

    Combination: The teenager, lanky and nervous, approached the microphone.

II. Appositives—nouns or noun phrases—rename or define another noun.

    Example: She is a corporate lawyer for an international firm. Ms. Thomas is also a scuba diver.

  Combination: Ms. Thomas, a corporate lawyer for an international firm, is also a scuba diver. (In this sentence, the noun phrase, *a corporate lawyer for an international firm,* is an appositive that states Ms. Thomas's occupation.)

                     Ms. Thomas, a scuba diver, is a corporate lawyer for an international firm. (In this sentence, the noun phrase, *a scuba diver,* is an appositive that describes Ms. Thomas's hobby.)

III. A relative-pronoun clause can act in the same manner as an appositive. It gives additional information about a noun by renaming it, defining it, or describing it. Beginning with *who, which, that, whose,* or *whom,* a relative-pronoun clause is a dependent clause—a group of words with a subject and a verb that cannot stand alone.

    Example: Because of the decline in oil prices, the local refinery has closed. The refinery employed five thousand workers.

  Combination: Because of the decline in oil prices, the local refinery, which employed five thousand workers, has closed. (The relative-pronoun clause, *which employed five thousand workers,* describes the noun *refinery.*)

IV. Present and past participles act as adjectives to modify a noun. Because they are formed from verbs, they carry the actions and visual images of verbs. (A present participle is formed by adding *ing* to the base form of the verb. A past participle is usually formed by adding *ed* to the base form of the verb.)

> **Example:** Tim was walking down a dark street. A man approached him. The man was wearing a mask.
>
> **Combination:** While walking down a dark street, Tim was approached by a masked man. (This sentence contains a participial phrase, *While walking down the street*, which modifies the noun *Tim*, and a participle, *masked*, which modifies the noun *man*.)

V. Coordination forms compound sentences, which contain two or more independent clauses. (An independent clause has a subject and a verb and can stand by itself as a complete sentence.) Compound sentences are formed in one of three ways.

A. Add a comma and a coordinate conjunction. There are seven coordinate conjunctions: *for, and, nor, but, or, yet,* and *so.*

Here are the relationships the seven coordinate conjunctions express:

For shows cause.

And shows addition.

Nor shows a negative choice.

But shows contrast or contradiction.

Or shows a choice.

Yet shows contrast.

So shows effect.

B. Add a semicolon (;). The use of the semicolon implies that the relationship between the sentences is clear. For example, the second sentence may define or give an illustration of the first sentence.

C. Add a semicolon and an adverbial conjunction, followed by a comma. There are four main adverbial conjunctions: *however, moreover, nevertheless,* and *therefore.* Here are the relationships the four adverbial conjunctions express.

However shows contrast or contradiction.

Moreover shows addition.

Nevertheless shows contrast.

Therefore shows result.

> **Example:** Her long hours in the gym were rewarded. She won the gold medal in gymnastics.
>
> **Compound-Sentence Combinations:** Her long hours in the gym were rewarded, for she won the gold medal in gymnastics. (The coordinate conjunction *for* indicates that winning the gold medal was the cause of the reward for the long hours in the gym.)
>
> Her long hours in the gym were rewarded; she won the gold medal in gymnastics. (The semicolon indicates that the two sentences are equal. The second sentence describes the reward of the long hours of practice.)
>
> She won the gold medal in gymnastics; therefore, her long hours in the gym were rewarded. (The adverbial conjunction *therefore* shows that her long hours in the gym were rewarded as a consequence of winning the gold medal.)

VI. Subordination forms complex sentences, which contain one independent clause and one or more dependent clauses. The dependent clause adds information and is subordinate to the independent clause because the independent clause contains the most important information in the sentence.

Example: The holiday recess was completed. The members of Congress returned to work on Capitol Hill.

Combination: After the holiday recess was completed, the members of Congress returned to work on Capitol Hill. (In this sentence, the dependent clause, *After the holiday recess was completed,* is not as important as the independent clause, *the members of Congress returned to work on Capitol Hill.* However, the dependent clause does tell when the members returned, so it adds more information to the sentence.)

Dependent clauses are usually preceded by subordinate conjunctions. Here is a partial list of subordinate conjunctions:

after	*than*
although	*unless*
as	*until*
because	*when*
before	*wherever*
if	*while*

EXERCISE 4 Combine each set of sentences below to form one sentence, and write it on the blank. Use whatever sentence-combining method seems to be most efficient. Identify the methods you use.

1. The hunter raised his gun.
   The hunter was dressed in bright orange clothing.
   The deer trotted into sight.

   _____

   _____

   Sentence-combining method _____

2. One industrious friend made popcorn.
   The rest of us sat and talked in front of a fire.
   The fire was crackling and popping.

   _____

   _____

   Sentence-combining method _____

3. At the edge of the swamp, the geese rested quietly.
   They broke into flight.
   A car approached.

   _____

   _____

   Sentence-combining method _____

4. Many nations in Africa face the effects of prolonged droughts.
   Industrial countries are offering aid to these victims of famine.
   Two industrial countries are the United States and England.

   _____

   _____

   Sentence-combining method _____

5. Travel to European countries offers Americans a chance to see other countries.
   Americans are able to experience different cultures.

   _____

   _____

   Sentence-combining method _____

6. The judge prepared to announce her decision.
   The defendant squirmed in his chair.
   He knew that the judge had found him guilty.

   _____

   _____

   Sentence-combining method _____

7. Many banks failed during the Great Depression.
   Franklin D. Roosevelt instituted the Federal Deposit Insurance Corporation.

   _____

   _____

   Sentence-combining method _____

8. San Francisco is a vibrant, exciting city.
   It has the Golden Gate Bridge and a magical Chinatown.

   _____

   _____

   Sentence-combining method _____

9. Women have made gains over the past few decades.
   The gains are in employment and economic opportunities.
   These changes are being appreciated by a new generation of women.

   _____

   _____

Sentence-combining method _____

10. *The Glass Menagerie* portrays the conflicts within a fragile family.
    The play is by Tennessee Williams.
    The play has long been a favorite of American theatergoers.

    _____

    _____

Sentence-combining method _____

11. The Sunbelt area is growing.
    It is the fastest growing area in the United States.
    The Sunbelt states offer mild climates and industrial expansion.
    The states offer a lower cost of living than the Northeast or the Midwest.

    _____

    _____

Sentence-combining method _____

12. Paul Newman's acting career has spanned three decades.
    He has directed films.
    He has started a food company.
    He has created a camp for children.

    _____

    _____

Sentence-combining method _____

13. On Halloween night, many of our friends enjoy old movies.
    The movies star Vincent Price.
    They read stories by Edgar Allan Poe.

    _____

    _____

Sentence-combining method _____

14. Many urban areas are experiencing a new type of homesteader.
    The middle and upper classes are returning to the hearts of cities.
    They are purchasing old homes.
    They carefully restore the homes.

    _____

    _____

Sentence-combining method _____

15. The great beauty of the American Southwest inspired Georgia O'Keeffe.
    Georgia O'Keeffe is a painter.
    She produced many impressionistic paintings of the desert's landscape.

    _____

    _____

    Sentence-combining method _____

16. Americans are concerned about fitness.
    Health clubs are enjoying a robust sales year.
    Businesses are enjoying a robust sales year.
    The businesses sell athletic equipment.

    _____

    _____

    Sentence-combining method _____

17. The rock band prepared to play its first song.
    The crowd roared its appreciation.

    _____

    _____

    Sentence-combining method _____

18. The Orient Express was one of the most famous trains in the world.
    The Orient Express epitomized luxury and comfort.

    _____

    _____

    Sentence-combining method _____

19. On the shores of Walden Pond, Henry David Thoreau built a small cabin.
    The cabin became the setting of one of the most famous books.
    The books were in American literature.
    The book was called *Walden*.

    _____

    _____

    Sentence-combining method _____

20. Many teenagers die each year in automobile accidents.
    The accidents involve drunk drivers.
    Most states have raised their legal drinking age to 21.

_____

_____

Sentence-combining method _____

Transitional Words and Expressions

Transitional words and expressions indicate specifically to the reader the types of relationships between sentences or ideas. These words or expressions mark the passage for readers so that they can easily understand how the writer links ideas. Analyze the relationship indicated by the transitional word *because*:

> Because the weather forecaster predicted torrential rains, we cancelled our beach trip.

In this sentence, the word *because* indicates a reason or cause. In this case, the reason that "we cancelled our beach trip" was the weather forecaster's prediction of rain. If the sentence did not contain the word *because*, then the reader would be forced to infer that the prediction of rain caused the change in plans. Hence, writers include transitions not only for their readers' benefit but also for clarity. Without transitions, readers can only guess, perhaps incorrectly, about the relationships between ideas.

Study the chart below; it indicates the types of relationships that each word or expression stresses. Notice that sometimes a transition can indicate two or three different types of relationships. To decide which transition to use, examine the stated ideas and the relationship that they suggest. While this chart gives you several options for transitional words, it does not include all transitions. As you discover others, add them to the list.

Relationship	*Transitional Words and Expressions*	
Addition	again	in addition
	also	likewise
	and	moreover
	as well as	next
	further	similarly
	furthermore	too
Cause	because	for this reason
	for	since
Chronology	after	in the meantime
	always	meanwhile
	at last	next
	before	soon
	briefly	suddenly
	currently	then
	finally	until
	first (second, etc.)	when
	frequently	
Comparison	all	both
	and	like
	as	similarly

Relationship	Transitional Words and Expressions	
Conclusion	finally	therefore
	hence	thus
	so	to conclude
Contrast	although	nevertheless
	but	on the contrary
	conversely	on the other hand
	despite	though
	difference	unlike
	even so	yet
	however	
Effect	as a result	so
	consequently	then
	for that reason	therefore
	hence	thus
	resulting	
Emphasis	above all	indeed
	especially	in fact
Example	for example	specifically
	for instance	such as
	in other words	to illustrate
Importance	finally	least
	first	next
	last	primarily
List	finally	moreover
	first	next
	furthermore	second
	last	third
Repetition	again	in summary
	as stated before	to reiterate
	i.e. (that is)	to repeat
Space	above	forward
	adjacent to	here
	alongside	in front of
	among	next to
	around	on top of
	below	over
	beside	there
	between	under
	beyond	where
	down	
Summary	finally	on the whole
	in brief	overall
	in short	

EXERCISE 5 In the following sentences, underline the transitional words and expressions. Identify the type of relationship they stress, and write it in the blank.

1. The crowd gasped in delight as the Thunderclouds performed their aerial maneuvers. _____

2. Because the weatherman had predicted snow showers, each child arrived at school in leggings and boots. _____

3. After limiting your topic, you should develop a thesis sentence. _____

4. The construction industry began to expand when interest rates declined to the single-digit level for the first time in seven years. _____

5. Furthermore, real estate agents experienced a sharp rise in their incomes.

   _____

6. The sales figures for this year remained flat despite a ten percent increase in catalog sales. _____

7. Overall, the company's performance this year was disappointing. _____

8. The support staff will be cut by one quarter as a direct consequence of the poor sales figures. _____

9. There will be a freeze on hiring until our profit margins are in the black.

   _____

10. To repeat, sales must improve, or the company will soon face bankruptcy.

    _____

EXERCISE 6 Provide transitional words or phrases that indicate the relationship in parentheses.

Example: Jane went to the dance, *but* Hank decided to see a movie.
                                    (contrast)

1. _____ his car was extremely old and in poor condition, Gerald
        (cause)
   decided to purchase a new one.

2. Making a cake requires several steps. _____, you must purchase
                                               (chronology)
   the ingredients the recipe requires. _____, you must combine the
                                            (chronology)
   ingredients in the correct order. _____, bake the cake at the cor-
                                         (chronology)

rect temperature for the required time. _____, let the cake cool,
(chronology)
and then frost it.

3. We had planned the perfect summer vacation at the beach; _____,
(contrast)
the weather was unseasonably cool and wet.

4. We have explored and used almost every inch of our country; _____,
(effect)
there are few true wilderness areas left.

5. _____ acid rain can occur several hundred miles from the source
(cause)
of pollution, we must legislate stricter pollution laws.

6. _____ the hockey team won every game in its regular season, it
(contrast)
was unable to win the championship game.

7. A vegetable garden provides fresh vegetables for the family; _____,
(addition)
it provides a productive hobby for the gardener.

8. Many occupations are dangerous; _____, police officers risk their
(example)
lives every day.

9. _____ the Industrial Revolution began in England in the 1830s, it
(contrast)
did not begin in America until after the Civil War.

10. The circus makes adults feel like children again; _____, there are
(result)
frequently more adults than children in the audience.

In a paragraph, you may use any number of transitions as you develop the topic sentence. Some transitions, though, are particularly suited to the types of support you might include. For example, when you are developing a series of steps that will direct the reader in performing an action, then transitions indicating chronology, importance, and enumeration (listing) would be appropriate for primary support sentences. In the same fashion, if you construct a paragraph that moves from the least important idea to the most important one, then transitions indicating importance would identify the primary supports. In addition, transitions that suggest examples would often identify secondary support sentences since these secondary supports usually illustrate, describe, or explain the primary supports.

Paragraphs, too, often have a dominant pattern of development that can be identified by the transitions a writer employs. For example, if a paragraph's topic sentence promises the reader a discussion of the effects of inflation, then transitions that indicate cause and result will appear frequently. Although the paragraph will not contain only one type of transition (for example, cause and result), one pattern will dominate. Therefore, be alert to an overall pattern of development in paragraphs.

EXERCISE 7   Underline the transitions used in each of the following paragraphs, and identify the relationships they stress. In the paragraph, also identify the supports that the transitions introduce. Finally, identify the dominant pattern of organization for the entire paragraph, in the blank to the right.

1. As a hobby, gardening is not the tranquil, bucolic exercise that promoters claim. Instead there are many problems and frustrations associated with "getting to know nature." First, Mother Nature does not smile and shed her warmth on the gardener during November and March, the prime months for planting bulbs and readying the soil. Spending hours on your knees digging in hard, cold soil is guaranteed to cause more arthritis than any tennis game ever could. Second, raking and hoeing the garden to prepare the soil are not the back-strengthening exercises recommended by the orthopedist. In fact, they are not recommended by anyone, other than your worst enemy. Then, once the soil is prepared and everything is planted, the real problems arrive: drought, flood, heat, and insects. There is nothing more frustrating than watching hours of back-breaking effort float away on a storm-produced stream or shrivel under record-breaking sunshine. In short, for tranquility, you should try a nice, quiet game of poker; at least then you can gamble away the proceeds of many hours of work in just two hours.

Dominant Pattern _____

2. Then the man drowsed off into what seemed to him the most comfortable and satisfying sleep he had ever known. The dog sat facing him and waiting. The brief day drew to a close in a long, slow twilight. There were no signs of a fire to be made, and, besides, never in the dog's experience had it known a man to sit like that in the snow and make no fire. As the twilight drew on, its eager yearning for the fire mastered it, and with a great lifting and shifting of forefeet, it whined softly, flattened its ears down in anticipation of being chidden by the man. But the man remained silent. Later, the dog whined loudly. And still later it crept close to the man and caught the scent of death. This made the animal bristle and back away. A little longer it delayed, howling under the stars that leaped and danced and shone brightly in the cold sky. Then it turned and trotted up the trail in the direction of the camp it knew, where were the other food-providers and fire-providers.

(from Jack London, "To Build a Fire")

Dominant Pattern _____

3. While the method of direct payments makes certain that those suffering most from the anguish of unemployment will receive direct aid, its total effect may be less than public spending in the form of public works. If the individual is given a direct payment, the bulk of the payment is spent for consumption. This increases the level of economic activity to some degree, provided the funds received do not come at the expense of consumption and investment elsewhere in the economy. Even if the individual is employed on a simple project such as leaf raking for the sake of respectability, the total effect is not much greater. The capital needed to put a group of individuals on such a job is limited to rakes, shovels, wheelbarrows, and perhaps a few trucks. Furthermore, the spending of a direct income

payment primarily for consumer goods may have no greater effect than decreasing excess inventories of consumer goods.

(from Thomas J. Hailstones, *Basic Economics*)

Dominant Pattern _____

4.   One of the many devastating effects of inflation on the middle class is the precipitous rise in tuition costs. As a direct consequence of annual tuition increases of fifteen to twenty percent, more and more students must combine schooling and working in order to be able to afford their education. Without the job, they cannot pay for school, yet, with the job, they have neither the time nor the energy required by school. After students have attended classes for five hours and worked for another five hours, homework commands little, if any, interest or effort. When homework done in a slipshod manner becomes the norm, grades suffer. Then, teachers must face students who do not know the material because they have not studied it. The final result is that the teacher becomes a remediator, a reviewer of basic skills, instead of an instructor in new materials. Therefore, despite the widespread belief in the value of working, there are instances when it is more advantageous for a student *not* to work.

Dominant Pattern _____

5.   More people should donate blood; giving blood is truly giving life. Unfortunately, too many adults have retained their childhood fear of needles, and so they refuse to face the blood technicians. Or, people don't understand the donating procedures, and this fear of the unknown prevents them from helping other human beings. Perhaps if the prospective donors knew all the uses to which their pint of blood is put and all the people who are helped by it, then they would be more willing to give fully of themselves. The whole blood is used, of course, but so are blood products. The pint can be separated into its components, and each part given to an ill person. Platelets help those whose bodies cannot resist infection; the red cells help those whose respiratory systems do not function properly. In addition, the white cells are used to help leukemia patients, and the blood serum provides needed fluids. When adults realize the multiple recipients of their gift, each one will be eager to donate at least four times a year.

Dominant Pattern _____

EXERCISE 8   Provide coherence in the following paragraphs by using the five methods discussed in this chapter: pronouns, transitional words and expressions, synonyms, limited repetition, and sentence combining. Identify the methods you use.

1.   The ideal office for a high school yearbook staff would be spacious and well equipped; however, the office of Hammon High School's yearbook, *The Village,* is not ideal. The space resembles a broom closet. It used to be one. During the winter months, the office reaches near-Arctic temperatures. It lacks any form of heating. The only thing that permits the habitation of the office in the winter is the

size. Its close proximity forces staff members to work together in a small area. The office contains three wooden desks. They are dilapidated. They leave very little room for movement. Because it is a closet, the space naturally lacks a storage closet. All pertinent papers and materials are crammed into two filing cabinets. The office lacks any sophisticated equipment. Two typewriters collect dust on the hard, cold floor of the office. The typewriters are broken. Editors must use outmoded computers in Wheeler Hall. They use the aging facilities of the Art Department's darkroom. These working conditions are not ideal.

2. In the eighteen years I lived with my parents, I had never done the laundry; washing my clothes for the first time was a new experience. The first time I performed the chore I emptied the entire contents of the hamper into the washer. I poured the detergent on top. I started the machine. I left to run a few errands. I returned twenty minutes later to check on the machine's progress. Soap suds were pouring out the top and down the sides of the machine. I ignored the mess. I let the machine complete the wash cycle. The wash cycle was complete. I transferred the laundry into the dryer. I set the timer on the machine. I pushed the start button. When the dryer was finished, I removed the wash. To my surprise, what had been white was hot pink. This was a costly error. It made me realize that the laundry should be separated before washing. Whites go with whites into hot water. Colors are washed in cool water. Fortunately, I have improved my technique. Since that first experience, I have not destroyed any more clothing.

3. Travelers can take an airplane or an ocean liner to a seaside destination; there are differences between the two in the way the travelers' time is spent. If travelers take the airplane, then they must arrive at the airport on time. They must check their baggage and board the plane. They have no time for extra sightseeing. Their main objective is to reach their destination quickly. They can relax later. While they are on the plane, they may be treated to a movie and a dinner. Those are the only luxuries. Travelers on an ocean liner spend their time differently. Once they are on board, there are many diversions for them. An ocean trip takes a long time. The ship is designed to cater to its passengers. There is a swimming pool. There are many activities the travelers can select. They can see movies, read at their leisure, enjoy nightclubs, and attend dances. They must relax. The ocean trip becomes a vacation in itself. The travelers arrive at an island refreshed. They can see the sights for a few days and return to their ship for the voyage home. Both ways of travel take vacationers to a specific location. They differ in the way the vacation is spent.

EXERCISE 9   In a paragraph of your own, provide coherence within sentences and the entire paragraph by using the five methods discussed in this chapter. After you have revised the paragraph, elicit responses and suggestions from a group of writers. Are your revisions effective? Do they add coherence to the paragraph? Are the relationships of ideas clearly identified for your audience?

Writing Strategies: COMPARISON/CONTRAST *and* CAUSE/EFFECT

Comparison/Contrast

You compare and contrast items each day when you shop for clothing, food, appliances, or cars. When you decided to attend college, you had already compared the advantages of a college education to the advantages of immediate full-time employment. In addition, you compared the costs, academic reputations, admissions standards, locations, and campus activities of different colleges. As you compared these items, you began to classify colleges by their contrasts, their differences. You might have even created a chart to aid you in identifying the particular characteristics of several colleges. Throughout this entire process, you analyzed a great number of items by comparing and contrasting.

As an organizational strategy, comparison-contrast paragraphs require a complete analysis of the two items by the writer. Since most readers will anticipate the obvious comparisons and contrasts between the items, you must move to more subtle differences, ones that are not quickly apparent to readers, to demonstrate the similarities and differences. For example, if you were to compare and contrast two restaurants, one fast-food and the other French, some differences are quite obvious: the French restaurant will cost more; the dinner will take longer at the French restaurant; you will have more options about food at the French restaurant; and you will be required to dress more formally there and to use your best table manners. Therefore, if you stress these differences in a paragraph, then you may lose the reader who is familiar with both types of restaurants. In this case, you should reconsider your original topic; you might instead compare two fast-food restaurants or compare two French restaurants. By doing this, you will indeed be able to offer your readers an analysis of the more subtle differences between the two establishments.

To organize your analysis effectively, present all of the information about one item first; then present information about the second item in the same sequence as you presented points in the first. Examine the subject-by-subject comparison of two restaurants below.

  I. Topic Sentence: Unlikely as it may seem, differences do exist between Joe's Burgers and the County Drive-In.

 II. Joe's Burgers

    A. Interior decorations

    B. Types of burgers

    C. Service

    D. Costs

III. County Drive-In

    A. Interior decorations

    B. Types of burgers

C. Service

D. Costs

IV. Conclusion

By using the subject-by-subject structure, you give the reader a complete analysis of one restaurant before you begin the second analysis. Readers will be able to distinguish the differences easily since they have already been given a description of one place.

Parentage and Parenthood

Ashley Montagu

It is apparently very necessary to distinguish between parenthood and parentage. Parenthood is an art; parentage is the consequence of a mere biological act. The biological ability to produce conception and to give birth to a child has nothing whatever to do with the ability to care for that child as it requires to be cared for. That ability, like every other, must be learned. It is highly desirable that parentage be not undertaken until the art of parenthood has been learned. Is this a counsel of perfection? As things stand now, perhaps it is, but it need not always be so. Parentage is often irresponsible. Parenthood is responsible. Parentage at best is irresponsibly responsible for the *birth* of a child. Parenthood is responsible for the development of a human being—not simply a child, but a human being. I do not think it is an overstatement to say that parenthood is the most important occupation in the world.

QUESTIONS

1. Why does Montagu begin this paragraph with the statement, "It is apparently very necessary to distinguish between parenthood and parentage"? What preconceptions might people hold about parenthood and parentage?

2. What are the primary distinctions between parentage and parenthood?

3. Which does Montagu believe is more important?

4. Explain Montagu's statement, "Parentage at best is irresponsibly responsible for the *birth* of a child."

Oranges:
Florida and California

John McPhee

An orange grown in Florida usually has a thin and tightly fitting skin, and it is also heavy with juice. Californians say that if you want to eat a Florida orange you have to get into a bathtub first. California oranges are light in weight and have thick skins that break easily and come off in hunks. The flesh inside is marvelously sweet, and the segments almost separate themselves. In Florida, it is said that you can run over a California orange with a ten-ton truck and not even wet the pavement. The differences from which these hyperboles arise will prevail in the two states even if the type of orange is the same. In arid climates, like California's, oranges develop a thick albedo, which is the white part of the skin. Florida is one of the two or three most rained-upon states in the United States. California uses the

Colorado River and similarly impressive sources to irrigate its oranges, but of course irrigation can only do so much. The annual difference in rainfall between the Florida and California orange-growing areas is one million one hundred and forty thousand gallons per acre. For years, California was the leading orange state, but Florida surpassed California in 1942, and grows three times as many oranges now. California oranges, for their part, can safely be called three times as beautiful.

QUESTIONS

1. Enumerate the differences between the two oranges.

2. To what cause does McPhee attribute the differences between the oranges?

3. Why are California oranges "three times as beautiful" as Florida oranges?

Two Attitudes Toward Success

Norman Podhoretz

My second purpose in telling the story of my own career is to provide a concrete setting for a diagnosis of the curiously contradictory feelings our culture instills in us toward the ambition for success, and toward each of its various goals: money, power, fame, and social position. On the one hand, we are commanded to become successful—that is, to acquire more of these worldly goods than we began with, and to do so by our own exertions; on the other hand, it is impressed upon us by means both direct and devious that if we obey the commandment, we shall find ourselves falling victim to the radical corruption of spirit which, given the nature of what is nowadays called the "system," the pursuit of success requires and which its attainment always bespeaks. On the one hand, "the exclusive worship of the bitch-goddess SUCCESS," as William James put it in a famous remark, "is our national disease"; on the other hand, a contempt for success is the consensus of the national literature for the past hundred years and more. On the one hand, our culture teaches us to shape our lives in accordance with the hunger for worldly things; on the other hand, it spitefully contrives to make us ashamed of the presence of those hungers in ourselves and to deprive us as far as possible of any pleasure in their satisfaction.

QUESTIONS

1. List the three major contrasts Podhoretz discusses in attitudes toward success.

2. What is the topic sentence of the paragraph? Where is it?

3. What do these contradictory feelings about the ambition for success tell us about our culture?

PARAGRAPH ASSIGNMENTS

1. Montagu presents the distinctions between parentage and parenthood. For an audience of expectant parents, compare and contrast two methods of raising children. Develop the distinctions between the two methods; as part of your purpose, defend one method as the better one.

2. McPhee compares two items that most of us would believe are too similar to be compared: Florida and California oranges. In a similar method, choose two items that are closely related and analyze their differences. Finally, compose a paragraph that will describe those differences. Identify both an audience and purpose for your paragraph.

3. Do Americans hunger for success? In what forms do we measure success? Compare and contrast two types of success valued by contemporary American society. (You may want to examine current magazine and television advertisements to determine how advertisers represent success.) Identify an audience who could benefit from your discussion and a purpose.

4. Contrast the differences between being a spectator at an event and being a spectator who watches the event on television. You might consider, for example, the different ways one sees a sporting event or a political rally or debate. Identify an audience and purpose for your paragraph.

Cause/Effect

We can use causal analysis each day when we ask "Why?" in response to a statement; in addition, we ask "What are the results?" of a particular event or situation. By asking these questions, we try to arrive at the causes of an event and the possible outcome of the event. For example, if your car fails to operate properly, your first question would be "What caused the malfunction?" (Even if you do not understand the technical language your mechanic uses, you will want an answer to this question before you pay the bill.) You also will want to know the consequences of the malfunction. Can the car be repaired? If so, can it be repaired quickly? What will you do for transportation while the car is being repaired? How will you pay for the repairs? Will this unexpected bill require an alteration in your budget? As you think the problem through you will analyze its causes and effects.

When first analyzing the causes and effects of a situation or event, brainstorm for ideas. In this manner, you may be able to trace a series of causes and a series of effects. In addition, you will analyze the situation more carefully and not rely upon first impressions about causes and effects. Consider, for example, the causes of inflation. If you state that inflation occurs because prices rise quickly as the value of the dollar drops, then you reduce a complex chain of events to a simple and incomplete analysis. In the same fashion, if you say that the effects of inflation are higher prices for everyone and increased unemployment, then you ignore many of the other effects of inflation. Therefore, make sure your analysis is as complete as possible.

Your purpose for writing determines the structure of a cause/effect paragraph. If you address only the causes or only the effects, then the paragraph will be more effective because you will have the necessary space to describe and explain thoroughly the causes or effects. You can choose to order your ideas in one of two ways: chronological order or order of importance. Your purpose in writing the paragraph will help you decide which one is more effective.

Why I Write

Anaïs Nin

Why one writes is a question I can answer easily, having so often asked it of myself. I believe one writes because one has to create a world in which one can live. I could not live in any of the worlds offered to me—the world of my parents, the world of war, the world of politics. I had to create a world of my own, like a climate, a country, an atmosphere in which I could breathe, reign, and recreate myself when destroyed by living. That, I believe, is the reason for every work of art.

1. Who is Nin's intended audience?

2. Why does Nin explain her reason for writing? What is her purpose?

3. What prompted her to put her ideas on paper?

4. Although Nin explains her personal motivations, she also comments on her "world." Explain how she does this.

The Arrest of Rosa Parks

Martin Luther King, Jr.

During 1955 and 1956, Martin Luther King, Jr. helped to organize the black community of Montgomery, Alabama, in a boycott against the city's segregated buses. The event described below was the catalyst for the boycott, one of many in the 1950s and 1960s. Through King's leadership, these peaceful, nonviolent protests changed the course of America's political, social, economic, and cultural life.

On December 1, 1955, an attractive Negro seamstress, Mrs. Rosa Parks, boarded the Cleveland Avenue Bus in downtown Montgomery. She was returning home after her regular day's work in the Montgomery Fair—a leading department store. Tired from long hours on her feet, Mrs. Parks sat down in the first seat behind the section reserved for whites. Not long after she took her seat, the bus operator ordered her, along with three other Negro passengers, to move back in order to accommodate boarding white passengers. By this time every seat in the bus was taken. This meant that if Mrs. Parks followed the driver's command she would have to stand while a white male passenger, who had just boarded the bus, would sit. The other three Negro passengers immediately complied with the driver's request. But Mrs. Parks quietly refused. The result was her arrest.

QUESTIONS 1. What does the fact that Rosa Parks was a seamstress tell you about those who defend their civil rights?

2. Why did Rosa Parks refuse to move to the back of the bus?

3. Was Mrs. Parks's action an heroic one?

4. What is the tone of this passage?

Credo

H. L. Mencken

I believe that "Huckleberry Finn" is one of the great masterpieces of the world, that it is the full equal of "Don Quixote" and "Robinson Crusoe," that it is vastly better than "Gil Blas," "Tristram Shandy," "Nicholas Nickleby" or "Tom Jones." I believe that it will be read by human beings of all ages, not as a solemn duty but for the honest love of it, and over and over again, long after every book written in America between the years 1800 and 1860, with perhaps three exceptions, has disappeared entirely save as a classroom fossil. I believe that Mark

Twain had a clearer vision of life, that he came nearer to its elementals and was less deceived by its false appearances, than any other American who has ever presumed to manufacture generalizations. I believe that, admitting all his defects, he wrote better English, in the sense of cleaner, straighter, vivider, saner English, than either Irving or Hawthorne. I believe that four of his books—"Huck," "Life on the Mississippi," "Captain Stormfield's Visit to Heaven," and "A Connecticut Yankee"—are alone worth more, as works of art and as criticisms of life, than the whole output of Cooper, Irving, Holmes, Mitchell, Stedman, Whittier and Bryant. I believe that he ranks well above Whitman and certainly not below Poe. I believe that he was the true father of our national literature, the first genuinely American artist of the blood royal.

QUESTIONS

1. Each sentence begins with the words "I believe." Explain the significance of these words.

2. Which sentence serves as the paragraph's topic sentence?

3. Mencken provides criteria by which to evaluate literary pieces. What are they?

PARAGRAPH ASSIGNMENTS

1. Sometimes people's motives and actions are misunderstood by others. These misunderstandings lead to friction and tension between friends, coworkers, or loved ones. Describe a time when your motives or actions were misunderstood, and discuss the effects this misunderstanding had on your relationship with that person. Address your comments to the person involved, and define a purpose for the paper.

2. As Anaïs Nin did, explain why you write. Develop an audience and purpose for the paragraph.

3. H. L. Mencken explores his reasons for believing *Huckleberry Finn* is a great masterpiece. In a similar way, explain a strongly held belief and your reasons for holding the belief. Develop an audience and purpose for the paragraph.

4. Each of us likes to believe that at some time we have behaved heroically. Describe such a time in your own life and discuss the effects of your action. Identify an audience and purpose for the paper.

5. For a review in your school newspaper, identify a movie, concert, or television show you saw recently. Provide a critical review of the show by discussing the reasons why you did or did not enjoy it. Include specific details about the event for your audience. Also, create a purpose for your review.

Diction

1. To use appropriate diction for achieving a specific purpose.
2. To avoid slang, jargon, regional expressions, clichés, and dead metaphors.
3. To be aware of a word's connotations and denotations.
4. To use context to define a word.
5. To recognize and create tone.
6. To explore composing through definition.

PREVIEW: Diction means the words you choose to interest your audience. Tone is the aural quality of your writing; it influences your audience and enhances the transmission of your message. Context is the prose surrounding a word.

Diction means word choice, the words you choose to convey your message. Depending on your choice of words, your message can be formal or informal, general or specific; moreover, your level of language adds precision to your sentences and helps to create tone. So you must be aware of the multiple meanings and suggestions of words as you decide which words to utilize.

Specific Words

One of the first aspects of diction to consider is the specificity of a word: how general or particular a word is. Whether a word is general (broad and all-inclusive) or specific (narrow and detailed) depends on the context in which it appears. For example, the word *mammal* is general if one then lists specific types of mammals; however, the same word can be specific if it appears under the heading *animals*, since it names a particular category of animals.

Frequently, beginning writers do not consider whether a word is specific or general. This failure to consider a word's level of specificity leads to imprecise and general sentences. Consider this example:

The man walked down the street.

Each of the major components of the sentence—the words *man, walked,* and *street*—is very general; these words are so vague, in fact, that a reader cannot easily visualize the person, his actions, or the street. Contrast the sentence above with this revision:

The man, almost seven feet tall, raced down the crowded city street.

This sentence, with its adjectives and descriptive verb, creates a sharper visual impression for the reader. The reader knows more about the person, his actions, and his location.

Hence, the sentence is more descriptive and precise because the words chosen are more specific.

As a writer, you should use specific words to help your reader precisely comprehend your message. On the other hand, if your goal is to confuse your audience deliberately and to avoid being tied to a particular opinion, then you *should* use general and abstract words. (Politicians and bureaucrats are noted for this vague diction.) By remembering your purpose, you can choose the appropriate level of specificity.

EXERCISE 1 Revise the following sentences to make them more specific because you want your audience to understand your message. You can improve your diction by adding nouns, descriptive verbs, adjectives, adverbs, or prepositional phrases.

Example: It was very hot today.

Revision: The temperature climbed into the high 90s, and no breeze rustled the tree leaves today.

1. Terry likes the beach in summer.

   _____

2. *Raiders of the Lost Ark* was a great movie.

   _____

3. The cat sat on the sofa.

   _____

4. The basketball player made two points.

   _____

5. The horse jumped the fence.

   _____

6. The judge passed sentence on the defendant.

   _____

7. The car was in poor condition.

   _____

8. It was a peaceful small town.

   _____

9. The concert was quite good.

   _____

10. The football game was exciting.

Slang, Jargon, and Regional Expressions

Another aspect of diction is the use of slang, jargon, and regional expressions. These types of vocabularies have very specific uses and are comprehensible only by particular groups. If you choose to use slang, jargon, or regional expressions, you must keep your audience in mind; make sure your readers are members of the target group and will understand your word choices. Otherwise, you will fail to communicate with the reader.

SLANG

Each generation and group has its own slang, its own language that has meaning only for the group. This language is extremely informal and can often be understood only by members of that particular group. During the Fifties, for example, the words *cool, cat, beat,* and *hip* were part of the slang used by teenagers, Beatniks, and college students. In the Sixties, hippies used the terms *groovy* and *freaked out*. For a brief period during the Eighties, "valley girl" slang was popular. Although this slang originated in Southern California, *awesome* and *barf* were used by teenagers around the country.

Within a particular group, slang is appropriate; it unifies the group, identifies its members, and serves as a "shorthand" or code vocabulary. However, slang is inappropriate when a writer wishes to address a larger audience that is *not* part of a particular group. By using slang here, the writer indicates a lack of concern for communicating ideas; therefore, the writer's message will not be understood by others.

JARGON

Like slang, jargon exists within groups. A particular vocabulary for a profession, business, or group, jargon may appear to be a rather formal vocabulary. For example, in a computer class, the terms *interface, modem,* and *access* have specific meanings and serve as a quick code for those who know the meanings. However, two problems occur when this specific language is used outside the particular group. First, people who use technical jargon in a discussion with those outside their field are inconsiderate and attempt to support their expertise through their use of this vocabulary and not through their ability to communicate ideas to others. Second, technical jargon loses its meaning when it is used outside the confines of a technical field; at best, it is inappropriate to say, "I accessed the information" without referring to a computer process. At worst, it is absurd to say, "The children interfaced with nature," when the children simply went outside to play.

REGIONAL EXPRESSIONS

Although regional expressions are used by larger groups of people than slang or jargon are, they also fall into the category of code words. One of the best features of the English language is its ability to be flexible. Within many geographical regions, certain names and terms have evolved over the years. As the expression *you all* typifies a Southerner, other phrases identify Americans from different sections of the country. The word *sub* can mean a submarine sandwich, stuffed with many types of cold cuts and cheeses; however, Philadelphians describe the sandwich as a *hoagy*. In New York, such combinations are called *heros*, and in New Orleans, the sandwich is a *poor boy*.

When a writer wishes to stress regional differences, these expressions are appropriate. However, without a specific context and purpose, these words can create the same problems that slang and technical jargon do; since regional expressions are used only by a specific group, they fail to communicate ideas effectively to those outside the region.

EXERCISE 2 The following sentences employ slang, jargon, or regional expressions. Revise the sentences so that they communicate ideas to a broader audience.

Example: Please extinguish all forms of illumination as you exit the room.

Revision: Please turn off the lights when you leave.

1. He's a bad dude.

_____

2. Jeremy considered his former friend an extraneous peripheral.

_____

3. She had to schlep all the way over to the elevated train.

_____

4. The flick was groovy.

_____

5. For sure, it's an awesome day.

_____

6. My cousins, both good old boys in Alabama, favor my sister's boys in Louisiana.

_____

7. That dirtbag stole the old woman's purse.

_____

8. Her pad is boss.

_____

9. His new state-of-the-art stereo interfaced with his television.

_____

10. In light of the applicant's present socioeconomic stratum, the bank officer believed that an additional advance of fiscal relief was untenable.

_____

Avoiding Clichés and Dead Metaphors

A third aspect of diction that you should be wary of is the use of clichés and dead metaphors. When you compare two concepts, the temptation to reach for the familiar can be strong, but you must resist it. Your goal as a writer is to communicate a *new* perspective to your reader; that is very hard to do if your wording is trite.

CLICHÉS

Clichés, expressions that have been used too often, contribute nothing to vivid writing. Comparisons such as *red as a rose, quiet as a mouse,* and *white as snow* have been so overused that they are no longer descriptive. Your readers should be able to visualize the action within a sentence; however, these phrases do not allow the readers to do that. They actually say very little, for the writer who resorts to them has not used imagination to create a new comparison, but has relied upon conventional, lifeless, overworked phrases instead.

DEAD METAPHORS

Dead metaphors are also overworked comparisons. (A metaphor is a comparison that does not use *like* or *as* to note the similarity between two items. For example, the clause *he is an oak* is a metaphor suggesting the person has the strong, stable qualities of an oak tree.) Many dead metaphors are used frequently: *Achilles' heel, swan song, flag waving, grandstanding,* and *explore every avenue* are heard daily. Like clichés, these metaphors have been heard so often that they really mean little, and rather than increase the vitality of writing, they actually reduce it.

Avoid dead metaphors and clichés in paragraphs. Using dead metaphors indicates that, while you wanted to make a comparison, you did not use your imagination to create a vivid one. These expressions interfere with the communication process by stifling your original thoughts and creating boredom in your reader.

EXERCISE 3 Identify the clichés and dead metaphors in the following sentences, and substitute original or vivid comparisons.

   Example: His money burned a hole in his pocket.

   Revision: He was a spendthrift; he spent his money as quickly as he earned it.

   1. That coach is as stubborn as a Tennessee mule.

   _____

   2. Sure as shooting, I'd be pleased as punch to do that for you.

   _____

   3. She's as pretty as a picture.

   _____

   4. At midnight, the house was as dark as a bottomless pit.

   _____

5. It's been a horrible day; it rained cats and dogs from morning until evening.

_____

6. We'll ride the problem out.

_____

7. As a negotiator, he's as tough as nails; as a person, he's a kitty cat.

_____

8. Nothing perturbs Ms. Jones; she's a rock.

_____

9. His Achilles' heel was his inability to reason under pressure.

_____

10. He let his hair down and joined the party.

_____

Connotations and Denotations

Most writers are consciously aware of a word's denotation when writing, but they may be less aware of its connotations. This is unfortunate because, by being aware of connotations and choosing words accordingly, authors create *tone,* the sound of their writing. In addition, they can generate specific responses from their readers, based on the different impressions conveyed by the chosen connotations.

Denotation is a word's accepted meaning(s) in a dictionary; **connotation** is a word's *suggested* meaning. For instance, compare the terms *house* and *home.* Both words share the same definition in a dictionary, but a smart real-estate agent will sell a prospective buyer a *home,* not a *house.* The agent might have the buyer picture his furniture in the new dwelling by saying, "How lovely your antique cabinet will look in this corner," or the agent might remind the buyer of the benefits of the dwelling by adding, "Your family will enjoy many comfortable evenings around the fireplace." Consider the old cliché: It takes a family to make a house a home. Americans tend to believe that homes are more valuable than houses. From this example, it is evident that the term *house* has little emotional appeal to us, but the term *home* connotes security, safety, companionship, and love.

Connotations are formed by two methods. First, connotations can be given to a word by a large group of people and spread by its use on television and radio. The word *appeasement,* for example, initially meant "to pacify or to soothe." However, in 1938, after British Prime Minister Neville Chamberlain said that he had *appeased* Hitler by not opposing Germany's military occupation of Czechoslovakia, the word *appeasement* acquired a negative connotation. Today, the word suggests an obsequious compromise in which moral principles are sacrificed for a temporary peace.

Advertisers also help create our general connotations. The word *natural,* for instance, has been applied not only to food grown without chemicals, but also to shampoos made from detergents and to ice cream made with chemical additives. Consider, too, the phrase *state-of-the-art.* The phrase itself is jargon and means little; it suggests, however, the most technologically advanced design. Many products today claim to be "state-of-the-art," and advertisers use our belief that what is new is better to sell cameras, cars, stereos, and computers.

Second, connotations can be personal, developed by individual experiences. Although the word *school* denotes an educational institution, the education one receives, or the members of an educational institution, its connotations can vary greatly. The word *school* may evoke one person's memories of the first day of school as a six-year-old child, or it may elicit another's memories of a particularly pleasant or frustrating academic year. The word may also remind one of a specific instructor or class. These personal connotations, however, are more difficult to convey to a general audience unless the writer recounts the experiences that helped to create the connotation.

EXERCISE 4 Consider some of the connotations, both general and personal, the following sets of words have. Explain when these words could be appropriately used.

1. teacher, instructor, professor, educator, lecturer, schoolmaster, pedagogue, mentor, coach

2. fat, hefty, corpulent, plump, stout, portly, obese

3. preppy, punk, jock, head, hippie

4. aristocracy, gentry, bourgeoisie, proletariat

5. love, adoration, respect, affection, sentiment, fondness, infatuation

6. friend, pal, chum, acquaintance, confidante, comrade, buddy, ally, companion

7. car, automobile, van, wagon, wheels, sports car, vehicle, jalopy, convertible

8. lawyer, barrister, prosecutor, defense attorney, counselor, advocate

9. talk, gab, converse, chatter, gossip, lecture, speak

10. hoax, trick, deception, lie, fraud, canard

SUGGESTED MEANINGS

By carefully choosing a word for its connotation, you can imply values that you would not want to state directly. You can also project an impression of the subject to your reader that will cause your reader to react in a predictable way. While seemingly being objective, you can control your reader's responses through diction and, perhaps, indulge your personal biases. Examine these three words for their connotations:

politician

statesman

diplomat

All three words have the same meaning, but each conveys a different impression. Many men in public life hunger to be called statesmen; they will probably even gladly accept being referred to as diplomats. Few, however, would describe their occupations as politicians. Therefore, if you refer to someone as a statesman, you create an aura of wisdom, power, and efficacy around the person; on the other hand, if a public servant is called a politician, you may imply that the person is pragmatic and corrupt. By simply choosing a word for its connotation, you can project specific images. Note the different connotations in the italicized words below:

1. The pilot was surprised to see his *crony* at the boat show.

2. The pilot was surprised to see his *friend* at the boat show.

3. The pilot was surprised to see his *acquaintance* at the boat show.

4. The pilot was surprised to see his *buddy* at the boat show.

Each of the above sentences has a different tone or sound because of the wording. Although the meaning of the sentence remains the same, the reader's responses to the given information will differ because of the impressions created by the author's choice of words.

EXERCISE 5   Read the following sets of paragraphs. Indicate specific words and their connotations that contribute to the paragraph's tone. Within each pair of paragraphs, contrast the tones, and indicate a probable audience for each paragraph.

1.   A politician has many cronies. He is willing to deal with them in a variety of settings: bars, convention halls, offices, and perhaps even back rooms. He is able to help them, and usually they are able to aid him; it is a mutually satisfying relationship. Each one recognizes the limits of the relationship and knows not to go beyond them. Most of the time, the public is unaware of all the goings-on.

Word	Denotation	Connotation
_____	_____	_____
_____	_____	_____
_____	_____	_____
_____	_____	_____
_____	_____	_____

Tone _____

Probable Audience _____

2.   A diplomat marvels at his many acquaintances. He enjoys their company in a wide range of circumstances: at receptions, parties, concerts, business meetings, and conferences. He prides himself on his ability to manipulate them tactfully, and they return the favor; both sides benefit from the relationship. Each party adheres to the proprieties and understands the bounds of their unspoken arrangement. Usually, the general public remains blissfully ignorant of all the undercurrents.

Word	Denotation	Connotation
_____	_____	_____
_____	_____	_____
_____	_____	_____
_____	_____	_____
_____	_____	_____

Tone _____

Probable Audience _____

WORDS IN CONTEXT

When you read and analyze material in order to synthesize its new ideas with your own knowledge and to utilize them in your own writing, you may read words that are unfamiliar. One way to deal with the problem would be to keep on reading and forget about a new word, but that rejection would probably interfere with your comprehending the material. Another way to deal with the unfamiliar word is to make it known: learn the meaning by looking the word up in the dictionary. That method, too, presents problems: you lose time, lose your train of thought, and must decide on the appropriate meaning. The practical way to define a new term *while you read* is to use its context to help you make an educated guess about its meaning, to help you approximate the dictionary definition.

The **context** of a word is the environment in which it is found—the writing in which the word is embedded. You can use context clues to determine a general meaning of an unfamiliar word. The context helps you define a word by providing a description, summary, explanation or example, a synonym or antonym; sometimes it even provides a definition by means of the punctuation used. Although the context will not always enable you to define a word, you should be aware of this possibility and be willing to try it. In this way, you can develop your vocabulary and incorporate your new knowledge into your writing. As a writer, you can help your readers to understand unfamiliar words by providing them with ample context clues.

Context: Punctuation

Certain elements of punctuation sometimes provide clues to the meaning of a word; they let the reader know that a definition is being provided. Analyze these sentences:

> Hanukkah (an eight-day Jewish holiday) is celebrated by exchanging gifts.

> The debate was enlivened by the participants' witty repartee: clever exchanges of comments and banter.

> Some political commentators have been harassed, continually annoyed, while lecturing on college campuses.

> Agoraphobia—fear of open spaces—prevents some people from even leaving their houses.

Define these words:

Hanukkah _____

repartee _____

harassed _____

agoraphobia _____

In each of the preceding sentences, punctuation clues alerted you to a forthcoming definition. In your writing, if you have one concept that is central to your argument, be sure to define it if there is any possibility that your reader will misunderstand or misconstrue your point. To do this, use punctuation clues: commas, parentheses, dashes, or colons. Your choice of a particular punctuation mark will depend on how much you want to emphasize the definition. Dashes and colons clearly separate the word's meaning from the rest of the sentence, so they tend to highlight and emphasize it. Commas help the word's meaning blend into the sentence, while parentheses indicate that extra information (e.g., the definition of a word) is included for those who need it.

Context: Synonyms and Antonyms

Synonyms are words that have the same meaning; antonyms are words that have opposing meanings. Both groups help to define unfamiliar words; synonyms include one concept in a larger group, and antonyms exclude a concept from a larger group. Here are some examples:

> The mother tried to assuage the toddler's anger by comforting and soothing him.

> The community strongly opposes any changes in the zoning laws; their aversion is based on a desire to maintain the historical character of the village.

> To paraphrase Marc Antony, have we come to extol the mayor or condemn him?

> Instead of abstaining from high-calorie foods, you have been gorging on them.

Using the context of the sentences, define these words:

assuage _____

aversion _____

extol _____

gorging _____

Context: Explanation or Example

Frequently, an author will signal that an explanation or example of an unfamiliar concept is being provided by using the abbreviations *i.e.* (that is) or *e.g.* (for example). Look at these examples:

> Because humans are bipedal—i.e., walk on two feet—their hands are free to use tools.

> The plot centered on several morbid events—e.g., the death of an infant, the suicide of a parent, and the kidnapping and murder of an heiress.

> Not only civilization but nature, too, supports parasites; for example, mistletoe derives nourishment from its host and kills the tree in the process.

> The instructor is overly concerned with picayune facts; that is, he asks questions about the color of a character's eyes, the style of the milkmaid's dress, and the exact location of the manor's kitchen.

Try to define these words:

bipedal _____

morbid _____

parasites _____

picayune _____

Remember: Examples provide only *some* information about an unfamiliar word. They do not include the whole group or the complete concept, as demonstrated in the following sentence:

> On the first warm day in spring, the forest resounded with the sounds of its denizens—i.e., the gobbles of turkeys, the chatter of squirrels, and the growls of bears.

Denizens mean inhabitants, but, obviously, there are more animals in a forest than just turkeys, bears, and squirrels. The examples provide you with enough information to define *denizen*, but they do not give you a complete picture of the forest environment.

Context: Description

Occasionally, in order to define a word for a reader, an author will describe, or present a picture of, the concept. Study these examples:

> If a figure has eight angles and eight sides, it is probably an octagon.

> Because the child reads two-and-a-half years below his grade level, he is classified as remedial.

> If he is less than one year behind his fellow student, he is considered developmental.

> Some fraternity parties become Bacchanalia, filled with carousing drunkards, noisy revelers, and riotous activity.

Try to define these words:

octagon _____

remedial _____

developmental _____

Bacchanalia _____

Context: Summary

Another way to define an unfamiliar word is to summarize it. This means providing familiar information first and then stating the unfamiliar concept. Here are some examples:

> By working from dawn to midnight, seven days a week, Oscar acquired a reputation as a workaholic.

> Because he donated untold sums of money to build libraries, orphanages, and even Carnegie Hall, Andrew Carnegie is remembered as a philanthropist, rather than a robber baron.

> Unfortunately for Jay Gould, he invested his ill-gotten gains in additional business enterprises and high living; therefore, his reputation has not been revised like Carnegie's. Jay Gould is still considered the premier robber baron.

Try to define these words:

workaholic _____

philanthropist _____

robber baron _____

Context: Definition

The easiest way for you to learn the meaning of a word is for the author to define it. This method is frequently utilized in textbooks when the reader must comprehend a word. Analyze these examples:

Bilingual means being literate in two languages.

A protist is a one-celled creature that is not clearly a plant or an animal; it has some of the characteristics of both kingdoms.

Generally, literacy means being able to write and comprehend on the fourth-grade level.

Few people know that a married man is also a benedict.

Define these words:

bilingual _____

protist _____

literacy _____

benedict _____

EXERCISE 6   Using context clues, define each of the italicized words on the line; then consult a dictionary to check your answers.

1. A CEO's *amanuensis* differs from other executives' secretaries in terms of status, glory, and longer working hours.

   _____

2. *Phobias* (irrational fears) afflict millions of Americans each year.

   _____

3. *Paraplegics*, persons paralyzed in their lower bodies, are still human beings with functioning brains and minds; they deserve attention.

   _____

4. Unlike the *carnivore*, the herbivore eats plants, not meat.

   _____

5. The *ego* is the self; the individual is aware of himself or herself.

   _____

6. *Neonatology*—i.e., the study of human newborns—is a relatively restricted field.

   _____

7. Although their appearances are markedly different, *mammals* (e.g., whales, dogs, and humans) are remarkably similar anatomically.

---

8. No one questions the motives behind giving overt financial aid because the aid is obvious to anyone who cares to examine the records; *covert* aid, on the other hand, is always being questioned.

---

9. *Autarchy,* unlimited sovereignty, is not a popular form of government these days.

---

10. Because he thinks of the concerns of others before his own, because he willingly sacrifices his goals to help others, Mr. Baumgartern is *altruistic.*

Recognizing and Creating Tone

Tone, the aural quality of prose, the sound of language, was mentioned earlier in this chapter. The tonal aspect of writing depends upon diction; diction and tone are inextricably linked. Tone can take many forms. Usually, it is discussed by citing opposites: formal or informal tone, ironic or sentimental tone, objective or subjective tone, and humorous or antagonistic tone. In speech, tone is easily recognized by the loudness, the pitch, and the inflection of a voice, and by facial expressions and body gestures. In your writing, your purpose and your intended audience control your choice of a particular tone, which you convey by using specific words and details. If you are discussing a serious topic, such as capital punishment, the need for unilateral disarmament, or civil rights, with a general audience, then your tone must be equally serious. It would be inappropriate to include jokes or colloquial language in such a discussion. In the same manner, you would create an inappropriate tone if you chose to use polysyllabic words in a description of a camping trip. In this case, the formality of the language would conflict with the recreation of a camping trip.

All writing uses a specific tone. If, for example, you want to convince a faculty committee to include a new course in the curriculum, then your tone must be objective to present the benefits of the course, formal to communicate with those who anticipate a well-articulated proposal, and, finally, persuasive to convince those who may be ambivalent about the proposition. Even writing that purports to be totally objective often has an identifiable tone created by the author's choice of details and words. Consider the example of an objective newspaper story. Assigned to report on the problems of unemployment, a journalist will certainly check current statistics and interview those people who administer programs for the unemployed and who are responsible to the state and federal governments for the allocation of funds. The journalist will also interview people who are unemployed. Although the writer will remain as objective as possible, he or she will select certain details that give the piece a specific tone. Contrast two possible introductions that could begin such a column. One introduction might begin by quoting statistics over the past year. The other might detail the daily routine of a person who has long been unemployed. Certainly, these introductions, in their approaches to the subject, create different tones. The first seeks to be authoritative in its use of statistics; the second focuses on the people who comprise the statistics and encourages the reader to react emotionally to the piece. Both introductions are acceptable; both describe the situation objectively. However, a reader will respond differently to each of the articles because the tones differ.

EXERCISE 7   Read the following pairs of paragraphs. Then, within each pair, identify and contrast each paragraph's tone and indicate which words and connotations contribute to it. Finally, indicate the paragraph's intended audience.

1. a. The portly executive assumed his most regal stance in an attempt to intimidate the insubordinate clerk. Then the awesome personage glanced disdainfully at the sniveling nonentity. Lastly, without even a whisper of sound, he turned on his heels and strode into the inner office, leaving the petitioner in a state of fear and wonder.

    Tone _____

Word	Denotation	Connotation
_____	_____	_____
_____	_____	_____
_____	_____	_____
_____	_____	_____
_____	_____	_____

    Audience _____

  b. The fat banker stood up, hoping to look a bit taller and perhaps overwhelm the rebellious clerk. Then he glared at his cringing subordinate. Finally, very quietly, he turned and walked out of the room, leaving a fear-filled and wondering person behind.

    Tone _____

Word	Denotation	Connotation
_____	_____	_____
_____	_____	_____
_____	_____	_____
_____	_____	_____
_____	_____	_____

    Audience _____

2. a. Today the bottom fell out of the stock market. The Dow Jones plummeted an unbelievable forty points, causing investors to scurry for their lives and their pocketbooks. The traders desperately tried to stonewall the shocking story in an attempt to belittle the events. But Mr. John Q. Public was not fooled; he cashed in his stock certificates and looked for the gold bugs.

    Tone _____

Word   Denotation   Connotation

_____   _____   _____

_____   _____   _____

_____   _____   _____

_____   _____   _____

_____   _____   _____

Audience _____

b. Stock prices declined today; the Dow Jones Industrial Average fell by forty points, probably due to a combination of factors: institutional profit-taking and shaky investor confidence. Traders noted that today's decline represented less than five percent of the market's value, a development not worth much media attention. However, the general public seemed apprehensive about falling stock prices. The number of shares traded increased by twenty-five percent, and the purchase of gold futures rose by eighteen percent.

Tone _____

Word   Denotation   Connotation

_____   _____   _____

_____   _____   _____

_____   _____   _____

_____   _____   _____

_____   _____   _____

Audience _____

Look again at paragraphs 1a and 1b on page 181. Basically, three actions take place:

1. a man stands up,
2. he looks at another person, and
3. the man leaves the room.

By supplying adjectives and adverbs to describe the people and their actions, and by selecting those modifiers carefully, the author not only created tone, he suggested who he thought was the better person: the portly executive or the insubordinate clerk? the fat banker or the rebellious clerk? The author controlled his reader's response by choosing his words carefully.

EXERCISE 8   Look again at paragraphs 2a and 2b on pages 181–182.

1. Which paragraph is more fact filled and objective? _____

2. Which paragraph is obviously subjective and conveys the author's opinion? ___

_____

3. List the words in the subjective paragraph that are opinion words: _____

_____

4. What is the purpose of paragraph 2a? Why did the author write it? _____

_____

_____

5. What is the purpose of paragraph 2b? What do you think the author is trying to

accomplish? _____

_____

_____

You have already compared the tone of each paragraph. Note that the choice of words is dictated by the author's purpose and his audience and that word choice clearly influences tone.

Consider the following selection, which describes a local boxing event. What details and words suggest a specific tone?

On this Saturday night, there are no reporters packing press row—no national television coverage, no Don King or Bob Arum, no cigar smoke curling about the hot lights above the ring. In fact, it proves somewhat difficult to find the arena: an antiseptic place called Novak Field House at Prince George's Community College outside Washington, D.C. Rather than the bright lights of a marquee, a fan encounters a hand-lettered poster, tacked onto a campus sign, pointing the way. Ninety minutes before fight time, the parking lot is nearly empty. Inside, workmen are still erecting the ring, and the Maryland State Boxing Commission's office proves to be a physical-education classroom.

A visitor is struck by the competence and calm with which the Commission staff handles the myriad forms and the inevitable problems. Seconds are licensed, as one of the officials remarks to no one in particular, "Can you believe this? A professional fighter forgot his shoes." Most of the young fighters come from nearby: Hyattsville, Laurel, Washington, Philadelphia. A number are eager but awkward; at least one is making his professional debut. The punches tend to be wide and the footwork somewhat sloppy. But the 400 fans, a family crowd containing a number of young children, seem generally pleased, especially with a rousing lightweight bout that generates sustained applause. Three bouts go the distance; three end in technical knockouts. The five ring officials, all widely experienced, alternate as judges and referee. They step in quickly to protect the fighters. One reluctant warrior is dispatched to the showers in the first round.

Generally sympathetic, the writer's tone also proves ironic at times. Consider the details he uses. The fight is held in a local college gym, not in Las Vegas or Atlantic City. The gym itself is "antiseptic," and with only a few minutes left before the scheduled bout, the ring is being assembled—this is not a major fight center. The boxers, although not described specifically, are identified as "young," "eager," and "awkward." They are not high-ranking professional fighters: one fighter has forgotten his shoes; their footwork is "sloppy"; and one leaves quickly after the first round. A "family" crowd watches the bouts; "young children" are present. Certainly, a fight such as this would not draw large crowds or press coverage; these are inexperienced fighters who are learning their trade as experienced referees "protect" the fighters from injury. Contrast this description of a local fight with the coverage a national title fight would receive. The writer stresses the difference between a local fight and a national championship by describing the place, the fans, the skill of the fighters, and the officials. These details and words create the author's tone.

EXERCISE 9 Construct a writing situation for the following topics. Identify an audience, purpose, and an appropriate tone for a paragraph. (Remember that each topic could be addressed to several audiences; be specific about identifying your listeners.)

1. a discussion of abortion

2. a discussion of requiring sex-education classes in high schools

3. a description of a stadium

4. a description of an athletic event

5. a discussion of health care for the elderly

EXERCISE 10 Rewrite the selection about the local boxing event on page 183. This time, imagine that you are the public relations manager for one of the contenders. Your intended audience is the sports writer for the *Washington Post*. Your purpose is to generate favorable publicity for your boxer.

EXERCISE 11 Complete one of the following exercises, and explain your choice of tone for each of the audiences.

1. Write three brief paragraphs that describe your classroom to each of the following audiences:

    ▪ the school administrators who want to know how to improve the educational setting

    ▪ a friend who has never visited the campus

    ▪ a brochure to be distributed to high-school seniors to encourage them to enroll at your school

2. Write three brief paragraphs that describe the campus student center for each of the following audiences:

    ▪ students who commute to campus daily

    ▪ a teacher who is interested in student activities

    ▪ your parents who will visit the campus soon

3. Write three brief paragraphs that describe a car from each of the following points of view:

    ▪ as a consumer

    ▪ as a salesman

    ▪ as an insurance agent

Writing Strategy: DEFINITION

A definition explains the meaning of a term. You are probably most familiar with dictionary definitions, which provide a word's most common, accepted meaning(s), subscribed to by a large number of people.

There are many ways to define a concept; one is the **logical method.** When defining a word this way, you provide the broad category to which the concept belongs and then you show in what ways the concept differs from all others in that category. For instance, an elephant is a very large land mammal with large ears and a long trunk, whereas a giraffe is a tall land mammal with an elongated neck. Other ways of defining a term include giving synonyms or antonyms of the concept, providing a visual representation, explaining the concept's function, giving examples, or showing what the concept is *not* by excluding a number of similar concepts.

The most useful definition to you is probably the **extended definition.** In a paragraph or an essay, the author explains why it is necessary to define a specific concept and then uses a combination of the aforementioned methods to provide as specific and concrete a definition as possible.

What is Terrorism?

Walter Laqueur

Terrorism is neither identical to guerrilla warfare nor a subspecies of it. The term "urban guerrilla" is as common as it is mistaken. Terrorism is indeed urban, but not "guerrilla" in any meaningful sense; the difference is not one of semantics but of quality. A guerrilla leader aims at building up ever-growing military units and eventually an army, in order to establish liberated zones in which propaganda can be openly conducted, and eventually to set up an alternative government. All this is impossible in cities. In many instances, guerrilla movements and other insurrectional groups do have footholds in cities, but they are usually not of much consequence, because in the urban milieu there are no opportunities for guerrilla warfare. There is a world of difference between a temporary zone of control and the establishment of an alternative government.

Some Western experts, and especially the media, have great difficulty accepting the basic differences among various forms of violence. "Terrorists," "commandos," "partisans," "urban guerrillas," "gunmen," "freedom fighters," "insurgents" and half a dozen other terms are often used interchangeably, frequently as a result of genuine confusion, sometimes probably with political intent, because the guerrilla has, on the whole, a positive public relations image, which the terrorist clearly does not possess.

QUESTIONS

1. Explain what terrorism is *not*.

2. Explain the purpose of a guerrilla leader.

3. What is the difference between a "temporary zone of control and the establishment of an alternative government"?

The Schlager

Struthers Burt

The schlager is an immensely long, thin sword, not much wider than a razor and ground to a razor's sharpness. It is slightly curved, and has a blunt end and a basket hilt to protect your hand. When you fight, you stand close together, one arm behind you, your sword arm crooked and above your head, and all the action is with the wrist. The object is to flick pieces of flesh from the scalp and face of your opponent, and you mustn't give way an inch, or grimace, and, under no circumstances, emit an "ouch!" or its German equivalent. The bouts take place in a hall, or cockpit, designed for the purpose, and there are numerous spectators, most of them members of the vereins involved. There is always a young surgeon in attendance whose duty it is to stop the fight if there is too much loss of blood, or between rounds, to sew up long wounds and doctor small ones. He operates in as brutal a manner as possible in order to further indoctrinate the young men in courage, also in order that the scars may heal badly. This, naturally, is good for the young surgeon, too—it teaches him not to be sentimental in his future practice. If you achieve good wounds, you put salt in them and keep them open to make spectacular scars.

QUESTIONS   1. Define a *schlager*.

2. What is the purpose of a schlager match?

3. Explain the derivation of the cliché "salt in the wound."

4. What is the tone in the paragraph?

The Common Reader

Virginia Woolf

There is a sentence in Dr. Johnson's Life of Gray which might well be written up in all those rooms, too humble to be called libraries, yet full of books, where the pursuit of reading is carried on by private people. ". . . I rejoice to concur with the common reader; for by the common sense of readers, uncorrupted by literary prejudices, after all the refinements of subtitle and the dogmatism of learning, must be finally decided all claim to poetical honours." It defines their qualities; it dignifies their aims; it bestows upon a pursuit which devours a great deal of time, and is yet apt to leave behind it nothing very substantial, the sanction of the great man's approval.

The common reader, as Dr. Johnson implies, differs from the critic and the scholar. He is worse educated, and nature has not gifted him so generously. He reads for his own pleasure rather than to impart knowledge or correct the opinions of others. Above all, he is guided by an instinct to create for himself, out of whatever odds and ends he can come by, some kind of whole—a portrait of a man, a sketch of an age, a theory of the art of writing. He never ceases, as he reads, to run up some rickety and ramshackle fabric which shall give him the temporary satisfaction of looking sufficiently like the real object to allow of affection, laughter, and argument. Hasty, inaccurate and superficial, snatching now this poem, now that scrap of old furniture without caring where he finds it or of what nature it may be so long as it serves his purpose and rounds his structure, his deficiencies as a critic are too obvious to be pointed out; but if he has, as Dr. Johnson maintained, some say in the final distribution of poetical honours, then, perhaps, it may be worthwhile to write down a few of the ideas and opinions which, insignificant in themselves, yet contribute to so mighty a result.

QUESTIONS

1. What does Woolf mean by the "common reader"?

2. List the criteria she uses to differentiate between the "common reader" and other readers.

3. If the common reader's opinion is of little significance, then why does the author state that it should be written down?

PARAGRAPH ASSIGNMENTS

1. Define a frequently used tool or implement.

2. "The common man," "John Doe," and "John Q. Public" are often-used terms. Define them and explain their significance to a recent immigrant who is just beginning to learn English.

3. For the benefit of someone who has never attended such an event, define a hot-rod race, marathon, horse race, boxing match, communion, bar mitzvah or bas mitzvah, or another sporting, social, or cultural event.

4. While trying to sound as non-partisan and impartial as possible, explain who or what democrats, republicans, conservatives, liberals, right-wingers, left-wingers, socialists, or fascists are. Write as if your readers are students in an introductory political science class.

OBJECTIVES: 1. To develop a style suitable to your audience, purpose, and message.
2. To create a suitable style by adeptly using voice, verbs, subordination, parallel constructions, and sentence variety, and by avoiding wordiness.

PREVIEW: Style is your individual way of communicating your message. Voice is the specific verb form used to indicate the relationship between a verb and its subject. Sentence variety comes from using different types of sentences, including periodic and loose sentences, as well as varied sentence beginnings.

As a final editing strategy, you should revise your work for an effective style. By completing this final revision, you can reduce wordiness, use active-voice and descriptive verbs, use subordination effectively, develop parallel constructions, and vary sentence structure.

Avoiding Wordiness

You can easily revise by eliminating unnecessary words. Consider this example of a wordy sentence:

> The school that is located in the valley has increased its enrollment with so many students to the point that the school is overcrowded and filled with students. (*Total number of words = 28*)

Now, consider this revision of the same sentence.

> Because the school in the valley has enrolled so many students, classes are overcrowded. (*Total number of words = 14*)

The revised sentence is more effective because it is not redundant. Here are the major revisions made in the sentence:

1. The relative clause *that is located in the valley* is wordy since the prepositional phrase *in the valley* tells where the school is located. Therefore, the words *that is located* can be eliminated.
2. The verb phrase *has increased its enrollment* can easily be reduced to *has enrolled*.
3. The phrase *to the point that* actually suggests a causal relationship; therefore, the word *because* can be substituted for the longer phrase, with no loss of meaning.
4. The phrase *filled with students* is synonymous with the word *overcrowded*. Hence, the phrase can be eliminated.

Each of these revisions was made without altering the meaning of the sentence. To reduce wordiness, first identify the main idea in the sentence; then locate and remove any repetitive elements; finally, consider one-word synonyms to replace longer phrases.

EXERCISE 1 Revise the following sentences to reduce wordiness. Be prepared to explain your revisions.

1. During the time of the year in the fall, Cheryl made a decision and determined that she should enlist in and join the army.

   _____

2. The gas occupies a space of four cubic feet.

   _____

3. The frozen precipitation, the snow, fell quickly and rapidly at 3 p.m. in the afternoon.

   _____

4. At that point in time, Thomas decided to move to the state of Oregon.

   _____

5. The student, a pupil of Ms. James, nervously and anxiously paced the floor and walked back and forth down the corridor as he awaited the decision of the principal about his conduct.

   _____

6. The parade, held in honor of St. Patrick's Day, attracted a large crowd with many people dressed in green clothes.

   _____

7. The vehicle, a four-wheel-drive Jeep, climbed the steep and narrow and winding road on the mountain easily and effortlessly.

   _____

8. The gymnast performed and executed several difficult tumbling maneuvers and routines.

   _____

9. The writer of newspaper articles reported on the latest and most current developments of the stock exchange on Wall Street in New York City, New York.

   _____

10. After he had appeared in several television programs and stories, the actor performed and starred in a movie.

   _____

Using Active Voice

Transitive verbs, those that can take a direct object, have either active or passive voice. An active-voice verb carries the action from the subject to the direct object. Look at the following example:

> Gerald wrote his term paper.

The subject of the sentence, *Gerald,* performs the action of the verb *wrote*; the direct object *paper* receives the action of the verb. (The direct object answers the question "What was written?") In this sentence, each element of the sentence performs its traditional role: the subject acts; the verb names the action; and the direct object receives the action of the verb. However, the focus of the sentence shifts when the verb is in passive voice:

> The term paper was written by Gerald.

In this sentence, the subject *paper* does not act as a subject traditionally does; instead of performing the action of the verb, this subject receives the action of the verb. In effect, the subject *paper* acts as a direct object would. The person who actually performed the action of writing is Gerald; however, the noun *Gerald* is the object of the preposition *by*. The importance of the actor has been reduced in the sentence. In fact, the actor could be eliminated entirely:

> The term paper was written.

In this version, there is no indication of who wrote the paper. The writer simply acknowledges that the paper has been completed.

In general, writers prefer active voice for several reasons. First, with active-voice constructions, the subject of the sentence does what it is supposed to do: it performs the action of the verb. Second, active voice indicates explicitly who or what performed an action. Third, active voice names the actor who must assume responsibility for the action. In a passive-voice construction, the actor is often hidden in a prepositional phrase and, therefore, takes no direct responsibility for the action. Fourth, sentences with active-voice verbs are usually more concise.

However, you can use the passive voice effectively in two cases:

1. When the identity of the actor is not known.

    > **Example:**   Before we tried to enter the gym, the door *had been locked.*

    In this sentence, the identity of the person who locked the door is not as important as the fact that the door was locked.

2. When, for whatever reason, the writer does not want to identify the actor. Usually, in this case, the writer wants to focus on the result of the action, not the actor.

    > **Example:**   The computer program *was completed* on time.

    In this sentence, the completion of the program is more important than the people who designed it.

The chart on p. 193 will help you identify active and passive verb constructions. The verb "to write" is presented in each tense.

Tense	Active Voice	Passive Voice
Present	*write* or *writes*	*am, is,* or *are written*
Past	*wrote*	*was* or *were written*
Future	*will write*	*will be written*
Present Perfect	*has* or *have written*	*has* or *have been written*
Past Perfect	*had written*	*had been written*
Future Perfect	*will have written*	*will have been written*
Present Progressive	*am, is,* or *are writing*	*am, is,* or *are being written*
Past Progressive	*was* or *were writing*	*was* or *were being written*
Future Progressive	*will be writing*	*will be being written*
Present Perfect Progressive	*has* or *have been writing*	*has* or *have been being written*
Past Perfect Progressive	*had been writing*	*had been being written*
Future Perfect Progressive	*will have been writing*	*will have been being written*

NOTE: The use of helping verbs, those verbs preceding the main verb and indicating the verb tense, in some cases is determined by the number and person of the subject. For example, note in the present progressive how subjects take different helping verbs: I *am* knowing, he/she *is* knowing, and they *are* knowing.

EXERCISE 2   In the following sentences, change the ineffective passive voice to active voice. Supply actors when necessary.

Example: The car was driven furiously by a reckless octogenarian.

Revision: A reckless octogenarian drove the car furiously.

1. The novel was written by a well-known historian.

   _____

2. The television program was cancelled after five weeks because of its poor ratings.

   _____

3. The windows were washed last week during our spring housecleaning.

   _____

4. The church doors were opened by the priest as the newly married couple walked up the aisle.

   _____

5. The information was gathered by Harriet, not by Jason.

   _____

6. The table was refinished by a master craftsman.

_____

7. The police were summoned to the scene of the crime by an anonymous caller.

_____

8. The elderly man was mugged by four adolescents.

_____

9. The forest was destroyed so that a shopping mall could be built.

_____

10. The bond bill, insuring funds for a new park, was passed by the county voters.

_____

Using Descriptive Verbs

Verbs, the most important element in a sentence, identify the action that the subject performs. Verbs that describe specific actions offer the reader a visual image. For example, the verbs *race, blaze, buzz,* and *warble* create immediate images and sounds for the reader. However, linking verbs, such as *to be, seem,* or *appear,* do *not* create images for the reader. Instead, these verbs offer equations or only approximations of actions: for example, he *is* an engineer, or she *seems* happy. Therefore, these linking verbs are not as vivid as verbs that describe actions.

Analyze the following paragraph. Pay particular attention to the verbs in this description of the Brooklyn Dodgers written by Roger Kahn, a sportswriter, long after the baseball team left Brooklyn for Los Angeles. In this passage, Kahn depicts the changes created by the passing of nearly twenty years.

> The team grew old. The Dodgers deserted Brooklyn. Wreckers swarmed into Ebbets Field and leveled the stands. Soil that had felt the spikes of Robinson and Reese was washed from the faces of mewling children. The New York *Herald Tribune* writhed, changed its face and collapsed. I covered a team that no longer exists in a demolished ball park for a newspaper that is dead.
>
> (from Roger Kahn, *The Boys of Summer*)

With its four monosyllabic words, the first sentence signals the passage of time. The years, like the words, move along quickly, and the verb *grew* marks the change from young baseball players to more mature men. In the second sentence, another terse construction not only tells what happened but also offers the writer's judgment, clearly a negative one, of the Dodgers' flight to Los Angeles in 1958. In the third sentence, Kahn turns from the Dodgers to the field where they performed. The verbs in this sentence, *swarmed* and *leveled,* tell the reader not only what happened but also the author's response to the change. Both verbs have negative connotations, and *swarmed,* a metaphor, effectively likens the workers to insects engaged in mindless destruction. Had Kahn chosen less vivid verbs—for example, "construction workers entered Ebbets Field and took apart the stands"—the sentence would have been much weaker. Sentence four strikingly juxtaposes past and present. The ground upon which numerous World Series were played now houses an apartment project. To emphasize such desecration, Kahn personifies *soil.* Previously, it had *felt* the spikes of Pee

Wee Reese and Jackie Robinson, the first black major-league player, as they turned double plays. Now, it is washed from the faces of young children as they cry and crawl where skilled athletes once strutted. Having dealt with the team and its stadium, Kahn moves in sentence five to the newspaper for which he covered the Dodgers in the early 1950s. To detail the demise of the New York *Herald Tribune,* Kahn uses three potent verbs—*writhed, changed,* and *collapsed*—with the first two personifying the newspaper to make its death throes more graphic. The final sentence, which serves as the paragraph's topic sentence and conclusion, records Kahn's sense of loss for the *team that no longer exists,* for the *demolished ball park,* and for the *newspaper that is dead.* Appropriately, the sentence ends with a sense of finality, as *dead* intensifies the theme of change that runs throughout the paragraph. Through his use of cogent verbs and appropriate participles, Kahn carefully orchestrates his idea that nothing good can last, that the boys of summer must inevitably become the men of winter.

EXERCISE 3   Replace the italicized weak verbs with strong, descriptive verbs. Revise the sentence as much as necessary.

1. The jogger *ran* down the street.

   _____

2. The football team *is* on the field.

   _____

3. The soprano *sang* the National Anthem well.

   _____

4. The bird *flew* from tree to tree.

   _____

5. The wolf *moved* toward the lamb.

   _____

6. St. Louis *is* on the Mississippi River.

   _____

7. The skaters *are* on the ice.

   _____

8. The play *is* an exciting one.

   _____

9. The child *is* at the playground.

   _____

10. The car's engine *sounds* strange.

   _____

Using Effective Subordination

Complex sentences contain one independent clause and one or more dependent clauses. Both types of clauses contain subjects and verbs; however, an independent clause expresses a complete thought and can stand alone as a sentence while a dependent clause cannot stand alone as a complete sentence. Dependent clauses usually begin with subordinate conjunctions (for example, *although, because, while, after, before,* and *as*), which introduce the clause, or relative pronouns (*who, which,* and *that*), which act often as the subjects in the dependent clause. Consider the following example of a complex sentence:

> Although the new television program received numerous awards, network executives cancelled the show because it failed to attract a large audience.

The independent clause *network executives cancelled the show* contains the most important information in the sentence. The dependent clause *although the new television program received numerous awards* presents a contrast, for the program was deleted from the schedule *even though* it was recognized as an outstanding program. The second dependent clause, *because it failed to attract a large audience,* provides the reason for the cancellation.

Since it can stand alone as a sentence, the independent clause should contain the most important piece of information in the sentence. The dependent clauses should contain only additional information, since these clauses are not capable of acting as complete sentences.

EXERCISE 4   Read the following paragraph carefully and answer the questions that follow it.

> College students appreciate their spring break for many reasons. First, there is the spring break, which is a well-deserved vacation for some students, who have worked diligently throughout the semester. Those students who spend their vacation by relaxing at one of their favorite beach resorts are lucky. Second, spring break is a time in which students who work part-time during the academic year can work more hours during the break to earn additional money to pay for their college expenses. Also, many seniors, who can use the time to apply for jobs and go on interviews, will be graduating in May or June. This extra time gives them an advantage over those students who do not apply for jobs until the summer. Finally, those students who use this time to complete assignments and readings and to prepare for upcoming final examinations often procrastinate during the first part of the semester. College students choose to spend their spring breaks in several ways since the break is a welcome week away from academic pressures and schedules.

1. What is the topic sentence of the paragraph?

_____

2. What is the controlling idea in the topic sentence?

_____

3. What items of information support this controlling idea?

_____

4. How many supporting ideas are located in dependent clauses? _____ How many supporting ideas are located in independent clauses? _____

5. Is there a problem with the focus of the sentences? If so, why? _____

_____

6. Revise the paragraph so that supporting ideas are located in independent clauses.

Using Parallel Constructions

In sentences, elements in a series should be parallel. These parallel constructions can be all nouns, verbs, participles, prepositional phrases, or all dependent clauses. However, within the series, all of the elements must take the same grammatical form. Consider the following example:

Hiking, jogging, and to swim are his favorite activities.

The subjects of the sentence—*hiking, jogging,* and *to swim*—are not parallel in grammatical form. The words *hiking* and *jogging* are gerunds (verbals ending in *ing* that act as nouns); however, the word *to swim* is an infinitive (a verbal using *to* plus the base form of the verb that acts as a noun, adjective, or adverb). Consider this revision:

Hiking, jogging, and swimming are his favorite activities.

In the revision, the subjects are now all gerunds, and the series is parallel. Here are some useful types of parallel constructions.

1. **Nouns** (A noun is a person, place, or thing.)

   Example: Ms. O'Connor excels as an *author, teacher,* and *administrator.*

2. **Verbs** (A verb describes action or existence. For instance, the verbs *run, act,* and *swim* describe actions. The verbs *be, seem, become,* and the verbs of the senses—*feel, taste, smell, look, sound*—describe existence.)

   Example: Jeremy *jokes, laughs,* and *teases* easily.

3. **Participles** (Present participles are formed by adding *ing* to the base form of a verb. Participles act as adjectives.)

   Example: *Joining* the health club and *exercising* every day, Hank soon acquired additional strength and confidence.

4. **Gerunds** (Gerunds are formed by adding *ing* to the base of a verb. Gerunds act as nouns.)

   Example: *Winning* the championship and *demonstrating* sportsmanship were important to the volleyball players.

5. **Infinitives** (Infinitives are formed by adding the word *to* to the base form of the verb. Infinitives act as nouns, adjectives, and adverbs.)

Example: Allie plans *to complete* her master's degree, *to obtain* an executive position, and *to scale* Pike's Peak within the next four years.

6. **Prepositional phrases** (Prepositional phrases are formed by a preposition—for example, *by, to, from, outside, behind,* and *through*—and a noun or pronoun, the object of the preposition.)

Example: *From every town, from every city,* and *from every farm* came volunteers for the armed forces.

7. **Dependent clauses** (Dependent clauses have a subject and a verb but cannot stand alone as a complete sentence. Dependent clauses are introduced by *subordinate conjunctions* or *relative pronouns*. The words *although, before, when, while,* and *because* are subordinate conjunctions; the words *who, which,* and *that* are relative pronouns.)

Example: Sally is a woman *who accepts a challenge, who works diligently,* and *who accomplishes her goals.*

EXERCISE 5 The following sentences do not have parallel constructions. Analyze the sentences and revise them so that items in a series are parallel.

1. After he had purchased a sleeping bag, backpack, and hiking shoes, Gawain was prepared to camp and hiking in the mountains.

_____

_____

2. Approaching the fence, jumping it cleanly, and to land gracefully, the rider received a round of applause from the spectators.

_____

_____

3. My grandmother enjoys cooking, to read, and singing.

_____

_____

4. The old cathedral with its stained-glass windows, high arches, and spires that towered was impressive.

_____

_____

5. For the audition, she planned to sing a favorite aria but preparing it poorly.

_____

_____

Varying Sentences

TYPES OF SENTENCES

Four types of sentences add variety to paragraphs: simple, compound, complex, and compound-complex. Each of these types is identified by clausal structure, either independent or dependent. Both types of clauses require subjects and verbs. Independent clauses can stand alone as complete sentences; however, dependent clauses cannot act as complete sentences. Consider the following examples of independent and dependent clauses.

Independent
clause: The whale swam slowly down the channel to the sea.

Dependent clause: Before we began the test.

The dependent clause leaves the reader wanting to know what happened before the test started, yet the writer has not included the information. Dependent clauses usually begin with subordinate conjunctions (*although, because, since, even though, until,* and *after*) or relative pronouns (*who, which,* and *that*), which often act as subjects for the dependent clauses.

Here are the four types of sentences listed according to their clausal structure.

1. A **simple sentence** contains **one independent clause.**

   The whale is a mammal.

2. A **compound sentence** contains **two or more independent clauses.** These clauses are joined in one of three ways: (1) with a comma and a coordinate conjunction (*for, and, nor, but, or, yet,* and *so*), (2) with a semicolon (;), or (3) with a semicolon (;) and an adverbial conjunction (*therefore, however, moreover,* and *nevertheless*) followed by a comma.

   The school bus arrived an hour late, for one of its tires was flat and had to be repaired.

3. A **complex sentence** contains **one independent clause and one or more dependent clauses.**

   After the track meet was over, we enjoyed a pizza at a local restaurant.

4. A **compound-complex sentence** contains **two or more independent clauses and one or more dependent clauses.**

   Because they hope to win a fortune, many people place a dollar bet on the lottery each week; however, few win the jackpot because the odds are simply against them.

Paragraphs using only one type of sentence become stale, repetitive, and predictable. Imagine, for example, a paragraph containing only simple sentences. Because there are few transitions and combinations of ideas, readers are forced to provide their own transitions and interest in the paragraph. A different type of problem exists with a paragraph filled with compound-complex sentences. Since these sentences can be long and involved, readers must be constantly alert to the intricacies of the prose. Both extremes, from the elementary simple sentence to the complicated compound-complex sentence, indicate the writer's unwillingness to adapt to an audience and failure to consider the most effective structure for the message. Therefore, a considerate writer varies sentence structure according to the audience's needs and according to the message.

EXERCISE 6   Combine the simple sentences in the paragraph below to form different sentence types. Consider your purpose for each sentence and construct an effective sentence for the message. Identify the types of sentences you use.

> The towns along the California coast have provided settings for many novels. John Steinbeck described Monterey in several of his novels. These novels ranged from *Cannery Row. Cannery Row* chronicles the adventures of the poor and a biologist in the town. Another of his novels to use the town of Monterey as its setting was *Tortilla Flat.* A little bit south of Monterey is the coastal town of Big Sur. Jack Kerouac used this town as the setting in his novel *Big Sur.* Big Sur is a small community, situated on high cliffs overlooking the Pacific. Raymond Chandler portrayed life in Los Angeles and its suburbs. He wrote detective novels. One of these novels was *Farewell, My Lovely.* Another novel was *The Big Sleep.* Other novelists also described Los Angeles and Hollywood. Nathanael West was one of these. He explored the falsity of Hollywood movies. He did this in his novel *The Day of The Locust.* Those novels all use the California coastal towns as their settings.

USING PERIODIC AND LOOSE SENTENCES

In addition to varying sentences by their clausal structure, you can vary the focus of sentences by using periodic and loose sentences. In a **periodic sentence,** the subject, verb, and direct object come at the end of the sentence. In this final position, the major elements of the sentence receive more attention and provide a climax for the sentence. The sentence may begin with prepositional phrases, participial phrases, adverbs, adjectives, or dependent clauses. Consider the following example of a periodic sentence:

> In the early spring morning, the first gentle day after the heavy snows and bitter winds of winter, a solitary robin appeared.

The last part of the sentence, *a solitary robin appeared,* provides a dramatic contrast to the description of a harsh winter. With the traditional spring bird as its subject, the independent clause also reinforces the first mention of the spring morning. Consider now the same sentence with its elements rearranged:

> A solitary robin appeared in the early spring morning, the first gentle day after the heavy snows and bitter winds of winter.

The sentence now begins with the subject and verb, but these parts of speech are no longer the focus of the sentence. Instead, the reader's attention is drawn to the description of winter. The opposite of a periodic sentence, this revision is called a **loose sentence.** With its subject and verb in an initial position, a loose sentence adds more information as it moves toward a conclusion. The loose sentence focuses on the accumulation of phrases or clauses rather than the central message contained in the subject and verb. Both types of sentences are effective, but they create different focuses for the reader.

EXERCISE 7   Identify the following sentences as periodic or loose. Revise the periodic sentences to create loose sentences. Revise the loose sentences to create periodic sentences.

1. The mass of men serve the state thus, not as men mainly, but as machines, with their bodies.

> (from H. D. Thoreau, "Civil Disobedience")

2. Brooklyn had been a heterogeneous, dominantly middle-class community, with remarkable schools, good libraries and not only major league baseball, but extensive concert series, second-run movie houses, expensive neighborhoods and a lovely rolling stretch of acreage called Prospect Park.

> (from Roger Kahn, *The Boys of Summer*)

3. By comparison with meaner looking places with a gas station, barbecue shack, general store, junkyard, empty lots and spilled gasoline, a redneck redolence of dried ketchup and hamburger napkins splayed around thin-shanked, dusty trees, Plains felt peaceful and prosperous.

> (from Norman Mailer, "Plains, Ga.")

4. In June she married Tom Buchanan of Chicago, with more pomp and circumstance than Louisville ever knew before.

> (from F. Scott Fitzgerald, *The Great Gatsby*)

5. Rather than love, than money, than fame, give me truth.

> (from H. D. Thoreau, *Walden*)

BEGINNING SENTENCES

If every sentence in a paragraph were a simple sentence, then the paragraph would be repetitive and juvenile. The same problem occurs if all sentences within a paragraph have the same basic structure of subject-verb-object. Because the English language lends itself so well to this traditional order, though, a beginning writer usually constructs this pattern. However, you can easily vary your sentences by altering the traditional order. Here are several types of beginnings that will keep your sentences interesting.

1. **A prepositional phrase:**

Through the woods was a lovely old mansion.

(In this sentence, the normal word order is reversed. The verb comes before the subject in this inverted sentence.)

2. **An infinitive phrase:**

To achieve her goal, Ellen must practice her skating routine every day.

3. **A participial phrase:**

Dancing around the ballroom, Fred and Ginger attracted everyone's attention.

4. **The direct object:**

The *book* I gave to him.

5. **A dependent clause:**

Even though the first day of spring had passed, the trees were bare of buds.

6. **An adverb:**

   Happily, James walked down the aisle to receive his diploma.

7. **An adjective:**

   Ecstatic, the young man laughed with his friends.

8. **A coordinate conjunction** (this method is usually considered to be informal usage):

   Jack approached the mountain curve cautiously. *For* he knew of the dangerous bend in the road and the drop to the canyon below.

9. **An absolute construction:**

   Book in hand, Katie returned to the classroom.

   (These absolute constructions are usually elliptical. In the sentence above, the phrase *book in hand* could actually mean *with her book in her hand,* a prepositional phrase, or *carrying her book in her hand,* a participial phrase.)

EXERCISE 8   Use at least five kinds of sentence beginnings to give the sentences below more interest. Identify the beginnings you use.

1. Tom handed Jill the tennis racquet.

   _____

2. The captain, energetic and courageous, boarded the alien vessel.

   _____

3. The swimmer was exhausted when he reached shore.

   _____

4. The children played joyfully at the beach.

   _____

5. The bear climbed the tree clumsily but steadily.

   _____

6. The desk had been stripped of its finish; now, it was ready for a coat of paint.

   _____

7. The instructor, with his briefcase filled with papers, faced several days of constant grading.

   _____

8. The baseball team, replete with ten rookies, hoped for a better season than it had last year.

_____

9. The city zoo first opened its doors on May 1, 1908.

_____

10. The movie won an Academy Award for its visual effects.

_____

EXERCISE 9   Revise a recent paper of your own for style. Edit sentences carefully to avoid wordiness; try to use active-voice and descriptive verbs, effective subordination, and parallel constructions, and be sure to vary sentence structure and beginnings. Identify the stylistic revisions you make, and share your paper with another student. Do others find your revisions effective?

The Whole Essay

OBJECTIVES: 1. To use the writing process to develop a coherent, organized, and unified essay.

2. To develop an effective thesis statement.

3. To develop an appropriate introductory paragraph.

4. To write a clear summary.

5. To write a useful critique.

6. To make an informed evaluation.

PREVIEW: A summary is a paragraph that delineates the key points of an essay. A critique examines the merits of an essay. An evaluation presents an informed judgment about the usefulness of an essay.

Longer and more thoroughly developed than the paragraph, the essay allows you to expand a description, narration, explanation, or argument. Consider, for example, a description of a favorite beach on a summer's day. In a single paragraph, you are forced to choose one very limited topic for development. You could, for instance, describe a particular group of people at the beach, the appearance of the beach within a certain restricted area, the activities available at the beach itself or at a surrounding area, or your own enjoyment of the day. In an essay, however, you have room to explore more ideas and include many observations. Specifically, you could describe three or four of the many types of people at the beach (from sun worshippers to tourists to residents at a beach town); you could narrate the day's events for a group of friends or discuss the problems of erosion and overdevelopment, which plague many beach towns, for a local environmental group. Hence, you can choose a broader topic and provide more information in an essay than in a paragraph.

Invention

Despite the differences in length and topic development, paragraphs and essays share the same composing process. In an essay, as in a paragraph, you must generate ideas and details, discover what you mean, identify your audience and purpose, organize your details, revise, edit, and, finally, proofread for correctness. (See "The Writing Process" in Chapter One of Part One.)

In the process of writing an essay, prewriting encourages your creativity, invention, and exploration of a topic. For example, before deciding upon a specific topic, many writers discuss potential topics with others, observe situations and places, play with ideas, and research topics. Through these activities, you can investigate many possibilities and discard those you choose not to develop.

Brainstorming and freewriting will guide you in the selection of a topic. During a brainstorming session, you should, in order to generate ideas, call upon your memory of personal experiences and knowledge gained through reading. If no ideas come to mind quickly, then use the questions newspaper reporters ask: who, what, when, where, why and how. The answers to these questions may direct you to specific topics and audiences. (See "Prewriting" in Chapter One of Part One and "Identifying Audience and Purpose" in Chapter Two of Part One.)

EXERCISE 1   In a brainstorming session, generate at least five possible essay topics for each category below. Include potential audiences and purposes for each topic.

1. Television news programs
2. Television comedies
3. Science-fiction movies
4. Computers
5. Divorce
6. Family structures
7. Police authority
8. Musicians
9. Popular music
10. Teachers

To test your knowledge of a specific essay topic, use freewriting. This method has a number of advantages. First, you can quickly determine whether you need to research a topic in order to develop it fully. Second, freewriting can eliminate any anxiety you might have about putting pen to paper; after a freewriting session, you know that you have something valuable to say about a topic. Finally, you can use freewriting at any point in the composing process. If you believe you have reached a dead end, then freewriting will enable you to generate additional ideas for your essay quickly.

EXERCISE 2   Choose two of the specific topics you generated for Exercise 1. Use a time limit of fifteen to twenty minutes for a freewriting session. When you have finished, compare your freewriting to that of other students. Which ideas can be incorporated into an essay? Which ideas need more development?

Thesis Statements

In a paragraph, the topic sentence states the writer's opinion, predicts what the writer will discuss in the paragraph, and controls the development of the paragraph. In an essay, the **thesis statement** functions in the same manner. Located in the first paragraph, the thesis statement is the main idea in the essay. Like the topic sentence, the thesis statement defines, predicts, and controls the essay.

First, the thesis must identify the writer's position; therefore, it must contain the writer's opinion. Consider this example:

> At Casebook College, sixty percent of the freshmen indicate that they plan to major in business administration.

This thesis is not adequate because it presents only factual information. Consider the revision on p. 208.

At Casebook College, sixty percent of the freshmen indicate that they plan to major in business administration because the program provides a solid background in theory, allows the students to operate a campus business for experience, and places students during their senior year in internships with businesses.

In the revised version, the writer retains the factual information and adds reasons, either identified from personal experience or from studies conducted, why the program is popular. By incorporating the reasons for the program's popularity, the writer also indicates that he or she will discuss these reasons in the essay's supporting paragraphs.

Second, a thesis statement, like a topic sentence, has a subject and a controlling idea. Consider these examples:

SUBJECT
Before graduation, *every college student* should
CONTROLLING IDEA
be required to take at least one computer course.

While commuting to college has many advantages,
SUBJECT   CONTROLLING IDEA
living on campus offers *valuable benefits* to students.

In the first example, the writer announces his position in an argument. In the second example, the writer obviously favors living on campus and is prepared to provide reasons for this position. In addition, the writer could easily compare the advantages of commuting to the advantages of living on campus. Notice that the writers avoid vague adjectives, such as *good, bad,* or *fantastic,* in their controlling ideas.

Finally, thesis statements control the development of the essay. Consider the following example:

SUBJECT
Popular with many Americans, the *Rambo movies* extol
CONTROLLING IDEAS
rugged individualism, patriotism, and private justice.

In this thesis statement, the writer identifies the essay's development and the controlling ideas. Each controlling idea will be thoroughly defined and explained in an individual supporting paragraph of the essay. Hence, this thesis statement automatically directs the content and organization of the paper.

EXERCISE 3   Analyze each thesis statement below. If the thesis statement is adequate (if it defines, predicts, and controls), then place a check beside it; circle the subject and underline the controlling idea. If the thesis is inadequate for any reason, then revise it.

_____ 1. Child abuse can have a devastating effect on an entire family.

_____ 2. Crime is a great problem in many urban areas.

_____ 3. Twenty percent of all faculty members at State College are women.

_____ 4. After the long decades of decay in urban areas, many cities are being revitalized by new tourist attractions, development of historic districts, and new cultural opportunities.

_____ 5. Mountain climbing is an excellent hobby.

_____ 6. Only forty percent of all college students graduate in four years.

_____ 7. American slang changes constantly.

_____ 8. Because of peer pressure, academic demands, and new social situations, high school can often be a bewildering experience for teenagers.

_____ 9. Each fast-food restaurant attracts its own clientele.

_____10. Americans are known for their optimism.

EXERCISE 4   For the general topics below, create at least two thesis statements for each topic. Identify an audience for each statement. *Or* return to Exercise 2 and create two thesis statements from each of your freewriting sessions.

1. Concerts

2. Movie videos

3. Amusement parks

4. Health clubs

5. A controversial topic (such as a local problem or major public concern)

Introductions

The beginning paragraph of an essay, the introduction, must perform three functions:

1. contain the thesis statement (the main idea and purpose),
2. suggest an audience to establish the writer's tone and opinion, and
3. attract the reader's attention and make the reader interested in the subject and its presentation.

The thesis statement can be placed at any point within the first paragraph. Its placement, however, is determined by your purpose. As the first sentence, the thesis immediately announces your opinion and subject; the rest of your introduction may list ideas and explanations that you will develop in the body paragraphs of the essay. If the thesis is in the middle of the introduction, then you catch your audience's interest, state your thesis, and discuss how it will be supported. If the thesis is the last sentence, then you attract the reader's attention, provide necessary explanation of a problem, and then identify your position.

The introduction should also establish the tone of the essay and identify its intended audience. Through your choice of words, you create one of many possible tones for the essay. For example, if you choose to use colloquial language, then you suggest that the essay is for your peers. A more formal level of language suggests the seriousness of the topic and an audience that must be informed of the topic's seriousness. To illustrate this formal tone, consider the seriousness with which you would persuade high-school students to avoid drugs and alcohol. Or consider the presentation of a proposal for a university-run day-care center that you might make to the president of the university. On the other hand, if the essay is to be a humorous account of a blind date, then you might establish your tone by incorporating some jokes, and you will identify the audience by the types of details you indicate you will develop in the essay. (See "Recognizing and Creating Tone" in Chapter Seven of Part One.)

Finally, your introduction must attract your reader's attention. Any number of methods will accomplish this goal; listed below are four of the many different types of introductions.

1. You can "focus down" from general to specific. This technique begins with a general, broad statement. Each successive sentence is narrower in scope than the preceding one. The thesis, the most precise statement in the paragraph, is last. Consider, for example, the problem of presenting in a history paper a thesis that requires background information before the writer can state the thesis. Specifically, a thesis presenting the causes of American involvement in World War I requires that background information be stated first. Hence, the thesis would be placed at the *end* of the introductory paragraph. Consider the following introductory paragraph.

> The average American participates in sports for many reasons: to exercise, to relieve tension, to get out of the house, or simply to have fun. Yet the seriousness with which many Americans play makes one wonder if sports do not cause more tension than they relieve. Is it how you play the game? Or is it whether you win or lose? My experiences in an adult softball league suggest that winning, not sportsmanship or fun, is what counts.

In this student paragraph, the writer moves from the general subject of Americans and sports in the first sentence to the more specific discussion of the seriousness with which Americans play. Finally, the writer connects the serious goal of winning to a specific sport.

2. You can begin with a commonplace statement. For example, even the title of Thomas Wolfe's novel *You Can't Go Home Again* could be used as an introduction to a paper describing a college student's first visit back to her home town after a few months at college. Analyze the following introductory paragraph from a long article on Ebbetts Field, the old home of the Brooklyn Dodgers.

> It was too small. The public urinals were fetid troughs. Its architecture suggested a mail-order tool shed, and every August the grass began to die. The work crews had to spray the outfield with green paint. There weren't enough seats and the parking was impossible and worst of all it had been designed in days when a baseball possessed the resiliency of a rolled sock. Later the ball would leap from bats, and pitchers working there developed sore arms, Jello-O hearts, shell shock. Ebbets Field, 1913-1957. RIP.
>
> (from Roger Kahn, "In the Catbird Seat")

Kahn begins with a commonplace remark, "It was too small." In *Sports Illustrated*, this remark appeared after the title and pictures of Ebbets Field. Hence, the readers knew what the pronoun *it* referred to. Without these guides, however, the reader can still understand the reference; the last two sentences (actually fragments) reveal the stadium's name. In addition, the last two sentences, arranged as an inscription on a tombstone, announce Kahn's thesis and subject: he will describe the history of the once-famous ballpark from its early days through its demolition.

3. You can begin with a pertinent quotation or statistic. (Quotations can easily be found in any number of dictionaries of quotations in the library. Statistics can be found in the

Statistical Abstracts of the United States, located in the reference room of major libraries.) Analyze the following introductory paragraph. Is the opening quotation effective?

> "Let us be thankful for the fools," said Samuel Clemens. "But for them the rest of us could not succeed." These "fools" think school is like taking a long walk under the pounding sun of a muggy summer day: it is quite unpleasant, but it is the only way for one to get where he or she is going. Serious students, on the other hand, know that school is more like climbing up a ski slope: all the hard work pays off when one gets to the top and can "swoosh" down the rest of the way. One's attitude toward school takes root early but becomes most evident in high school. This attitude can later be seen in the student's reasons for going to college. Furthermore, a student's outlook on education may even reflect his or her outlook on life. Many students simply do not care about learning, while others actually see the importance of an education.

This introductory paragraph links the quotation about "fools" to a type of student who simply does not care about his or her education. The paragraph then compares two types of students: those who are unconcerned about their education and those who are concerned.

Consider this paragraph, which begins with a statistic:

> After years of inflation and high unemployment, the current unemployment figure of 7.3% seems to be relatively low. While this single-digit figure is small, it represents approximately 30 million Americans who live below the poverty level because there is no work for them. Until this figure can be reduced by an increase in American production and jobs, the federal government should be responsible for fulfilling the needs of the unemployed.

This introductory paragraph contrasts the seemingly low unemployment rate with the vast numbers of Americans who are affected by unemployment. The writer then argues for governmental support for the unemployed.

4. You can begin dramatically by repeating a conversation or by telling a story. This method has many variations, each with the same intent: to make your reader aware of realistic situations and to encourage your reader to respond to the situations. Consider, for example, the effect of describing the living conditions of the poor in ghettos as the introduction to an essay on the plight of the poor. Certainly your reader would be more sympathetic to the essay and its arguments if you make the statistics of poverty come alive by describing people who live under those conditions. Analyze the following lead paragraph of a newspaper article that discusses the crisis of illiteracy.

> One afternoon two years ago, the telephone rang in my English Department office. Barely had I said hello when the voice of an unidentified caller barked: "Do you know about Chaucer and all them writers who wrote around him?" Before I had a chance to reply, the voice barked again: "Did he write different than we write now?" This phone call was startling. Was it the glaring lack of manners? Was it the absence of correct English? Was it the caller's bewilderment about the history of his native tongue? Or was the most disturbing factor the laziness—that lack of intellectual curiosity—that kept the caller from going to the nearby library and seeing quite easily that Chaucer did, indeed, "write different than we write now"? Illiteracy is a pressing problem—a problem so urgent that it threatens to rend the fabric of American culture.
>
> (from Vincent Fitzpatrick, "Why Something Must
> Be Done About Illiteracy")

This paragraph could easily begin with statistics demonstrating the problem of illiteracy; however, the dramatic lead, with an unidentified caller demanding information, proves to be more effective. Although many people may not have studied Chaucer, most would head to the library to find the answer to the caller's question. In addition, the caller's question, filled with errors, does point to the insidious nature of illiteracy: the caller wants someone else to tell him the answer rather than researching the question himself.

EXERCISE 5 Analyze the following introductions, written by students. Identify the type of introduction each writer used. Also, identify the thesis statement in each paragraph. If an introduction does not adequately develop the reader's interest, lacks a thesis statement, or fails to suggest an audience and purpose, then revise the paragraph.

1. As I planned my vacation to Jamaica, travel agencies and brochures provided what I thought to be a complete picture of the island paradise. I found, however, that this perfect picture excluded many hard realities of life in Jamaica. There were parts of the island which were as beautiful as I had expected, but there was an abundance of problems such as poverty and crime which contrasted sharply with my preconceived visions of the island.

2. More often than not, people assume that any kind of professional dance is all the same. This is not true. Two distinct types of dance are classical ballet and modern dance. The dictionary defines *ballet* as "dancing in which conventional poses and steps are combined with light flowing figures (such as leaps and turns)." To illustrate one of their differences, modern dance is not even defined in the dictionary. Modern dance is only about twenty years old and was pioneered by Martha Graham. The main differences between ballet and modern dance are the way that the body's turn out is used and the different footwear worn. Both types of dance are expressive, but each in its own style.

3. To a newcomer, the barrio was a farming ghetto with people just above the poverty line. In this farming suburb of Manila, all wore haggard faces and blistered hands. Day in and day out, they slaved over their crops to produce minimal income. Poverty was evident in their faces, their homes, and their lives. But in this pathetic condition, the barrio produced hard-working people bent on improving their situation. One of these rare individuals who displayed insurmountable supplies of hope, determination, and perseverance was my uncle.

4. Of all the home computers on the market, the Excel 600X and the Discovery 128 are two of the most competitive. Many people do not investigate the advantages and disadvantages of both and, thus, buy the more advertised of the two—the Discovery. Only through careful comparison of the two would one find that the Excel is the better buy for the money.

5. A town like hundreds of other G.I. towns across America, Leesville, Louisiana blossomed with the influx of military pay vouchers and raced headlong from insignificance to prosperity. Seemingly overnight, whole blocks of bars, pawn shops, and liquor stores appeared, eager to give the soldiers a place to spend their money. Typical of these places was the Golden Nugget.

EXERCISE 6   Return to Exercise 4, in which you developed thesis statements for five topics. Choose two of these thesis statements and create two different introductory paragraphs, one for each thesis.

Supporting Details

Contained in the middle paragraphs, the body of the essay supports the thesis statement by supplying illustrations, examples, definitions, points of comparison and contrast, separate causes or effects, or points in an argument. These body paragraphs develop the thesis in much the same way that primary and secondary supports develop the topic sentence in a paragraph. The chart below demonstrates the similarities between paragraphs and essays.

Paragraph	*Essay*
1. The *topic sentence* defines the writer's opinion, predicts the discussion, and controls the paragraph.	1. The *thesis statement* defines the writer's opinion, predicts the discussion, and controls the essay.
2. The *primary support sentences* develop the controlling idea in the topic sentence.	2. The *body paragraphs* develop the controlling idea in the thesis statement. Each body paragraph has a topic sentence that directly supports the thesis statement.
3. The *secondary support sentences* provide additional information, such as examples, descriptions, or explanations, about the primary support sentences.	3. Individual body paragraphs have primary and secondary supports that provide additional information about the topic sentence of the body paragraph.
4. The *concluding sentence* restates the topic sentence and primary supports, or provides a logical conclusion.	4. The *conclusion* summarizes the thesis statement and the topic sentences of the body paragraphs or provides a logical conclusion and suggestions.

An essay's thesis statement is supported by body paragraphs that explain, narrate, describe, or argue points of the thesis. Consider this thesis statement:

> While commuting to college has many advantages, living on campus offers valuable benefits to students.

Each body paragraph of this essay would develop one benefit of living on campus. Also, since these are paragraphs, each body paragraph needs a topic sentence and supporting details.

After generating a thesis statement, try brainstorming for specific supporting ideas. This method will give you many ideas for body paragraphs and probably provide some details. Consider this example.

Thesis: While commuting to college has many advantages, living on campus offers valuable benefits to students.

Brainstorming
   Ideas: chance to live on one's own for first time

able to participate in campus activities easily

closer to library and school's facilities

able to make friends with others in dorm

able to participate in social activities in dorms

set schedule for oneself

responsible for own actions

do not have to waste time commuting

can join campus clubs

can seek help from friends

learn valuable interpersonal skills of dealing with others

Organizing
   Ideas: Paragraph 1. Living on campus allows the student to take advantage of many campus facilities to develop academic skills.

A. The library offers not only resources but also a quiet place to study, something students may not have at home.

B. Students can use the campus computers at any time.

C. By living on campus, students can more readily meet with professors and instructors.

D. Students can use labs and workshops in the evenings.

Paragraph 2. Living on campus allows students to participate in campus activities more fully.

A. Since they live on campus, students have more access to nighttime cultural events, such as concerts and lectures.

B. Students can join clubs and participate more directly in the organization of the campus.

C. Students can enjoy activities in the dorms, such as intramural sports and social gatherings.

Paragraph 3. Finally, living on campus allows students to become more mature since they are responsible for their actions.

A. Students must learn to budget their time carefully since no one will remind them of their responsibilities.

B. Students must learn to budget their money carefully.

C. Students must learn to perform domestic chores for themselves.

D. While living in the dorms, students must learn how to deal with others.

As you can see, a brainstorming session can yield topics that can be developed into separate paragraphs and also details for those paragraphs. This method can save time as well; you not only generate ideas quickly, but also you can determine an organization for those ideas. In addition, you can quickly judge whether or not your supports are unified. As the sentences in a paragraph must be unified, so too must the paragraphs in an essay be unified. Each paragraph and its sentences must develop the thesis statement. Finally, for those who have difficulty devising a thesis, brainstorming for details about a topic might identify particular ideas that can be used for the thesis. (See Chapter Four in Part One.)

You have explored various writing strategies for organizing details in paragraphs. These same strategies apply to essays as well. During the first few drafts of an essay, you should remain open to new ideas and details that you might discover. Also, you should take the time in the first few drafts to explore what you want to say and how it can be said more effectively. As you have seen, any number of writing strategies can provide a structure for details; however, your audience and purpose should guide you in developing an appropriate structure and selecting the most convincing details for your essay.

Analyzing Essays

Analyzing an essay requires that you consider its contents, structure, and purpose. During this process, keep your personal reading goals in mind: you are reading the essay to analyze, synthesize, and utilize the information it provides. Three steps will enable you to read an essay effectively. "Effectively" is the key word in this process; you don't just want to let your eyes roam the page. Instead, because you want to comprehend the essay, you must summarize, critique, and evaluate it.

SUMMARIZING

Summarizing is a frequently used technique. When you tell a friend a condensed version of a movie's plot, when you provide the highlights of a basketball game, and when you review a lecture class, you are summarizing. You should also be using summaries to help you study; rather than rereading an entire chapter before an exam, you should read the chapter's summary. Instead of hastily skimming all of your supplementary readings, you should read the summary you wrote for each article. Likewise, businesses rely on summaries; executives demand brief reports about business transactions, conferences, and important events. They do not want blow-by-blow descriptions; they want summaries.

Summarizing is essential to the reading process also. Being able to compose an accurate summary indicates that you, the reader, were able to analyze the written material, to comprehend its key points, and to take the first step towards synthesizing and utilizing new information.

What exactly is a summary? It is a shortened version of an original article, book, event, etc. A summary reviews a thesis and key supporting ideas. A summary should include the major arguments and/or reasons given by the author to support his or her point of view and perspective of the situation. In effect, the summary provides an outline of the given material in paragraph form.

How do you develop a summary? You cannot expect to write an accurate summary without comprehending the material; therefore, you must read and analyze the material carefully. Then, skim the essay. (Remember that when you skim you are trying to determine the author's thesis and essential support. See "Skimming" in *To the Student*.) After reading and skimming, you should thoroughly understand the topic. Then, you can begin to assess the relative importance of all the material you have just assimilated; decide what is most important, what is least important, and what are really just details and examples. Outlining will probably aid you at this point because it will enable you to visualize the relationships between ideas, to weigh the relative importance of each concept, and to organize the important ones. Finally, write the summary in one paragraph. Be sure to use complete sentences in your paragraph and to paraphrase the author. (In other words, use your own words; don't quote.)

EXERCISE 7   Read the essay, "On Friendship," pages 217–219, and write an accurate summary of it. Remember that your audience will use your summary to decide whether the article is worth reading completely.

CRITIQUING

Remember the definition of an essay: a short composition discussing one topic, presenting a personal perspective on the topic and not, therefore, attempting to discuss that topic in exhaustive detail. Although essay writers present a personal perspective, their goal is to convince, persuade, or suggest to readers that their personal viewpoints are *not* subjective; they want their audience to concur that their opinions are the logically correct ones because they are founded on reliable evidence.

As a reader, you must determine whether the authors have achieved their goals. By critiquing an author's material, you can determine the validity of his or her perspective. Then, if the opinion is valid, you can synthesize the newly learned information and the newly gained perspective with your own knowledge and perspectives, arrive at a new body of information, and develop new insights into the topic.

What, then, is meant by "critiquing an essay," and how do you do it? You critique an essay when you judge the merits of its arguments, when you objectively determine its strengths and weaknesses. To judge fairly, you must read and analyze carefully; here, your summary will help you. In the summary, you noted the author's thesis and reasons. Now, when critiquing, continue the analytical process. Look at the facts, statistics, examples, etc. provided by the author. Do they really explain each topic sentence, provide more details about the topic, and support the author's viewpoint?

The following questions may help you to critique new material:

1. What is the author's thesis?
   State the topic.
   State the author's viewpoint.

2. List the reasons given to support the author's opinion.

3. What details does the author provide to explain each reason?
   Are the details relevant to the thesis?
   Are the details factual and easily verifiable?
   Are the details based on subjective or objective experience?

4. Does the author make a strong case to support his or her belief?
   Does the author provide enough evidence to convince a skeptic that the personal opinion is logical and valid?

If you answer "yes" to the last question, then you can synthesize the essay's information because you have decided that it is worthwhile to incorporate that information into your store of knowledge.

EXERCISE 8   Critique the essay, "On Friendship," pages 217–219. Use the questions above to decide whether the authors have presented a strong argument for their point of view.

EVALUATING

The last step in processing an essay is evaluating it. This means deciding whether or not you will utilize the essay's information. If the evaluation is favorable, then you will act upon the information and incorporate it into your writing. However, if the evaluation is unfavorable, then you will not utilize the given material because you don't want your ideas to be inadequate or unacceptable.

When evaluating an essay, you must remember that it is not an exhaustive examination of a topic. After all, it is not a book. Because of its comparatively short length, an essay omits much information. The decision to include or exclude material is made by the author, based on his or her purpose, intended audience, and desired length of the essay. Consequently, the author may decide to exclude some important material because it may undermine or contradict his or her thesis.

What, then, is evaluating? It is deciding whether the author has presented a thorough analysis of the topic, whether he or she has fairly presented both sides of the issue, and whether the evidence justifies the author's conclusion.

How do you evaluate an essay? You must familiarize yourself with additional evidence and opposing views. In that way, you can judge for yourself whether an author is completely honest in presenting this viewpoint or whether he or she omitted material that is potentially devastating. To complete this step, you must be well informed or, at the very least, familiar with your library and with research techniques.

The following questions may help you to evaluate an essay.

1. What would be the most likely opposing thesis?
   State it.
2. How would opponents of the author's opinion support their viewpoint?
   What reasons would they give for their opposition?
3. Does the author refer to his or her opponents' views?
   Does the author try to refute their ideas?
   Is this refutation successful?
4. What facts, statistics, details, etc. contradict the author's viewpoint?
   What facts, statistics, details, etc. weaken his or her case?
5. Are there acknowledged experts on the topic whose opinions differ from the author's?
   Who are they?
   Are their conclusions valid?
   Do they support their views with facts, studies, etc.?

EXERCISE 9   Brainstorm the topic in the essay, "On Friendship," pages 217–219, to develop an opposing perspective. If you need additional evidence, research the topic. Then decide whether the authors' viewpoint is valid. Finally, write an essay on the topic that incorporates all the information you have gathered and synthesized.

On Friendship

Margaret Mead and Rhonda Metraux

1   Few Americans stay put for a lifetime. We move from town to city to suburb, from high school to college in a different state, from a job in one region to a better job elsewhere, from the home where we raise our children to the home where we plan to live in retirement. With each move we are forever making new friends, who become part of our new life at that time.

2   For many of us the summer is a special time for forming new friendships. Today millions of Americans vacation abroad, and they go not only to see new sights but also—in those places where they do not feel too strange—with the hope of meeting new people. No one really expects a vacation trip to produce a close friend. But surely the beginning of a friendship is possible? Surely in every country people value friendship?

3   They do. The difficulty when strangers from two countries meet is not a lack of appreciation of friendship, but different expectations about what constitutes friendship and how it comes into being. In those European countries that Americans are most likely to visit, friendship is quite sharply distinguished from other,

more casual relations, and is differently related to family life. For a Frenchman, a German or an Englishman friendship is usually more particularized and carries a heavier burden of commitment.

4   But as we use the word, "friend" can be applied to a wide range of relationships—to someone one has known for a few weeks in a new place, to a close business associate, to a childhood playmate, to a man or woman, to a trusted confidant. There are real differences among these relations for Americans—a friendship may be superficial, casual, situational or deep and enduring. But to a European, who sees only our surface behavior, the differences are not clear.

5   As they see it, people known and accepted temporarily, casually, flow in and out of Americans' homes with little ceremony and often with little personal commitment. They may be parents of the children's friends, house guests of neighbors, members of a committee, business associates from another town or even another country. Coming as a guest into an American home, the European visitor finds no visible landmarks. The atmosphere is relaxed. Most people, old and young, are called by first names.

6   Who, then, is a friend?

7   Even simple translation from one language to another is difficult. "You see," a Frenchman explains, "if I were to say to you in France, 'This is my good friend,' that person would not be as close to me as someone about whom I said only, 'This is my friend.' Anyone about whom I have to say *more* is really less."

8   In France, as in many European countries, friends generally are of the same sex, and friendship is seen as basically a relationship between men. Frenchwomen laugh at the idea that "women can't be friends," but they also admit sometimes that for women "it's a different thing." And many French people doubt the possibility of a friendship between a man and a woman. There is also the kind of relationship within a group—men and women who have worked together for a long time, who may be very close, sharing great loyalty and warmth of feeling. They may call one another *copains*—a word that in English becomes "friends" but has more the feeling of "pals" or "buddies." In French eyes this is not friendship, although two members of such a group may well be friends.

9   For the French, friendship is a one-to-one relationship that demands a keen awareness of the other person's intellect, temperament and particular interests. A friend is someone who draws out your own best qualities, with whom you sparkle and become more of whatever the friendship draws upon. Your political philosophy assumes more depth, appreciation of a play becomes sharper, taste in food or wine is accentuated, enjoyment of a sport is intensified.

10   And French friendships are compartmentalized. A man may play chess with a friend for thirty years without knowing his political opinions, or he may talk politics with him for as long a time without knowing about his personal life. Different friends fill different niches in each person's life. These friendships are not made part of family life. A friend is not expected to spend evenings being nice to children or courteous to a deaf grandmother. These duties, also serious and enjoined, are primarily for relatives. Men who are friends may meet in a café. Intellectual friends may meet in larger groups for evenings of conversation. Working people may meet at the little *bistro* where they drink and talk, far from the family. Marriage does not affect such friendships; wives do not have to be taken into account.

11   In the past in France, friendships of this kind seldom were open to any but intellectual women. Since most women's lives centered on their homes, their warmest relations with other women often went back to their girlhood. The special relationship of friendship is based on what the French value most—on the mind, on compatibility of outlook, on vivid awareness of some chosen area of life.

12   Friendship heightens the sense of each person's individuality. Other relationships commanding as great loyalty and devotion have a different meaning. In

World War II the first resistance groups formed in Paris were built on the foundation of *les copains*. But significantly, as time went on these little groups, whose lives rested in one another's hands, called themselves "families." Where each had a total responsibility for all, it was kinship ties that provided the model. And even today such ties, crossing every line of class and personal interest, remain binding on the survivors of these small, secret bands.

13   In Germany, in contrast with France, friendship is much more articulately a matter of feeling. Adolescents, boys and girls, form deeply sentimental attachments, walk and talk together—not so much to polish their wits as to share their hopes and fears and dreams, to form a common front against the world of school and family and to join in a kind of mutual discovery of each other's and their own inner life. Within the family, the closest relationship over a lifetime is between brothers and sisters. Outside the family, men and women find in their closest friends of the same sex the devotion of a sister, the loyalty of a brother. Appropriately, in Germany friends usually are brought into the family. Children call their father's and their mother's friends "uncle" and "aunt." Between French friends, who have chosen each other for the congeniality of their point of view, lively disagreement and sharpness of argument are the breath of life. But for Germans, whose friendships are based on mutuality of feeling, deep disagreement on any subject that matters to both is regarded as a tragedy. Like ties of kinship, ties of friendship are meant to be irrevocably binding. Young Germans who come to the United States have great difficulty in establishing such friendships with Americans. We view friendship more tentatively, subject to changes in intensity as people move, change their jobs, marry, or discover new interests.

14   English friendships follow still a different pattern. Their basis is shared activity. Activities at different stages of life may be of very different kinds—discovering a common interest in school, serving together in the armed forces, taking part in a foreign mission, staying in the same country house during a crisis. In the midst of the activity, whatever it may be, people fall into step—sometimes two men or two women, sometimes two couples, sometimes three people—and find that they walk or play a game or tell stories or serve on a tiresome and exacting committee with the same easy anticipation of what each will do day by day or in some critical situation. Americans who have made English friends comment that, even years later, "you can take up just where you left off." Meeting after a long interval, friends are like a couple who begin to dance again when the orchestra strikes up after a pause. English friendships are formed outside the family circle, but they are not, as in Germany, contrapuntal to the family nor are they, as in France, separated from the family. And a break in an English friendship comes not necessarily as a result of some irreconcilable difference of viewpoint or feeling but instead as a result of misjudgment, where one friend seriously misjudges how the other will think or feel or act, so that suddenly they are out of step.

15   What, then, is friendship? Looking at these different styles, including our own, each of which is related to a whole way of life, are there common elements? There is the recognition that friendship, in contrast with kinship, invokes freedom of choice. A friend is someone who chooses and is chosen. Related to this is the sense each friend gives the other of being a special individual, on whatever grounds this recognition is based. And between friends there is inevitably a kind of equality of give-and-take. These similarities make the bridge between societies possible, and the American's characteristic openness to different styles of relationship makes it possible for him to find new friends abroad with whom he feels at home.

The same methods you use to analyze a professional writer's essay can be applied to a student's writing as well. Within the composing process, an analysis of an essay will enable you to identify areas that need to be revised and to evaluate the essay's effectiveness in the areas of audience, purpose, organization, and supporting details.

EXERCISE 10   Read and analyze the following student essay. Consider the writer's thesis and the supporting body paragraphs. Be prepared to answer the questions that follow the essay.

I grew up in the Garden of Eden. This land of milk and honey provided me with the essentials of boyhood: a park with baseball diamonds, friends for companionship, and a haunted house. As I grew older, my garden died. A specific combination of intangibles separated my neighborhood of Mayfield from the other neighborhoods in the city. The school down the block, St. Francis of Assisi School, educated me. The kids who went there taught me. The dreams I believed in still live there in Mayfield. Only when I left did I realize what I was leaving behind. As a boy in Mayfield, I learned through my school, my friends, my dreams, and my departure.

In many ways, Mayfield differed from other neighborhoods. In a section of the city near Lake Roland, Mayfield resembles any other neighborhood. Maybe Mayfield was special because I lived there. Walking down the street, one felt as if he were reading *Our Town*. Each family owned a house with a small yard and sidewalk. The Protestant church, St. Matthew's Church, sat at the corner of Mayfield and Norman Avenues. A few streets over, the Catholic church and school held masses and classes. The Irish and Italian families dwelt among the German and English families. My family stood alone as the only Asian family in Mayfield. Everyone knew everyone else through the church, the PTA, or through gossip.

St. Francis of Assisi School initiated me into the life of Catholic education. Sister Grace Christie introduced my pure mind to the realm of *A, B, C*'s and 1, 2, 3's. She did not scare me as some of the other nuns did: "Oh, another Lee! I can't wait until I have you in my class!" Sister Edwards would screech while pinching my left cheek. The youngest child in the family often deals with these uncomfortable occasions. The first year of my formal education amused me. But by the second grade, Mrs. Young informed me that I was no longer a child. I was a student. Eager at first, I soon was overwhelmed by spelling tests and two-digit addition. I wanted to go home.

When I got home from school, I often spent my free time playing with the many kids in Mayfield. Usually the youngest, I envied and imitated the big kids. I thought the big kids in fifth grade could do anything. Wanting to be accepted, I would practice doing the things that big kids did. Dave, a kid my age, and I rode our bikes without using our hands, pretended to patrol Kinley Avenue as the cops did, and even spoke those bad words the big kids used. Sometimes the kids would elect someone to steal apples from the yard of the haunted house. I promised myself that when I finally got big I would never make the little kids do what I had to do. The big kids would teach me important stuff that Sister Grace did not know like how to play baseball or where babies come from. Competing with the other kids, I often wondered about being big.

At Mayfield, I dreamed the usual boyhood dreams that still exist in other kids. As a child who never experienced the world outside Mayfield, I assumed that since I made the pee-wee league baseball team as a seven-year-old, I would play in the American League. Not only would I make the professional baseball team, but I would go to the moon and visit Mars. Maybe I could save the president and win the Olympics. More practical dreams came to me later as my parents felt my destiny to follow a medical route. The other kids in the neighborhood dreamed themselves to be firemen, movie stars, nurses, teachers, and scientists. Dreams change, and some die as kids grow older.

When I moved from Mayfield on September 7, 1977, I could not pack everything I wanted to take. So many items, some good and some bad, remained. I wanted to take my friends. Mom and Dad swore that they would buy me a new two-wheeler when they decided to leave the old one behind. I wondered if we would ever come home. Although still too young to understand, I knew that I could follow my dreams elsewhere. So I left most everything behind, but I packed away my hope which remained after such a trauma.

Looking back, I wonder what happened to my hopes. Growing up in the Garden of Eden, I possessed everything. Somehow I let it slip away. The friends I had still exist. My education still frustrates me. I still dream like a child. But I am one of the big kids. In my quest for fulfilling my hopes, I perverted my intentions. My curiosity forced me to grow up too fast.

QUESTIONS

1. What type of introduction does the writer use? Does it capture the audience's attention? What is the writer's thesis? How will the writer develop the thesis? Has the writer developed a specific tone?

2. Examine each body paragraph carefully. Note the topic sentences for each one. Do they substantiate the thesis?

3. Write an outline for each body paragraph. Identify the specific supports for each topic sentence. Are any sentences unnecessary or unclear? List the primary and secondary supports in each body paragraph. What transitional words or expressions connect the paragraphs?

4. What type of conclusion does the writer use? Does the writer remind the reader of the introductory paragraph?

EXERCISE 11

In Exercise 6, you developed introductions and thesis statements. Choose one of those introductions now, and brainstorm for ideas for supporting body paragraphs. Organize your list of details, and write at least two body paragraphs for your thesis. Compare your paragraphs with those of other students. Are your paragraphs unified?

EXERCISE 12 Choose one of the topics below, and write an essay.

1. Describe a portion of your childhood.

2. Describe your high school by focusing on teachers, students, activities, and buildings.

3. Describe your favorite place.

After you have completed your essay, ask your classmates to analyze it with you. What process did you use to create the essay? Why did you choose this process?

Revising

Many beginning writers simply stop after the first draft of an essay; they do not evaluate the essay's unity or organization. While the essay may be somewhat organized, these writers do not make the commitment to revise the essay and provide transitions and effective details. However, through revision, you can make your essays more effective and discover more about the topic. Revision requires many stages. First, you must consider the essay's topic and organization. Second, you must analyze your details carefully. Did you include the best examples, descriptions, or arguments? Are these details specific? Third, you should determine whether your paragraphs are effective. Would any paragraph be better placed elsewhere in the essay? Does each paragraph have a topic sentence and supporting details? Fourth, you must provide transitions for the reader. Are your transitions appropriate?

Since it is almost impossible to perform all of these checks at once, you can revise in stages so that each area of the essay is analyzed carefully and not merely pronounced "adequate." Answers to the following questions will guide you in the revision process.

I. *Thesis*

   A. Is there a thesis?

   B. Is the thesis accurate?

   C. Does the thesis define your opinion, predict the discussion, and control the essay?

   D. Could the thesis be worded more clearly?

   E. If there is no thesis, then what seems to be the main idea in the essay?

II. *Organization*

   A. Is the final organization of the essay effective? If, for instance, you are narrating an event, then is the narration in chronological order?

   B. Would your paragraphs be better arranged in another manner?

III. *Body Paragraphs*

   A. Does each body paragraph in the paper have a topic sentence?

   B. Does each topic sentence refer to or support the thesis?'

   C. Do these body paragraphs present the best ideas possible to support the thesis? Or can you now think of other examples that might be more effective and interesting?

   D. Did you include specific details?

   E. Do the sentences in each paragraph support the topic sentence?

   F. Are these paragraphs unified?

IV. *Introduction*

   A. Does the introduction develop the reader's interest?

   B. Does the introduction supply enough information about the background of the topic?

   C. Is the introduction too short?

   D. Would another type of introduction be more effective?

V. *Transitions*

   A. Are there transitions between paragraphs?

   B. Are there effective transitions between the sentences within paragraphs?

   C. Can the reader easily follow the ideas presented in the essay?

EXERCISE 13   Use the questions above to analyze the following student essay. Where should the student revise the essay? Make specific suggestions about the types of revision the student should make. Compare your comments to those of other students. Finally, revise the essay yourself.

There are many memorable places that captivate one's mind from time to time. One of the most memorable places to me is a secluded place located in my elementary school's yard. When I was in elementary school, my friends and I used to meet every day after school to decide our plans for that afternoon; our meetings took place at a beautiful, small bridge next to the school yard.

The bridge, which is a footbridge, spans a man-made creek. It unites the neighborhood, in which most of the students live, with the school. The bridge is made of concrete and seems as if it has been standing for many years. It extends approximately thirty-five feet long and hangs ten feet above the water. Two green, solid-metal railings guard each side of the bridge. Both railings are constructed with three parallel bars running the length of the bridge. These guardrails are designed to prevent small children from falling into the creek.

At the foot of the neighborhood side of the bridge there is a small pathway. This pathway leads from one of the neighborhood streets to the bridge. It is made of scattered gravel and loose dirt. Trees shelter the street, and the swaying branches produce a very serene atmosphere. A few of the branches hang very low, so adults find it difficult to pass through; however children can easily run under the branches.

Once on the bridge, the view captures the winding creek. The water in the creek is shallow, and fallen leaves float downstream. Along the creek, trees are suspended over the water and throw shadows on the small bridge. The trees and bridge complement each other in forming a beautiful, relaxing scene.

At the school yard end of the bridge stands an enormous oak tree, which seems as if it has been standing longer than any of its neighbors. It looks as if kids have been playing on and around it for years. The beaten path, around the oak tree, clearly shows this. The oak tree has etchings of long-forgotten school-yard crushes.

The bridge is a beautiful sight and structure. The surroundings overwhelm the viewer, and the place is calm. But to me the bridge is a meeting place, a place where I spent many hours with my young friends. This bridge is a sentimental landmark to me. It brings back memories which have been misplaced, but not forgotten.

EXERCISE 14   Look carefully at the essay you wrote in Exercise 12. With the assistance of other students, decide what revisions would make the essay more effective. List them, and then revise the essay. Use the revision checklist as a guide.

Editing

While editing a paper, you must focus upon the individual sentences in each paragraph. At this stage, you can ensure that the sentences themselves are effective, concise, and correct. This act of "polishing" the essay gives you another chance to evaluate your essay.

Since there are many points to consider, editing, like revision, can best be accomplished in stages. You should edit each paragraph separately and read it aloud. Often the act of reading aloud will alert you to potential problems. If, for example, sentences are unclear when the paper is read aloud, then you know that you must edit them. The list below can help you edit a paper easily.

I. *Clarity*

   A. Do all of your sentences mean what they say? Or are they ambiguous?

   B. Have you used the correct words to communicate your meaning?

II. *Coherence* (See Chapter 6 in Part One.)

   A. Did you use pronouns to achieve coherence? Are any pronouns ambiguous in their reference?

   B. Did you use synonyms? Are they accurate?

   C. Did you use limited repetition to achieve coherence?

   D. Did you use sentence combining to achieve coherence?

III. *Diction* (See Chapter 7 in Part One.)

   A. Did you use specific words?

   B. Did you avoid slang, jargon, and regional expressions?

   C. Did you use clichés? Can you think of another way to express your meaning?

   D. Did you create a specific, identifiable tone through word choice? Is this tone appropriate for the intended audience?

IV. *Style* (See Chapter 8 in Part One.)

   A. Are sentences wordy?

   B. Did you use active voice and descriptive verbs?

   C. Did you subordinate ideas effectively?

   D. Did you vary your sentence structure?

V. *Correctness*

   A. Are there any fragments, run-ons, or comma splices? (See Chapters 6, 7, and 8 in Part Two.)

   B. Do subjects and verbs agree in number? (See Chapter 9 in Part Two.)

   C. Are there any unnecessary shifts in verb tense? (See Chapters 1, 2, and 3 in Part Two.)

   D. Are there any unnecessary shifts in point of view?

   E. Are your pronouns correct in case, number, and gender? (See Chapter 10 in Part Two.)

   F. Did you check marks of punctuation? Are commas, semicolons, colons, and other marks of punctuation used correctly? (See Chapters 11, 12, and 13 in Part Two.)

   G. Are words spelled correctly? (See any good dictionary.)

EXERCISE 15   Use the guidelines above to edit the following essay for sentence problems. Make
your corrections here.

When I look back on my life to see which stage of developement
has influenced my attitudes the most, I see that my childhood had a
major impact. The values and interests I picked up during this period
have stayed with me throughout my life. My love of sports and athletic
competition stem from my childhood experiences. Specifically, my family
and childhood environment have caused, to a great degree, the intense
competition and sometimes unsportsmanlike conduct that I exhibited
when I play sports.

The intensity with which I play sports has been evident since early
childhood. As a young boy, I often played different sports with my
father, and I can well remember our on-going rivalry in basketball. As I
grew taller and more skilled, I was able to beat him almost every time,
however, there were games in which the "old man" would get lucky and
beat me. I never took defeat lightly, and I usually stomped off the court
in anger after a loss. Maybe that fact that I seldom lost made defeat
harder to swallow.

Whereas my fierce competition in playing against my dad almost
reached the point of being unsportsmanlike. It certainly reached this
point when I competed with my younger brother. Since we lived in a
small community, my brother and me usually played games, such as
football, baseball, soccer, and basketball one-on-one rather than with
other boys. When we played I always won, which is not surprising considering that I was three years older than him and several inches
taller. Still, despite my obvious advantages, I never gave him an inch
and prided myself on the fact that he had never beaten me in any of
the sports we played. When he did come close to winning, I would usually go into a rage and preceded to double my efforts to defeat him.
Sometimes I even resorted to cheating to keep from losing. I did whatever it took to win, and after doing so, I would jump and holler in cele-
bration as if I had just won the World Series or the Super Bowl.

When I played sports outside of my family, I usually controlled my intensity, but must of the same behavior was displayed. I always played to win; even if I am just playing in an intramural games, and sometimes I become quite depressed when I lost. Losing also led me to do some very childish acts, such as slamming down balls and bats, yelling unmentionables, and stomping off the playing field in anger. There actions mirrored the behavior I exhibited playing against my father and brother, but now my conduct was being witnessed outside of my family.

The causes of this behavior are threefold, and all three are linked to my childhood experiences. Foremost is the competition within my family, especially with my brother. My behavior was worst when I played against him, because of my need to dominate him since I was older. I never had to accept defeat playing against my brother because I never lost. My love of sports and the great importance I placed on them also led to the intensity I exhibited. I was introduced to sports at a young age and participated in them throughout my childhood. The importance I placed on sports is linked with an underlying cause; my need to be a sports superstar. While I had done well on the teams I played on, I had never been a superstar. However, when I played against my brother I was able to dominate him and, in effect, become the star I never was. Even when I played against my peers, I always strive to be the best.

The seriousness with which I play sports has led to unfortunate results. This attitude has cause unnecessary tension and immature behavior that has, in turn, caused embarrassment. I have not set a good example for my brother and as a result, he has displayed similar actions at times. If I had played sports just for fun and not take them so seriously, then I would surely have enjoyed playing much more.

EXERCISE 16   Return to the essay you revised in Exercise 14 and edit it now for sentence-level problems. Ask others to assist you, and compare your ideas with theirs.

Proofreading

After revising and editing an essay, you must copy or type it neatly for submission. Since you may be rushed at this point, you may overlook typing errors (such as transposed letters in words), omitted words, and stray marks of punctuation. Therefore, you should proofread the final copy of the paper for such errors. Corrections can easily be made in pen, and words can be inserted neatly. (Most instructors will accept final papers with some corrections on them.) Use the following guidelines for proofreading the final copy.

1. Is each word spelled correctly? (Too often when writers proofread quickly, they see what they anticipate they will see, and they will miss simple spelling or typing errors. To break this pattern of anticipation, read the paper backwards. In this manner, you can focus on each word in isolation and easily check its spelling.)

2. Are words omitted? Or are words repeated? (Again, writers anticipate what they meant to say and misread what is actually on the paper. Read each sentence aloud slowly and carefully. Listen closely to the words. Are there any errors?)

3. Are there stray marks of punctuation? (Isolate each sentence by placing pieces of paper around it; read the sentence carefully.)

EXERCISE 17   Read the following two paragraphs of a student essay. Proofread this final copy carefully. Make any necessary corrections here:

> The running craze has reached enormous proportions in recent years. One can not help but notic the increase in the number of runners; the streets and sidewalks ahve been invaded by these fitness freak. Anumber of them are serious competitiors, entering any number of the countless races held held every week end. Of these racers, no two follow exactly the same training regiment; still all routines are based on either high-milage running or speed-oriented workouts, or a combination of the two. Each method has its benefits and drawbacks.
>
> Both training methods can be use to prepare for middle-distance and long-distance racing. Distance traiining consists running at least a couple of miles at a steady and is used to develope stamina. Speed-oriented workouts, on the other hand, involve running short distances of under one mile at a fast pace. This training is used to build spped and to simulate the final mile of a race in terms of pace and intensity.

EXERCISE 18   Make a final copy of your edited paper from Exercise 16 for submission to your instructor. Use the guidelines to proofread the copy carefully.

Writing Assignments

1. Tell about a time when your world seemed to have turned upside down. Consider the larger social implications of this event. What can others gain from your narration? Write the article for an appropriate magazine and identify the magazine's audience.

2. For a newspaper, cover a local event of some importance (such as a demonstration, a town meeting, a natural disaster, or a political rally), or narrate other activities (such as a day at the race track, a rock concert, or a sports event). Identify your audience and purpose.

3. Describe a person in his or her environment. Be specific about the qualities and characteristics of the person that are evident in this environment. Consider, for example, how you might describe a businessperson in the office, a lawyer investigating a case, or a homeless person on the street. Identify an audience and purpose for your piece.

4. Describe for a local city council the condition of a section of town that should be rehabilitated. Your purpose will be to demonstrate to the city council members that the project is worthwhile.

5. Before financial speculators commit themselves to a project, they demand market research to prove the profitability of the investment. Therefore, classify shoppers at a local mall to show your financial backers that another, more upscale mall is needed.

6. For a foreign-exchange student who has just arrived at your school, type the American student. What specific types of students does the exchange student need to understand in order to adapt to American culture?

7. Arrange interviews with several people of the same age, for example, young adults, middle-aged adults, or older adults. In the interviews, ask each person what he or she perceives to be the advantages and disadvantages of not only his or her own age but also other ages. In an essay for a sociology class, present your findings. Illustrate the age group by providing examples from your interviews.

8. Others often hold great expectations for us. Describe a time you surprised someone by surpassing his or her expectations for you. Direct the paper to the person you surprised and create a purpose for the paper.

9. Choose a task you know how to perform well. In a directional process analysis, guide a novice through the process so that he or she can complete the task by reading your instructions. Also, provide a reason for him or her to wish to learn this task.

10. Describe in an informational process analysis the method by which you compose an essay. Be as specific about your writing process as possible, and identify the type of writing you do most frequently. Your audience should be the members of your composition class; remember that your explanation may assist others in the writing process.

11. Interview a member of another generation to learn that person's views about the changes in American life during his or her lifetime, about the problems he or she identifies today in American society, and about his or her attitudes on traditions and values in American life. Compare or contrast your own views with this other person's to present this paper to the members of an introductory sociology class. (Before interviewing the other person, create specific questions that will guide the person to a discussion of his or her values.)

12. As a travel agent or travel writer, compare or contrast two vacation spots or two regions of the country for publication in a local newspaper. To prepare for this assignment, read the travel section of a local paper or national magazine.

13. Most major events in our lives (graduation, first car, first job, death of a family member) are remembered as isolated incidents; they have no before and after. Yet, of course, these events do have causes and effects. Write about an important occurrence in your life and analyze its causes and effects.

14. Students attend college, rather than getting a full-time job or enrolling in a trade school, because they expect that the college experience and a college degree will ultimately benefit them. This may be a misperception. Write an essay about the results—both good and bad—of attending college as if you were presenting college as one of several possible options to a group of high-school seniors.

15. Many words we use frequently have different meanings for others. Choose one of the following terms and define it in an essay for a specific audience: *educated, gifted, brave, adventurous,* and *humorous.*

16. Part of the American dream is to become successful. Examine several major magazines carefully and determine how each one portrays success. In an essay, define *success* for a group of foreign businesspeople who will be working in the United States.

17. There are many injustices in today's world. Limit your essay to a discussion of one injustice and your proposed course of action to remedy the injustice. Direct your piece to an appropriate audience.

18. America is a society of laws, yet many of those laws are considered misguided, unenforced, and/or poorly administered. Discuss a law you think should be changed and explain your views to your local state legislator.

19. Nearly every town in America has homeless people on its streets. For your local city council, argue that the city or state is or is not responsible for the needs of the poor.

20. Identify a campus problem that needs to be addressed. In an essay to the appropriate administrator, present your arguments concerning this issue.

The following writing assignments are based upon the photographs included in Part I.

1. Using the picture on page 21 as your guide, describe your most memorable day at a beach or lake. Focus on the sensory images created by the sun, sand, and water.

2. Examine the photograph of the cyclists on page 1 carefully. What do you notice in particular about the composition of the photo? In a short piece for your school paper, describe this section of the race.

3. In the photograph on page 23, the players are blocking a volleyball shot. Consider the techniques or skills that certain sports require. Explain these skills to a beginning player.

4. On page 41, consider the risks that the climber is taking as she moves slowly up the rock face of the mountain. Create an analogy of her risks to the ones you might take when you compose. What points of the processes are similar? Include a discussion of the rewards of taking such risks in your piece.

5. While the photograph on page 61 focuses on the player dribbling the ball, what do the expressions on the spectators' faces tell you? For a piece in the sports section of your campus newspaper, describe the reactions of the spectators to this fast break down the court.

6. In the photograph on page 85, two football teams from large universities are competing. For a group of alumni, explain the functions of college athletics at large universities.

7. Consider the photograph on page 117 carefully. Although ballet usually requires a number of people to create a dance, what are the responsibilities of an individual? How does this picture demonstrate the individual's responsibilities? In an essay, enumerate the dancer's responsibilities.

8. Compare or contrast the two styles of jumping that are demonstrated in the photograph on page 137. Provide this analysis for a sports magazine devoted to track and field events.

9. As the photograph on page 167 demonstrates, each group of athletes has its own jargon, yet often these terms are used interchangeably in other sports and in casual conversations. For a paper describing this use of metaphor, examine the terms *home run, touchdown, striking out, going the distance, fumble, covering all the angles,* or any other terms specific to a sport. Explain how these terms are used in situations outside their original sports context.

10. The photograph on page 189 juxtaposes a diver and the American flag. What is the connection of sports and patriotism? Examine the role of the Olympics as a political and athletic event.

11. Describe the picture of the windsurfer (page 21) to someone who has no experience with the sport. What can you infer about the windsurfer's characteristics and personality? What details in the picture support these inferences?

12. By examining the pictures of the volleyball players (page 23) and the football players (page 85), define *teamwork* to a group of students who are organizing a team sport.

13. Both the photographs of the weightlifter (page 167) and the diver (page 189) have flags as their backgrounds. Consider the basic elements of patriotism. Must one of these elements be self-denial, either by athletes or soldiers? Present your definition of *patriotism* to a group of new American citizens.

14. As a writer for a sports magazine, compare or contrast the pictures of the football players (page 85), the cyclists (page 1), and the basketball player (page 61). Can you distinguish a sports fan's personality by the type of sport he or she watches? In your piece, explain how each sport attracts a specific type of fan.

15. What types of people would be most likely to be windsurfers (page 21) or rock climbers (page 41)? Compare or contrast the attitudes and characteristics of these two athletes.

Grammar Review

Introduction

1. To review the parts of speech.

2. To introduce identification of subjects and verbs.

3. To introduce four basic sentence formats.

KEY CONCEPT: A sentence must fulfill two requirements:

1. It must have a subject and a verb.

2. It must express a complete thought.

Parts of Speech

There are eight parts of speech. Because most of these terms will be used throughout the book, it is helpful if you can recognize these terms.

1. **Nouns** name people, places, or things. There are two kinds of nouns: common and proper. A common noun provides a general name for a person, place, or thing; a proper noun identifies a specific person, place, or thing and is capitalized.

   Examples: The *doctor* operates daily. (*Doctor* is a common noun naming a person.)
   Captain Lewis whistled softly.
   (*Captain Lewis* is a proper noun naming a person.)

   We crossed the *valley*. (*Valley* is a common noun naming a place.)
   We saw the *Grand Canyon*.
   (The *Grand Canyon* is a proper noun naming a place.)

   The *boat* raced away. (*Boat* is a common noun naming a thing.)
   We visited the *Queen Elizabeth II*.
   (The *Queen Elizabeth II* is a proper noun naming a thing.)

   A noun can also be abstract or concrete. Abstract nouns name intangible ideas, ideals, or qualities. Concrete nouns name tangible people, places, or things. Concrete nouns can be perceived through at least one of the five senses: touch, taste, smell, sight, or sound.

   Examples: The terms *love, honor,* and *patriotism* are difficult to define precisely.
   (*Love, honor,* and *patriotism* are abstract nouns.)

The *animals* at the *zoo* pleased the *tourists.*
(*Animals, zoo,* and *tourists* are concrete nouns.)

2. **Verbs** are words that describe action or existence.

Examples: Each afternoon, the children *run, skip,* and *jump* during recess.
(*Run, skip,* and *jump* are verbs that show action.)

Ellen *seems* very happy. She *is* a certified public accountant.
(*Seems,* the present tense of the verb *seem,* and *is,* the present tense of the verb *be,* are verbs that show existence.)

In addition to describing action or existence, some forms of specific verbs can be used as *helping verbs;* these helping verbs aid the reader in determining the correct time and conditions of an action. (These helping verbs are always used with another *main verb* that shows action or describes existence.) The chart below lists a number of helping verbs that can be used to determine the time and condition of the verb *to go.*

Examples:

is going, are going	will go
was going, were going	has gone, have gone
will be going	had gone
has been going, have been going	will have gone
had been going	shall go
will have been going	did go
should have gone	may go
can go	could go
could have gone	might go
might have gone	would have gone

Although the basic action in each of the above examples is the same (*to go*), the time (present, past, and future) and the conditions (obligation, possibility, ability, emphasis, and permission) of the action change in each example.

Below is a list of the most common helping verbs:

can	is/are/am	may	shall
could	was/were	might	should
do	has/have	must	used to
does	had	ought to	will
did			would

3. **Pronouns** are words that take the place of nouns.

Examples: The pronoun *he* can take the place of the nouns *Bill, Jack,* or *man* (or any other noun that is masculine and singular).

The pronoun *they* can take the place of a number of people.

The many types of pronouns are listed below.

• Personal Pronouns

Subjective or Nominative case: I, you, he, she, it, we, they
Objective case: me, you, him, her, it, us, them
Possessive case: my, mine, your, yours, his, her, hers, its, our, ours, their, theirs

- Indefinite Pronouns

  all, anyone, anything, anybody, each, everybody, everyone, everything, no one, nobody, nothing, several, some, someone, somebody

- Relative Pronouns

  who, whom, whose, which, that, whoever, whomever, whichever

- Demonstrative Pronouns

  this, that, those, these

- Intensive/Reflexive Pronouns

  myself, yourself, himself, herself, itself, ourselves, yourselves, themselves

- Interrogative Pronouns

  who, which, whom, whose, what

4. **Adjectives** describe nouns. They tell what color, shape, size, amount, mood, or temperature a noun is.

   Examples: Our trip to the beach was marred by the *cold, gray* day.
   (The words *cold* and *gray* describe the day in terms of temperature and color.)

   The *large, octagonal,* brightly *colored* rug was a gift.
   (The words *large, octagonal,* and *colored* describe the rug in terms of its size, shape, and color.)

   NOTE: The words *a, an,* and *the* are adjectives; these three words are called articles.

5. **Adverbs** modify verbs, adjectives, or other adverbs. They tell when, where, how, and to what degree.

   Examples: The cat jumped *gracefully.*   (*Gracefully* tells how the cat jumped.)

   We have been *here before.*   (*Here* tells where, and *before* tells when.)

   She thanked him *very graciously* for the flowers.
   (*Very* tells to what degree she thanked him; *graciously* describes how she thanked him.)

6. **Conjunctions** join words or groups of words. There are three major types of conjunctions.
   Coordinate conjunctions join words, word phrases, or sentences of equal value.

   Examples: Ann *and* Hilda   (*And* joins the names of two people.)

   The girls tried to open the window, *but* it was painted shut.
   (*But* joins two sentences.)

There are seven coordinate conjunctions: *for, and, nor, but, or, yet,* and *so.*
   Subordinate conjunctions join a dependent clause (a group of words with a subject and a verb which does not make a complete thought) and an independent clause (a group of words with a subject and a verb which does form a complete thought).

   Examples: *After* the flood waters had receded, the townspeople began to remove the debris left behind.
   (*After,* a subordinate conjunction, joins the dependent clause to the independent clause, "the townspeople began to remove the debris left behind.")

The dog acted *as if* he had never seen a cat before.
(*As if,* a subordinate conjunction, joins the dependent clause to the independent clause, "The dog acted.")

Below is a list of frequently used subordinate conjunctions:

after	since	whenever
although	so that	when
as (as if)	unless	where
because	until	whether
even though	wherever	while
if		

Conjunctive adverbs (or *adverbial conjunctions*) are used with a semicolon to join two or more independent clauses to form one compound sentence.

Examples: The house was overpriced; *moreover,* the couple did not need so many rooms.
(*Moreover* joins two independent clauses.)

The couple planned a small wedding; *however,* their parents invited over two hundred friends.
(*However* joins two independent clauses.)

Below is a partial list of conjunctive adverbs:

consequently	however	otherwise
furthermore	moreover	therefore
hence	nevertheless	thus

7. **Prepositions** are used to show the relationship between a noun or a pronoun and another word in a sentence.

Examples: The island *across* the bay is owned *by* the city.
(*Across* is a preposition. It helps describe which island, and it connects *bay* and *island* to describe the location. *By* is also a preposition; it describes who owns the island.)

The thief ran *behind* the house *on* the corner.
(*Behind* is a preposition; it describes the location of the hiding place of the thief. *On* is a preposition; it identifies the location of the house.)

Here is a sample list of prepositions:

about	inside
after	outside
around	since
behind	through
below	to
during	under
due to	with

8. **Interjections** are words that are used to express strong emotions, such as anger, joy, sorrow, or surprise. Often an exclamation point comes after the interjection.

Examples: *Wow!* She won five million dollars in the weekly state lottery.
(*Wow* expresses happiness and surprise.)

Whew! It sure is hot today.
(*Whew* expresses discomfort.)

PRACTICE

Write the part of speech of each italicized word in the following sentences above the word.

1. *In* the past four years, college *tuition has risen* three times faster than the rate of inflation.

2. *Boy!* That's a *gorgeous* Maserati.

3. Alice *and* Arlene *must serve* detention for a week.

4. The air conditioner *seems* to be malfunctioning.

5. Each *society* photographer seeks to catch his subject in a *revealing* and *memorable* pose.

6. The dancers swayed *slowly* and *gracefully; however,* they did not win a prize.

7. *Although she* had walked on the moon *and* flown to Jupiter, she decided to retire from the space program.

8. *Oh my gosh!* The *kerosene* heater *has* exploded.

9. *Everyone should* complete one year of service *to* the community.

10. *Warden James* just paroled "The Shark," a *vicious mass* murderer.

11. The children *danced* and *sang before* the program ended.

12. A car *with* a blue hood and *purple* wheels has been found abandoned *by* the railroad tracks.

13. *Shyness* and introspection are the *characteristics of* an introvert.

14. *We* can go to the movies, *or* we can go *to* the beach.

15. *You* lost *my* book; *that* wasn't *very* nice.

16. *Jerome failed his* comprehensive examination, *for* he had not completed the required course work.

17. *On* our vacation this *summer,* we saw Naples *by* the sea, *Andorra near* the Pyrenees, and Oslo *at* the tip *of* a fjord.

18. Even though a thesaurus is helpful, I find a dictionary more *useful* and *informative.*

19. The kindergarten students laughed *gleefully as* they *quickly* raced *through* the tunnel.

20. "I *have been rejected* for a promotion once *too* often!" he shouted.

Check the answer key.

Subjects and Verbs

Subjects and verbs provide the core portion of a sentence, because they tell who performed an action and what the action was. **Subjects** must be nouns or pronouns. **Verbs** show action or existence. The easiest test for locating the subject and verb in a sentence is to ask these questions:

1. What is the action? or What word shows existence? The answer is the *verb.*
2. Who or what is performing the action? The answer is the *subject.*

Locate the subject and verb in the following sentence.

Example: Barry sang.

1. What is the action? *sang* (the verb)
2. Who is performing the action? *Barry* (the subject)

Sentence Formats

There are four basic sentence formats in American English. You should be able to recognize each of these, because they are used frequently. These formats give information about the construction of sentences.

1. Format 1 is **Subject/Verb.**

    Example: Teresa laughed.

    The subject is *Teresa.*
    The verb is *laughed.*

2. Format 2 is **Subject/Verb/Direct Object.**

    Example: The lawyer won the case.

    The subject is *lawyer.*
    The verb is *won.*
    The direct object, which receives the action of the verb, is *case.*

3. Format 3 has two forms:

    A. **Subject/Linking Verb/Predicate Adjective**

    Example: Grammar seems difficult.

    The subject is *grammar.*
    The linking verb, which shows existence, is *seems.*
    The predicate adjective, which modifies the subject, is *difficult.*

B. **Subject/Linking Verb/Predicate Nominative**

Example: Writing is an exercise in thought.

> The subject is *writing*.
> The linking verb is *is*.
> The predicate nominative, which renames the subject, is *exercise*.

4. Format 4 is **Subject/Verb/Indirect Object/Direct Object.**

Example: She handed him a plate.

> The subject is *she*.
> The verb is *handed*.
> The direct object is *plate*.
> The indirect object, which tells to whom the plate was handed, is *him*.

NOTE: See Chapter 4 in Part Two for further explanation of subjects, verbs, and sentence formats.

Verbs I:
The Present, Past, and Future Tenses

1. To recognize and use the basic verb tenses—past, present, and future.

2. To form correctly regular and irregular verbs in past, present, and future tenses.

3. To use a consistent and appropriate verb tense when writing.

KEY CONCEPT: To communicate accurately and effectively, a writer must know and use the correct present, past, and future tenses of the appropriate verb.

Action Verbs and Linking Verbs

Verbs are divided into two categories:

1. **Action verbs** are words that show movement. For example, *to run, to dance,* and *to see* are action verbs.
2. **Linking verbs** are verbs that do not show action. Instead, they convey existence, being, becoming, and, sometimes, one of the five senses (touch, taste, smell, hearing, or sight). For example, the verbs *to be, to seem,* and *to become* are linking verbs. Linking verbs connect, or make equal, the subject and the word after the linking verb.

NOTE: The basic verb form is the word *to* plus the basic verb—*to be, to run.* This form is called the **infinitive.** All verb forms are made from the infinitive.

PRACTICE 1

Identify the following verbs as action verbs or linking verbs.

1. to jump _____

2. to be _____

3. to drive _____

4. to dance _____

5. to seem _____

6. to become _____

7. to sing _____

8. to work _____

9. to draw _____

10. to read _____

Check the answer key.

Conjugating Verbs

In order to use the various forms of a verb correctly, you must learn to **conjugate** the verb—that is, produce its different forms from the basic form, the infinitive. You can determine the verb forms by using the following pronouns as subjects (a pronoun takes the place of a noun—a person, place, or thing):

First Person: *I* is singular (you are talking about your own actions)
we is plural (you are talking about your actions and the actions of one or more people; for example, if you wanted to substitute a pronoun for "Joe and I," you would use the pronoun *we*)

Second Person: *you* is singular (you are talking directly to another person)
you is plural (you are talking directly to two or more people)

Third Person: *he, she, it* are singular (you are talking about one other person or thing)
they is plural (you are talking about two or more people or things)

Pronouns must agree in number (the number of people, places, or things) and in gender (masculine, feminine, or neuter) with the nouns they replace.

PRACTICE 2

Substitute pronouns for the nouns listed below.

Example: Joe and I __*we*__

1. Tom _____

2. Mrs. Jones _____

3. a horse _____

4. the test _____

5. a rose _____

6. the house _____

7. Sam, Tim, and Helen _____

8. the buildings _____

9. the firefighters _____

10. Mr. Duff and I _____

Check the answer key.

When you conjugate a verb, use the following chart:

Singular	*Plural*
I _____	we _____
you _____	you _____
he, she, it _____	they _____

The Present Tense

All verb tenses indicate time. The present tense has four functions:

1. It describes what is taking place now.

    Example: The soccer player *kicks* the ball.

2. It shows an habitual action, one that is often repeated.

    Example: Each weekday morning, the children *go* to school.

3. It identifies an action that will take place in the near future.

    Example: The play *starts* in ten minutes.

4. As the historical present, it is used primarily in the analysis of a literary text. In discussing *Hamlet*, for example, a writer should not say, "Hamlet procrastinated because he doubted his father's ghost," or "Hamlet said, 'To be, or not to be. . . .' " Rather the student should write, "Hamlet *procrastinates*," or "Hamlet *says*." The historical present is used for two reasons: the text as a living entity endures beyond the date of composition, and, for the reader encountering the text, the action actually does exist in the present.

    Example: In *The Adventures of Huckleberry Finn*, Mark Twain *creates* many memorable characters.

The present tense is formed from the infinitive of the verb. **Regular verbs** follow a set pattern in the present tense. **Irregular verbs** do not follow this pattern; you must learn those verbs individually. Fortunately, most verbs are regular ones.

For example, the verb *to run* is a regular verb. Say the word aloud and use the pronoun chart for conjugation. Your conjugation of the verb *to run* in the present tense should be:

I run	we run
you run	you run
he, she, it runs	they run

Because this is a regular verb, what conclusion can you draw about the conjugation of regular verbs in the present tense? Consider where the verb changes. Which pronoun form takes a different ending? Your answer should be third-person singular (the *he, she,* or *it* form). How does that form change? It adds an *s* to the end of the verb.

You have now developed a rule for conjugating regular verbs in the present tense. The basic form of the verb does not change from the infinitive except for the third-person singular. Add *s* or *es* to the third-person singular to form this conjugation.

PRACTICE 3

Conjugate the following verbs in present tense.

1. to walk: I _____   we _____

          you _____   you _____

          he, she, it _____   they _____

2. to read: I _____   we _____

          you _____   you _____

          he, she, it _____   they _____

3. to dance: I _____   we _____

          you _____   you _____

          he, she, it _____   they _____

4. to hide: I _____   we _____

          you _____   you _____

          he, she, it _____   they _____

5. to call: I _____   we _____

          you _____   you _____

          he, she, it _____   they _____

Check the answer key.

Irregular verbs do not follow this pattern for the present tense. You must simply memorize the forms. Sometimes, if you simply say the verb and its conjugation aloud, you may recognize the forms. Two familiar irregular verbs are *to be* and *to have*. Learn the conjugations of these verbs.

to be

I <u>am</u>	we <u>are</u>
you <u>are</u>	you <u>are</u>
he, she, it <u>is</u>	they <u>are</u>

to have

I <u>have</u>	we <u>have</u>
you <u>have</u>	you <u>have</u>
he, she, it <u>has</u>	they <u>have</u>

PRACTICE 4

Fill in the blanks with the appropriate present-tense form of the verb. Use the verbs provided for the sentences.

Example: I _____ *go* _____ to school each weekday.
                             (to go)

1. He _____ to his girlfriend every day.
                (to talk)

2. Doris _____ four miles each day.
                    (to run)

3. You _____ one library book, but he _____ the one you need.
                (to have)   (to have)

4. It _____ a very hot August day.
            (to be)

5. The Allegheny Mountains _____ a lovely sight in the fall.
                                        (to be)

6. Ted and I _____ a joint checking account.
                    (to have)

7. Many thousands of people _____ the state of Kentucky.
                                        (to visit)

8. She _____ very well; her sketches _____ now on display at the
            (to draw)   (to be)
   local museum.

9. On family trips, my father _____ .
                                        (to drive)

10. Many luxuries _____ now necessities. The telephone _____
                    (to be)   (to be)
    one example.

Check the answer key.

The Past Tense

The *past tense* of verbs describes an action that took place in the past and that was completed before the present time. Look at the following sentence:

Example: Bill Rodgers *won* the New York City Marathon in 1980.

The verb *won* is in the past tense. The action took place in 1980, so it was in the past. Also, the action was completed before the current year.

Look at the following conjugations of the verbs *to walk* and *to revolve* in the past tense:

to walk

I walked	we walked
you walked	you walked
he, she, it walked	they walked

to revolve

I revolved	we revolved
you revolved	you revolved
he, she, it revolved	they revolved

Because these are regular verbs, what conclusion can you draw about how regular verbs are formed in the past tense? Both verbs add what endings? *d* or *ed*

You have now developed a rule for forming the past tense of regular verbs: add *d* or *ed* to the basic form of the verb.

PRACTICE 5

Form the past tense of the following regular verbs:

1. to dance: I _____ we _____

   you _____ you _____

   he, she, it _____ they _____

2. to pour: I _____ we _____

   you _____ you _____

   he, she, it _____ they _____

3. to mark: I _____ we _____

   you _____ you _____

   he, she, it _____ they _____

4. to paint: I _____ we _____

   you _____ you _____

   he, she, it _____ they _____

5. to call: I _____ we _____

   you _____ you _____

   he, she, it _____ they _____

Check the answer key.

Irregular verbs in the past tense are formed in a number of ways:

1. by changing the vowels in the basic verb form. For example, *to know* becomes *knew* in the past tense.
2. by changing the vowels and adding a *t*. For example, *to teach* becomes *taught* in the past tense.
3. by changing a *d* to a *t*. *To build* becomes *built* in the past tense.
4. by changing the entire form. For example, the verbs *to be, to have,* and *to do* follow no set pattern.

NOTE: If you are uncertain about the formation of a verb in the past tense, check a dictionary. Look at the following entry for the verb *to draw* from *Webster's Collegiate Dictionary.* (9th ed.).*

¹**draw** \'drȯ\ *vb* **drew** \'drü\; . . .

The second form of the verb is the past tense. Therefore, to conjugate the verb *to draw* in the past tense, one would write the following:

I drew	we drew
you drew	you drew
he, she, it drew	they drew

The following chart identifies many frequently used irregular verbs in their infinitives, past tenses, and present and past participles. (Present participles are used to form the progressive tenses. Past participles are used to form the perfect tenses. In the progressive and perfect tenses, present and past participles require helping verbs, such as *is, am, are, has, have,* or *had,* to identify the time periods. See Chapter 2 in Part Two for information on the progressive and perfect tenses.)

Infinitive	Past	Present Participle	Past Participle
1. to be	was or were	being	been
2. to become	became	becoming	become
3. to begin	began	beginning	begun
4. to bite	bit	biting	bitten
5. to blow	blew	blowing	blown
6. to break	broke	breaking	broken
7. to bring	brought	bringing	brought
8. to build	built	building	built
9. to burst	burst	bursting	burst
10. to buy	bought	buying	bought
11. to catch	caught	catching	caught
12. to choose	chose	choosing	chosen
13. to come	came	coming	come
14. to deal	dealt	dealing	dealt
15. to dive	dove (dived)	diving	dived
16. to do	did	doing	done
17. to draw	drew	drawing	drawn
18. to drink	drank	drinking	drunk
19. to drive	drove	driving	driven
20. to fall	fell	falling	fallen
21. to feel	felt	feeling	felt
22. to fly	flew	flying	flown
23. to forget	forgot	forgetting	forgotten
24. to freeze	froze	freezing	frozen
25. to go	went	going	gone

*By permission. From *Webster's Ninth Collegiate Dictionary,* © 1984 by Merriam-Webster, Inc., publisher of the Merriam-Webster ® Dictionaries.

Infinitive	Past	Present Participle	Past Participle
26. to grow	grew	growing	grown
27. to have	had	having	had
28. to hit	hit	hitting	hit
29. to hold	held	holding	held
30. to know	knew	knowing	known
31. to lay (place)	laid	laying	laid
32. to lead	led	leading	led
33. to lie (recline)	lay	lying	lain
34. to make	made	making	made
35. to read	read	reading	read
36. to ride	rode	riding	ridden
37. to ring	rang	ringing	rung
38. to rise	rose	rising	risen
39. to run	ran	running	run
40. to see	saw	seeing	seen
41. to shake	shook	shaking	shaken
42. to shrink	shrank (shrunk)	shrinking	shrunk (shrunken)
43. to sing	sang	singing	sung
44. to sink	sank	sinking	sunk
45. to sit	sat	sitting	sat
46. to speak	spoke	speaking	spoken
47. to spring	sprang	springing	sprung
48. to sting	stung	stinging	stung
49. to stride	strode	striding	strode
50. to strike	struck	striking	struck
51. to swim	swam	swimming	swum
52. to take	took	taking	taken
53. to teach	taught	teaching	taught
54. to tear	tore	tearing	torn
55. to tell	told	telling	told
56. to throw	threw	throwing	thrown
57. to wake	woke	waking	waken
58. to wear	wore	wearing	worn
59. to weave	wove	weaving	woven
60. to write	wrote	writing	written

PRACTICE 6

Fill in the blanks with the correct form of the past-tense verb. Use the verbs provided.

Example: The dog _____*ran*_____ down the street.
(to run)

1. Julie _____ the same song over and over for an hour.
(to sing)

2. Faulkner _____ many of his stories about a mythical county in Mississippi.
(to write)

3. Sherri _____ home early because she _____ ill.
   (to go)   (to feel)

4. The spring of 1987 _____ many unusual weather patterns; many states
   (to bring)

   _____ excessive rainfall and floods.
   (to experience)

5. We _____ the book *Animal Farm* by George Orwell.
   (to read)

6. Pope John Paul II _____ many countries in 1983; he _____
   (to visit)   (to go)

   to Poland and countries in Central America.

7. India _____ part of the British Empire until 1947.
   (to be)

8. The American Revolution _____ a new country into existence.
   (to bring)

9. During World War I and World War II, many Americans _____ in the
   (to enlist)

   armed services.

10. Unemployment _____ 10 percent in 1982; it subsequently
    (to reach)

    _____ to 6 percent in 1987.
    (to drop)

Check the answer key.

The Future Tense

The *future tense* indicates actions that will take place in the future. The time could be within the next few minutes: I *will begin* dinner in five minutes. Or it could be in thousands of years: In the year 3000, the world *will be* very different from what we know today.

Look at the following conjugations of the verbs *to write* (a regular verb) and *to be* (an irregular verb):

to write

I shall/will write	we shall/will write
you will write	you will write
he, she, it will write	they will write

to be

I shall/will be	we shall/will be
you will be	you will be
he, she, it will be	they will be

What pattern is followed? The word *will* is combined with the infinitive base of the verb. Thus, the rule for forming the future tense for both regular and irregular verbs is to add the word *will* to the infinitive base of the verb.

When the future tense is used to form a question, the helping verb *will* precedes the subject of the sentence and the infinitive base of the verb follows.

Example: *Will* you *meet* us for dinner tonight at the new French restaurant?

NOTE: In first-person singular and plural forms of the future tense, the word *shall* is used (for example, I *shall go* home). However, in current American English, many people prefer to use *will* in place of *shall*. When you use *will* and the *infinitive base* in first-person singular and plural forms in the future tense, you indicate a great conviction (for example, I *will go* home). This form of the future shows that you are determined to go and that you have made a definite choice.

PRACTICE 7

Supply the future-tense forms of the verbs in the following sentences. Use the verbs provided.

Example: Harry ___*will come*___ to dinner on Thursday.
(to come)

1. I _____ my homework tonight.
   (to complete)

2. Jason _____ Mary to the Senior Dance.
   (to ask)

3. _____ you _____ home tonight?
   (to be)

4. A serious runner _____ over fifty miles a week.
   (to run)

5. Before we move to Seattle, we _____ our house in Los Angeles.
   (to sell)

6. _____ they _____ their father at the airport?
   (to meet)

7. Each presidential candidate _____ across the country to gain the
   (to travel)

   voters' support.

8. The new industry _____ the town in a number of ways.
   (to benefit)

9. College _____ a testing ground for many students.
   (to be)

10. With determination and effort, students _____ academically in college.
    (to succeed)

Check the answer key.

Consistency of Verb Tenses

Since verbs indicate the time an action occurred, you should make certain that all verbs in a sentence use the appropriate tense. For example, if you are describing an event from your childhood, then you should use only the past tense. You would confuse your reader if you included future or present actions in the paragraph. Examine the following sentences with inconsistent verbs tenses and their revisions.

Example: When she *was* fifteen years old, Barbara *trains* horses.
Revision: When she *was* fifteen years old, Barbara *trained* horses.

Example: As soon as the train *arrived,* we *board* it quickly.
Revision: As soon as the train *arrived,* we *boarded* it quickly.

PRACTICE 8

Read the following paragraph carefully. Check all italicized verbs for consistent tense. Change any verb that is not consistent.

(1) My first cooking experience *was* a memorable one. (2) I *decide* to bake some chicken; not knowing what to do, I *will fumble* my way through all the steps of a recipe. (3) The end result *is* a cooked piece of rawhide; the chicken *was* so tough that it *begun* to solidify while it *cooks*. (4) Not knowing where I *went* astray, I *will scrape* the contents of my plate into the garbage can and *proceeded* to go out to dinner. (5) When I *return* home, the dirty pots, pans, and dishes *wait* to be cleaned; I *will toss* them into the sink where they *sat* for nearly a week. (6) In addition, this cooking experience *created* an aversion to doing the dishes. (7) In my house, I *will do* the dishes when I *ran* out of plates, or I can no longer find the sink. (8) In either case, I eventually *did* the dishes. (9) However, I *am* too lazy to scrub them, and into the dishwasher they *went* untouched. (10) After the dishwasher *completes* its cycle, I *will put* the clean dishes away; the dirty ones *remained* in the dishwasher for another wash. (11) Fortunately, I *will learn* to correct my cooking errors and cleaning habits.

Check the answer key.

Verbs II: The Perfect Tenses and the Progressive Forms

OBJECTIVES:	1. To recognize and use the three perfect tenses correctly.
	2. To recognize and use the six progressive verb forms correctly.
	3. To use a consistent and appropriate verb tense when writing.
KEY CONCEPT:	To communicate clearly and effectively, a writer must be able to choose the correct perfect tense or progressive form.

The Perfect Tenses

You have learned the three basic tenses that tell when an action took place—the past, the present, and the future. In addition, there are periods of time that other verb tenses cover. The perfect tenses help to describe these other times.

You now know two major forms of the verb: the infinitive and the past tense. Now, in order to conjugate the perfect tense verbs, you must use and recognize the **past participle** as the third major verb form. Consider the following examples of the verb *to see*:

1. Mike *saw* the bus. (*Saw* is the past tense of the verb *to see*; at a definite time in the past, Mike did see a particular bus.)
2. Mike *has seen* the bus. (*Seen* is the past participle of the verb *to see,* and *has* is a helping verb—it helps determine the time period; in this sentence, Mike did see a bus at some point before the present, but the tense does not indicate a particular or definite time in the past.)

Past participles are formed from the infinitive of the verb. For regular verbs, the past tense and the past participle will be the same form.

Example: to dance (infinitive)
danced (past tense)
danced (past participle)

NOTE: The past and the past participle of the verb *to dance* are formed by adding *d* or *ed* to the infinitive.

Irregular verbs, of course, take different past-participle forms. The past participles may be formed in a variety of ways:

1. add *n* or *en* to the infinitive (for example, *known* is the past participle of *to know*).
2. change the vowels in the verb form (for example, *begun* is the past participle of *to begin*).
3. change the vowels and add *n* or *en* (for example, *frozen* is the past participle of *to freeze*).
4. change the vowels and add a *t* (for example, *felt* is the past participle of the verb *to feel*).
5. change a *d* to a *t* (for example, *sent* is the past participle of *to send*).

For all cases of irregular verbs with which you are unfamiliar, check a good dictionary. The dictionary will provide the correct form of the past participle.

PRACTICE 1

Complete the chart below by forming the past and the past participle of the given verbs.

Infinitive	Past	Past Participle
Example: to swim	*swam*	*swum*

Infinitive	Past	Past Participle
1. to dive		
2. to sing		
3. to write		
4. to fly		
5. to drink		
6. to steal		
7. to teach		
8. to learn		
9. to give		
10. to receive		

Check the answer key.

The Present Perfect Tense

The present perfect tense indicates one of two conditions:

1. that at an undetermined time in the past, an action took place.

   Example: He *has gone* to his grandmother's many times.
   Can you give a specific time when he went?

2. that an action took place in the past and is continuing in the present.

Example: He *has attended* this school for two years.
He obviously started in the past, and he is presently a student.

The **present perfect tense** is formed by using *has* or *have* (the present tense of the verb *to have*) and the past participle of the verb. Your use of *has* or *have* is determined by the noun. If it is third-person singular, use *has*. If it is plural or first- or second-person singular, then use *have*. Consider the following conjugation of the verb *to walk* in the present perfect tense:

I have walked	we have walked
you have walked	you have walked
he, she, it has walked	they have walked

EXERCISE   Write the rule for forming the present perfect tense:

_____

_____

Have your instructor or tutor check your work.

PRACTICE 2

Fill in the blanks with the correct form of the present perfect tense of the verb. Use only the verbs given.

Example: He ___*has strolled*___ down this street many times.
(to stroll)

1. I _____ a good school year.
(to have)

2. Terry _____ to Europe several times.
(to be)

3. In presidential campaigns, foreign policy _____ a major issue between
(to be)
the two candidates.

4. They _____ us many times.
(to visit)

5. He _____ a fine young man.
(to become)

6. Women _____ many of the rights they fought for during the 1960s and
(to receive)
1970s.

7. Stella _____ the dress she wanted.
(to buy)

8. He _____ in several marathons.
   (to race)

9. Mary and I _____ the movie *Psycho* four times.
   (to see)

10. Students _____ for the fall semester at the college.
    (to enroll)

Check the answer key.

The Past Perfect Tense

The past perfect tense describes a time in the past that occurred before another past action.

> **Example:** Bob *had passed* his examination before he received his license.
> By the time he received his license (an action that took place in the past), he had already passed the exam (an action that took place *before* he got the license).

Examine this sentence and explain the time sequence:

> **Example:** After he *had run* ten miles, he *fainted.*
> Which past action occurred first? *had run*
> Which past action occurred last? *fainted*

The rule for forming the past perfect tense is a simple one: use *had* and the *past participle*. Here is the conjugation of the verb *to drive* in the past perfect tense:

I had driven	we had driven
you had driven	you had driven
he, she, it had driven	they had driven

PRACTICE 3

Fill in the blanks with the correct form of the past perfect tense of the verb. Use the verbs given.

1. If he _____ home, we would have visited him.
   (to be)

2. When the teacher _____ the lesson, the class applauded.
   (to finish)

3. After the bank teller _____ the transaction, the robbers left.
   (to complete)

4. The lawyer _____ his star witness before the defendant confessed.
   (to call)

5. Before the bomb could have exploded, the police officers _____ it.
   (to defuse)

6. Before the referee blew his whistle, he _____ the foul.
   (to determine)

7. After the star basketball player _____ his foul shot, the crowd in the gym exploded.
   (to make)

8. After the college students _____ their tour of London, they boarded a train to Scotland.
   (to complete)

9. The student _____ his topic before he began to write his essay.
(to choose)

10. After we _____ the heavy chest upstairs, we decided that it was too
(to move)

large for the small room.

Check the answer key.

Future Perfect Tense

The future perfect tense tells about a future event that will have been completed before another event. Look at the following sentence:

Example: I *will have worked* for three months by the time I start school this fall.

Both actions will take place in the future. Which action will be completed first? *will have worked*. This action must be in the future perfect tense.

The rule for forming the future perfect tense is simple: add *will have* or *shall have* to the *past participle of the verb*. Here is the verb *to go* in the future perfect tense:

I will have gone	we will have gone
you will have gone	you will have gone
he, she, it will have gone	they will have gone

NOTE: See "The Future Tense" in Chapter 1, Part Two, for a discussion of *shall* and *will*.

PRACTICE 4

Fill in the blanks with the correct form of the future perfect tense of the verb. Use only the verbs given.

1. The satellite _____ in orbit for five years before its power source is
(to be)

depleted.

2. The archaeologists _____ for seven years at the dig before they un-
(to work)

cover the first layer of the forgotten city.

3. By the end of the week, Kerri _____ her project.
(to finish)

4. When he completes graduate school, he _____ in school continuously
(to be)

for twenty years.

5. By the year 2000, Disneyworld _____ over three billion visitors.
(to welcome)

6. Professor Abbot _____ for thirty years by the end of this semester.
(to teach)

7. Sheila _____ the novel *Crime and Punishment* by Friday.
(to read)

8. By July, the North Carolina Outer Banks _____ their four hundredth
   (to celebrate)

   anniversary.

9. By March, the architects _____ their proposals for the new city hall.
   (to submit)

10. When he wins his 300th game, the pitcher _____ about 10,000
    (to throw)

    baseballs.

Check the answer key.

The Progressive Forms

The progressive forms of verbs indicate an action that is, was, or will be in progress. The progressive form requires a present participle as the base of the form. The present participle is formed by adding *ing* to the infinitive base. For example, *jumping* is the present participle of *to jump*.

EXERCISE   Form the present participle of the following verbs.

1. to hop _____

2. to sleep _____

3. to become _____

4. to honk _____

5. to work _____

Have your instructor or tutor check your work.

The progressive forms exist in the present, past, and future. The forms are constructed by adding the appropriate form of the verb *to be* to the present participle.

Look at the following conjugations of the verb *to show*:

- **Present Progressive** (The action is taking place now.)

I am showing	we are showing
you are showing	you are showing
he, she, it is showing	they are showing

  NOTE: Use the *present* tense of the verb *to be* to form the present progressive.

- **Past Progressive** (The action was taking place in the past.)

I was showing	we were showing
you were showing	you were showing
he, she, it was showing	they were showing

  NOTE: Use the *past* tense of the verb *to be* to form the past progressive.

- **Future Progressive** (The action will be taking place in the future.)

I will be showing	we will be showing
you will be showing	you will be showing
he, she, it will be showing	they will be showing

NOTE: Use the *future* tense of the verb *to be* to form the future progressive.

The three perfect tenses—the past perfect, the present perfect, and the future perfect—also have progressive forms. These perfect progressive forms follow the rules of the perfect tense (in telling when an action occurred) and the progressive (an action in progress).

Here are the conjugations of the verb *to practice* in the perfect progressive forms. These are also constructed by adding the appropriate form of the verb *to be* (to indicate the time) to the present participle:

- **Present Perfect Progressive** (The action began in the past and continues to the present; this form stresses the continuing action.)

I have been practicing	we have been practicing
you have been practicing	you have been practicing
he, she, it has been practicing	they have been practicing

Example: The band *has been practicing* for five weeks for the state contest.

- **Past Perfect Progressive** (The action in progress was completed in the past before another event.)

I had been practicing	we had been practicing
you had been practicing	you had been practicing
he, she, it had been practicing	they had been practicing

Example: I *had been practicing* my violin when Mother told me to stop.

- **Future Perfect Progressive** (The action will continue into the future and be completed before another future action.)

I will have been practicing	we will have been practicing
you will have been practicing	you will have been practicing
he, she, it will have been practicing	they will have been practicing

Example: We *will have been* practicing our songs for three weeks before the contest begins.

PRACTICE 5

Complete the progressive forms of the verbs indicated below.

1. The present progressive of *to ask*   I _____

2. The past perfect progressive of *to do*   They _____

3. The future progressive of *to sing*   We _____

4. The present perfect progressive of *to hit*   He _____

5. The future perfect progressive of *to deal*   You _____

6. The past progressive of *to swim*   They _____

Check the answer key.

PRACTICE 6

Fill in the blanks with the correct progressive forms of the verbs indicated. Pay particular attention to the time sequence; the time will tell you which tense to use.

1. We _____ for four hours when the fireworks begin.
   (to dance)

2. He _____ his work now.
   (to complete)

3. She _____ the dog when the phone rang.
   (to bathe)

4. The lawyer _____ on this case for two years.
   (to work)

5. Jean _____ to her grandmother's house since she was five.
   (to go)

6. The guests _____ soon.
   (to leave)

7. Last year, she _____ on her law degree; this year, she
   (to work)

   _____ law.
   (to practice)

8. The toaster _____ not _____ properly; I _____ my toast
   (to work)   (to burn)

   every morning for the past week.

9. Last year, Harold _____ for a city council post; this year, he
   (to run)

   _____ a concession stand at the stadium.
   (to operate)

10. The college football team _____ its rivals next week.
    (to play)

Check the answer key.

Helping Verbs

As you have seen in the perfect tenses and progressive forms, some verbs have a dual function. When acting alone, they describe action or existence; when acting as part of a verb phrase, they help the reader correctly determine the time frame, conditions, and tone (in some tenses) of an action. When they act as **helping verbs,** these verbs will precede the main verb.

Helping Verbs (Condition)

meaning	*verb*	*tense*	*example*
able to	can could	present past	I can pay I could pay, I could have paid
permitted to	may might	present past	I may pay I might pay, I might have paid
expected to	shall should	present past	I shall pay I should pay, I should have paid
willing to	will would	present past	I will pay I would pay, I would have paid

Helping Verbs (Time and Tone)

helping verb	*tense*	*example*
has, have	present perfect	I have swum He has swum
had	past perfect	He had swum
shall, will	future perfect	I shall have swum He will have swum
am, is, are	present progressive	I am swimming He is swimming They are swimming
was, were	past progressive	I was swimming They were swimming
will be	future progressive	He will be swimming
has been, have been	present perfect progressive	He has been swimming They have been swimming
had been	past perfect progressive	He had been swimming
will have been	future perfect progressive	He will have been swimming

Helping Verbs (Time and Tone)

helping verb	tense	example
do, does	present emphatic	I do swim He does swim
did	past emphatic	He did swim

PRACTICE 7

Fill in the blank with the verb and tense that are requested in the parentheses.

1. My mother told me that I _____ with my cousin at least once tonight. (conditional past tense of *to dance*)

2. This professor _____ at the college for over thirty years. (present perfect progressive of *to teach*)

3. The candidate _____ to correct the misstatements in his résumé. (present emphatic of *to plan*)

4. The infant _____ across the floor to retrieve his favorite toy. (past perfect of *to crawl*)

5. Her counselor indicated that she _____ able to take physics if she wanted to, but she opted for a calculus course instead. (past tense of *to be*)

6. The patient _____ well after surgery, but then his condition deteriorated. (past perfect progressive of *to do*)

7. Even though the patient died, let us remember that he _____ for over one hundred days with an artificial liver. (past emphatic of *to live*)

8. By the time he qualifies for the Olympic team, Charles _____ for more than ten years. (future perfect progressive of *to compete*)

9. If the party _____ me, I would have been proud to serve in the office. (past perfect of *to nominate*)

10. She _____ the committee's draft report. (present perfect of *to accept*)

Check the answer key.

Consistency of Verb Tenses

Verb tenses should be consistent in most cases. Because verb tenses show time, it is important that they express exactly what time you wish to describe. For example, if you are writing about an event that occurred in the past, use the past tense. Imagine how confused your reader would be if he read a sentence like this:

Example: Tomorrow, the pilot *flew* the plane.

   When is the action taking place? The verb *flew* is the past tense form of *to fly*, yet the time is *tomorrow*.

With this confusion corrected, the sentence would read:

Example: Tomorrow, the pilot *will fly* the plane.

When you write a paragraph or an essay, make sure that the verb forms you use are in the same tense, or time period.

PRACTICE 8

Make the verb tenses of the underlined verbs consistent. Use the first verb in the sentence as your guide. If it is present tense, make the second verb present tense, also. If it is past tense, make the second verb past tense, also.

Example: When I ran home, I ~~find~~ *found* the front door open.

1. Before he called Alice to ask her for a date, he takes a deep breath.

2. As the band marched onto the football field, the football players are still on the gridiron.

3. College offers many activities to students, yet many students failed to take advantage of the extracurricular activities.

4. The mechanic tested the car's engine, only to find that it is not working.

5. Dreiser's novel *An American Tragedy* was written in 1925; the same year, Fitzgerald's novel *The Great Gatsby* is published.

6. The typewriter will become obsolete one day because the word processor replaced it.

7. When the football player caught the ball, he turns to look at his coach.

8. After the photographer took the picture, he will develop the film.

9. Before the Olympic Games begin, many thousands of athletes arrived in Seoul.

10. The train trip across Canada took so many days that we will miss our appointment in Seattle, Washington.

Check the answer key.

PRACTICE 9

Read the following paragraph carefully. Check the italicized verbs for consistent tense. Change any verb that is not consistent.

(1) "If I had been able to study, I *will have passed* the test," exclaims a distraught teenager. (2) "But I *do* not *have* a sufficient amount of time." (3) All parents *have heard* this excuse at one time or another. (4) Helping teenagers become mature, responsible adults *was* a difficult job. (5) Unfortunately, some parents do not succeed, but that it is not because they *had* not *tried*. (6) They diligently read books and articles on the topic; they faithfully *attended* parenting classes, and they regularly set aside "quality time" for family discussions. (7) But all their efforts *have been* in vain. (8) Some people *managed* to cross the threshold into so-called adulthood even though they are still self-indulgent, egocentric, and petty.

Check the answer key.

Verbs III: The Finer Points—Voice, Mood, Verbals, and Style

| | OBJECTIVES: | 1. To recognize transitive and intransitive verbs in context. |
| | | 2. To recognize and use active and passive voice. |

OBJECTIVES:

1. To recognize transitive and intransitive verbs in context.
2. To recognize and use active and passive voice.
3. To recognize the three moods of verbs.
4. To recognize and use verbals—infinitives, gerunds, and participles.
5. To use verbs in developing writing style.

KEY CONCEPT: To communicate effectively, the writer must choose the proper voice and mood for the verb used, learn to use verbal forms when needed, and use verbs to develop an effective style.

Transitive and Intransitive Verbs

Consider a typical English sentence:

Example:

subject verb object
Helen wrote a paper.

The sentence moves from *Helen* (the subject, who performed the action) to the verb *wrote* (the action) to *paper* (the object that received the action, or what was written).

In the first chapter on verbs, you learned that there are two types of verbs: action verbs and linking verbs. Action verbs can be further divided into transitive and intransitive verbs. Linking verbs are always intransitive.

Transitive Verbs

A **transitive verb,** such as *build,* has an object. The transitive verb's action is transferred from the subject to the object, as we saw in the sentence *Helen wrote a paper.* To test for transitive verbs, simply ask, "What receives the action of the verb?" or "What was acted upon (in this case, what was written)?" For your use, substitute the verb in your sentence. Test the following sentence:

Example: Jerry threw the ball.

The subject (the actor) is *Jerry.*
The verb (the action) is *threw.*
What was thrown? *ball.* So, *ball* is the object of the verb *threw,* a transitive verb.

Intransitive Verbs

An **intransitive verb** does not have an object.

Example: She laughed.

> The subject (the actor) is *She*.
> The verb (the action) is *laughed*.
> But there is no word to receive the action, so there is no object; therefore, the verb *laughed* is intransitive.

PRACTICE 1

Determine whether the following italicized verbs are transitive or intransitive.

Example: Captain Williams *caught* a shark. _____*transitive*_____

1. He *caught* a fish. _____

2. Susie *swam*. _____

3. The choir *sang* an opera. _____

4. He *drove* the car. _____

5. The children *cleared* the table. _____

6. It *rained*. _____

7. Sara *baked* a cake. _____

8. The gorilla *frightened* the child. _____

9. Steve *jumped*. _____

10. The goat *climbed*. _____

Check the answer key.

The same verb can be transitive or intransitive, depending upon how it is used in the sentence.

Example: The four-year-old child *acts* like an adult. (*Acts* is intransitive; there is no word that receives the action.)

He *acted* the role of Othello. (*Acted*, in this case, is transitive; *role* is the object—it receives the action of the verb.)

NOTE: Check a dictionary if you are unsure whether a verb is transitive or intransitive. A good dictionary will list the word and categorize it. Here is an entry from *Webster's Dictionary*:

> ²**act** *vt* [verb transitive] . . . **1** *obs*: ACTUATE, ANIMATE **2a:** to represent or perform by action esp. on the stage . . . *vi* [verb intransitive] **1a:** to perform on the stage. . . .*

Voice

Transitive verbs have voice. A transitive verb can have either active or passive voice. A transitive verb with **active voice** will carry the action to an object. The subject actually performs the action of the verb. Look at this sentence:

Example:
subject verb object
Ted played tennis.

Ted is the subject, and he is also the actor.

Examine this sentence:

Example:
subject   verb   object
Jane is playing basketball.

Does *Jane* (the subject) actually perform the action? If the subject performs the action, then the verb is in active voice. In this case, the verb, *is playing,* is active.

A transitive verb with **passive voice** will not carry the action forward to an object. Instead, the subject will be acted upon:

Example: The ball *was caught* by Bill.

The subject of the sentence is *ball.* But did the ball perform the action of the verb? No, it was simply caught. Bill, the person who caught the ball, is not the subject. Instead, the actor, Bill, has been placed in a prepositional phrase. Actually, the normal order of the sentence (subject-verb-object) has been reversed. The action of the verb moves backwards to *ball*, not forward as in active voice. In fact, the sentence could easily be rewritten in normal order:

Example: Bill caught the ball.

In most cases, the active voice is more powerful and more realistic than the passive voice. The reason for this is simple: in a sentence with active voice, the subject *performs* the action of the verb. In a sentence with passive voice, the subject *receives* the action of the verb, a job usually performed by the object of the sentence.

---

*By permission. From *Webster's Ninth New Collegiate Dictionary,* © 1984 by Merriam-Webster, Inc., publisher of the Merriam-Webster Dictionaries.

However, there are two cases in which the passive voice is the better choice:

1. when you don't know who performed an action.

   Example: The door was slammed.

   This sentence indicates that you do not know who slammed the door.

2. when, for whatever reason, you do not wish to disclose the name of the actor.

   Example: The report was submitted late.

   In this case, the author of the report does not want to admit that he submitted the paper after the deadline.

PRACTICE 2

Change the following passive verbs to active ones.

Example: The report *was delivered* by David.

Correction: David __*delivered*__ the report.

1. The announcement *was made* by John.

   John _____ the announcement.

2. The horse *was saddled* by the jockey.

   The jockey _____ the horse.

3. Birthday presents *were received* by the child.

   The child _____ birthday presents.

4. The radio station *was changed* by me.

   I _____ the radio station.

5. The dinner *was cooked* by the gourmet chef.

   The gourmet chef _____ the dinner.

6. The fire *was lit* by Sam.

   Sam _____ the fire.

7. The proclamation *was announced* by the president.

   The president _____ the proclamation.

8. A new law *was passed* by Congress.

   Congress _____ a new law.

9. The ruling *was made* by the Supreme Court.

The Supreme Court _____ the ruling.

10. The gift *was given* by my aunt.

My aunt _____ the gift.

Check the answer key.

Transitive verbs can be conjugated in passive voice through all the tenses. Compare the following conjugations of the verb *to give* in active and passive voice.

	Active Voice	*Passive Voice*
Present	gives/give	am/is/are given
Past	gave	was/were given
Future	will give	will be given
Present Perfect	has/have given	has/have been given
Past Perfect	had given	had been given
Future Perfect	will have given	will have been given
Present Progressive	am/is/are giving	am/is/are being given
Past Progressive	was/were giving	was/were being given
Future Progressive	will be giving	will be being given
Present Perfect Progressive	has/have been giving	has/have been being given
Past Perfect Progressive	had been giving	had been being given
Future Perfect Progressive	will have been giving	will have been being given

PRACTICE 3

Change the following active verbs to passive voice; use the same verb tense given in the sentences.

Example: I *gave* the present.

Correction: The present _*was given*_____ by me.

1. He *will give* the speech.

The speech _____ by him.

2. The Joneses *sent* the roses.

The roses _____ by the Joneses.

3. James *had driven* the car.

   The car _____ by James.

4. The major *will have commanded* the troops.

   The troops _____ by the major.

5. I *wrote* the report.

   The report _____ by me.

Check the answer key.

Mood

Verbs are classified also by mood. There are three moods: indicative, imperative, and subjunctive.
   The **indicative mood** makes a statement.

Example: I *ran* home.

The indicative mood is most frequently used. In fact, almost all the verbs in the book have been in the indicative mood.

   The **imperative mood** expresses a command or a request.

Example: Please *close* the door.

   The **subjunctive mood** has been replaced in everyday spoken English, for the most part, by the indicative mood. However, the present and past tenses of the subjunctive mood are still valuable in expressing certain concepts, and the subjunctive mood is required in formal writing.
   The present tense of verbs in the subjunctive mood is conjugated the same throughout the form. The present subjunctive is the same as the infinitive. The present subjunctive is used rarely and only in conjunction with verbs of insistence (verbs like *demand, insist, require,* and *request*). In the sentence construction, the speaker demands that someone complete an action.
   Here is the present-tense conjugation of the verb *to be* in the subjunctive mood:

I be	we be
you be	you be
he, she, it be	they be

Examples: John requires that we *be* on time.
   The president demands that all citizens *be* registered voters.
   It is necessary that Mary *be* ready at five o'clock exactly.

The past subjunctive is formed from the past tense of a verb. The verb used most frequently in the past subjunctive is the verb *to be*. Look at the past subjunctive of the verb *to be*:

I were	we were
you were	you were
he, she, it were	they were

The past subjunctive is used in one of two cases:

1. *To express a situation contrary to fact.* Use an *If . . . then* sentence construction.

    Example: If I *were* a millionaire, then I would buy a huge estate.

    The implication is obvious: I am not a millionaire. This use of the past subjunctive shows that the premise (the phrase following *If*) is not true.

2. *To express a wish.* Use a sentence construction that includes a verb that expresses a wish, hope, or desire.

    Example: I wish that it *were* Saturday.

    The statement was made on a day other than Saturday. The speaker wants the weekend to come.

PRACTICE 4

Insert the correct form of the subjunctive of the verb *to be* into the following sentences.

1. I wish that Mary _____ here.

2. If Tom _____ a scientist, then he would qualify as an astronaut.

3. My job demands that I _____ at work at 5:00 a.m.

4. The senator requests that aides _____ at the briefing.

5. If you _____ the instructor, then I know you would correct the problems.

Check the answer key.

Verbals

Infinitives, gerunds, and participles are derived from verbs and are used frequently. These verbals and verbs share some characteristics. For example, verbals can describe actions and have objects. Verbals also can describe states of existence and have subject complements. However, these verbals are *not* the verbs in sentences. Instead, verbals act as different parts of speech.

Infinitives

You should recognize these as the basic form of verbs. The infinitive consists of the word *to* plus the verb. An infinitive can function as a noun (a person, place, or thing), an adverb (modifies a verb, adverb, or adjective), or an adjective (modifies a noun or pronoun).

Consider the following sentences:

Examples: 1. *To run* is my favorite sport.
    To run is a noun used as the subject of the sentence.

2. His desire *to eat too much* made him gain weight.
The infinitive phrase *to eat too much* is used as an adjective; it describes his desire.

3. She ran *to see who was at the door*.
The infinitive phrase *to see who was at the door* is used as an adverb; it tells why she ran.

EXERCISE Underline the infinitives and the infinitive phrases in each of the following sentences. Identify each infinitive by its part of speech: noun, adjective, or adverb.

1. To become a good pianist, you must practice an hour each day.

2. His ability to run quickly made him an excellent sprinter.

3. Terrance hopes to travel to Europe next summer.

4. To enjoy a visit to another country, you should be willing to explore the country's cities and to visit historical sites.

5. Our trip to the library allowed us to complete our research.

Have your instructor or tutor check your work.

Gerunds

A gerund is used frequently. It is made by adding *ing* to the verb. A gerund has only one function: it serves as a noun. The words *rowing, sailing,* and *hiking* in the following sentences are all gerunds and used as nouns.

Examples:
1. *Sailing* is a favorite sport on the Gulf of Mexico.
Sailing is a gerund and is used as the subject of the sentence.

2. The campers enjoyed *rowing, hiking, sailing,* and *backpacking*.
The words *rowing, hiking, sailing,* and *backpacking* are all gerunds used as objects of the verb.

EXERCISE Underline the gerunds and gerund phrases in each of the following sentences. Identify each gerund by its part of speech.

1. Many adventurous tourists enjoy rafting down the Colorado River.

2. Hiking the length of the Appalachian Trail requires at least six months.

3. Wind surfing has become a popular sport.

4. Many actors and actresses like preparing for the annual *Circus of the Stars*.

5. Many people appreciate picnicking on warm spring days.

Have your instructor or tutor check your work.

Participles

A participle is a verbal used only as an adjective to modify a noun or pronoun.

A **present participle** is made from the verb and *ing*. You constructed these when you studied the progressive forms of verbs. Although a present participle and a gerund are constructed in the same manner, you can tell them apart. Remember that a gerund is used solely as a noun, and a participle is used only as an adjective.

Examples: 1. People of all ages enjoy *dancing.*
               Dancing is a gerund, a noun.

             2. *Dancing* gracefully, they won the audience's heart.
               In this sentence, *dancing* is the present participle of the verb *to dance*; it describes the subject *they.*

You have already seen past participles when you constructed the perfect tenses of verbs. The past participle is the form of the verb that follows *has* or *have* and *had*. A past participle is usually made from the verb and *d* or *ed*. However, past participles derived from irregular verbs do not follow this rule. To review the formation of irregular past participles, check the list of the various formations in "The Perfect Tenses," Chapter 2, Part Two.

The participle, present or past, is used as an adjective to describe a noun or pronoun. Look at the following sentences:

Examples: 1. He is a well-*known* author.
               Known is the past participle of the verb *to know*; it modifies *author.*

             2. After *hitting* the ball, she ran to first base.
               The participial phrase *After hitting the ball* modifies the subject *she*; it tells what she did.

             3. The baseball, *hit* by Mickey Mantle, sailed over the outfield wall.
               The participial phrase *hit by Mickey Mantle* describes the baseball by telling who hit it.

NOTE: By themselves, present and past participles cannot be the verbs in sentences; instead, these participles will modify nouns or pronouns. However, present and past participles are used to construct the perfect tenses and the progressive forms of verbs. In this usage, the participles are preceded by helping verbs, such as *am, is, are, have, has,* or *had*. Review the conjugations of the perfect tenses and the progressive forms in Chapter 2, Part Two.

EXERCISE   Underline the participles and participial phrases in each of the following sentences. Identify each participle by its part of speech.

1. Sharon is an accomplished pianist; she recently won the coveted Prix de France.

2. Jumping for joy, the children raced to the entrance of the amusement park.

3. The recently injured man applied for government benefits.

4. Listening intently to the radio, Jules failed to hear the ringing telephone.

5. The steaming soup quickly boiled over the sides of the pot.

Have your instructor or tutor check your work.

PRACTICE 5

Identify all verbal phrases in the sentences by circling them, and label each type of verbal. The verbs in the sentence have been identified for you; they are in italic type.

Example: Roller (skating) *is* great fun.   _____ *a gerund* _____

1. To earn an A on the test *is* my goal.   _____

2. Their mother, a noted scientist, *received* the Nobel Prize.   _____

3. Driving to the store, I *saw* an old friend.   _____

4. He *wants* to earn extra money this summer.   _____

5. Water skiing *is* a marvelous way to spend a summer afternoon.   _____

6. The child playing in the yard *is* Hank's brother.   _____

7. We *took* a well-deserved vacation.   _____

8. Shakespeare's famous line "To be, or not to be" *is* often *quoted*.   _____

9. The middle-aged man *enjoyed* photographing birds.   _____

10. He *enjoys* his job of ringing the church bells.   _____

11. Dashing to the finish line, Jenny *placed* first in the 800-meter race.

_____

12. After receiving her bachelor's degree, Carrie *plans* to attend law school.

_____

13. Typing the final word, the novelist *finished* her first work.   _____

14. To dance the limbo, you *must* be very flexible.   _____

15. The couple *planned* to see a movie, dine at a good restaurant, and dance until midnight.   _____

16. The quarterback, fading back for a pass, *was hit* by the rushing tackles.

_____

17. Pivoting quickly, the band members *marched* past the parade judge.

_____

18. The feuding families *decided* to settle their differences in court.   _____

19. Building a fire *requires* effort, skill, and a little luck.   _____

20. Frank *enjoys* camping and biking as his hobbies.   _____

Check the answer key.

Style

Verbs are the core portion of a sentence. Therefore, they are vitally important when you write a sentence, a paragraph, or an essay. The following guidelines will help you when you write:

1. *Use action verbs.* These convey more movement than the linking verbs. They also convey a visual image, much more so than the verb *to be.* Compare these sentences:

   Examples: The horse *was* in the pasture.
   The horse *grazed* in the pasture.

   Which verb gives a better image of the scene? *grazed,* the action verb.

2. *Use active voice in preference to the passive voice.* The active voice conveys action from the subject (the actor) to the object (the receiver of the action). In other words, the subject fulfills its function—to act. Compare these two sentences:

   Examples: a. The article was written by Ms. Abrams.
   b. Ms. Abrams wrote the article.

   Which is the stronger sentence? *b*

3. *Keep verb tense consistent.* Do not confuse your reader by changing tenses unnecessarily.

4. *To give a clear, visual image, use more verbs and verbals than adjectives.*

Subjects, Verbs, and Prepositional Phrases

Subjects

A sentence must have a subject. A **subject** is a *noun* (a person, place, or thing) or a *pronoun* (a word that takes the place of a noun).

Types of Nouns

A **proper noun** names a specific person, place, or thing. It is always capitalized.

Examples: *Mr. Smith, Professor Thomas, New York City, Ford.*

A **common noun** names an object, place, or person. It does *not* name a *specific* object, place, or person.

Examples: *dog, animal, tree.*

A **concrete noun** names anything you can perceive through one of the five senses—touch, taste, smell, hearing, or sight.

Examples: *chair, room, ball, wind, music, paint.*

An **abstract noun** names an emotion, quality, or idea. You cannot perceive this noun through one of the five senses.

Examples: *love, hate, anger, philosophy.*

A **collective noun** names a group of individuals.

Examples: *army, jury, team, committee.*

Types of Pronouns

A **pronoun** takes the place of a noun.

Example: Meredith went to the movies; she saw the Bogart movie *The African Queen.*
In this sentence, *she* is a pronoun that takes the place of the proper noun *Meredith.*

Each of the following pronouns could be used as the subject of a sentence:

Personal pronouns: *I, you, she, he, it, we, you, they*

Indefinite pronouns: *everyone, everybody, somebody, someone, each, nobody, no one, none, anybody, anyone, some, all, several*

PRACTICE 1

a. List five proper nouns:

1. _____

2. _____

3. _____

4. _____

5. _____

b. List five common nouns:

1. _____

2. _____

3. _____

4. _____

5. _____

c. List five concrete nouns:

1. _____

2. _____

3. _____

4. _____

5. _____

d. List five abstract nouns:

1. _____

2. _____

3. _____

4. _____

5. _____

e. List five collective nouns:

1. _____

2. _____

3. _____

f. List five pronouns:

1. _____

2. _____

3. _____

4. _____   4. _____

5. _____   5. _____

Have your instructor or tutor check your work.

Verbs

A sentence also must contain a **verb.** There are two types of verbs:

1. **Action** verbs are words that show movement. For example, *to sing, to joke, to run,* and *to walk* are action verbs.

2. **Linking** verbs are verbs that do not show action. Instead, they convey existence, being, becoming, and sometimes, one of the five senses. For example, the verbs *to be, to seem, to appear,* and *to become* are linking verbs. Linking verbs connect, or make equal, the subject and the word after the linking verb.

PRACTICE 2

a. List five action verbs: b. List three linking verbs:

1. _____   1. _____

2. _____   2. _____

3. _____   3. _____

4. _____

5. _____

Have your instructor or tutor check your work.

Identifying Subjects and Verbs

The easiest way to identify the subject and verb in a sentence is to ask these questions:

- What is the action? or What word links two or more other words? the *verb.*
- Who or what is performing the action? the *subject.*

Examples: 1. Barbara sang.

What is the action? *sang* (verb)
Who sang? *Barbara* (subject)

2. Robert leaped.

What is the action? *leaped* (verb)
Who leaped? *Robert* (subject)

PRACTICE 3

Identify the subjects and verbs in the sentences below.

1. Terry laughs.

   verb _____

   subject _____

2. Children play.

   verb _____

   subject _____

3. The bullet hit the target.

   verb _____

   subject _____

4. I swam.

   verb _____

   subject _____

5. The doctor fainted.

   verb _____

   subject _____

Check the answer key.

Simple and Compound Subjects and Verbs

If a sentence has only one subject, it is called a **simple subject.** If the sentence has only one verb, it is called a **simple verb.** However, a sentence may also contain a **compound subject** (two or more nouns—singular or plural—or pronouns performing the same action) and/or a **compound verb** (two or more actions that the subject performs). The three possible combinations of simple and compound subjects and verbs follow.

Compound Subject/Simple Verb. In this case, two or more subjects perform one action.

Example: George and Frank went to Mexico.

What is the action? *went*
Who went? *George* and *Frank*

In this sentence, both *George* and *Frank* are performing the same action. The compound subject is *George and Frank.*

Simple Subject/Compound Verb. The simple subject of the sentence performs two or more actions. Answer the questions in this example:

Example: The audience booed and hissed the performer.

What are the two actions performed? _____
What is the subject? _____

In this sentence, the audience performed two actions—booed and hissed. The compound verb is *booed* and *hissed.*

Compound Subject/Compound Verb. This means that two or more subjects perform two or more actions. Answer the questions in this example.

Example: Curly, Larry, and Moe danced and ate all night.

What is the compound verb? _____

What is the compound subject? _____

Curly, Larry, and *Moe* are all performing the same actions—*danced* and *ate.*

PRACTICE 4

Find the subjects and verbs in the following sentences.

1. Fords and Chevrolets are two makes of American cars.

   verb _____   subject _____

2. The cat hissed and scratched.

   verb _____   subject _____

3. Caleb and Rachel read and study.

   verb _____   subject _____

4. Angela became a doctor.

   verb _____   subject _____

5. Carl and Martha took a vacation last spring.

   verb _____   subject _____

6. Tina seemed sad.

   verb _____   subject _____

7. Ice cream and cake are his favorite foods.

   verb _____   subject _____

8. Puerto Rico and St. Thomas are beautiful vacation spots.

   verb _____   subject _____

9. Nita appears happy.

   verb _____   subject _____

10. The dolphin leaped and swam.

   verb _____   subject _____

Check the answer key.

Exceptions

The words *there, here,* and *where* can never be the subject of a sentence, so you must look for another word—a noun or a pronoun—as the subject of the sentence.

> Example: There is my car.
>
> What is the verb? *is*
> What is the subject? *car*

PRACTICE 5

Find the subjects and verbs in each of the following sentences.

1. There are my best friends.

   verb _____   subject _____

2. Here is the manuscript for the new television series.

   verb _____   subject _____

3. Where are Harry's ball and bat?

   verb _____   subject _____

4. Here is the answer to your question.

   verb _____   subject _____

5. Here come Linda's boyfriend and another girl.

   verb _____   subject _____

Check the answer key.

Helping Verbs

In the previous examples and practice exercises, you might have noticed that most of the verbs have consisted of only one word. Because most of the sentences used the present tense (present time), only one word was needed for the verb. However, because verbs tell us about time, it is sometimes necessary for a verb to have more than one word in order to convey a particular time. The **main verb** (major action) may be accompanied by **helping verbs** that help describe the time of the action.

> Example: Look at the following sentences. All of them contain a form of the verb *to ask.* Notice the helping verbs.
>
> | | |
> |---|---|
> | I ask. | I am asking. |
> | I asked. | I was asking. |
> | I will ask. | I will be asking. |
> | I have asked. | I have been asking. |
> | I had asked. | I had been asking. |
> | I will have asked. | I will have been asking. |

PRACTICE 6

Find the subjects and the verbs in the following sentences. Be sure to include any helping verbs.

1. Tom will have left school by 4 o'clock.

verb _____   subject _____

2. The senator will have been in office four years this spring.

verb _____   subject _____

3. The car had been demolished in the wreck.

verb _____   subject _____

4. The animals at the zoo will be released into a natural-habitat park.

verb _____   subject _____

5. The disc jockey was playing records by Willie Nelson and Hank Williams, Jr.

verb _____   subject _____

Check the answer key.

NOTE: Do not include negatives (such as the word *no*) in the verb.

Example: Helen is not going to the dance.
The subject is *Helen*.
The verb is *is going*.

Prepositional Phrases

A sentence may have many phrases and additional words. One type of phrase that can seem confusing and make a sentence seem more complex is a prepositional phrase. A prepositional phrase consists of a **preposition** (for example, *of, for, to, in, out, around, through*) and a noun or pronoun (called the **object of the preposition**); it may also contain adjectives and/or adverbs.

Prepositions are easily recognized. Prepositional phrases provide additional information to the reader of the sentence. Usually, prepositions express the time of the action or other relationships. The following prepositions introduce information in the categories of time, place, and other:

Time	*Place*		*Other*
after	under	behind	because
before	in/into	through	of
during	out	up	with
since	around	inside	from
	outside	to	except
	between	among	in order of
	over	by	due to
			because of
			by
			like
			such as

The following are examples of prepositional phrases:

under the forbidding mountain   behind the door
into the green room   since May
after the game   with her

NOTE: To help determine if a word is a preposition, use this test: A preposition expresses any relationship that makes sense with regard to a house.

Example: *into* the house
around the house
to the house
outside the house
into, around, to, and *outside* are prepositions
This test will help you locate prepositions that describe place; it will not help locate those that express time.

A number of prepositional phrases in a sentence may make it difficult to find the subject and the verb. Remember: The *noun* or *pronoun* in a prepositional phrase is *the object of the preposition;* this word can never be the subject of the sentence!

To find the subject and verb in a sentence, simply eliminate the prepositional phrases in the sentence.

Example: The Board of Trustees of the college is meeting now in the conference room of the Administration Building.

Cross out the prepositional phrases (as well as any other adjectives and adverbs) in the above sentence, and find the subject and the verb. Your sentence should now look like this:

~~The~~ Board ~~of Trustees of the college~~ is meeting ~~now in the conference room of the Administration Building.~~

What is the verb? *is meeting*
What is the subject? *Board*

PRACTICE 7

Cross out any prepositional phrases in the following sentences. Then, underline the subjects and the verbs and label them.

Example: ~~In the center~~ of the room <u>stood Jim</u>.
(verb) (subject)

1. The cat ran under the porch.

2. Broncho Davis was a famous football player for twenty years.

3. The greyhound with the matted coat and an evil look in his eyes frightened the school

   children.

4. The drive to Orlando is a pleasant one.

5. Bing Crosby and Bob Hope were a successful team for more than fifteen years.

Check the answer key.

Sentence Formats

Sentence Format 1: Subject and Verb

An example of a Format 1 sentence is: Birds sing.

The abbreviation for Sentence Format 1 is S-V. Consider the abbreviation and explain it by using terms you have already encountered.
(S stands for _____ . V stands for _____ .)

The Subject. What words other than *birds* can be substituted into the sentence? Remember, construct a sentence that will have meaning.

_____ sing.   _____ sing.

_____ sing.   _____ sing.

_____ sing.   _____ sing.

What types of words are *birds* and the ones you substituted? Words that can be substituted for each other belong to the same format. The words you supplied have the same relationship with *sing* as the word *birds* has with *sing*. They are all the same type of words—nouns or pronouns.

If you used *he, she, we, I, it, they,* or *you* for the subject, then you used **pronouns,** not nouns. Pronouns take the place of nouns, so they can be used as the subject of a sentence.

EXERCISE Fill in the blanks with words that follow Sentence Format 1.

1. _____ squawk.   5. _____ jump.

2. _____ yell.   6. _____ sink.

3. _____ meow.   7. _____ swim.

4. _____ dance.   8. _____ leap.

Have your instructor or tutor check your work.

The Verb. The noun or pronoun—the subject—is only part of Sentences Format 1; the second portion of the format is the **verb.** In the example sentence, *Birds sing,* what words can be substituted for *sing*? These are **action verbs,** because they name an action.

Birds _____   Birds _____   Birds _____ .

A word that can be substituted for *sing* is a verb.

EXERCISE Fill in the blanks with verbs to complete the sentences.

1. Dogs ————————————— . 5. Windows ————————————— .

2. Monkeys ————————————— . 6. Joggers ————————————— .

3. Cars ————————————— . 7. Airplanes ————————————— .

4. Houses ————————————— . 8. Radios ————————————— .

Next, using Sentence Format 1 (S-V), write your own sentences.

1. ———————————————————————

2. ———————————————————————

3. ———————————————————————

4. ———————————————————————

5. ———————————————————————

Have your instructor or tutor check your work.

EXERCISE Using Format 1, write five sentences with pronouns as the subjects.

1. ———————————————————————

2. ———————————————————————

3. ———————————————————————

4. ———————————————————————

5. ———————————————————————

Have your instructor or tutor check your work.

Sentence Format 2: The Direct Object

Sentence Format 2 builds upon Sentence Format 1 (S-V). It simply adds another word and relationship to the format.

Example: Harry hit the baseball.

Consider carefully the relationships among the words. You should recognize that *Harry* is the subject and *hit* is the verb. However, what relationship does *baseball* have to *hit*? *Baseball* is the **direct object** of the verb. Nouns and pronouns can act as direct objects. The direct object receives the action of the verb. When you ask, "What was hit?" and locate an answer, then you have found the direct object.

The abbreviation for Sentence Format 2 is S-V-DO.

EXERCISE   Fill in the blanks with one word that will complete the sentence. Identify the word you used. Is it a subject, a verb, or direct object?

1. _____ threw a ball.

2. Tom _____ his lunch.

3. I dropped my _____ .

4. Grandmother _____ her knitting.

5. _____ read the book.

6. Dad drove the _____ .

7. My little brother _____ the dog.

8. The bus hit the _____ .

9. He bought the _____ .

10. The cat _____ its kittens.

Have your instructor or tutor check your work.

PRACTICE 8

Label each of the following sentences Format 1 or Format 2. Write the format for each sentence in the blank to the right. Also, identify subjects, verb, and direct objects.

Example: S V
          I ran.   *Format*
                    I S-V

                              Format

1. Tom forgot.   _____

2. The band won the contest. _____

3. Helen read a book.   _____

4. I swam.   _____

5. The dog crossed the road. _____

6. The arrow struck a tree.   _____

7. The baseball team lost.   _____

8. The child broke the vase. _____

Check the answer key.

EXERCISE   In the above set of sentences, three sentences followed Format 1. Add a word or words to those three sentences to make them Format 2 sentences.

1. _____

2. _____

3. _____

Have your instructor or tutor check your work.

PRACTICE 9

Label each sentence either Format 1 or Format 2. Identify the subjects, verbs, and direct objects.

                     S   V   DO   *Format*

Example: The runner won the New York City Marathon. **2   S-V-DO**

                                                           Format

1. The police caught the thief. _____

2. Our television broke. _____

3. The horse won the Triple Crown. _____

4. The children jumped the fence. _____

5. Mary cried. _____

6. The moon rose over the field. _____

7. The fullback caught the football. _____

8. The rooster crowed at dawn. _____

9. The airplane left the runway. _____

10. The scuba diver speared a barracuda. _____

11. His shoelaces broke. _____

12. The president of the corporation fired

    his assistant. _____

13. The speaker declined the invitation. _____

14. The chair fell. _____

15. Children like ice cream. _____

Check the answer key.

EXERCISE   Write five sentences of your own that follow Format 2.

1. _____

2. _____

3. _____

4. _____

5. _____

Have your instructor or tutor check your work.

Sentence Format 3: The Predicate Adjective and the Predicate Nominative

The third sentence format introduces two new elements. Look at these examples.

Examples: Harry is tall.
Harry is a freshman.

Notice that a new type of verb is included: a **linking verb.** Any form of the verb *to be* is a linking verb, as are the verbs *seem, feel, appear,* and *become.* Linking verbs (LV) connect the word that follows them to the subject in a special relationship. It almost seems as if the linking verb equates both sides.

The Predicate Adjective. Consider these Format 3 sentences:

Examples: Cathy is cute.
The sky appears cloudy.
Horses are strong.
The runners appear tired.

In these sentences, the words connected to the subjects by the linking verbs are **adjectives;** they describe or characterize the nouns that are the subjects. You could write *cute Cathy, cloudy sky, strong horses,* or *tired runners.* These adjectives in Sentence Format are called *predicate adjectives,* because they describe the subject.

NOTE: If you took only the subjects and verbs of the sentences, then you would not have complete sentences: *Cathy is, The sky appears, Horses are,* and *The runners appear.* The predicate adjective is needed to describe the subject and to complete the sentence.

The format for the sentence *Harry is tall* is: S-LV-PA

PRACTICE 10

In the following sentences, underline the linking verbs. Write the predicate adjective and the subject together and identify the format.

	PA-S	LV	Format
Example: The weather <u>is</u> bad.	*bad weather*	*is*	S-LV-PA
	PA-S	LV	Format
1. The weightlifter is powerful.	_____	_____	_____

2. Tom appears sad.   _____   _____   _____

3. Mary looks happy.   _____   _____   _____

4. The dinner tasted good.   _____   _____   _____

5. Earl Bruce was cooperative.   _____   _____   _____

6. The cat sounds angry.   _____   _____   _____

7. He seems tired.   _____   _____   _____

8. The onion smells sour.   _____   _____   _____

9. The road becomes rough.   _____   _____   _____

10. The apple was red and delicious.   _____   _____   _____

Check the answer key.

EXERCISE Complete the following sentences by adding predicate adjectives.

1. He becomes _____ .

2. The mouse was _____ .

3. The movie seemed _____ .

4. The sky turned _____ .

5. Sam is _____ .

6. Baseball seems _____ .

7. The book appeared _____ .

8. The oranges are _____ .

9. The cake tasted _____ .

10. The dessert was _____ .

Have your instructor or tutor check your work.

PRACTICE 11

Both Format 2 and Format 3 sentences will be found in the following exercise. Identify each format. Underline the linking verb twice and write the predicate adjective in the blanks and label them. Underline action verbs once and write the direct objects in the blanks and label them DO.

NOTE: Linking verbs never take direct objects.

Format

Examples: 1. He suddenly <u>became</u> weak.

weak – PA 3

2. Tom <u>bounced</u> a ball.

ball – DO 2

Format

1. The cowboy branded the calf.   _____

2. His car looks expensive.   _____

3. I enjoy comic books.   _____

4. The arrow struck a rock.   _____

5. His shoes are dirty.   _____

6. The girls were pretty.   _____

7. Gerry's Restaurant serves good food.   _____

8. The Gulf of Mexico has quite blue water.   _____

9. The teacher looks interested.   _____

10. The audience seemed uneasy.   _____

Check the answer key.

EXERCISE   Write five sentences of your own that follow the format S-LV-PA.

1. _____

2. _____

3. _____

4. _____

5. _____

Have your instructor or tutor check your work.

The Predicate Nominative. The second example sentence for Format 3 was:

Harry is a freshman.

The format is basically the same as S-LV-PA. *Harry* is the subject, and *is* is the linking verb. However, *freshman* is a noun, not a predicate adjective. A noun following a linking verb is called a **predicate nominative.** The predicate nominative might define the subject, identify it, or rename it. In other words, the predicate nominative, a noun, is equal to the subject, a noun. For example, in the example sentence, *Harry* and *freshman* are equivalent. The abbreviation for this second type of Format 3 sentence is: S-LV-PN

S   LV   PN
Harry is a freshman.

PRACTICE 12

Identify the predicate nominatives in the following sentences. Write the predicate nominative and the subject on the lines to the right of the sentence. Use an equal sign to indicate their equality. Also, label the subjects and linking verbs.

Example:
           S LV   PN   PN = S
Tom is the team captain. *captain = Tom*

                                                             PN   =   S

1. The senator is the chairman of a major committee. _____

2. Annapolis is the state capital of Maryland. _____

3. The mahogany desk is an antique. _____

4. Shawn became an astronaut. _____

5. Because of his ability as a blocker, John is a complete

    football player. _____

6. With her ability as a writer of feature stories, Jane is a

    considerable force in Houston journalism. _____

7. Television is one of the primary news media today. _____

8. She is a good actress. _____

9. The girl with the red hair is my cousin. _____

10. An alligator on a shirt is a symbol of preppies. _____

Check the answer key.

EXERCISE Complete the following sentences by adding predicate nominatives.

1. Novels are _____ .

2. My car is _____ .

3. The captain was _____ .

4. Besides being test pilots, astronauts must also be _____ .

5. The pretty little girl became _____ .

6. Besides being students, many college students are also _____ .

7. The cowboy is also a _____ .

8. Jim is a _____ .

9. To Michelangelo, sculpture was _____.

10. Multinational corporations are _____.

Have your instructor or tutor check your work.

EXERCISE   Write five sentences of your own that conform to the format S-LV-PN.

1. _____

2. _____

3. _____

4. _____

5. _____

Have your instructor or tutor check your work.

PRACTICE 13

Label each sentence by one of two formats: S-LV-PA or S-LV-PN. Label each part of the sentence.

Example: Harry is a good debater. S-LV-PN

1. She is an attractive girl in my opinion.   _____

2. His ideas about politics are ambiguous.   _____

3. Students always seem busy with their work.   _____

4. Doctors and lawyers are our highest-paid professionals.   _____

5. Most teachers are enthusiastic.   _____

6. Discos, once places for a popular entertainment, are now

    bowling alleys.   _____

7. Records and tapes are expensive.   _____

8. The latest dress craze is the mini-skirt.   _____

9. William Faulkner was one of the greatest American novelists.   _____

10. Silence and patience are virtues.   _____

Check the answer key.

EXERCISE   The following questions will test your understanding of the first three sentence formats.

1. What are linking verbs? Name some.

_____

2. Do linking verbs take direct objects?

_____

3. What is the relationship of a direct object to the verb?

_____

4. What is the relationship of a direct object to the subject?

_____

5. What is the relationship of a predicate nominative to the subject?

_____

6. What is the relationship of a predicate adjective to the subject?

_____

7. Give the codes for the first three sentence patterns.

_____

If you had trouble answering any of these questions, review the sections on Formats 1, 2, and 3 before you continue.

Sentence Format 4: The Indirect Object

Identify and label the following sentence:

Hector threw the ball.

You should be familiar with this format; it is Sentence Format 2. Now, label the next sentence:

Hector threw me the ball.

In the sentence above, *Hector* is the subject, *threw* is the verb, and *ball* is the direct object. But the sentence has an additional word—*me*. *Me* is a pronoun; it tells to whom the ball was thrown. A pronoun or a noun with this relationship to the verb is called an *indirect object*. You could construct the sentence in this manner: Hector threw the ball to me. Notice that *me* is now the object of the preposition *to*. You can place *to* or *for* in front of the indirect object.

To test for indirect objects in a sentence, follow these two steps:

1. Rewrite the sentence to follow Format 2 (S-V-DO).
2. Add *to* or *for* plus the word in question to the end of the sentence.

Example: May gave me the book.

In order to decide if *me* is the indirect object,
follow the two steps of the test:

Step 1.   Rewrite the sentence to follow Format 2:

May gave the book. (S-V-DO)

Step 2.   Add *to* or *for* plus the word in question to the end of the sentence:

May gave the book to me.

Because *me* can be placed into a prepositional phrase, *me* is the indirect object. *Me*, finally, holds the book.

Examples: Harold gave Tracy the roses.

Apply the two-step test:

_____

Dad gave Vicki her allowance.

Apply the two-step test:

_____

Do the sentences make sense? If they do, you have found the indirect objects.

The abbreviation for Sentence Format 4 is S-V-IO-DO.

PRACTICE 14

Label all subjects, verbs, indirect objects, and direct objects.

          S V   IO   DO
Example: I gave Jim the award for academic excellence.

1. Tim awarded Henry the prize.

2. The boy bought the girl a flower.

3. The nervous young man handed his girlfriend a diamond ring.

4. My English teacher gave me a high mark on my test.

5. Tim fed the dog his dinner.

6. The bird built his mate a nest.

7. I gave my friend an umbrella.

8. She brought Jim a soda.

9. The kidnappers gave the child a candy bar.

10. Sharon bought her father a wool sweater.

Check the answer key.

EXERCISE   Write ten sentences of your own that follow Format 4.

1. _____

2. _____

3. _____

4. _____

5. _____

6. _____

7. _____

8. _____

9. _____

10. _____

Have your instructor or tutor check your work.

PRACTICE 15

Identify each of the following sentences either Format 1, 2, 3, or 4. Label each part of the sentence.

	Abbreviation	*Format*
Example: S LV PN He is my basketball coach.	S-LV-PN	3

	Abbreviation	*Format*
1. She is the star of our class play.	_____	_____
2. The coach gave Tom his football equipment.	_____	_____
3. The bread tastes stale.	_____	_____
4. The dog caught the stick.	_____	_____
5. The wealthy man gave the poor child a dollar.	_____	_____
6. I walked into the room.	_____	_____

7. The marathon runner became an Olympic hero.   _____   _____

8. Women have joined many traditional men's clubs.   _____   _____

9. Kim sang an aria from *Aida*.   _____   _____

10. The horse tripped on the last jump.   _____   _____

11. Jimmy Connors is a marvelous tennis player.   _____   _____

12. The lawyer gave his client some advice.   _____   _____

13. The student was sick yesterday.   _____   _____

14. Maria invited Brad to the dance.   _____   _____

15. The dog growled at the letter carrier.   _____   _____

16. Freshly cut roses are an expensive gift.   _____   _____

17. Bob caught a fish for dinner.   _____   _____

18. Doctors seem quite intelligent.   _____   _____

19. He gave me a present for my birthday.   _____   _____

20. The television picture appears faded.   _____   _____

Check the answer key.

Classes of Sentences

There are four types of sentences, classified according to their purpose: declarative, interrogative, imperative, and exclamatory.

A **declarative** sentence makes a statement. You have been working primarily with declarative sentences. Notice that the sentence ends with a period.

Example: The car will not start.
            It is raining today.

An **interrogative** sentence asks a question. It ends with a question mark.

Example: Will you go to the movies with me?
            Subject: *you*
            verb: *Will go*

NOTE: In a question, usually the helping verb comes before the subject and the main verb comes after it.

An **imperative** sentence expresses a command or a rhetorical question (you expect that the listener will comply with your request). It usually ends with a period, but an imperative sentence can also end with an exclamation mark (for added emphasis).

Examples: Help.
                Help!

NOTE: This particular imperative sentence contains only one word. What is the verb in the sentence? *help*. But where is the subject? Consider this for a moment. Aren't you commanding or requesting that someone help you? Then, you are actually addressing someone else; it is as if you are saying, "*You* help." The subject of the sentence is called an **understood you.** It is written like this: (you)

Example: Please pass the cake.
             verb: *pass*
             subject: *(you)*

An **exclamatory** sentence expresses surprise or shock. It ends with an exclamation mark.

Example: The house is on fire!

PRACTICE 16

Classify each of the following sentences as one of the four classes: declarative, imperative, interrogative, or exclamatory.

1. Watch out for that man. _____

2. Have you done your homework? _____

3. Time can be measured. _____

4. The car caught fire! _____

5. Tell me your name. _____

6. Exercise is good for you. _____

7. Do you like summer sports? _____

8. Help. _____

9. I got an A! _____

10. Horses are patient animals. _____

Check the answer key.

EXERCISE   Now, write a sentence of your own as an example of each class.

1. Declarative: _____

2. Interrogative: _____

3. Imperative: _____

4. Exclamatory: _____

Have your instructor or tutor check your work.

Types of Sentences

1. To recognize simple sentences.

2. To recognize compound sentences.

3. To recognize complex sentences.

4. To recognize compound-complex sentences.

5. To write all four types of sentences correctly.

KEY CONCEPT: There are four types of sentences:

1. simple

2. compound

3. complex

4. compound-complex
   Because all types of sentences are built upon clauses (a group of words that has a subject and a verb), a writer must be able to recognize the two kinds of clauses:

   • independent
   • dependent

Simple Sentences

A **simple sentence** contains a single independent clause. A clause is a group of words that has a subject and a verb. There are two kinds of clauses:

1. independent (or main) and
2. dependent (or subordinate).

PRACTICE 1

Read each of the following groups of words and decide if the group of words is a clause. Place a *C* beside the groups that are clauses.

_____ 1. In the rain.

_____ 2. When he finished.

_____ 3. Because the movie is over.

_____ 4. Hilda screamed.

_____ 5. When jogging home.

Check the answer key.

An **independent clause** has a subject and a verb, and it expresses a complete thought. As its name suggests, an independent clause can stand by itself. A simple sentence is an independent clause.

Examples: The lecture was over.
              The Colorado River travels through many western states.
              In the fall, the Blue Ridge Mountains are spectacular.
              The ship is owned by Ridder Company, a firm in Miami.

PRACTICE 2

Write five simple sentences of your own.

1. _____

2. _____

3. _____

4. _____

5. _____

Have your instructor or tutor check your work.

A **dependent clause** has a subject and a verb, but it does not express a complete thought. A dependent clause does *not* make a sentence.

Example: While Dan was driving.

              This group of words does have a subject (*Dan*) and a verb (*was driving*), but it does not express a complete thought. The writer did not tell us what happened while Dan was driving.

Look at these two versions of the same idea:

Examples: The dog barked all night.
              Because the dog barked all night.

              The first sentence is complete; the second sentence is not, because it does not tell us the result of the dog's barking. Both groups of words, *While Dan was driving* and *Because the dog barked all night,* contain subjects and verbs, but do not express complete thoughts; both word groups are dependent clauses.

The following words are commonly used **subordinate conjunctions** and **relative pronouns**. If a group of words that has a subject and a verb begins with one of these subordinate conjunctions or relative pronouns, the clause is a dependent clause. Be able to recognize these words.

Subordinate Conjunctions

after	if	what
although	since	when
as	so that	whenever
as if	than	where
because	though	whereas
before	unless	wherever
even though	until	whether
how		while

Relative Pronouns

that	whoever
which	whom
whichever	whomever
who	whose

If one of these words precedes a group of words containing a subject and a verb, then you have a dependent clause.

> **NOTE:** The pronouns *who, which, that,* and *whoever* can be the subject of the dependent clause.

Since many of the words listed as subordinate conjunctions are also other parts of speech, check each group of words carefully. If one of these words precedes a group of words containing a subject and a verb, then you have a dependent clause. Consider the following example:

> While he enjoyed the play.

In this group of words, the word *while* is a subordinate conjunction since it precedes the subject *he* and the verb *enjoyed*.

However, many of the words in the list are also adverbs or prepositions. As such, they will not precede a subject and a verb; hence, the group of words will not be a dependent clause. Consider the following examples:

> While running for the train.

> Because of her competence.

Neither group of words above is a complete sentence nor a dependent clause. Instead, the first group, *while running for the train,* is a participial phrase. There is no subject or verb in this group of words. (See "Verbals" in Chapter 3, Part Two.) The second group of words, *because of her competence,* is a prepositional phrase. The compound preposition *because of* has as its object the noun *competence.* (See "Prepositional Phrases" in Chapter 4, Part Two.)

Always check the complete group of words before you determine the function of the group in the sentence.

PRACTICE 3

Read the clauses below. If the clause expresses a complete thought, place an *I* (for independent clause) next to it. If the clause does not express a complete thought, place a *D* (for dependent clause) next to it.

_____ 1. Although the day was bright and sunny.

_____ 2. Because she is so vain and conceited.

_____ 3. I believe in motherhood and apple pie.

_____ 4. When we reach our destination.

_____ 5. He completed his work.

_____ 6. If the recession ever ends.

_____ 7. Before the play starts.

_____ 8. Tonight is a night for merrymaking.

_____ 9. While Anne was driving east.

_____ 10. She received an *A* in English.

Check the answer key.

As you saw in Chapter 4, simple sentences can contain any combination of simple and compound subjects and verbs. Simple sentences may also contain prepositional and verbal phrases, and they follow the formats listed in Chapter 4, Part Two. For more information on word combinations that appear in simple sentences, see "Sentence Combining" in Chapter 6, Part One, and "Beginning Sentences" in Chapter 8, Part One.

PRACTICE 4

For each of the simple sentences below, label the subject(s), verb(s), prepositional and verbal phrases, and the format.

Example: $\underline{S - V - DO - II}$ Tad enjoys hiking (in the mountains) each weekend.

_____ 1. Each spring, the college sponsors a career day for students.

_____ 2. During the president's vacation, the vice-president was solely responsible

for the administration of the college.

_____ 3. Swimming is an excellent sport.

_____ 4. The sentry, supposedly standing guard duty, had fallen asleep at his post.

_____ 5. Harold and Maude made an improbable couple because of the contrast in

their ages.

_____ 6. Our hiking club plans to visit Pike's Peak this summer.

_____ 7. Distraught, the accident victim refused to answer questions.

_____ 8. At the sound of the approaching train, the deer scrambled for safety.

_____ 9. To enjoy a stage production of one of Shakespeare's plays, you should read the play prior to the performance.

_____ 10. Sheila's chief ambition is to become an actress.

Check the answer key.

Compound Sentences

A **compound sentence** contains two or more independent clauses. Read the following sentences, and determine how they differ:

Examples: 1. Mickey and Marvin sang a song and played their guitars.
2. Mickey sang a song, and Marvin played his guitar.

In sentence 1, both Mickey and Marvin are performing both actions—*sang* and *played*. In sentence 2, only Mickey sang, while Marvin played. Sentence 2 is a compound sentence; it is made of two independent clauses: (1) *Mickey sang a song,* and (2) *Marvin played his guitar.* A compound sentence is punctuated in one of three ways:

1. The two independent clauses are joined by a comma (,) and one of the seven coordinate conjunctions: *for, and, nor, but, or, yet,* and *so.* You can remember the coordinate conjunctions by remembering the word FANBOYS (composed of the first letter of each word).

   IMPORTANT: When you use one of these seven coordinate conjunctions, pay attention to the relationship each word stresses:

   a. *And* makes the independent clauses equal; both clauses carry the same weight and have the same value.
   b. *But* and *yet* show contrast between the two independent clauses.
   c. *Or* indicates a choice between the two statements; *nor* indicates a negative choice between the two clauses.
   d. *For* and *so* show cause and effect.

   Example: Read each of the following sentences, and determine how the coordinate conjunctions change the meaning of the sentences:

   a. Helen is going to the mall, *and* Cynthia is going to town.
   b. Helen is going to the mall, *but* Cynthia is going to town.
   c. Helen is going to the mall, *so* Cynthia is going to town.

2. The two independent clauses are joined by a semicolon (;).

   Example: Terry hurried home; the house was on fire.

   IMPORTANT: Use a semicolon only when the two independent clauses are closely related and the relationship is implied.

3. The two independent clauses are joined by a semicolon (;) and an adverbial conjunction. The adverbial conjunction indicates the type of relationship between the two independent clauses. The following list contains many of the adverbial conjunctions.

also	indeed	primarily
consequently	likewise	rather
currently	moreover	similarly
finally	nevertheless	then
hence	next	therefore
however	overall	thus

Since each adverbial conjunction stresses a particular relationship between the two independent clauses, consider your choice of an adverbial conjunction carefully. For example, the adverbial conjunctions *therefore, consequently,* and *thus* indicate that the second independent clause is a logical conclusion or result of the first clause. Check a dictionary for the relationships the other adverbial conjunctions stress.

When you use one of these adverbial conjunctions to join two independent clauses, you must place a semicolon before the adverbial conjunction and a comma after it.

Examples: Ms. McBride was the city council president for many years; currently, she is mayor.

The supply of crude oil dropped tremendously; thus, the price of gasoline climbed rapidly.

PRACTICE 5

Combine each pair of simple sentences into a compound sentence. Use six of the seven coordinate conjunctions. Remember that a comma must precede the coordinate conjunction.

1. The student was sick. She missed the test.

   _____

2. The administration has decided to raise salaries. The cost of living has risen.

   _____

3. The recession continued. Steel output increased.

   _____

4. I lost my wallet. I cannot buy the record.

   _____

5. Harold will go to law school. He will go to medical school.

   _____

6. It may snow. I am still going on my vacation.

_____

Have your instructor or tutor check your work.

PRACTICE 6

Using three of the seven coordinate conjunctions and three adverbial conjunctions from the preceding lists, write six compound sentences of your own.

1. _____

2. _____

3. _____

4. _____

5. _____

6. _____

Have your instructor or tutor check your work.

PRACTICE 7

Classify each of the following sentences as either simple or compound. Identify all subjects and verbs.

Example: <u>*compound*</u> School started late today, for it had snowed.

_____ 1. Governor Toll was nominated for a second term, but he declined the opportunity.

_____ 2. The Kentucky Derby, the Preakness, and the Belmont Stakes form the Triple Crown of horse racing.

_____ 3. Before the turn of the century, firefighters used horse-drawn trucks; today, they use motorized vehicles.

_____ 4. Many musicians and composers were employed by kings in the seventeenth century.

_____ 5. Mexico has many interesting buildings; some, in fact, go back to the time of the Mayas.

Check the answer key.

Complex Sentences

A complex sentence contains one independent clause and one or more dependent clauses.

Examples:
              s   v
1. They wanted to manage a restaurant.

    Sentence 1 is an independent clause; it has a subject and a verb, and it expresses a complete thought.

                    s   v
2. Although they had no cooking skills or management experience.

    This group of words is a dependent clause. It has a subject and a verb, but it does not express a complete thought, so it is not a sentence. Notice, also, that the clause begins with the subordinate conjunction *although*.

        Independent Clause   Dependent Clause
3. They wanted to manage a restaurant, although they had no cooking skills or management experience.

    Sentence 3 is a complex sentence, because it has both an independent clause and a dependent clause.

Subordination

In a compound sentence, both independent clauses carry the same amount of weight; they are equally important. However, in a complex sentence, the independent clause is more important than the dependent clause because an independent clause can stand by itself. The dependent clause in a complex sentence should give only additional information about the independent clause.

Example:
        Independent Clause   Dependent Clause
The students finished the test (that their teacher had given them.)

Which clause is more important? _____
The main idea of the sentence is that the students finished the test. The dependent clause, *that their teacher had given them,* is not as important; the dependent clause simply adds extra information about who gave the test to the students.

PRACTICE 8

Review the subordinate conjunctions and relative pronouns on page 000. Identify the word or groups of words by writing one of the following labels: *IC* (independent clause), *DC* (dependent clause), *PP* (prepositional phrase), *SW* (subordinate word).

_____ 1. before the storm

_____ 2. if he goes

_____ 3. since she is rich

_____ 4. because

_____ 5. millions have cable television

_____ 6. nearly every American drives a car

_____ 7. in the spring

_____ 8. beyond the blue horizon

_____ 9. when she took her seat

_____ 10. on the beach

_____ 11. when

_____ 12. after the clock struck twelve

_____ 13. he gave a dazzling performance

_____ 14. despite the blizzard

_____ 15. Henry who is a sailor

_____ 16. on the roof

_____ 17. at the party in the old house

_____ 18. Marge can be intriguing

_____ 19. after the race begins

_____ 20. while she was dancing

Check the answer key.

PRACTICE 9

Combine each pair of sentences into a complex sentence by making one of the clauses dependent. Remember to keep the most important idea as the independent clause.

1. The book was difficult. It was worth the effort.

   _____

2. The brunette cried. She had won the contest.

   _____

3. The riverboat capsized. It struck a log.

   _____

4. The wallet was returned. The credit cards were missing.

   _____

5. Jane received the school award. The teachers voted for her.

_____

Have your instructor or tutor check your work.

PRACTICE 10

Write five complex sentences of your own.

1. _____
2. _____
3. _____
4. _____
5. _____

Have your instructor or tutor check your work.

PRACTICE 11

Identify the dependent clauses and the independent clauses in each of the following sentences. Underline the independent clause and label it. Place parentheses around the dependent clause and label it.

Example: *dependent clause* *independent clause*
(Because it is so hot,) the children want to go to the beach.

1. Whenever the weather is beautiful, they have a picnic.

2. Although he had household chores, he decided to see a movie.

3. It began to rain before the boat reached shore.

4. We knew that he did not go home.

5. Because she has an exam tomorrow, Kate will study tonight.

6. After the movie ended, all thirty of us headed to the local pizza parlor.

7. Before Marvin could shout a warning, the firecracker exploded.

8. After they buy a house, they will purchase new furniture.

9. Harriet decided to go on the ski trip, even though she had a broken leg.

10. Because many parents believe that their children should know how to operate computers, they are purchasing home computers.

Check the answer key.

PRACTICE 12

Identify each of the following sentences by type: simple, compound, or complex. Label all clauses, as in Practice 11.

_____ 1. Betsy goes to the beach whenever she can.

_____ 2. It is a warm day; the temperature is now 95 degrees.

_____ 3. In order to earn enough money to go to college, Terry worked as a waitress all summer.

_____ 4. Jack and Mary entered the haunted house cautiously, for they believed all the stories about ghosts.

_____ 5. When the rain was over, the children ran outside.

_____ 6. Because the battery was dead, the car refused to start.

_____ 7. You must hurry, or you will miss the last bus.

_____ 8. Marcello and his brothers gritted their teeth and began the long, slow climb to the top of the mountain.

_____ 9. He told you that your plan was impossible.

_____ 10. With its varied historical background, New Orleans is a fascinating place to visit; the Mardi Gras is one example of its French heritage.

Check the answer key.

Compound-Complex Sentences

A compound-complex sentence is just what its name says: it is a compound sentence that contains one or more dependent clauses. A compound-complex sentence has two or more independent clauses and one or more dependent clauses.

Example:

Dependent Clause   Independent Clause   Independent

The doctor, (who was also a golfer,) examined his last patient; then he headed for

Clause

the golf course.

PRACTICE 13

The following sentences are compound-complex. Underline each independent clause, and place parentheses around the dependent clause. Label the clauses.

                    dependent clause   independent clause   independent clause
Example: (When he listens to the radio) he turns the volume up, and the neighbors complain.

1. When the monster appeared on the screen, one girl fainted, and the audience clapped.

2. The movie's visual effects, which cost fifteen million dollars, were fantastic; later, the graphic artists won an Academy Award for their work.

3. I wish that you had seen the film; we could discuss it.

4. Knitting, which is a relaxing pastime, can be profitable, for handmade sweaters have become a fashion item.

5. Order the pizza when you get home; I'll be there soon.

6. Because England was America's first mother country, many people believe that the English do everything better; however, these Americans are not correct.

7. If you will wait for me, I'll finish my work, and then we can go to the beach.

8. Before you purchase your textbooks, go to class; the instructor may have changed the reading list.

9. Our surprise birthday party for Jerry failed; before he entered the room, everyone was practicing "Happy Birthday."

10. My father always told me to turn the lights off when I leave a room; he claimed that such a practice would save money.

Check the answer key.

PRACTICE 14

Write five compound-complex sentences of your own.

1. _____

2. _____

3. _____

4. _____

5. _____

Have your instructor or tutor check your work.

PRACTICE 15

Identify each of the following sentences by type: simple, compound, complex, or compound-complex. Label all clauses, as in Practice 13.

_____ 1. She is a person whom we admire.

_____ 2. The dog that wins the contest will be used in the commercial.

_____ 3. Because he has left, we must stay here.

_____ 4. Because the panda's natural habitat in China is threatened, many Chinese zookeepers wish to export them to other countries, and the Chinese government has agreed.

_____ 5. Close the door when you enter.

_____ 6. Before we leave for a vacation, we always have the car checked for problems.

_____ 7. Have Dave and Hank decided when they will paint the house?

_____ 8. We decided to see *The Rocky Horror Picture Show* at midnight.

_____ 9. Curt and Stacy played the romantic leads in *Romeo and Juliet;* however, the performance reminded one of *The Taming of the Shrew.*

_____ 10. Each section of the country, from New England to the West Coast, boasts of its native foods.

Check the answer key.

A Final Hint

There is a pattern of logical steps you can follow to identify the type of sentence. Follow these guidelines, and you cannot make a mistake:

Step 1:   Circle the subordinate conjunctions or relative pronouns in the sentence. Do a subject and a verb follow a subordinate word? Does a verb follow a relative pronoun? If so in either case, label the group of words a *dependent clause.*

Step 2:   Circle any commas and the coordinate conjunctions, and circle any semicolons. If there are independent clauses on either side of the coordinate conjunction or semicolon, label the clauses *independent clauses.*

Step 3:   Count the number of independent clauses and dependent clauses in the sentence, and decide what type of sentence you have.

   Example: Look at the following sentence:

   If you will do the dishes, I will vacuum the house, and then we can go to the movies.

Step 1: (If) you will do the dishes, I will vacuum the house, and then we can go to the movies.

dependent clause

Step 2: If you will do the dishes, I will vacuum the house, (and) then we can go to the movies.

independent clause   *independent clause*

Step 3: one dependent clause: *If you will do the dishes*

two independent clauses: a) *I will vacuum the house*
b) *then we can go to the movies*

One dependent clause and two independent clauses make this a *compound-complex sentence.*

PRACTICE 16

Use the guidelines above to determine what type the following sentence is. Write out the steps as you apply them.

Although her father had forbidden her to see him, Maude continued to meet Harold.

Step 1: _____

_____

Step 2: _____

_____

Step 3: _____

_____

Have your instructor or tutor check your work.

Style

Ideas can be presented in any of the types of sentences; however, one way is usually more effective than others. If you understand how sentences are made, then you can begin to manipulate them to create the most effective one.

You should also strive for sentence variety and complexity in your writing. A paragraph that contains only simple sentences will probably bore your reader. On the other hand, a paragraph that contains only compound-complex sentences will cause your reader to spend more time on each sentence, and the complexity of thought may cause confusion. Try to write sentences that are effective and concise. (See "Sentence Combining" in Chapter 6, Part One, for an explanation of combining sentences effectively.)

Fragments

OBJECTIVES: 1. To recognize fragments, individually and in paragraphs.

2. To correct fragments.

3. To use the editing symbol for fragment (*Frag*) when proof-reading.

KEY CONCEPT: A sentence is a group of words that expresses a complete thought. If a sentence is not complete, it is called a *fragment*. In other words, a fragment is an incomplete thought punctuated as if it were complete, as if it were a sentence. There are four sentence errors that can produce fragments.

Fragment Type 1: No Subject

Usually, in order to express a thought completely, a sentence must contain a subject and a verb. Sometimes, however, it may contain only a verb. This particular type of sentence, called an imperative sentence, is used to express commands: for example, "Stop!" The verb is *stop;* the subject is called an **understood you,** because the speaker is commanding someone else to stop.

A group of words written without a subject is a fragment.

Example: Were walking down the street in a great hurry.

Obviously, you don't write this type of sentence frequently, but it does happen. The mistake can be corrected by simply adding a subject.

Correction: *The children* were walking down the street in a great hurry.

EXERCISE   Follow the above example, and correct the following fragments.

1. Stopped on the side of the road.

_____

2. Hit the curb.

_____

3. Ran into the store.

_____

Have your instructor or tutor check your work.

Fragment Type 2: No Verb

A group of words written without a verb is a fragment.

    Example: The woman in the yellow-striped dress.

Again, this type of fragment isn't usually mistaken for a sentence, but it can happen. When it does, the simplest way to correct the error is to add a verb.

    Correction: The woman in the yellow-striped dress is my teacher.

    NOTE: Often the reason for mistakenly punctuating this type of fragment as a sentence is that the group of words is used in apposition.

    Example: That's my teacher. The woman in the yellow-striped dress.

If this is the basis for the mistake, then correct the fragment by attaching it to the sentence to which it is related.

    Correction: That's my teacher, the woman in the yellow-striped dress.

    EXERCISE   Follow the example above, and correct the following fragments.

1. The child in the clown costume.

    The child is in the clown costume

2. The tiger in the cage.

_____

3. The duck pond in the center of town.

_____

Have your instructor or tutor check your work.

Fragment Type 3: -ing Verb with No Helping Verb

A sentence containing an -ing verb without a helping verb (such as *is, are, was, were, have been, will be*) is a fragment.

Example: Barry battling bravely against the encroaching ants.

This fragment can easily be corrected by adding an appropriate helping verb.

Correction: Barry *was* battling bravely against the encroaching ants.

EXERCISE   Follow the above example, and correct the following fragments.

1. The wolves circling the injured doe.

_____

2. The helicopter hovering overhead.

_____

3. The plane landing on the runway.

_____

Have your instructor or tutor check your work.

Fragment Type 4: No Complete Thought

A dependent clause (a group of words that contains a subject and a verb but does *not* express a complete thought) punctuated as a sentence is a fragment.

Example: That the children were very unhappy.

When editing very quickly, you might see a subject and verb in this dependent clause and incorrectly label it a sentence. But if you read the clause carefully, you can *hear* that it is not a complete thought. The fragment leaves the reader hanging in mid-air, asking who, when, or why.

NOTE: A dependent clause usually begins with a subordinate conjunction or a relative pronoun. (See Chapter 5 in Part Two for a detailed explanation of dependent clauses.) The following words are some of the most common subordinate conjunctions and relative pronouns; you should be able to recognize most of them.

Subordinate Conjunctions

after	since	when
although	so that	where
as (if)	than	whereas
because	though	wherever
before	unless	whether
even though	until	while
how	what	unless
if		until

Relative Pronouns

that	which	whom
what	whichever	whomever
whatever	who	whose
	whoever	

(*Whichever, whoever,* and *whomever* are not often used.)

There are two ways to correct a dependent-clause fragment. Choose whichever method is more appropriate for your message.

1. Because it is the subordinate conjunction that transforms the independent clause (simple sentence) into a dependent clause, *get rid of the subordinate conjunction,* which will leave you with a simple sentence.

   Fragment: That the children were very unhappy.

   Correction: The children were very unhappy.

   NOTE: This method does not always work, because a relative pronoun serves as the subject of the dependent clause.

   Example: Which was difficult.

   If you omit the subordinate conjunction, you still would not have an independent clause:

   Was difficult.

   Instead, you would still have a fragment, because your group of words now does not have a subject. In such a case, use the second method to correct the fragment.

2. *Connect the dependent clause to an independent clause,* and create a complex sentence.

   Fragment: That the children were very unhappy.

   Correction: Anyone could see that the children were very unhappy.

   Fragment: Which was difficult.

   Correction: We had to take a make-up exam, which was difficult.

EXERCISE   Follow the above examples as models, and correct the following fragments.

1. Because new cars get better gas mileage.

   _____

2. Because it began to snow.

   _____

3. Although we raced to the scene of the accident.

   _____

Have your instructor or tutor check your work.

PRACTICE 1

Decide whether each group of words below is a sentence or a fragment. If the sentence is correct, write *C* in the blank. If the group of words is a fragment, write *Frag* in the blank. Correct all fragments.

1. Man's best friend ~~'s~~ a dog.   *Frag*

2. The summer ~~which~~ is a pleasant season.   *Frag*

3. Mr. Jones is my English teacher.   *C*

4. ~~Which~~ *Math* is a difficult subject.   *Frag*

5. Many people vacation in Maine because the state offers outdoor activities

   and historical sites.   *C*

6. Taking tests can be a grueling experience.   *C*

7. The boy *was* in the scuba outfit.   *Frag*

8. The Roseland Ballroom ~~'s~~ a good place to dance.   *Frag*

9. Many people buy designer jeans because they fit better.   *C*

10. Harold ~~was~~ *went* swimming the English Channel.   *Frag*

Check the answer key.

Kathy

KATHY N STEVE

KATHY N STEVE

7

Comma Splices

OBJECTIVES:
1. To recognize comma splices in individual sentences and in paragraphs.

2. To correct comma splices.

3. To use the editing symbol for comma splices (*CS*) when proofreading.

KEY CONCEPT:
A *comma splice* occurs when two independent clauses (in compound and compound-complex sentences) are spliced (joined) by a comma and punctuated as a single sentence.

Using only a comma to join two or more complete thoughts is incorrect.

Example: The teacher was not smiling, he was frowning.

In this example, there are two complete sentences: *The teacher was not smiling,* and *he was frowning.*

Identifying the Problem

Comma splices occur only in compound or compound-complex sentences; these are the sentence types that have at least two independent clauses. To identify comma splices, look at the break between the two independent clauses. If the two independent clauses are joined by only a comma at this break, then the entire sentence is a comma splice. You must then correct the comma splice.

PRACTICE 1

Read the following sentences. If a sentence is correctly punctuated, place *C* beside it. If the group of words is actually a comma splice, place *CS* beside the sentence, and draw a vertical line separating the two independent clauses.

1. The exhibit of Andrew Wyeth's paintings was excellent, we particularly appreciated the recently unveiled "Helga" series. _____

2. Many films have been made of the conditions in Germany during the 1930s, *Cabaret* is one of the best of these. _____

3. Jason decided to see a movie, he should have completed his work first. _____

4. The space shuttle program has been devastated by the *Challenger* accident, no new shuttles will be launched for eighteen months. _____

5. Before Harriet enrolled in college, she worked as a bank teller, she plans now to major in business. _____

Check the answer key.

Correcting the Problem

There are three acceptable ways to correct the comma splice.

1. *Make the two independent clauses into two separate, complete sentences.*

   Comma Splice: The teacher was not smiling, he was frowning.
   Correction: The teacher was not smiling. He was frowning.

EXERCISE   Correct these comma splices by making two complete sentences.

1. George is an expert skier, he won three trophies.

   _____

2. Morgan enjoys adventure movies, he saw *Raiders of the Lost Ark* ten times.

   _____

   _____

Have your instructor or tutor check your work.

2. *Join the independent clauses with a comma and an appropriate coordinate conjunction.* The coordinate conjunction tells the reader that there is a relationship between the two independent clauses; furthermore, the conjunctions provide clues to the type of relationship. There are seven coordinate conjunctions: *for, and, but, so, yet, nor,* and *or.*

   Example: The teacher was not smiling, and he seemed very grumpy.

   NOTE: Learn what types of relationships each of the coordinate conjunctions stresses (see Chapter 5, Part Two, also):
   1. *For* shows cause.
   2. *And* makes two independent clauses equal.
   3. *Nor* shows negative choice.
   4. *But* shows opposition.
   5. *Or* shows choice.
   6. *So* shows result.
   7. *Yet* shows opposition.

EXERCISE Correct this comma splice by joining the two independent clauses with a comma and a coordinate conjunction.

The blizzard forced us to change our plans for a five-mile hike, we decided to stay home and build a fire.

_____

_____

Have your instructor or tutor check your work.

3. *Join the two independent clauses with a semicolon (;).*

Example: The dean was not smiling; he seemed very grumpy.

NOTE: The semicolon tells the reader that a relationship exists between the two independent clauses; however, the semicolon does not identify the relationship. Although it is correct to use a semicolon to join two independent clauses, the clauses should be closely related. For example, the second independent clause can explain the first or provide an example of the first. This connection should be clear to your reader.

Example: Many Civil War battlefields have been preserved by the Park Service; the Antietam battlefield is one of these.

In this example, the second independent clause provides a direct example of the first clause. The reader can easily understand the relationship between the two clauses.

EXERCISE Correct these comma splices by joining the two independent clauses with semicolons.

1. We did not buy the self-cleaning oven, the high cost of electricity to operate it would be beyond our budget.

_____

_____

2. Tammi's membership in the club was important to her, the club provided her with activities and social contacts.

_____

Have your instructor or tutor check your work.

NOTE: Often when you use a semicolon, you may want to include an **adverbial conjunction** (sometimes called a **conjunctive adverb**) to indicate what kind of relationship exists between the two independent clauses. There are four major adverbial conjunctions: *however, therefore, moreover,* and *nevertheless*. When you use one of these four adverbial conjunctions, you must place a semicolon before the adverbial conjunction and a comma after it.

Example: It was raining constantly; nevertheless, we continued our climb up the mountain.

Here are the relationships that these adverbial conjunctions indicate:

1. *however* means "contradiction" or "opposition."
2. *moreover* means "in addition to" and "also."
3. *therefore* means "in conclusion."
4. *nevertheless* means "in spite of."

The following list provides additional adverbial conjunctions.

also	indeed	rather
consequently	likewise	similarly
currently	next	then
finally	overall	thus
hence	primarily	

If you are unfamiliar with these adverbial conjunctions, check a dictionary for the relationships these conjunctions stress.

If you have only a comma in front of the adverbial conjunction in a sentence with two independent clauses, you still have a comma splice, so be careful.

Comma Splice: On the Fourth of July, all the banks were closed, moreover, all of the stores were closed.

Correction: On the Fourth of July, all the banks were closed; moreover, all of the stores were closed.

Adverbial conjunctions can be used in a simple sentence, as well. If an adverbial conjunction is located in a simple sentence—one with only one independent clause—you must enclose it within commas.

Examples: A dog is, moreover, man's best friend.

              Therefore, you must work harder.

EXERCISE   Correct these comma splices by joining the two independent clauses with semicolons and appropriate adverbial conjunctions.

1. Students must have free time during a school day, they must not spend all of their time in the student center.

2. Our opponents won the state championship three times in a row, we were confident of our abilities.

Have your instructor or tutor check your work.

PRACTICE 2

In the blank at the right of each sentence, write *C* if the sentence is correct. Write *CS* if the sentence is a comma splice. Correct the comma splices.

1. April is a lovely month, but I like June best. _____

2. Sally got a good promotion at her job, she also managed to take courses in the evening. _____

3. The cost of living in Paris is very high, I heard that an apartment could cost as much as a thousand dollars a month. _____

4. Last summer, Jerry spent most of his time at the beach, however, he never learned how to surf. _____

5. One of the best jobs I ever had was as a lifeguard at Wildwood State Park, I could meet many new people. _____

6. Photography is a good hobby; many people like to take pictures of people they know and places they have visited. _____

7. Teachers prefer typed papers, yet many students don't own a typewriter. _____

8. The parking facilities at this university are inadequate, each day I must drive around for at least thirty minutes before I find a space. _____

9. I prefer good restaurants, but I like fast-food places also. _____

10. Walt Whitman was a major American poet, he lived in Camden, New Jersey. _____

Check the answer key.

Run-Ons

OBJECTIVES:	1. To recognize run-ons, individually and in paragraphs.
	2. To correct run-ons.
	3. To use the editing symbol for run-ons (RO) correctly when proofreading.

KEY CONCEPT: A run-on (sometimes called a **fused sentence** or a **run-together sentence**) contains two or more independent clauses that have been punctuated as one sentence; that is, no punctuation separates the two independent clauses.

Consider this example:

Example: The lawyer pleaded her client's case well she won the case.
In this example, there are two complete sentences:

The lawyer pleaded her client's case well, and *she won the case.*

Identifying the Problem

Run-ons are found only in compound or compound-complex sentences; these are the sentences with two or more independent clauses. To identify run-ons, look at the break between the two sentences. If there is no punctuation at this point, then the sentence is a run-on.

PRACTICE 1

Read the following sentences. If a sentence is correct, place *C* beside it. If the group of words is actually a run-on, place *RO* beside the sentence, and draw a vertical line separating the two independent clauses.

Example: __RO__ I work at a factory during the night / I go to school during the day.

__C__ Drag racing is an exciting sport.

1. Harry is my best friend he will do anything for me. _____

2. Chemistry is a difficult subject. _____

3. America is a nation on the move many families move four times in a ten-year

   period. _____

4. Shelly is a good dancer she has been selected to appear with the New York

   Ballet Company. _____

5. The United Nations was formed from an older organization, the League of

Nations.

Check the answer key.

Correcting the Problem

There are three ways to correct a run-on sentence.

1. *First, break the run-on into two separate sentences with a period and a capital letter in each.*

Run-on: The dean smiled at the new freshmen they had survived their first week of classes.

Correction: The dean smiled at the new freshmen. They had survived their first week of classes.

EXERCISE   Correct these run-ons by following the above example.

1. The students went to the dean's office they wanted to complain about a teacher.

_____

2. The accountant sighed as she left her office she had worked for fifteen consecutive hours.

_____

_____

3. Smoke detectors do not cost very much they have helped save many lives.

_____

_____

Have your instructor or tutor check your work.

2. *Connect the two independent clauses with a comma and the appropriate coordinate conjunction.* There are seven coordinate conjunctions: *for, and, nor, but, or, yet,* and *so.* Each coordinate conjunction tells the reader what kind of relationship exists between the two independent clauses.

   Look at the following sentences and determine the relationship between the two independent clauses. Pay particular attention to the coordinate conjunctions.

   a. Sue is going shopping, and her husband is going bowling.
   b. Sue is going shopping, but her husband is going bowling.
   c. Sue is going shopping, so her husband is going bowling.
   d. Sue is going shopping, for her husband is going bowling.

In sentence a, the *and* tells the reader that neither one of the two independent clauses is more important than the other. In other words, the fact that *Sue is going shopping* is as important as the fact that *her husband is going bowling.*

In sentence b, the *but* shows opposition; it tells the reader that Sue and her husband are doing different things.

In sentence c, the *so* tells the reader that *her husband's going bowling* is the result of *Sue's going shopping.* You might imagine that her husband didn't want to go shopping, and he decided to go bowling while Sue was shopping.

In sentence d, the *for* tells the reader that *Sue is going shopping* because *her husband is going bowling.* In other words, Sue didn't want to go bowling, and she chose to go shopping instead.

> **NOTE:** See Chapter 7 in Part Two for a list of the relationships each coordinate conjunction stresses.

EXERCISE Following the example, correct these run-ons.

1. The snow thrilled us we wanted to go skiing.

   _____

2. Doug gently unlocked the front door he did not want to awaken his parents at 4:00 A.M.

   _____

   _____

3. Nearly half of all car accidents involve a drunk driver many states have tightened their laws concerning driving under the influence of alcohol.

   _____

   _____

Have your instructor or tutor check your work.

> **NOTE.** Using only a comma is not enough. You must use *both* the comma and the coordinate conjunction.

3. *Connect the two independent clauses with a semicolon* (;). The semicolon implies to the reader that a relationship exists between the two sentences; however, it does not indicate the *type* of relationship. Use a semicolon when the two independent clauses are closely related. For instance, the second clause can provide an example of the first one or explain the first.

Run-on:	The giant black and white pandas are native to China in fact they are the national animals of China.
Correction:	The giant black and white pandas are native to China; in fact, they are the national animals of China.

EXERCISE   Correct these run-ons by using a semicolon to separate the two independent clauses.

1. We could not buy the house it was priced at $150,000.

   _____

2. You must dress warmly in an Alaskan winter the average temperature is 0 degrees Fahrenheit.

   _____

   _____

3. In the 1800s, life in the American West was treacherous a pioneer might fall victim to natural disasters or wild animals.

   _____

   _____

Have your instructor or tutor check your work.

NOTE: Often when you use a semicolon, you may want to include an **adverbial conjunction** (sometimes called a **conjunctive adverb**) to indicate what kind of relationship exists between the two independent clauses. There are four major **adverbial conjunctions:** *however, moreover, therefore,* and *nevertheless*. When you use one of these four adverbial conjunctions, a semicolon must come before the adverbial conjunction and a comma after it.

Example: We were supposed to be at school at 9:00 A.M.; however, our car wouldn't start.

Below is a list of other adverbial conjunctions. Each of these identifies a particular relationship between the two independent clauses. Check a dictionary to learn these relationships.

also	indeed	primarily
consequently	likewise	rather
currently	next	similarly
finally	overall	then
hence		thus

PRACTICE 2

In the blank at the right of each sentence, write *C* if the sentence is correctly punctuated. Write *RO* if the sentence is a run-on. Correct the run-on sentences.

1. It was a cold, wet day; however, we still had our picnic at the beach.   _____

2. I plan to go to law school I hope that I am accepted.   _____

3. Mathematics is my hardest course English is my favorite course.   _____

4. Thelma will be a lawyer Thelma will be a doctor.   _____

5. Running is a good exercise; moreover, it relieves tension. _____

6. My uncle has a cabin in Maine, and he has a cottage at Cape Cod. _____

7. The lake was crystal clear and warm the sky was a brilliant blue. _____

8. Cumberland's basketball team won the semifinals now the team will compete in the state finals. _____

9. College demands quite a lot from a student; however, it offers many rewards. _____

10. Skiing is a difficult sport moreover it can be dangerous. _____

Check the answer key.

9

Subject-Verb Agreement

OBJECTIVES:
1. To make subjects and verbs agree in number.
2. To correct problems in subject-verb agreement.
3. To use the editing symbol for subject-verb agreement (*S-V Agr*) correctly while proofreading.

KEY CONCEPT: Agreement of subjects and verbs means exactly what it says: in a sentence, the subject and verb must agree in **number.** If the subject is singular (one item), then the verb must also be singular. If the subject is plural (two or more items), then the verb must also be plural.

Singular and Plural Forms

Most singular subjects add an *s* or *es* to make a plural noun. For example, *dog* is singular, and *dogs* is plural.

PRACTICE 1

Label each of the following words either singular (*S*) or plural (*P*).

_____ 1. cat   _____ 6. miles

_____ 2. cats   _____ 7. ideas

_____ 3. he and I   _____ 8. his aunts

_____ 4. car   _____ 9. home

_____ 5. records   _____ 10. happiness

Check the answer key.

Most present-tense verbs that are singular end in *s* or *es;* most present-tense plural verbs do not end in *s*. For example, "She danc*es*" is singular, and "They danc*e*" is plural. Look at the following chart:

Number	Subjects	Verbs
Singular	—	*es* or *s*
Plural	*s* or *es*	—

The chart provides the basic rule for subject-verb agreement. By looking at the chart, you can easily see that, in general, *either* the subject or the verb, but not *both*, will end in *s* or *es*.

Examples:
                    s   v
          The <u>cat</u> <u>carries</u> her kittens.
          Cat is singular.
          Carries is singular.

                  s   v
          The <u>cats</u> <u>carry</u> their kittens.
          Cats is plural.
          Carry is plural.

This chart provides a good test for subject-verb agreement. If both the subject and the verb end in *s* or *es*, check your work carefully. Usually, this will not occur.

PRACTICE 2

Revise the following sentences to make the subjects and verbs plural. The subjects have been underlined once, and the verbs twice.

Example: The <u>tree</u> <u>grows</u> straight.

The trees grow straight.

1. The <u>boy</u> <u>laughs</u> at the clown.

_____

2. The <u>mouse</u> <u>hides</u> in the pantry.

_____

3. The <u>examination</u> <u>seems</u> difficult.

_____

4. The <u>puppy</u> <u>nips</u> at my heels.

_____

5. The <u>girl</u> <u>dives</u> into the water.

_____

Check the answer key.

Verbs

There are some exceptions to the basic rule of singular and plural verb forms.

Regular Verbs

Regular verbs (most English verbs are regular) follow a pattern of conjunction in the present tense. Learn this pattern:

Singular	*Plural*
I (verb)	we (verb)
you (verb)	you (verb)
he, she, or it (verb + es or s)	they (verb)

Example: The verb *to dance* is a regular verb, and it is conjugated in the present tense as follows:

to dance

I *dance*	we *dance*
you *dance*	you *dance*
he, she, it *dances*	they *dance*

Which form of the verb changes? *he, she,* or *it* (third-person singular) *dances*
How does the third-person singular form change? It adds an *s* to the end of the verb.

Irregular Verbs

Some English verbs that we use frequently are irregular; that is, these irregular verbs do not follow the pattern of conjugation of regular verbs. For example, the verbs *to be, to have,* and *to do* are irregular verbs. Learn the present-tense and past-tense forms of these verbs.

Present-tense form of *to be:*

I *am*	we *are*
you *are*	you *are*
he, she, or it *is*	they *are*

Past-tense form of *to be:*

I *was*	we *were*
you *were*	you *were*
he, she, or it *was*	they *were*

Present-tense form of *to have:*

I *have*	we *have*
you *have*	you *have*
he, she, or it *has*	they *have*

Past-tense form of *to have:*

I *had*	we *had*
you *had*	you *had*
he, she, or it *had*	they *had*

Present-tense form of *to do:*

I *do*	we *do*
you *do*	you *do*
he, she, or it *does*	they *do*

Past-tense form of *to do:*

I *did*	we *did*
you *did*	you *did*
he, she, or it *did*	they *did*

PRACTICE 3

In the following sentences, put one line under the subject and two lines under the verb. In the blank space, write *S* if the subject is singular or *P* if the subject is plural. The first sentence is already done for you.

__S__ 1. The <u>cat</u> <u>carried</u> her kittens into the next room.

____ 2. The child screamed for her mother.

____ 3. Dolphins are supposedly the most intelligent marine animals.

____ 4. Hank Thompson always answers the office phone.

____ 5. Gardens grow quickly with lots of rain and sunshine.

____ 6. A student's grades depend upon his own efforts.

____ 7. Tim works in an automobile factory.

____ 8. Chrysler was able to recover from bankruptcy.

____ 9. The dogs bark all night long.

____ 10. They sat in the car.

____ 11. Many millionaires own oil wells in Texas.

____ 12. Headaches are often caused by stress.

____ 13. The desk was in the middle of the room.

____ 14. His favorite actor is Martin Sheen.

____ 15. Hemingway's books make valuable reading.

____ 16. An adolescent faces many problems.

____ 17. The pewter bowl is on sale at the department store.

——— 18. The reclining chair is very comfortable.

——— 19. The bird's song was very pleasing.

——— 20. The tennis player smashes the ball into his net.

Check the answer key.

Subjects

Always locate the subject first, because it determines whether the verb will be singular or plural. Also, remember that the noun in a prepositional phrase cannot be the subject of the sentence.

                                  s   v

Examples: The <u>Board</u> of Directors <u>meets</u> on Thursdays.

Board is the subject of the sentence, and it controls the verb. *Directors* is the object of the preposition *of,* so it cannot be the subject.

Simple Subjects

Most subjects in sentences are usually one word. The most common type of subject is the simple subject (one noun or pronoun).

Pronouns. Pronouns can take the place of nouns. For example, in the sentence "Mary went to the store because she needed a loaf of bread," *she* is a pronoun that takes the place of *Mary.* Here is a chart of the pronouns that are most commonly used as subjects:

Singular	*Plural*
I	we
you	you
he, she, it	they
this	these
that	those

Examples: Those <u>doctors</u> <u>believe</u> in the holistic theory of medicine. (simple subject—plural form)

She <u>has</u> agreed to render him an apology.
(simple subject—singular form)

You should not have any problem making most simple subjects agree with their verbs.

PRACTICE 4

In each sentence, change the plural subjects to singular ones; then, make any necessary changes in the verbs.

1. Students always feel tired after exams.

2. Dogs are usually considered man's best friend.

3. Children love to receive gifts.

4. The nations have amassed a budget surplus.

5. The plants need to be repotted.

Check the answer key.

Indefinite Pronouns. However, some simple subjects do cause problems. Below is a list of ndefinite pronouns. All of them take a *singular* verb.

anybody	either	nobody
anyone	everybody	no one
anything	everyone	somebody
each	neither	some one

Examples: Anybody is allowed into the school.

Each one is responsible for his own gear.

Some indefinite pronouns (for example, *all, any, more, most, none, some*) can be either singular or plural, depending on the words that modify them. This situation usually occurs when the subject is a portion or percentage.

Examples:

S — modifier — V
Most (of the swimmers) refuse to enter the water. (plural)

S — modifier — V
Most (of the summer) is gone. (singular)

S — modifier — V
Ten percent (of the money) was recovered. (singular)

S — modifier — V
Seventy percent (of all women) want equality of the sexes. (plural)

In these cases, in order to determine whether the subject is singular or plural, you must look at the modifier (usually a prepositional phrase):

- If the modifier is singular, then the subject is singular and takes a singular verb.
- If the modifier is plural, then the subject is plural and takes a plural verb.

EXERCISE   Using the previous example sentences as models, change the subject in each of the sentences as indicated and make any necessary changes in the verb.

Change "of the semester" to "of my college years":

1. A quarter of the semester was spent studying Milton.

Change "of the child's day" to "of the class's time":

2. Ten percent of the child's day is devoted to art history.

Have your instructor or tutor check your work.

PRACTICE 5

Identify the subject in each sentence and indicate whether it is singular (*S*) or plural (*P*). Circle the verb that agrees with the subject.

Example: <u>P</u>^S   Many students (participates, (participate)) in organized sports.

_____ 1. Each person (enjoy, enjoys) the rights established by the Constitution.

_____ 2. All of the cake (was, were) eaten last night.

_____ 3. Some of the boys (has, have) decided to go camping.

_____ 4. Each of the boys (play, plays) hockey.

_____ 5. Neither of the girls (wants, want) to work tonight.

_____ 6. All of the students (enjoys, enjoy) holidays.

_____ 7. Each teenager (wants, want) his own car.

_____ 8. The horses (gallops, gallop) along the fence.

_____ 9. Most adults (enjoys, enjoy) a vacation.

_____ 10. Half of the cherry pie (was, were) gone.

Check the answer key.

Collective Nouns

A collective noun is also a simple subject, so it takes a *singular verb*. (Remember, a collective noun is one that refers to a group of individuals as a unit.) Here is a short list of collective nouns:

family	team	battalion	jury
crew	squad	company	union
herd	class	army	division
committee	crowd	quartet	mob

Examples: The <u>class</u> <u>has</u> decided to go to Central Park for a picnic.
             s   v

<u>Congress</u> <u>has</u> adjourned for the Fourth of July holiday.
s   v

EXERCISE   Using the example sentences as models, make the suggested change in the subject in each of the following sentences and make any necessary changes in the verb.

Change "children" to "family":

1. The children are unhappy about foregoing a spring vacation this year.

Change "committee" to "executives":

2. The committee is undecided about the company's future plans.

Have your instructor or tutor check your work.

Titles

The title of a written work, a movie or television show, an artistic creation, or a musical composition takes a *singular* verb.

Examples: "Hansel and Gretel" is a well-loved children's tale.

The Ring and the Book presents a tangled web of lies and half-truths.

EXERCISE Using the above sentences as models, make the suggested change in each of the following sentences.

Change "This" to "*All the King's Men*":

1. This is my favorite book.

Change "The Kiss" to "The Destructors":

2. "The Kiss" was not a very interesting short story.

Have your instructor or tutor check your work.

Plural-Form Singular-Meaning Nouns

Some nouns are plural in form but singular in meaning; they take a singular verb. Here are some examples:

aerobics	calisthenics	mathematics
aesthetics	economics	news

Example: The news is not good.

Economics was not my best course.

On the other hand, "jeans," "pants," and "trousers" always take a plural verb.

Example: Designer jeans are the hottest clothing item right now.

"Scissors" can be treated as singular or plural; base your choice on the sense of the sentence and its style. When in doubt about the number (singular or plural) of a word, consult your dictionary.

EXERCISE Make the suggested change in each of these sentences.

Change "history" to "physics":

1. Without a doubt, history is a boring subject.

Change "decor" to "aesthetics":

2. The decor of the room requires a restrained piece of statuary in the alcove.

Have your instructor or tutor check your work.

Nouns of Quantities. *Nouns* that refer to a *quantity* or to items that are considered a *single unit* take a *singular verb.*

Examples: $\overset{s}{\underline{\text{Ten kilos}}}$ $\overset{v}{\underline{\underline{\text{is}}}}$ too much for one person to lift.

One thousand $\overset{s}{\underline{\text{dollars}}}$ $\overset{v}{\underline{\underline{\text{was}}}}$ a lot to bet on the flip of a card.

EXERCISE   Make the suggested change in each of these sentences.

Change "This" to "Two miles":

1. This is too far to walk.

Change "One gallon" to "Two gallons":

2. One gallon provides about an hour's worth of motorcycle riding.

Have your instructor or tutor check your work.

PRACTICE 6

Identify the subject (S) in each sentence and indicate whether it is singular (S) or plural (P). Circle the verb that agrees in number with the subject.

Example: _S_ The flock of starlings (seems, seem) nervous.

_____ 1. This year, the gaggle of geese (has, have) stayed in this area for more than a month.

_____ 2. *The Crusaders* (is, are) a long-forgotten work by Margaret du Pleny.

_____ 3. Measles (is, are) no longer considered the scourge of mankind.

_____ 4. Trousers (has, have) made a fashion comeback.

_____ 5. One hundred pounds of potato salad (is, are) a lot to make each week.

Check the answer key.

Not all agreement problems are caused by simple subjects, however.

Compound Subjects

Whether a *compound subject* requires a singular or a plural verb depends on the sentence.

REMEMBER: A compound subject means that there is more than one subject in the sentence.

If the elements of the compound subject joined by *and* are still considered separate entities, they require a *plural* verb:

Examples: Tom, Harry, Joe, and Hank are in the classroom now.

Swimming and golf are my favorite sports.

However, if the nouns that are joined by *and* are considered one unit or refer to a single person, then a singular verb is required:

Examples: Ham and eggs is my favorite breakfast.

Meat and potatoes seems to be the only meal fit for this man.

My friend and confidante, Lucille, has been stricken by pneumonia.

EXERCISE Following the above examples, make the suggested change in each sentence and change the verb, if necessary.

Add "and one cat":

1. One dog is about all this apartment can hold.

Add "and Susan":

2. Sally is going to the movies tonight.

Have your instructor or tutor check your work.

If the compound subject is joined by "or," "either . . . or," or "neither . . . nor," then the number of the subject that is closer to the verb determines the number of the verb.

Examples: Either Sally or the boys are supposed to pick your father up at the station.

Neither the teachers nor the administration wants a strike this year.

EXERCISE Using the above sentences as models, make the suggested change in each sentence.

Change "Susan" to "the company":

1. Susan or Herman has to make a decision.

Change "media" to "*Congressional Record*":

2. Neither Congress nor the media report results accurately.

Have your instructor or tutor check your work.

PRACTICE 7

Underline the subject in each sentence. Decide whether the subject is singular (*S*) or plural (*P*), and fill in the blank at the left. Circle the correct verb.

_____ 1. Jack and Eileen (wants, want) to get married.

_____ 2. Neither the foreman nor the union representatives (wants, want) to discipline the errant worker.

_____ 3. Harold or George (swims, swim) faster than you do.

_____ 4. My friend and her husband (has, have) slipped into alcoholism. (same person)

_____ 5. Quiche and hash just (doesn't, don't) seem to complement each other.

Check the answer key.

The last two sources of confusion about subject-verb agreement stem from different types of sentences.

Relative-Pronoun Clauses

If you have a relative pronoun (*who, which,* or *that*) as the subject of the dependent clause in a complex sentence, then you must determine the noun to which it refers before you can decide whether the pronoun should be singular or plural.

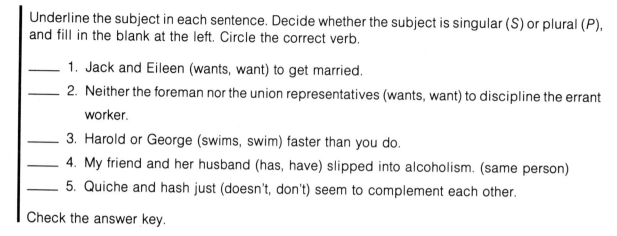

Examples: Her father, <u>who is</u> an Army major, is buying a new car. (*who* refers to *father*)

Terry's book, <u>which is</u> on the table, costs ten dollars. (*which* refers to *book*)

EXERCISE   Make the suggested change in each of the following sentences.

Make "brother" plural:

1. His brother, who is joining the Navy, likes the sea.

Make "friends" singular.

2. My friends, who are standing in the doorway, have just returned from a dance.

Have your instructor or tutor check your work.

NOTE: Be careful with relative pronouns in the construction "one of." Consider the following examples:

Examples: He is one of the men who receive their pay on Friday.
The doctor is the only one of the staff members who understands the patient's condition.

In the first example, the relative pronoun "who" replaces the word "men"; hence, the verb must be plural. (In this sentence, the subject "he" is part of a group of men who receive their pay on Friday.)

In the second example, the relative pronoun "who" substitutes for the word "one"; thus, the verb must be singular. (In this example, the doctor is identified as the "only one" who understands the problem.) If the construction "one of" is preceded by the word "only," then the verb will be singular. However, if the construction "one of" does not have the word "only" preceding it, then you must analyze the sentence and its meaning to determine the noun or pronoun the relative pronoun replaces. Then, decide whether the verb should be singular or plural.

PRACTICE 8

Underline the relative pronoun in each sentence; then, identify the noun to which the relative pronoun refers. Decide whether the subject is singular (*S*) or plural (*P*), and fill in the blank at the left. Circle the correct verb.

_____ 1. F. Scott Fitzgerald, who (was, were) a major literary figure in the 1920s, worked in Hollywood during the late 1930s.

_____ 2. Harris is one of the lawyers who (selects, select) their cases carefully.

_____ 3. This final calculus problem is the only one that (is, are) difficult.

_____ 4. The Stonehenge monument, which (is, are) in England, served as the site of many religious ceremonies.

_____ 5. Sam is the only one of her friends who (enjoys, enjoy) tennis.

Check the answer key.

Inverted Sentences

In inverted sentences, which often begin with the adverbs *there, here,* or *where* or with prepositional phrases, the subject follows the verb. You must look for the subject after the verb before you can determine the number.

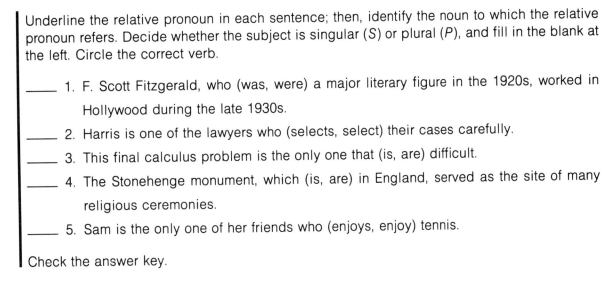

Examples: There is the book.

Here are the children.

EXERCISE Make the suggested change in each of the following sentences.

Make "outfits" singular:

1. There are the new outfits.

Change "dog" to "animals":

2. Here is the last dog.

Have your instructor or tutor check your work.

PRACTICE 9

Underline the subject of each sentence. Decide whether the subject is singular (*S*) or plural (*P*), and fill in the blank at the left. Circle the correct verb.

_____ 1. There (is, are) too many people in this elevator.

_____ 2. At the end of the shady lane (stands, stand) the county courthouse and a church.

_____ 3. Here (is, are) your letters of recommendation.

_____ 4. For each of the applicants, there (was, were) long forms to complete.

_____ 5. Behind these locked doors (lies, lie) a fortune in gold bullion.

Check the answer key.

Pronoun Reference

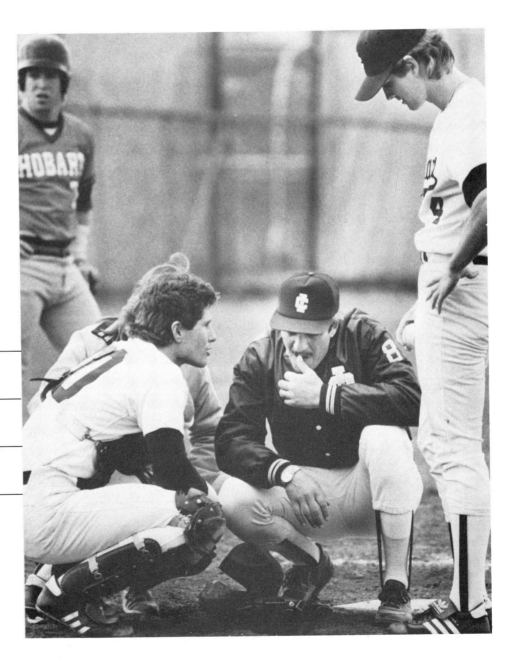

OBJECTIVES: 1. To recognize pronoun-reference problems.

2. To correct pronoun-reference problems.

3. To proofread an essay for pronoun reference. The editing symbol for pronoun reference is *pro. ref.*

KEY CONCEPT: A **pronoun** usually takes the place of a noun. The noun the pronoun replaces is called the **antecedent.** Usually, the pronoun takes the place of the closest noun.

antecedent   pronoun

Example: *Jill* was happy; in fact, *she* was ecstatic.

Personal Pronouns and Cases

The following chart lists personal pronouns; become familiar with them.

Personal Pronouns

Person	Nominative Case		Objective Case		Possessive Case	
	Singular	Plural	Singular	Plural	Singular	Plural
First	I	we	me	us	my, mine	our, ours
Second	you	you	you	you	your, yours	your, yours
Third	he	they	him	them	his	their, theirs
	she		her		her, hers	
	it		it		its	

The **nominative** (or subjective) case is used when the pronoun is the subject of the sentence or when the pronoun is a predicate nominative.

antecedent   pronoun

Examples: The *girls* ate lunch in a Chinese restaurant; *they* enjoyed the meal greatly.

(In this sentence, the pronoun *they* is a subject.)

antecedent   pronoun

In last night's basketball game, *Ira* played very well. In fact, it was *he* who was chosen the most valuable player of the game.

(In this sentence, the pronoun *he* is a predicate nominative.)

The **objective** case is used when the pronoun is a direct object, an indirect object, or the object of a preposition.

Examples: Jerry called *them* last night. (a direct object)
Time gives *us* grey hairs. (an indirect object)
Julie gave the textbook to *him*. (the object of a preposition)

To test for the objective case, place a *to* or *for* before the pronoun. If the sentence is clear, then you need to use the objective case.

Example: The teacher gave *her* the test.
The teacher gave the test to *her*.

The **possessive** case indicates ownership.

Example: The class gave *its* approval to the plan.
Mr. Mason made *his* famous chocolate cheesecake.

PRACTICE 1

Provide the correct pronoun for each of the following nouns. Pay particular attention to the case of the pronoun.

	Nominative	Objective	Possessive
1. a dock	_____	_____	_____
2. dog	_____	_____	_____
3. Harry and Ellen	_____	_____	_____
4. James and I	_____	_____	_____
5. Sara	_____	_____	_____

Check the answer key.

Pronoun Agreement

Number Agreement

A pronoun must agree in number with its antecedent; that is, if a noun is singular, then the pronoun that replaces it must be singular. If a noun is plural, then the pronoun that replaces it must be plural.

antecedent   pronoun   pronoun

Example: The sophomore *women* decided that *they* would return to *their* rooms.

Gender Agreement

Pronouns must agree with their antecedents in gender; that is, if the noun is masculine, then the pronoun must also be masculine. If the noun is feminine, then the pronoun must be feminine. If the noun is neuter (or has no determined sex), then the pronoun must be neuter.

antecedent pronoun

Example: The little *boy* lost *his* toy.   (singular, masculine)

antecedent   pronoun

The elderly *woman* dropped *her* keys.   (singular, feminine)

antecedent   pronoun

The *chair* is missing one of *its* legs.   (singular, neuter)

NOTE: Ships, planes, and countries are usually feminine.

Person Agreement

Pronouns must also agree with their antecedents in person. You must be able to identify the speaker (first person), the person spoken to (second person), and the person spoken about (third person).

antecedent   pronoun

Examples: *I* dropped *my* wallet.   (first person, singular—the speaker)

antecedent   pronoun

Your grandfather told only *you* to stay here.
(second person, singular—the person spoken to)

antecedent   pronoun

Harold believes *he* can win a gold medal in the Olympics.
(third person, masculine, singular—the person spoken about)

PRACTICE 2

Use the pronoun chart to fill in the blanks with the correct pronoun.

1. Maria revealed that _____ had been married recently.

2. The actors decided that _____ did not like the script.

3. At student union meetings, only full-time students are allowed to express _____

   opinions.

4. I realized that I would never get _____ dream car.

5. The baby waved _____ tin cup at each passerby.

Check the answer key.

PRACTICE 3

In each of the following sentences, circle the pronoun and its antecedent. Write the pronoun and its antecedent in the columns to the right.

Example: We saw (The Return of the Jedi;) (it)   _*it*_   *The Return of the Jedi*

was a marvelous film.   Pronoun   Antecedent

1. Maria gave her money to Hank.   _____   _____

2. Mr. Roberts, you must do your homework.   _____   _____

3. The teacher announced the test results to her class.   _____   _____

4. The radiologist completed his work.   _____   _____

5. The famous trial lawyer made her opening state-

ment to the jury.   _____   _____

6. Steve and I decided that we had spent too much

money on the new car.   _____   _____

7. The horse threw its rider.   _____   _____

8. Bring the books to me; then, take them to Mr. Stone.   _____   _____

9. The lamp, a gift from my grandmother, had been in

her home for years.   _____   _____

10. The film industry caters to the public's interests;

recently it has produced many science-fiction

movies.   _____   _____

11. Give the pen to me; it needs to be refilled.   _____   _____

12. Bonnie and Jack, will you please talk softly?   _____   _____

13. The plants need to be watered; I have not watered

them for three weeks.   _____   _____

14. The mother rushed into the house to see her child.   _____   _____

15. The novel was read by many people; it sold over six

million copies.   _____   _____

Check the answer key.

PRACTICE 4

The antecedents for the pronouns in the sentences appear in parentheses. Choose the pronoun that would most logically refer to the antecedent.

Example: (Harriet) __*She*__ answered the phone.

1. Add some spices to the casserole; (the casserole) _____ is bland.

2. (Paula) _____ takes violin lessons twice a week.

3. (Mary and I) _____ decided to take a vacation.

4. After John finished working, (John) _____ went straight home.

5. The musician played a song that (the musician) _____ had written.

6. The congresswoman gave (the congresswoman's) _____ support to the loyal mayoral candidate.

7. Mr. Willis, my chemistry instructor, told (Mr. Willis's) _____ students how to complete the experiment.

8. Martha bought a new suit. (The suit) _____ fits her well.

9. The principal and the faculty will drive (the principal's and the faculty's) _____ cars to the convention.

10. The reporter asked the president very tough questions. (The president) _____ refused to comment.

11. Please check the oil in the car. (The oil) _____ needs to be changed.

12. Whales have been hunted for many years, but now (whales) _____ have become an endangered species.

13. (Samantha and Janice) _____ plan to become vice presidents in the firm.

14. Take the meat out of the freezer. (The meat) _____ needs to thaw.

15. (The hockey players) _____ practice for five hours each day.

Check the answer key.

Special Problems

Split Subjects

Either . . . or and *neither . . . nor* often confuse writers. For sentences that contain *either . . . or* or *neither . . . nor,* the antecedent closer to the pronoun controls the number and gender of the pronoun.

antecedent   pronoun

Example: Neither *Tim* nor his *friends* have *their* own cars.

antecedent pronoun

Neither his *friends* nor *Tim* has *his* own car.

antecedent   pronoun

Either *Major Banks* or the *captains* will issue *their* orders.

antecedent   pronoun

Either the *captains* or *Major Banks* will issue *his* orders.

Plural Subjects

Subjects joined by *and* are usually plural, and they take a plural pronoun.

antecedent   antecedent   pronoun

Example: The *seniors* and the *juniors* will plan *their* party.

Collective Nouns

Collective nouns are words that stand for a group of members, but they are considered to be singular because the group acts as a unit. For example, the following words are collective nouns:

army	committee	trio
team	group	jury
pair	family	flock
class	herd	society

antecedent   pronoun

Example: The *army* is planning *its* practice maneuvers.

antecedent   pronoun

The Smith *family* is planning *its* vacation.

However, if the collective noun refers to a group as a number of individuals, then it may be plural and require a plural pronoun.

antecedent   pronoun

Example: The *jury* are casting *their* ballots.

However, this plural form sometimes sounds awkward. It would be better to revise the sentence: *The members of the jury are casting their ballots.*

Indefinite Pronouns

The following words are *singular* indefinite pronouns:

each	every
someone	somebody
anybody	anyone
everybody	everyone
no one	one

These singular indefinite pronouns usually take masculine, singular pronouns.

antecedent   pronoun
Example: Does *everyone* have *his* book?

You will notice that this traditional use of masculine, singular pronouns to replace indefinite pronouns excludes the women in the audience. The same problem can occur when you want to provide a pronoun for a noun that does not identify gender, such as *student, officer, doctor,* or *athlete.* Certainly, this usage is not always appropriate, as the following sentence demonstrates:

Each *student* must register *his* car before *he* parks on campus.

This sentence, similar to many in college catalogs, is appropriate only at an all-male institution. It is inappropriate for a catalog that addresses both men and women. To avoid sexist language, you can use a number of methods.

1. Use the correct form of the expression *he or she.*

   Example: Each student must register *his or her* car before *he or she* parks on campus.

   However, if you use this alternative in a lengthy passage, you will find that the constant repetition of *he or she* is awkward and can distract your readers.

2. Alternate masculine and feminine pronouns throughout a passage.

   Example: Each student must register *his* car before *he* parks on campus. To register a car, each student must present *her* current campus identification, the car's registration, and a check for twenty dollars to the bursar.

   At best, this usage is confusing to your readers.

3. Use only nouns, instead of pronouns, in a passage.

   Example: Each student must register the student's car before the student parks on campus.

   Certainly, this method will become repetitive for your readers.

4. Use plural nouns or plural indefinite pronouns.

   Examples: Students must register *their* cars before *they* park on campus.
   All students must register *their* cars before *they* park on campus.

   This usage includes everyone, male and female, in the audience. In addition, it avoids confusion and repetition.

The following indefinite pronouns can be *singular* or *plural: all, some, many, most,* and *none.* The number of these pronouns is determined by the number of the noun in the prepositional phrase that follows the indefinite pronoun.

antecedent   pronoun
Examples: *All* of the police officers are required to report to *their* posts at once.

In this sentence, *all* is plural because the noun in the following prepositional phrase, *police officers,* is plural.

Some of the cake was left.
In this sentence, *some* is singular because the noun in the prepositional phrase, *cake,* is singular.

antecedent   pronoun
Some of the swimmers have completed *their* laps.

Since the word *some* is followed by the prepositional phrase *of the swimmers, some* is plural.

EXERCISE   Fill in the correct pronoun in the following sentences. Circle the antecedent.

1. Every freshman must complete _____ housing request as soon as possible.

2. Some of the sophomore women called _____ parents the first week of classes.

3. Every man and woman in the armed forces serves _____ country proudly.

4. Half of the seniors plan to apply to graduate school before _____ complete this semester.

5. All of the cars on this lot need repair because _____ have been driven over sixty thousand miles.

Have your instructor or tutor check your work.

Singular Pronouns

A singular pronoun is used with nouns that appear to be plural but are actually singular. For example, the nouns *news, physics, economics, mathematics,* and *genetics* are all singular and require singular pronouns.

antecedent   pronoun
Example: *Physics* operates by *its* own principles.

Mistaking the Antecedent

Sometimes prepositional phrases and relative pronouns (*who, which, that*) can cause confusion if they come between the pronoun and its antecedent.

antecedent   prep phrase   pronoun
Examples: *Each* (of the dogs) buried *its* bone.

antecedent   pronoun
Jean is just one of the senior *women* who have already received *their* awards.

Ambiguous Antecedents

Be very careful not to confuse your reader by writing a sentence that has an ambiguous pronoun reference.

Example: Jim told Pablo that he should go home.

Can you tell from this sentence who should go home? Instead, use dialogue to resolve the reference problem.

Example: Jim told Pablo, "I should go home." (Jim is going home.)

Jim told Pablo, "You should go home." (Pablo is going home.)

PRACTICE 5

Fill in the correct pronoun in each sentence. Write the antecedent on the line to the right of the sentences.

Example: The jury is making ___*its*___ final decision.   ___*jury*___

1. Most societies care for _____ older people and infants.   _____

2. The herd of cattle is approaching _____ favorite watering hole.   _____

3. Everybody must bring _____ books.   _____

4. Neither the coach nor her players are happy about _____ loss.   _____

5. Some of the fathers are bringing _____ children.   _____

6. The company offered _____ employees a sizable raise.   _____

7. The class must learn _____ lesson.   _____

8. Neither of the two girls is capable of repairing _____ car.   _____

9. The board of trustees had _____ final meeting.   _____

10. She is one of the women who are making major strides in _____

    fields.   _____

11. The flock of birds sighted _____ nesting ground.   _____

12. Do all of the freshmen students have _____ registration cards?   _____

13. The dean and his associates are discussing _____ options.   _____

14. The doctor and her staff plan to present _____ research findings on

    Monday.   _____

15. *The New England Journal of Medicine* announced _____ new

    board of directors.   _____

Check the answer key.

Commas to Separate

OBJECTIVES:
1. To recognize the need for commas in sentences and in paragraphs.

2. To use commas correctly.

3. To proofread a paper for comma mistakes, and to use correctly the editing symbol for comma mistakes (*P*).

KEY CONCEPT: Commas are used to separate six different parts or elements in a sentence:

1. Independent clauses joined by coordinate conjunctions,

2. Items in a series,

3. Coordinate adjectives,

4. Long introductory elements,

5. Dates and addresses, and

6. Any elements that might be misread and misunderstood if they were not separated by commas.

Independent Clauses

An independent clause is a group of words that contains a subject and a verb and can stand alone. In other words, it is a simple sentence and may be punctuated as such. However, you may want to join two independent clauses and write them as one compound sentence; in that case, you must use one of two methods:

1. *Join two independent clauses with a **semicolon.***

Examples: The teachers elect their representatives. (independent clause)
The administration approves them. (independent clause)

The teachers elect their representatives; the administration approves them. (compound sentence)

The children decided to buy their parents a gift. (independent clause)
They raided their piggy banks. (independent clause)

The children decided to buy their parents a gift; they raided their piggy banks. (compound sentence)

2. *Join two independent clauses by adding a **comma** and a **coordinate conjunction.***

Examples: The teachers elect their representatives, but the administration approves them.

The children decided to buy their parents a gift, so they raided their piggy banks.

NOTE: The comma comes before the coordinate conjunction. There are only seven coordinate conjunctions: *and, but, for, so, or, yet,* and *nor.* (See "Compound Sentences" in Chapter 5, Part Two.)

EXERCISE   Join the following independent clauses to form a compound sentence by using a comma and a coordinate conjunction.

Independent clauses: Susan cooked an elaborate dinner.
John washed the dishes afterwards.

Compound sentence:

_____

Independent clauses: The manager reviewed the sales figures.
He was not happy with what he saw.

Compound sentence:

_____

Have your instructor or tutor check your work.

NOTE: Remember that the comma precedes the coordinate conjunction only when it is joining two independent clauses, but usually not when the conjunction is joining words, phrases, or dependent clauses.

Examples: The boys decided to swim and fish. (joins prepositional words)

The girls are either at the beach or at the pool. (joins phrases)

A child must know that his parents love him and that they will care for him. (joins dependent clauses)

PRACTICE 1

If there is a comma error in a sentence, write *P* in the blank, and then correct the sentence by inserting a comma wherever necessary. If a sentence is correctly punctuated, write *C* in the blank.

1. The boys and girls could not decide whether to swim or fish.   *C*

2. On Thursday the governing board will decide on next year's budget and this year's dues obligation.   *C*

3. The children played in the schoolyard, for the teachers were attending a faculty conference.   *P*

4. The bride wanted to party for another hour, but the groom was anxious to begin the honeymoon.   *P*

5. The cake must bake for an hour, and the cookies have to bake for forty minutes.   *P*

Check the answer key.

Items in a Series

Commas are used to separate each item in a series from the preceding item. Remember that a series is a group of three or more items having the same function and form in the sentence.

> Examples: Sara, Mike, and Elton are good friends. (series of words)
>
> In the living room, in the playroom, and in the basement are radios. (series of phrases)
>
> Mary Jean promised that she would be a good girl, that she would not bite her brother, and that she would not climb onto the television. (series of clauses)

EXERCISE   Add commas wherever necessary in the following sentences.

1. We bought apples, peaches and bananas at the fruit store today.

2. The instructor looked through his briefcase, through his desk, and around the office for the lost grade book.

3. Despite the facts that she was only 5'2" tall, that she weighed 180 pounds, and that she had dyed her hair green, Marcie believed she could get a job as a high-fashion model.

   Have your instructor or tutor check your work.

PRACTICE 2

If there is a comma error in a sentence, write *P* in the blank and then correct the sentence by inserting a comma wherever necessary. If a sentence is correctly punctuated, write *C* in the blank.

1. People who want to buy a foreign car have a wide range of choices: Datsuns, Toyotas, and Volkswagens.   P

2. Milky Ways, M&Ms, and Mounds are my favorite candies.   P

3. I bought a dress and a coat the other day.   C

4. She buys gifts for Christmas, Thanksgiving, and Easter.   P

5. I have to stop at the cleaner's, buy some milk and pick up the twins at school.   P

optional

Check the answer key.

Coordinate Adjectives

Commas are used to separate coordinate adjectives. Coordinate adjectives are two or more adjectives that modify a noun or pronoun and that have equal value in modifying the noun or pronoun.

> Examples: happy, lively children
>
> beautiful, sophisticated woman

To test whether two adjectives are coordinate, reverse the order of the adjectives and insert *and* between them. If the phrase still makes sense, then the adjectives *must* be separated by a comma.

Examples: happy, lively children
lively and happy children

beautiful, sophisticated woman
sophisticated and beautiful woman

wholesome Italian food
Italian and wholesome food

NOTE: Obviously, the last phrase does not contain coordinate adjectives; therefore, it should not contain a comma.

EXCEPTIONS: Adjectives that describe size, age, or color generally are not separated by a comma.

Examples: big black Cadillac
little old lady

EXERCISE   Follow the above examples, and insert a comma where necessary in the following sentences.

1. He acted the part of the charming, convivial host.

2. That fancy, expensive sports car has too many gadgets for my taste.

Have your instructor or tutor check your work.

PRACTICE 3

Insert a comma wherever necessary in the following sentences. If a sentence is correctly punctuated, mark it *C*.

1. The little old woman seemed to shrink even more under her son's harsh, impersonal gaze.
2. The yellow foreign roadster sped from the scene of the accident.
3. A dirty, dingy file cabinet creates a bad impression in an executive's office.
4. The short blond-haired youngster was the prime troublemaker in the group.
5. The Irish setter with the long red hair seemed out of place among the poodles.

Check the answer key.

Long Introductory Elements

These must be separated from the rest of the sentence by a comma. The key words here are *long* and *introductory*. If the element is short, or if it is not at the beginning of the sentence, no comma is needed.

Examples: On Tuesday we went to the movies. (short prepositional phrase)
            On that fateful and fear-filled Tuesday, we went to the movies. (long prepositional phrase)

            People feel guilty when they reject another's plea for help. (clause at end of sentence)
            When they reject another's plea for help, people feel guilty. (introductory clause)

EXERCISE   Correct these sentences by following the above examples.

1. Before going home, the man decided to play one last game of pool.

2. After Susan decided to sue for divorce, she moved out of the apartment.

Have your instructor or tutor check your work.

PRACTICE 4

If there is a comma error in a sentence, write *P* in the blank, and then insert a comma wherever necessary. If a sentence is correctly punctuated, write *C* in the blank.

1. Having been introduced to the star once before, Harry felt at ease in her presence.   _P_

2. Tonight, I want to go straight home.   _P or C_

3. Before the group moved down the road, each member checked his equipment.   _P_

4. In the total darkness, with, only the ticking of the clock to guide him, the burglar stumbled on the carpet.   _P_

5. Because the tests are machine-graded, it is unlikely that there would be an error.   _P_

Check the answer key.

Dates and Addresses

Commas are used to separate individual items in a date or an address.

Examples: Ty Cobb hit his last home run on September 11, 1927, at Wrigley Field.
            The new Regency House is at 42 Marston Lane, Ridgefield, Ohio, a major metropolis.

NOTE: The comma is optional when only the month and year are given.

Example: Most people believe the Great Depression began in October 1929 and ended with the advent of World War II.

EXERCISE   Correct the following sentences by inserting a comma where necessary.

1. My parents were married on August 14,1975,and divorced in May 1985.
2. Their first home was at 1225 Elm Street,Florham Station,Arizona.

Have your instructor or tutor check your work.

PRACTICE 5

If there is a comma error in a sentence, write *P* in the blank and then correct the error. If a sentence is correctly punctuated, write *C* in the blank.

1. December 7,1941,is a date few people will ever forget.

2. One famous address for Americans is 1600 Pennsylvania Avenue,Washington,D.C.

3. The real-estate broker just mentioned that the house at 27-01 32nd Avenue, Flushing, is for sale.

4. Before you leave, let me remind you that the term project is due November 2, and not a day later.

5. Even though you prefer the apartment at 227 Oak Crest Drive, it will not be available until July 1993.

Check the answer key.

Elements That Might Be Misread or Misunderstood

The reason for a comma in this situation is obvious. Some sentences might be easily understood when you hear them but misunderstood when you read them. In order to prevent this, separate any phrases that might cause confusion by inserting a comma.

Example: Before eating the children washed their hands.

Correction: Before eating, the children washed their hands.

The sentence should be punctuated with a comma; otherwise, your reader might assume that you eat children.

Example: Although we were expecting only three fifty guests arrived.

Correction: Although we were expecting only three, fifty guests arrived.

The above sentence needs a comma to prevent a misunderstanding about the number of guests.

EXERCISE   Correct the following sentences by inserting a comma where necessary.

1. At eleven,fifty Boy Scouts began the hike up Stone Face Mountain.

2. After mile,twenty five more people dropped out of the race.

Have your instructor or tutor check your work.

PRACTICE 6

If there is a comma error in a sentence, write *P* in the blank, and then correct the error. If a sentence is correctly punctuated, write *C* in the blank.

1. After jumping,the dog raced toward the cat.   _____

2. Exactly at nine,thirty men raced home.   _____

3. When old, horses should be put out to pasture.   _____

4. Before Byron was thirty,one masterpiece had been published.   _____

5. Precisely at twelve o'clock,four blasts were sounded on the horn.   _____

Check the answer key.

Commas to Enclose

OBJECTIVES:
1. To recognize poorly punctuated sentences, in isolation and in paragraphs.

2. To use commas to enclose or set off words, phrases, and clauses correctly.

3. To proofread a paper for comma errors and to use the editing symbol for a comma error (*P*).

KEY CONCEPT: Commas are used to enclose or set off six major elements that interrupt sentences:

1. Direct address,

2. Speaker in a dialogue,

3. Apposition,

4. Out-of-place adjectives,

5. Nonrestrictive clauses and phrases, and

6. Parenthetical expressions.

Interrupters are extra words or ideas added to the basic thought of a sentence. Because they are not necessary to the basic sentence, interrupters must be enclosed or set off by commas. Depending on its placement in the sentence, the interrupter will require either one or two commas to isolate it.

Examples: If I'm not mistaken, his pay averages about $200 per week. (beginning of the sentence—one comma)

His pay, if I'm not mistaken, averages about $200 per week. (middle of the sentence—two commas)

His pay averages about $200 per week, if I'm not mistaken. (end of the sentence—one comma)

Commas in Direct Address

When the speaker in a sentence talks to another person and names that person, the process is called *direct address* because the speaker is addressing his audience directly.

Example: I think, dear, you're wrong.

The speaker is talking to a person whom he calls "dear." Therefore, "dear" must be enclosed within commas. Because the interrupter is placed in the middle of the sentence, two commas are used to enclose it.

Example: Your performance is poor, Nancy.

The speaker is talking to a person, and that person is named at the end of the sentence. Therefore, one comma is used to set off the noun in direct address, "Nancy."

Example: You poor little waif, you seem frozen.

The speaker is addressing a person whom he calls "you poor little waif." Because that direct-address interrupter is placed at the beginning of the sentence, one comma is used to isolate it.

EXERCISE   Correct the following sentences by inserting the necessary commas.

1. The children don't trust any authority figure sir.
2. Let me assure you boss there's a reason for my tardiness.

Have your instructor or tutor check your work.

PRACTICE 1

Correctly punctuate the following sentences.

1. Professor MacBride may I ask a question?
2. He really thinks Charles that he has grounds for a lawsuit.
3. Your Honor I object to the tone of his question.
4. Tomorrow you will go to the parade children.
5. Let's go to the game tonight Mary.

Check the answer key.

Commas in Dialogue

A dialogue is a conversation between two or more people. If the speaker (not the listener) in the conversation is identified, his name (or the noun or pronoun used to refer to the speaker) and the verb that refers to his speaking are enclosed within commas.

Examples: Mary said, "I dislike concerts because the music is too loud."

"I dislike concerts because the music is too loud," said the girl.

"I dislike concerts," proclaimed the teenager, "because the music is too loud."

In each of these sentences, the speaker is identified. Therefore, in the first sentence the phrase "Mary said," which is at the beginning of the sentence, is set off by one comma. The phrase "said the girl" is at the end of the second sentence, so one comma is used. Finally, the phrase "proclaimed the teenager" is in the middle of the last sentence, so it is enclosed by two commas.

NOTE: Dialogue is usually punctuated by quotation marks. So, if you see quotation marks, check to see whether there is a speaker stated in the sentence, and, if so, enclose the speaker and the verb within commas.

EXERCISE   Correct the following sentences by inserting a comma where necessary.

"I'm as happy as a lark" yelled George.

She screamed "Don't you say another word."

Have your instructor or tutor check your work.

PRACTICE 2

Correctly punctuate the following sentences.

1. "Teachers don't understand" screamed the disgusted student.
2. "Bugs" said the little girl quite primly "are dirty creatures."
3. Before he left home, six-year-old John stated very emphatically "I will not return."
4. "I am not at all interested" said Mother to the salesrepresentative.
5. The proud owner of a prize-winning Persian unequivocally declared "Cats are much smarter than dogs."

Check the answer key.

Commas with Appositives

When a noun is immediately followed by a group of words that explain or rename it, the group of words is called an appositive and must be enclosed within commas.

Example: Alexander Pope, the Neo-Classic poet, is famous for his monologues.

Alexander Pope is famous for his monologues.

"The Neo-Classic poet" gives additional information about Pope; therefore, it is in apposition and is enclosed within commas. The appositive could be omitted, and the sentence would still make sense and provide enough information to be understood.

Example: The New York Jets, the underdogs, surprised everyone by winning the Super Bowl.

The New York Jets surprised everyone by winning the Super Bowl.

"The underdogs" gives the reader additional information about the football team, but the phrase is not necessary for comprehending the sentence. Thus, "the underdogs" is in apposition and is enclosed by commas.

NOTE: When an appositive offers additional, *nonessential* information about the noun, it is enclosed in commas. However, some appositives are necessary to identify the noun. In this case, the appositive is not enclosed in commas. Consider the differences in meaning between these examples.

Examples: The poet Dryden is famous for his satire.

My neighbor Mr. Taracks is the neighborhood busybody.

Neither of the above sentences could be rewritten without losing the sense of the sentence.

Examples: The poet is famous for his satire. *Which poet?*

My neighbor is the neighborhood busybody. *Which neighbor?*

The sense of the sentences has been lost. The information was necessary to identify the noun; therefore, no commas were used to enclose the information.

EXERCISE Using the example sentences as models, insert commas wherever necessary in the following sentences.

1. My only sister Sue is studying engineering.

2. *Childe Roland to the Dark Tower Came* an epic poem was written by Robert Browning.

3. Sally the class busybody loves to take charge of every project.

Have your instructor or tutor check your work.

PRACTICE 3

In the blank to the right of each sentence, write *C* if the sentence is correctly punctuated or *P* if there is a comma error. Correct the comma errors.

1. My history teacher Professor Jones gives difficult tests. _____

2. Mrs. Smith Sally's neighbor likes to wear hot-pink shorts in the summer. _____

3. Old Lyin' George a famous panhandler died peacefully last night in a nursing home. _____

4. President Carter the nation's thirty-ninth chief executive refused to return to the peanut business. _____

5. My only brother Harry wants to join the Peace Corps. _____

Check the answer key.

Commas with Out-of-Place Adjectives

Because adjectives usually precede the nouns they modify, any deviation from that usual pattern catches the reader's attention and interrupts the flow of thought. When that happens, the out-of-place adjective(s) must be enclosed by commas.

Examples: 1. The tall, slender girl attracted everyone's attention. (usual pattern)

2. The girl, tall and slender, attracted everyone's attention. (out-of-place)

3. The grand, imposing house required a large housekeeping staff. (usual pattern)

4. The house, grand and imposing, required a large housekeeping staff. (out-of-place)

EXERCISE Using the example sentences as models, correctly punctuate these sentences.

1. The woman witty and sophisticated charmed her hostile audience.
2. The toddler sturdy and daring was determined to climb out of the crib.

Have your instructor or tutor check your work.

PRACTICE 4

In the blank to the right of each sentence, write *C* if the sentence is correctly punctuated or *P* if there is a comma error. Correct the comma errors.

1. My child bright and witty will be famous some day.   _____

2. The old man tired but undaunted faced his accusers.   _____

3. The fresh air of spring exhilarating and uplifting should be packaged and sold
   for use during the winter.   _____

4. The young boy senile before his time was a victim of a dreaded disease.   _____

5. The beautiful and happy baby laughed at the puppy's antics.   _____

Check the answer key.

Commas with Nonrestrictive Clauses and Phrases

A nonrestrictive clause or phrase gives extra information about the word it modifies, so it is not essential to the sentence and is enclosed by commas.

Example:	My brother, who has a weak knee, should not play football.
	The basic thought of this sentence is that the speaker's brother should not play football. Because the speaker obviously knows his brother, he is able to offer the reason for that prohibition, but that reason is not essential to the sentence. Therefore, because the clause acts as an interrupter, stopping the flow of the sentence, it must be punctuated as one. Enclose it within commas.
Example:	Steven Stomes, whose show you like, will host a party next week for disabled vets.

EXERCISE Using the example sentence as a model, correctly punctuate the following sentences.

1. Mary who is a great athlete is also an outstanding scholar.
2. King George III who lost the American colonies is not considered an outstanding monarch.

Have your instructor or tutor check your work.

NOTE: Remember, *non*restrictive clauses and phrases are enclosed within commas. Anything that is essential to the meaning of the sentence should be left as an integral part of the sentence and *not* enclosed.

Example: The man who is standing by the door is a security policeman.

"Who is standing by the door" is essential for identifying the man; without this clause, the reader would have no means of identifying the security policeman. Consequently, no commas are used in the sentence.

Now, note the effect commas can have on the meaning of a sentence.

Example: Journalists, who write well about crucial issues, are rewarded with a large audience.

The basic thought of the sentence is that journalists have large audiences; the nonrestrictive clause (which has been enclosed by commas) merely gives the reason for the large audiences. It provides extra information to the reader.

Example: Journalists who write well about crucial issues are rewarded with a large audience.

The meaning has changed. Now, it is only proficient journalists who reach large audiences. The clause is essential to the sentence because it identifies the journalists. Therefore, no commas are used.

PRACTICE 5

In the blank to the right of each sentence, write *C* if the sentence is correctly punctuated or *P* if there is a comma error. Correct the comma errors.

1. Parrots although notorious for their ability to mimic speech are really shy birds.   _____

2. Puppies while amusing you with their tricks can turn a house upside-down.   _____

3. Fashionable dress because the criteria change so often should not be used to

   judge another person's worth.   _____

4. The parishioners who often leave early disrupt the service.   _____

5. The gentleman who is standing by the fireplace is a well-known composer.   _____

Check the answer key.

Commas with Parenthetical Expressions

When a word or phrase is inserted into a sentence to explain or comment on that sentence, it is called a parenthetical expression. Because the word or phrase is not essential to the sentence (it is merely providing additional information), it is enclosed by commas.

Example: The dean, on the other hand, believes in vigorously recruiting students.

The basic thought of this sentence is the dean's desire to seek students actively. The phrase "on the other hand" serves as a *transition*; it helps to move the reader from one idea to another, in this case contrasting, idea. Because it acts as an interrupter in the middle of the sentence, it is enclosed by two commas.

EXERCISE   Following the above examples, correctly punctuate these sentences.

1. In fact the author believes his works were plagiarized.

2. The original cowboy to tell the truth would not match today's idealized version of a cowpuncher.

Have your instructor or tutor check your work.

Following is a discussion of the two most common types of parenthetical expressions.

Transitional Expressions

In general, transitional expressions help give unity and coherence to an essay or paragraph. They influence the style of the writing, so they are enclosed by commas.

Below is a chart of some commonly used transitions and the type of relationship each one indicates.

Type of Relationship	*Transition*
Cause and Effect	consequently, hence, therefore, thus
Chronological	first, second, third, last, finally, later
Comparison/Contrast	similarly, however, nevertheless, on the other hand, in contrast, on the contrary
Example	for example, to illustrate, for instance
Importance/Repetition	as a matter of fact, generally speaking, in addition, in fact, on the whole, to say the least, to tell the truth, moreover
Summary/Conclusion	in brief, in short, to conclude, to summarize, therefore

Note that these expressions require the reader to pause while reading the sentence, so they are enclosed by commas.

On the other hand, some short parenthetical expressions of one or two words do *not* force the reader to pause; therefore, they would not be enclosed by commas. Here are some examples:

actually	at worst	perhaps
also	if any	then
at best	indeed	too
at least	of course	

Examples: Then everyone decided to leave the dance hall.

Of course the inflation rate had also climbed to 20 percent by that time.

EXERCISE   Correctly punctuate these sentences.

1. Perhaps the hospital expects too much from its volunteers.

2. Actually they have always expected too much.

Have your instructor or tutor check your work.

Mild Interjections

Mild interjections are words such as *oh, wow,* and *ah.* They are usually placed at the beginning of a sentence to comment on it. Again, because they are not essential to the sentence and because they interrupt its thought, they are considered parenthetical elements and are enclosed by commas.

Examples: Oh, I didn't know you were here.

Wow, that's some black eye!

EXERCISE   Correctly punctuate these sentences.

1. Ah how I appreciate a fine cigar.
2. Oh that was an unexpected move.

Have your instructor or tutor check your work.

PRACTICE 6

In the blank to the right of each sentence, write *C* if the sentence is correctly punctuated or *P* if there is a comma error. Correct the comma errors.

1. In fact she is quite a good cook.   _____

2. He is, I believe, determined to ascend the corporate ladder.   _____

3. Surprisingly Calhoun's Clogs won the steeplechase easily.   _____

4. To conclude productivity has improved, but not by as great a percentage as we
   had hoped.   _____

5. John Darlingston believe it or not is an accomplished pianist.   _____

Check the answer key.

13

Apostrophes

OBJECTIVES:
1. To recognize the need for apostrophes.
2. To use apostrophes correctly.
3. To proofread a paper for apostrophe errors. The editing symbol for apostrophes is *apos*.

KEY CONCEPT: Apostrophes are used for three purposes:
1. To indicate possession,
2. To form contractions, and
3. To form plurals of certain words.

Use of Apostrophes to Indicate Possession

An apostrophe is used to demonstrate possession. The apostrophe takes the place of omitted words of ownership. If you can reverse the order of the words and use *of* or *for*, then you need an apostrophe. For example, *child's book* becomes *the book of the child.*

Examples: son's chores (the chores of the son)
sons' chores (the chores of more than one son)
Octavia's cake (the cake of Octavia)
Nelson's journey (the journey of Nelson)

NOTE: An apostrophe is not required for possessive pronouns. The pronouns *my, mine, your, yours, his, her, hers, its, our, ours, their,* and *theirs* do not need apostrophes to make them possessive.

Examples: *His* car is not here. Shall we take *yours* or *mine?*
Each cat had *its* favorite spot in the house.

Rules for Forming the Possessive

1. *Add the apostrophe plus an* s *('s) to show possession in these cases:*

   a. a singular noun—

   Examples: a cat's cry
   the astronaut's suit

b. an indefinite pronoun—

Examples: someone's keys
everyone's answers

c. plural nouns that do not end in *s*—

Examples: children's coats
women's responsibilities
men's roles

d. compound (more than one word) expressions used as a singular noun—

Examples: her father-in-law's chair
the chief-of-police's gun

e. joint possession and separate possession—

Examples: Libby and Cindy's rooms (same rooms)
Libby's and Cindy's rooms (different rooms)

PRACTICE 1

Make the following items possessive.

1. the rules of the school _____

2. the idea of someone _____

3. the responses of some people _____

4. the regulations of the agency _____

5. the child whose parents are Thelma and Gene _____

6. the families of Mr. Grant and Mr. Stone _____

7. the quilt of my mother-in-law _____

8. the motives of the thief _____

9. the responses of the congregation _____

10. the insults of the crowd _____

Check the answer key.

2. *Add an apostrophe (') or an apostrophe plus an* s *('s) to singular words ending in* s.

a. Add the apostrophe plus the *s* to singular words of one syllable.

Examples: my boss's schedule
the bus's tires

    b. Add an apostrophe plus an *s* or an apostrophe only to singular words of two syllables. Your choice depends upon sound.

        Examples: Thomas's or Thomas' dog
                    discus' flight or discus's flight

    c. Singular words of three or more syllables use only an apostrophe to make them possessive.

        Examples: Martinkus' book
                    Pythagoras' theory

EXERCISE   Make the following proper nouns possessive.

the inhabitants of the Ozarks _____

the boat of Ross _____

Have your instructor or tutor check your work.

   3. *Add only an apostrophe (') to plural nouns ending in* s.

       Examples: goats' pasture
                  bridges' supports

EXERCISE   Make the following words possessive.

the engines of the tractors _____

the caps of the swimmers _____

Have your instructor or tutor check your work.

Use of Apostrophes to Form Contractions

Use apostrophes in place of some letters to form contracted words or numbers. Make sure that the apostrophe is in the same place as the omitted letters or numbers.

Examples:	of the clock	o'clock
	he did not	he didn't
	she will	she'll
	Kim will not	Kim won't
	he is	he's
	I am	I'm
	they are	they're
	1965	'65

Usually, except for a contraction like *o'clock,* you should not use contractions in formal writing.

Use of Apostrophes to Form Plurals

Use apostrophes to form plurals of letters, numbers, abbreviations, and words referred to as words.

Examples: Please distinguish between your *i*'s and your *t*'s.
Nathan's 7's often look like 9's.
The VIP's arrived at the gala opening of the new play.
You used too many *and*'s in your last paper.

EXERCISE   Make the following words and letters plural.

1. the letters *t* and *b* _____

2. the abbreviations IBM PC (Personal Computer) and MP (Military Police) _____

3. the numbers 17 and 1,000 _____

4. the words *make* and *sing* _____

Have your instructor or tutor check your work.

NOTE: In current usage, the plurals of this century's decades—the '20's, for example—are written without the apostrophe plus *s*. Instead, these decades appear with only the initial apostrophe to indicate that the first numbers are absent and the *s* to indicate plural. The Sixties are now written numerically as the '60s.

PRACTICE 2

Use an apostrophe to make the following sets of words possessive, contractions, or plurals.

1. the ball of the team   _____

2. the work of a rabbi   _____

3. the passengers of the bus   _____

4. the passengers of the buses   _____

5. the record of someone   _____

6. the credit cards of Ms. Jones   _____

7. the racquet of the tennis pro   _____

8. the weather conditions of today   _____

9. the motto of the Marines   _____

10. the national anthem of America   _____

11. the responsibilities of the commander-in-chief   _____

12. the refrigerator of his grandparents   _____

13. the restaurants of Jack and Tony (same restaurants)   _____

14. the restaurants of Jack and Tony (different restaurants)   _____

15. the special effects of the movie   _____

16. the concern of the people   _____

17. I will not   _____

18. he cannot   _____

19. they have   _____

20. the plural of the word *several*   _____

21. the plural of the word *yet*   _____

22. the jungles of Brazil   _____

23. the wares of the salespeople   _____

24. the uniform of the soldier   _____

25. the plural of the letter *z*   _____

Check the answer key.

Introduction
PRACTICE

1. In—preposition
   tuition—noun
   has risen—verb
2. Boy!—interjection
   gorgeous—adjective
3. and—coordinate conjunction
   must serve—verb
4. seems—verb (linking)
5. society—adjective
   revealing—adjective
   memorable—adjective
6. slowly, gracefully—adverbs
   however—adverbial conjunction
7. although—subordinate conjunction
   she—personal pronoun, nominative case
   and—coordinate conjunction
8. Oh my gosh!—interjection
   kerosene—adjective
   has—helping verb
9. Everyone—indefinite pronoun
   should—helping verb
   to—preposition
10. Warden James—proper noun
    vicious—adjective
    mass—adjective
11. danced, sang—verbs
    before—subordinate conjunction
12. with—preposition
    purple—adjective
    by—preposition
13. Shyness—noun
    characteristics—noun
    of—preposition
14. We—personal pronoun, nominative case
    or—coordinate conjunction
    to—preposition
15. You—personal pronoun, nominative case
    my—personal pronoun, possessive case
    that—demonstrative pronoun
    very—adverb
16. Jerome—proper noun
    failed—verb
    his—personal pronoun, possessive case
    for—coordinate conjunction
17. On—preposition
    summer—noun
    by—preposition
    Andorra—proper noun
    near—preposition
    at—preposition
    of—preposition
18. useful—adjective
    informative—adjective
19. gleefully—adverb
    as—subordinate conjunction
    quickly—adverb
    through—preposition
20. have been rejected—verb
    too—adverb

Chapter 1
PRACTICE 1

1. action	6. linking
2. linking	7. action
3. action	8. action
4. action	9. action
5. linking	10. action

PRACTICE 2

1. he	6. it
2. she	7. they
3. it	8. they
4. it	9. they
5. it	10. we

PRACTICE 3

1. I walk / we walk
   you walk / you walk
   he, she, it walks / they walk
2. I read / we read
   you read / you read
   he, she, it reads / they read
3. I dance / we dance
   you dance / you dance
   he, she, it dances / they dance
4. I hide / we hide
   you hide / you hide
   he, she, it hides / they hide
5. I call / we call
   you call / you call
   he, she, it calls / they call

PRACTICE 4

1. talks	6. have
2. runs	7. visit
3. have, has	8. draws, are
4. is	9. drives
5. are	10. are, is

PRACTICE 5

1. all forms take *danced*
2. all forms take *poured*
3. all forms take *marked*
4. all forms take *painted*
5. all forms take *called*

PRACTICE 6

1. sang	6. visited, went
2. wrote	7. was
3. went, felt	8. brought
4. brought, experienced	9. enlisted
5. read	10. reached, dropped

PRACTICE 7

1. will (shall) complete
2. will ask
3. Will be
4. will run
5. will sell
6. Will meet
7. will travel
8. will benefit
9. will be
10. will succeed

PRACTICE 8

1. correct
2. decided, fumbled
3. was, began, cooked
4. scraped
5. returned, waited, tossed
6. correct
7. do, run
8. do
9. go
10. put, remain
11. learned

Chapter 2
PRACTICE 1

	Infinitive	Past	Past Participle		Infinitive	Past	Past Participle
1.	to dive	dived (dove)	dived	6.	to steal	stole	stolen
2.	to sing	sang	sung	7.	to teach	taught	taught
3.	to write	wrote	written	8.	to learn	learned	learned
4.	to fly	flew	flown	9.	to give	gave	given
5.	to drink	drank	drunk	10.	to receive	received	received

PRACTICE 2

1. have had
2. has been
3. has been
4. have visited
5. has become
6. have received
7. has bought
8. has raced
9. have seen
10. have enrolled

PRACTICE 3

1. had been
2. had finished
3. had completed
4. had called
5. had defused
6. had determined
7. had made
8. had completed
9. had chosen
10. had moved

PRACTICE 4

1. will have been
2. will have worked
3. will have finished
4. will have been
5. will have welcomed
6. will have taught
7. will have read
8. will have celebrated
9. will have submitted
10. will have thrown

PRACTICE 5

1. I am asking
2. They had been doing
3. We will be singing
4. He has been hitting
5. You will have been dealing
6. They were swimming

PRACTICE 6

1. will have been dancing
2. is completing
3. was bathing
4. has been working
5. has been going
6. will be leaving
7. was working, is practicing
8. is working, have been burning
9. was running, is operating
10. will be playing

PRACTICE 7

1. should dance
2. has been teaching
3. does plan
4. had crawled
5. was
6. had been doing
7. did live
8. will have been competing
9. had nominated
10. has accepted

PRACTICE 8

1. he *took*
2. players *were*
3. students *fail*
4. it *was working*
5. *The Great Gatsby was published*
6. work processor *will replace*
7. he *turned*
8. he *developed*
9. thousands of athletes *will have arrived*
10. we *missed*

PRACTICE 9

1. would have passed
2. did have
3. correct
4. is
5. have tried
6. attend
7. are
8. manage

Chapter 3
PRACTICE 1

1. transitive
2. intransitive
3. transitive
4. transitive
5. transitive
6. intransitive
7. transitive
8. transitive
9. intransitive
10. intransitive

PRACTICE 2

1. made
2. saddled
3. received
4. changed
5. cooked
6. lit
7. announced
8. passed
9. made
10. gave

PRACTICE 3

1. will be given
2. were sent
3. had been driven
4. will have been
   commanded
5. was written

PRACTICE 4

1. were
2. were
3. be
4. be
5. were

PRACTICE 5

1. To earn—infinitive
2. noted—past participle
3. Driving to the store—present participle
4. to earn extra money this summer—infinitive
5. skiing—gerund; to spend a summer afternoon—infinitive
6. playing in the yard—present participle
7. deserved—past participle
8. "To be, or not to be"—infinitives
9. aged—past participle; photographing birds—gerund
10. ringing the church bells—gerund
11. Dashing to the finish line—present participle
12. After receiving her bachelor's degree—present participle
    to attend law school—infinitive
13. Typing the final word—present participle
14. To dance the limbo—infinitive
15. to see a movie, (to) dine at a restaurant, and (to) dance until midnight—infinitives
16. fading back for a pass—present participle
    rushing—present participle
17. Pivoting quickly—present participle
18. feuding—present participle
    to settle their differences in court—infinitive
19. Building a fire—gerund
20. camping, biking—gerunds

Chapter 4

PRACTICE 3

	Verb	Subject
1.	laughs	Terry
2.	play	children
3.	hit	bullet
4.	swam	I
5.	fainted	doctor

PRACTICE 4

	Verb	Subject
1.	are	Fords, Chevrolets
2.	hissed, scratched	cat
3.	read, study	Caleb, Rachel
4.	became	Angela
5.	took	Carl, Martha
6.	seemed	Tina
7.	are	ice cream, cake
8.	are	Puerto Rico, St. Thomas
9.	appears	Nita
10.	leaped, swam	dolphin

PRACTICE 5

	Verb	Subject
1.	are	friends
2.	is	manuscript
3.	are	ball, bat
4.	is	answer
5.	come	boyfriend, girl

PRACTICE 6

	Verb	Subject
1.	will have left	Tom
2.	will have been	senator
3.	had been demolished	car
4.	will be released	animals
5.	was playing	jockey

PRACTICE 7

      S   V
1. The *cat ran* ~~under the porch~~.

       S   V
2. *Bronco Davis was* a famous football player ~~for twenty years~~.

          S   V
3. The *greyhound* ~~with the matted coat and an evil look in his eyes~~ *frightened* the school children.

      S   V
4. The *drive* ~~to Orlando~~ *is* a pleasant one.

      S   S   V
5. *Bing Crosby* and *Bob Hope were* a successful team ~~for more than fifteen years~~.

PRACTICE 8

	Subject	Verb	Object	Format 1 or 2
1.	Tom	forgot		1 S-V
2.	band	won	contest	2 S-V-DO
3.	Helen	read	book	2 S-V-DO
4.	I	swam		1 S-V
5.	dog	crossed	road	2 S-V-DO
6.	arrow	struck	tree	2 S-V-DO
7.	team	lost		1 S-V
8.	child	broke	vase	2 S-V-DO

PRACTICE 9

	Subject	Verb	Object	Format 1 or 2
1.	police	caught	thief	2 S-V-DO
2.	television	broke		1 S-V
3.	horse	won	Triple Crown	2 S-V-DO
4.	children	jumped	fence	2 S-V-DO
5.	Mary	cried		1 S-V
6.	moon	rose		1 S-V
7.	fullback	caught	football	2 S-V-DO
8.	rooster	crowed		1 S-V
9.	airplane	left	runway	2 S-V-DO
10.	diver	speared	barracuda	2 S-V-DO
11.	shoelaces	broke		1 S-V
12.	president	fired	assistant	2 S-V-DO
13.	speaker	declined	invitation	2 S-V-DO
14.	chair	fell		1 S-V
15.	Children	like	ice cream	2 S-V-DO

PRACTICE 10

PA-S	LV	Format
1. powerful weightlifter	is	S-LV-PA
2. sad Tom	appears	S-LV-PA
3. happy Mary	looks	S-LV-PA
4. good dinner	tasted	S-LV-PA
5. cooperative Earl Bruce	was	S-LV-PA
6. angry cat	sounds	S-LV-PA
7. tired He	seems	S-LV-PA
8. sour onion	smells	S-LV-PA
9. rough road	becomes	S-LV-PA
10. red, delicious apple	was	S-LV-PA

PRACTICE 11

Verb	PA or DO		Verb	PA or DO
1. branded	calf-DO		6. were	pretty-PA
2. looks	expensive-PA		7. serves	food-DO
3. enjoy	books-DO		8. has	water-DO
4. struck	rock-DO		9. looks	interested-PA
5. are	dirty-PA		10. seemed	uneasy-PA

PRACTICE 12

Subject	Linking Verb	Predicate Nominative
1. senator	is	chairman
2. Annapolis	is	capitol
3. desk	is	antique
4. Shawn	became	astronaut
5. John	is	player
6. Jane	is	force
7. Television	is	one
8. She	is	actress
9. girl	is	cousin
10. alligator	is	symbol

PRACTICE 13

Subject	LV	PA	PN	Format
1. She	is		girl	S-LV-PN
2. ideas	are	ambiguous		S-LV-PA
3. Students	seem	busy		S-LV-PA
4. Doctors, lawyers	are		professionals	S-LV-PN
5. teachers	are	enthusiastic		S-LV-PA
6. Discos	are		alleys	S-LV-PN
7. Records, tapes	are	expensive		S-LV-PA
8. craze	is		mini-skirt	S-LV-PN
9. Faulkner	was		one	S-LV-PN
10. Silence, patience	are		virtues	S-LV-PN

PRACTICE 14

	Subject	Verb	IO	DO
1.	Tim	awarded	Henry	prize
2.	boy	bought	girl	flower
3.	man	handed	girlfriend	ring
4.	teacher	gave	me	mark
5.	Tim	fed	dog	dinner
6.	bird	built	mate	nest
7.	I	gave	friend	umbrella
8.	She	brought	Jim	soda
9.	kidnappers	gave	child	bar
10.	Sharon	bought	father	sweater

PRACTICE 15

	Subject	Verb	IO	DO/PA or PN	Format
1.	She	is		star-PN	S-LV-PN
2.	coach	gave	Tom	equipment-DO	S-V-IO-DO
3.	bread	tastes		stale-PA	S-LV-PA
4.	dog	caught		stick-DO	S-V-DO
5.	man	gave	child	dollar-DO	S-V-IO-DO
6.	I	walked			S-V
7.	runner	became		hero-PN	S-LV-PN
8.	Women	have joined		clubs-DO	S-V-DO
9.	Kim	sang		aria-DO	S-V-DO
10.	horse	tripped			S-V
11.	Connors	is		player-PN	S-LV-PN
12.	lawyer	gave	client	advice-DO	S-V-IO-DO
13.	student	was		sick-PA	S-LV-PA
14.	Maria	invited		Brad-DO	S-V-DO
15.	dog	growled			S-V
16.	roses	are		gift-PN	S-LV-PN
17.	Bob	caught		fish-DO	S-V-DO
18.	Doctors	seem		intelligent-PA	S-LV-PA
19.	He	gave	me	present-DO	S-V-IO-DO
20.	picture	appears		faded-PA	S-LV-PA

PRACTICE 16

1. Imperative
2. Interrogative
3. Declarative
4. Exclamatory
5. Imperative
6. Declarative
7. Interrogative
8. Imperative
9. Exclamatory
10. Declarative

Chapter 5
PRACTICE 1

1.
2. C
3. C
4. C
5.

PRACTICE 3

1. D
2. D
3. I
4. D
5. I
6. D
7. D
8. I
9. D
10. I

PRACTICE 4

1. college—subject
   sponsors—verb
   day—direct object
   for students—prepositional phrase
   Format: S-V-DO
2. During the president's vacation—prepositional phrase
   vice-president—subject
   was—verb
   responsible—predicate adjective
   for the administration—prepositional phrase
   of the college—prepositional phrase
   Format: S-V-PA
3. Swimming—subject
   is—verb
   sport—predicate nominative
   Format: S-V-PN
4. sentry—subject
   standing guard duty—participial phrase
   had fallen—verb
   asleep—predicate adjective
   at his post—prepositional phrase
   Format: S-V-PA
5. Harold, Maude—subjects
   made—verb
   couple—direct object
   because of the contrast—prepositional
   phrase
   in their ages—prepositional phrase
   Format: S-V-DO

6. hiking—participle
   club—subject
   plans—verb
   to visit—direct object
   Format: S-V-DO
7. Distraught—participle
   victim—subject
   refused—verb
   to answer—direct object
   Format: S-V-DO
8. At the sound—prepositional phrase
   of the approaching train—prepositional
   phrase (approaching—participle)
   deer—subject
   scrambled—verb
   for safety—prepositional phrase
   Format: S-V
9. To enjoy—infinitive
   of one—prepositional phrase
   of Shakespeare's plays—prepositional phrase
   you—subject
   should read—verb
   play—direct object
   to the performance—prepositional phrase
   Format: S-V-DO
10. ambition—subject
    is—verb
    to become—predicate nominative
    Format: S-V-PN

PRACTICE 7

1. compound   Governor Toll was nominated   he decided
              (S)   (V)   (S) (V)

2. simple   Derby, Preakness, Belmont Stakes   form
            (subjects)   (V)

3. compound   firefighters   used   they   use
              (S)   (V)   (S)   (V)

4. simple   musicians, composers   were employed
            (subjects)   (V)

5. compound   Mexico   has   some   go
              (S)   (V)   (S)   (V)

PRACTICE 8

1. PP (prepositional phrase)
2. DC (dependent clause)
3. DC
4. SW (subordinating word)
5. IC (independent clause)
6. IC
7. PP
8. PP
9. DC
10. PP
11. SW
12. DC
13. IC
14. PP
15. DC
16. PP
17. PP
18. IC
19. DC
20. DC

PRACTICE 11

1. dependent clause / independent clause
(Whenever the weather is beautiful), they have a picnic.

2. dependent clause / independent clause
(Although he had household chores), he decided to see a movie.

3. independent clause / dependent clause
It began to rain (before the boat reached shore).

4. independent clause / dependent clause
We knew (that he did not go home).

5. dependent clause / independent clause
(Because she has an exam tomorrow), Kate will study tonight.

6. dependent clause / independent clause
(After the movie ended), all thirty of us headed to the local pizza parlor.

7. dependent clause / independent clause
(Before Marvin could shout a warning), the firecracker exploded.

8. dependent clause / independent clause
(After they buy a house), they will purchase new furniture.

9. independent clause / dependent clause
Harriet decided to go on the ski trip (even though she had a broken leg.)

10. dependent clause / dependent clause
[Because many parents believe (that their children should know computers)], they are
independent clause
purchasing home computers.

PRACTICE 12

1. complex
independent clause / dependent clause
Betsy goes to the beach (whenever she can.)

2. compound
independent clause / independent clause
It is a warm day; the temperature is now 95 degrees.

3. simple
independent clause
In order to earn enough money to go to college, Terry worked as a waitress
all summer.

4. compound
independent clause / independent clause
Jack and Mary entered the haunted house cautiously, for they believed all the
stories about ghosts.

5. complex
dependent clause / independent clause
(When the rain was over), the children ran outside.

6. complex
dependent clause / independent clause
(Because the battery was dead), the car refused to start.

7. compound
independent clause / independent clause
You must hurry, or you will miss the last bus.

> independent clause

8. simple   <u>Marcello and his brothers gritted their teeth and began the long, slow climb to the top</u>

<u>of the mountain.</u>

> independent clause   dependent clause

9. complex   <u>He told you</u> (that your plan was impossible).

> independent clause

10. compound   <u>With its varied historical background, New Orleans is a fascinating place to visit;</u>

> independent clause

<u>the Mardi Gras is one example of its French heritage.</u>

PRACTICE 13

> dependent clause   independent clause   independent clause

1. (When the monster appeared on the screen,) <u>one girl fainted</u>, and <u>the audience clapped.</u>

> independent clause   dependent clause

2. <u>The movie's visual effects</u>, (which cost 15 million dollars,) <u>were fantastic</u>; later, <u>the graphic</u>

> independent clause

<u>artists won an Academy Award for their work.</u>

> independent clause   dependent clause   independent clause

3. <u>I wish</u> (that you had seen the film); <u>we could discuss it.</u>

> independent clause   dependent clause   independent clause

4. <u>Knitting</u>, (which is a relaxing pastime,) <u>can be profitable</u>, for <u>handmade sweaters have become</u>

<u>a fashion item.</u>

> independent clause   dependent clause   independent clause

5. <u>Order the pizza</u> (when you get home); <u>I'll be there soon.</u>

> dependent clause   independent clause

6. (Because England was America's first mother country), <u>many people believe</u> (that the English

> dependent clause   independent clause

do everything better); however, <u>these Americans are not correct.</u>

> dependent clause   independent clause   independent clause

7. (If you will wait for me), then <u>I'll finish my work</u>, and <u>we can go to the beach.</u>

> dependent clause   independent clause   independent clause

8. (Before you purchase your textbooks), <u>go to class</u>; <u>the instructor may have changed the reading</u>

<u>list.</u>

> independent clause   dependent clause

9. <u>Our surprise birthday party for Jerry failed</u>; (before he entered the room), <u>everyone was</u>

> independent clause

<u>practicing "Happy Birthday."</u>

> independent clause   dependent clause   independent clause

10. <u>My father always told me to turn the lights off</u> (when I leave a room); <u>he claimed</u> (that such

> dependent clause

a practice would save money).

PRACTICE 15

1. complex

    independent clause   dependent clause
    She is a person (whom we admire.)

2. complex

    independent clause   dependent clause   independent clause
    The dog (that wins the contest) will be used in the commercial.

3. complex

    dependent clause   independent clause
    (Because he has left), we must stay here.

4. compound-
    complex

    dependent clause
    (Because the panda's natural habitat in China is threatened), many Chinese

    independent clause
    zookeepers wish to export them to other countries, and the Chinese

    independent clause
    government has agreed.

5. complex

    independent clause   dependent clause
    Close the door (when you enter).

6. complex

    dependent clause   independent clause
    (Before we leave for a vacation), we always have the car checked for problems.

7. complex

    independent clause   dependent clause
    Have Dave and Hank decided (when they will paint the house)?

8. simple

    independent clause
    We decided to see *The Rocky Horror Picture Show* at midnight.

9. compound

    independent clause
    Curt and Stacy played the romantic leads in *Romeo and Juliet*; however, the

    independent clause
    performance reminded one of *The Taming of the Shrew*.

10. simple

    independent clause
    Each section of the country, from New England to the West Coast, boasts of its

    native foods.

Chapter 6
PRACTICE 1

1. Frag	3. C	5. C	7. Frag	9. C
2. Frag	4. Frag	6. C	8. Frag	10. Frag

Have your instructor or tutor check your corrections.

Chapter 7

PRACTICE 1

1. CS
2. CS
3. CS
4. CS
5. CS

PRACTICE 2

1. C
2. CS job; she *or* and, she
3. CS high; I
4. CS beach; however,
5. CS Park, for
6. C
7. C
8. CS inadequate; each
9. C
10. CS poet; he

Chapter 8

PRACTICE 1

1. RO   friend/he
2. C
3. RO   move/many
4. RO   dancer/she
5. C

Have your instructor or tutor check your corrections

PRACTICE 2

1. C	6. C
2. RO	7. RO
3. RO	8. RO
4. RO	9. C
5. C	10. RO

Chapter 9

PRACTICE 1

1. S	6. P
2. P	7. P
3. P	8. P
4. S	9. S
5. P	10. S

PRACTICE 2

1. The boys laugh at the clown.
2. The mice hide in the pantry.
3. The examinations seem difficult.
4. The puppies nip at my heels.
5. The girls dive into the water.

PRACTICE 3

S or P	Subject	Verb
1. S	cat	carried
2. S	child	screamed
3. P	dolphins	are
4. S	Hank Thompson	answers
5. P	gardens	grow
6. P	grades	depend
7. S	Tim	works
8. S	Chrysler	was
9. P	dogs	bark
10. P	They	sat
11. P	millionaires	own
12. P	headaches	are caused
13. S	desk	was
14. S	actor	is
15. P	books	make
16. S	adolescent	faces
17. S	bowl	is
18. S	chair	is
19. S	song	was
20. S	player	smashes

PRACTICE 4

1. The student always feels. . . .
2. A dog is usually considered. . . .
3. A child loves. . . .
4. The nation has amassed. . . .
5. The plant needs. . . .

PRACTICE 5

S or P	Subject	Verb
1. S	each	enjoys
2. S	All	was
3. P	Some	have
4. S	Each	plays
5. S	Neither	wants
6. P	All	enjoy
7. S	teenager	wants
8. P	horses	gallop
9. P	adults	enjoy
10. S	Half	was

PRACTICE 6

S or P	Subject	Verb
1. S	gaggle	has
2. S	*The Crusaders*	is
3. S	measles	is
4. P	trousers	have
5. S	pounds	is

PRACTICE 7

S or P	Subject	Verb
1. P	Jack and Eileen	want
2. P	union representatives	want
3. S	George	swims
4. S	husband	has
5. P	quiche, hash	don't

PRACTICE 8

S or P	Subject	Verb
1. S	who (refers to Fitzgerald)	was
2. P	who (refers to lawyers)	select
3. S	that (refers to one)	is
4. S	which (refers to monument)	is
5. S	who (refers to only one)	enjoys

PRACTICE 9

S or P	Subject	Verb
1. P	people	are
2. P	courthouse, church	stand
3. P	letters	are
4. P	forms	were
5. S	fortune	lies

Chapter 10

PRACTICE 1

	Nominative	Objective	Possessive
1. dock	it	it	its
2. dog	it	it	its
3. Harry and Ellen	they	them	their, theirs
4. James and I	we	us	our, ours
5. Sara	she	her	her, hers

PRACTICE 2

1. she
2. they
3. their
4. my
5. its/her/his

PRACTICE 3

	Pronoun	Antecedent
1.	her	Maria
2.	you	Mr. Roberts
3.	her	teacher
4.	his	radiologist
5.	her	lawyer
6.	we	Steve and I
7.	its	horse
8.	them	books
9.	her	grandmother
10.	it	industry
11.	it	pen
12.	you	Bonnie and Jack
13.	them	plants
14.	her	mother
15.	it	novel

PRACTICE 4

1. it	6. her	11. It
2. She	7. his	12. they
3. We	8. it	13. They
4. he	9. their	14. It
5. he or she	10. He	15. they

PRACTICE 5

	Pronoun	Antecedent
1.	their	societies
2.	its	herd
3.	his/her	Everybody
4.	their	players
5.	their	some
6.	its	company
7.	its	class
8.	her	neither
9.	its	board
10.	their	women
11.	its	flock
12.	their	students
13.	their	dean, associates
14.	their	doctor
15.	its	*New England Journal of Medicine*

Chapter 11

PRACTICE 1

1. C
2. C
3. P   schoolyard, for
4. P   hour, but
5. P   hour, and

PRACTICE 2

1. P   Datsuns, Toyotas, and
2. P   Ways, M&Ms, and
3. C
4. P   Christmas, Thanksgiving, and
5. P   cleaner's, . . . milk, and

PRACTICE 3

1. P   harsh,
2. C
3. P   dirty,
4. P   short,
5. C

PRACTICE 4

1. P   before,
2. C
3. P   road,
4. P   him,
5. P   graded,

PRACTICE 5

1. P   December 7, 1941
2. P   Avenue, Washington, D. C.
3. C
4. C
5. P   July, 1993

PRACTICE 6

1. P   jumping,
2. P   nine,
3. P   old,
4. P   thirty,
5. C

Chapter 12

PRACTICE 1

1. MacBride,
2. thinks, Charles,
3. Honor,
4. parade,
5. tonight,

PRACTICE 2

1. understand,"
2. "Bugs," . . . primly, "are
3. emphatically,
4. interested,"
5. declared,

PRACTICE 3

1. C
2. P   Smith, Sally's neighbor,
3. P   George, a famous panhandler,
4. P   Carter, . . . executive,
5. P   brother, Harry,

PRACTICE 4

1. P   child, bright and witty,
2. P   man, . . . undaunted,
3. P   spring, . . . uplifting,
4. P   boy, . . . time,
5. C

PRACTICE 5

1. P   Parrots, . . . speech,
2. P   Puppies, . . . tricks,
3. P   dress, . . . often,
4. C
5. C

PRACTICE 6

1. P   fact,
2. C
3. P   Surprisingly,
4. P   conclude,
5. P   Darlingston, . . . not,

Chapter 13

PRACTICE 1

1. school's rules
2. someone's idea
3. some people's responses
4. agency's regulations
5. Thelma and Gene's child
6. Mr. Grant's and Mr. Stone's families
7. my mother-in-law's quilt
8. the thief's motives
9. the congregation's responses
10. the crowd's insults

PRACTICE 2

1. the team's ball
2. the rabbi's work
3. the bus's passengers
4. the buses' passengers
5. someone's record
6. Ms. Jones's credit cards
7. the tennis pro's racquet
8. today's weather conditions
9. the Marines' motto
10. America's national anthem
11. the commander-in-chief's responsibilities
12. his grandparents' refrigerator
13. Jack and Tony's restaurants
14. Jack's and Tony's restaurants
15. the movie's special effects
16. the people's concern
17. I won't
18. he can't
19. they've
20. *several*'s
21. *yet*'s
22. Brazil's jungles
23. the salespeople's wares
24. the soldier's uniform
25. z's